READINGS IN CLASSICAL RHETORIC

Readings in
Classical Rhetoric

Edited by

THOMAS W. BENSON

MICHAEL H. PROSSER

Indiana University Press

Bloomington and London

Copyright © 1969 by Allyn and Bacon, Inc.
Copyright © 1972 by Thomas W. Benson and Michael H. Prosser

Published in Canada by Fitzhenry & Whiteside Limited, Don Mills, Ontario

Library of Congress catalog card number: 76-80478
ISBN: 0-253-34864-1

Manufactured in the United States of America

TO OUR PARENTS
Walter A. and *Beatrice N. Benson*
Marshall H. and *Clydia C. Prosser*

PREFACE

Philosophers and statesmen rarely find themselves intent upon a single unifying tradition, and yet George Kennedy writes that at the core of classical learning:

> one of the principal interests of the Greeks was rhetoric. . . .In its origin and intention rhetoric was natural and good: it produced clarity, vigor and beauty, and it rose logically from the conditions and qualities of the classical mind. . . .Though a practical and philosophical tradition may be discerned, and though there were temporary vagaries, the history of ancient rhetoric is largely that of the growth of a single, great, traditional theory to which many writers and teachers contributed.[1]

Rhetoric, the theory of oral discourse, affected and indeed pervaded all aspects of classical thought. Bearing the stamp of its impact were the Homeric hymns, the *Iliad* and the *Odyssey*, Aeschylus' *Eumenides*, the great dramatic tragedies, the elegiac and lyric poetry, and the literature of the Romans, often formed in the Greek image. The rhetorical notion of probability had direct implications for the classical philosopher and mathematician as it does today. The philosophical method of a dialectical search for truth complemented and was enriched by the rhetorician's concern for an argument's consistency with the real world. And "the significance of rhetoric and oratory in Greek and Roman intellectual life is further evident in education and criticism. It is not too much to say that rhetoric played the central role in ancient education."[2] The Romans, fervent imitators of the Greeks, used rhetoric and oratory to form their laws, politics, literature, philosophy and religion.

The rhetorical tradition exerts no less an influence in our own times as changing patterns of communication and technology force us to reconsider

---

[1] George Kennedy, *The Art of Persuasion in Greece* (Princeton, New Jersey, 1963), pp. 3-7.

[2] *Ibid.*, p. 7.

the premises of a democratic society. Now, more than ever, we need to understand and develop new answers to questions that troubled classical rhetoricians. Can decision-making in a complex society be based upon the knowledge which is available to the common man? Can training in rhetoric provide one with the tools and attitudes he needs to contribute to a stable and open community?

Many modern writers have emphasized the contributions of rhetoric to all phases of ancient life. Among representative titles are: *Ancient Rhetoric and Poetic; Rhetoric in Graeco-Roman Education; Greek Thinkers; Attic Orators; The Art of Persuasion in Greece; Greek Rhetoric and Literary Criticism; Rhetoric at Rome;* and *Speech Criticism.* Other studies have complemented these titles by demonstrating the relevance of ancient rhetoric to contemporary life, including: *Classical Rhetoric for the Modern Student; Public Speaking as a Liberal Art; Readings in Speech; The Relevance of Rhetoric; Rhetoric: A Philosophical Inquiry; New Rhetorics; Essays on Rhetoric; Public Speaking: A Rhetorical Perspective; Readings in Rhetoric;* and *The Province of Rhetoric.*

Departments of speech, English, philosophy and classics provide the key centers of interest in the new and the classical rhetorics. Despite the considerable enthusiasm for the study of rhetoric, no single work provides large selections of primary materials written by the classical rhetoricians themselves. Until now, we have had to content ourselves with secondary sources containing tiny excerpts, or with entire and expensive translations of the ancient rhetorical writings. To fill this large gap, we have edited this anthology of primary readings of the classical rhetoricians in translation. We have sought to emphasize especially the continuity and coherence of the ancient rhetorical traditions, organizing large excerpts into the topical divisions which later classical writers agreed upon. Additionally, we have been at pains to select excerpts which illustrate the major conflicts within the unfolding tradition. Most excerpts are sufficiently long to enable a sampling of not only the major points of view, but also the arguments supporting them. We have included selections not only from writings of the standard classical rhetoricians but also from less typical works which have special value, such as *Ad Alexandrum* and *Ad Herennium,* and the writings of Philodemus, Petronius, Longinus, Tacitus and Augustine. We have utilized the best accessible translations, remaining absolutely faithful to their texts, except that we have eliminated most of the copious footnotes offered by the translators. Since this anthology is intended to create a new interest in the classical rhetoricians, readers are encouraged to return to the larger single translations from which these selections are taken for a more comprehensive discussion by the translators and authors.

We wish to acknowledge our indebtedness to Professor Carroll Arnold, who examined the entire manuscript, making many suggestions for improvement which we adopted, and to our teachers, Herbert Wichelns, John F. Wilson, Karl Wallace, Ray Nadeau, Otto Dieter and Marie

Hochmuth Nichols. We appreciate the assistance given us by the Department of Speech Communication at the State University of New York at Buffalo; the advice of our colleagues, Professors Louis Swift and John Peradotto of the Department of Classics at the State University of New York at Buffalo; and the editorial counsel of Jon Verplanck, Associate Editor of Allyn and Bacon. We offer our thanks to the publishers, and particularly the Loeb Classical Library, for their generous permission to reprint the varied materials included in this volume. In any anthology of excerpted materials, there are preferences which must be unsatisfied. We accept responsibility for choices of scope and emphasis, as well as any errors of judgment.

THOMAS W. BENSON
MICHAEL H. PROSSER

Buffalo, New York

CONTENTS

Page

PREFACE   vii

UNIT I: RHETORIC: ITS DEFINITIONS, VALUE AND SCOPE   1
Plato, *Gorgias,* Translated by W.R.M. Lamb   3
Plato, *Phaedrus,* Translated by H. N. Fowler   22
Isocrates, "Against the Sophists," Translated by George Norlin   43
Isocrates, *Antidosis,* Translated by George Norlin   47
Aristotle, *The Rhetoric,* Translated by Richard Claverhouse Jebb   53
Rhetorica Ad Alexandrum, Translated by H. Rackham   63
Philodemus, *The Rhetoric of Philodemus,* Translated by H. M. Hubbell 76
Cicero, *De Oratore,* Translated by E. W. Sutton and H. Rackham   91
Petronius, "Among the Rhetoricians," Translated by William
    Arrowsmith   108
Tacitus, *Dialogus,* Translated by William Peterson   112
Quintilian, *Institutio Oratoria,* Translated by H. E. Butler   116
Augustine, *On Christian Doctrine,* Translated by D. W. Robertson, Jr. 133

UNIT II: INVENTION   141
Quintilian, *Institutio Oratoria,* Translated by H. E. Butler   143
Aristotle, *The Rhetoric,* Translated by Richard Claverhouse Jebb   149
Aristotle, *The Rhetoric,* Translated by Richard Claverhouse Jebb   154
Cicero, *De Oratore,* Translated by E. W. Sutton and H. Rackham   171
Augustine, *On Christian Doctrine,* Translated by D. W. Robertson, Jr. 180

UNIT III: ARRANGEMENT   189

Aristotle, *The Rhetoric*, Translated by Richard Claverhouse Jebb   191
Rhetorica Ad Herennium, Translated by Harry Caplan   193
Cicero, *De Inventione*, Translated by H. M. Hubbell   196
Quintilian, *Institutio Oratoria*, Translated by H. E. Butler   206

UNIT IV: STYLE   215

Quintilian, *Institutio Oratoria*, Translated by H. E. Butler   217
Cicero, *Orator*, Translated by H. M. Hubbell   232
Aristotle, *The Rhetoric*, Translated by Richard Claverhouse Jebb   240
Cicero, *De Oratore*, Translated by E. W. Sutton and H. Rackham   251
Demetrius, *On Style*, Translated by G.M.A. Grube   256
Longinus, *On the Sublime*, Translated by A.O. Prickard   266
Augustine, *On Christian Doctrine*, Translated by D. W. Robertson, Jr.   273

UNIT V: MEMORY AND DELIVERY   287

Rhetorica Ad Herennium, Translated by Harry Caplan   289

APPENDIX: CHRONOLOGY OF CLASSICAL RHETORIC   300
SELECTED BIBLIOGRAPHY   314
INDEX   329

UNIT ONE:
RHETORIC—ITS DEFINITIONS,
VALUE AND SCOPE

PLATO: GORGIAS

Translated by W. R. M. Lamb

The formal study of rhetoric is said to have begun in Sicily in the fifth century B.C. when Corax wrote the first treatise on the subject. Sicilian rhetoric was brought to Athens by Gorgias, perhaps in the year of Plato's birth. It was Plato who submitted rhetoric to its first searching philosophical dissection. In the earliest of his two major dialogues on rhetoric, Plato cast Gorgias, with his supporters Polus and Callicles, into a devastating investigation and rejection of rhetorical, as opposed to philosophical culture. The selection offered here is from the opening of the dialogue, concentrating on the exchange between Socrates and Gorgias and ending with Socrates' long speech condemning rhetoric. The passage contains Plato's most cogently stated attack against rhetoric, although later in the dialogue Socrates deals more roughly with Polus and Callicles than with Gorgias.

447A — 465E

CHARACTERS: CALLICLES, SOCRATES, CHAEREPHON, GORGIAS, POLUS

CALL. To join in a fight or a fray, as the saying is, Socrates, you have chosen your time well enough.

SOC. Do you mean, according to the proverb, we have come too late for a feast?

Reprinted by permission of the publishers and THE LOEB CLASSICAL LIBRARY from W. R. M. Lamb, translator, Plato, *Gorgias,* Cambridge, Mass.: Harvard University Press.

CALL. Yes, a most elegant feast; for Gorgias gave us a fine and varied display but a moment ago.

SOC. But indeed, Callicles, it is Chaerephon here who must take the blame for this; he forced us to spend our time in the market-place.

CHAER. No matter, Socrates: I will take the curing of it too; for Gorgias is a friend of mine, so that he will give us a display now, if you think fit, or if you prefer, on another occasion.

CALL. What, Chaerephon? Has Socrates a desire to hear Gorgias?

CHAER. Yes, it is for that very purpose we are here.

CALL. Then whatever you have a mind to pay me a call – Gorgias is staying with me, and he will give you a display.

SOC. Thank you, Callicles: but would he consent to discuss with us? For I want to find out from the man what is the function of his art, and what it is that he professes and teaches. As for the rest of his performance, he must give it us, as you suggest, on another occasion.

CALL. The best way is to ask our friend himself, Socrates: for indeed that was one of the features of his performance. Why, only this moment he was pressing for whatever questions anyone in the house might like to ask, and saying he would answer them all.

SOC. What a good idea! Ask him, Chaerephon.

CHAER. What am I to ask?

SOC. What he is.

CHAER. How do you mean?

SOC. Just as, if he chanced to be in the shoe-making business, his answer would have been, I presume, a shoemaker. Now, don't you see my meaning?

CHAER. I see, and will ask him. Tell me, Gorgias, is Callicles here correct in saying that you profess to answer any questions one may ask you?

GORG. He is, Chaerephon; indeed, I was just now making this very profession, and I may add that nobody has asked me anything new for many years now.

CHAER. So I presume you will easily answer, Gorgias.

GORG. You are free to make trial of that, Chaerephon.

POL. Yes, to be sure; and, if you like, Chaerephon, of me. For I think Gorgias must be quite tired out, after the long discourse he has just delivered.

CHAER. Why, Polus, do you suppose you could answer more excellently than Gorgias?

POL. And what does that matter, if I should satisfy you?

CHAER. Not at all; since it is your wish, answer.

POL. Ask.

CHAER. Then I ask you, if Gorgias chanced to be skilled in the same

art as his brother Herodicus, what should we be justified in calling him?
What we call his brother, should we not?

POL. Certainly.

CHAER. Then we should make a right statement if we described him
as a doctor.

POL. Yes.

CHAER. And if he were expert in the same art as Aristophon, son of
Aglaophon, or his brother, what name should we rightly give him?

POL. Obviously that of painter.

CHAER. But as it is, we would like to know in what art he is skilled,
and hence by what name we should rightly call him.

POL. Chaerephon, there are many arts amongst mankind that have
been discovered experimentally, as the result of experiences: for
experience conducts the course of our life according to art, but
inexperience according to chance. Of these several arts various men
partake in various ways, and the best men of the best. Gorgias here is one
of these, and he is a partner in the finest art of all.

SOC. Fine, at any rate, Gorgias, is the equipment for discourse that
Polus seems to have got: but still he is not performing his promise to
Chaerephon.

GORG. How exactly, Socrates?

SOC. He does not seem to me to be quite answering what he is asked.

GORG. Well, will you please ask him?

SOC. No, if you yourself will be so good as to answer, why, I would
far rather ask you. For I see plainly, from what he has said, that Polus has
had more practice in what is called rhetoric than in discussion.

POL. How so, Socrates?

SOC. Because, Polus, when Chaerephon has asked in what art Gorgias
is skilled, you merely eulogize his art as though it were under some
censure, instead of replying what it is.

POL. Why, did I not reply that it was the finest?

SOC. You certainly did: but nobody asked what was the quality of
his art, only what it was, and by what name we ought to call Gorgias. Just
as Chaerephon laid out the lines for you at first, and you answered him
properly in brief words, in the same way you must now state what is that
art, and what we ought to call Gorgias; or rather, Gorgias, do you tell us
yourself in what art it is you are skilled, and hence, what we ought to call
you.

GORG. Rhetoric, Socrates.

SOC. So we are to call you a rhetorician?

GORG. Yes, and a good one, if you are pleased to call me what — to
use Homer's phrase — "I vaunt myself to be."

SOC. Well, I am pleased to do so.

GORG. Then call me such.

SOC. And are we to say that you are able to make others like yourself?

GORG. Yes, that is what I profess to do, not only here, but elsewhere also.

SOC. Then would you be willing, Gorgias, to continue this present way of discussion, by alternate question and answer, and defer to some other time that lengthy style of speech in which Polus made a beginning? Come, be true to your promise, and consent to answer each question briefly.

GORG. There are some answers, Socrates, that necessitate a lengthy expression: however, I will try to be as brief as possible; for indeed it is one of my claims that no one could express the same thing in briefer terms than myself.

SOC. That is just what I want, Gorgias: give me a display of this very skill — in brevity of speech; your lengthy style will do another time.

GORG. Well, I will do that, and you will admit that you never heard anyone speak more briefly.

SOC. Come then; since you claim to be skilled in rhetorical art, and to be able to make anyone else a rhetorician, tell me with what particular thing rhetoric is concerned: as, for example, weaving is concerned with the manufacture of clothes, is it not?

GORG. Yes.

SOC. And music, likewise, with the making of tunes?

GORG. Yes.

SOC. Upon my word, Gorgias, I do admire your answers! You make them as brief as they well can be.

GORG. Yes, Socrates, I consider myself a very fair hand at that.

SOC. You are right there. Come now, answer me in the same way about rhetoric: with what particular thing is its skill concerned?

GORG. With speech.

SOC. What kind of speech, Gorgias? Do you mean that which shows by what regimen sick people could get well?

GORG. No.

SOC. Then rhetoric is not concerned with all kinds of speech.

GORG. No, I say.

SOC. Yet it does make men able to speak.

GORG. Yes.

SOC. And to understand also the things about which they speak.

GORG. Of course.

SOC. Now, does the medical art, which we mentioned just now, make men able to understand and speak about the sick?

GORG. It must.

SOC. Hence the medical art also, it seems, is concerned with speech.

GORG. Yes.

SOC. That is, speech about diseases?

GORG. Certainly.

SOC. Now, is gymnastic also concerned with speech about the good and bad condition of our bodies?

GORG. Quite so.

SOC. And moreover it is the same, Gorgias, with all the other arts; each of them is concerned with that kind of speech which deals with the subject matter of that particular art.

GORG. Apparently.

SOC. Then why, pray, do you not give the name "rhetorical" to those other arts, when they are concerned with speech, if you call that 'rhetoric" which has to do with speech?

GORG. Because, Socrates, the skill in those other arts is almost wholly concerned with manual work and similar activities, whereas in rhetoric there is no such manual working, but its whole activity and efficacy is by means of speech. For this reason I claim for the rhetorical art that it is concerned with speech, and it is a correct description, I maintain.

SOC. Now, do I understand what sort of art you choose to call it? Perhaps, however, I shall get to know this more clearly. But answer me this: we have arts, have we not?

GORG. Yes.

SOC. Then amongst the various arts some, I take it, consist mainly of work, and so require but brief speech; while others require none, for the art's object may be achieved actually in silence, as with painting, sculpture, and many other arts. It is to such as these that I understand you to refer when you say rhetoric has no concern with them; is not that so?

GORG. Your supposition is quite correct, Socrates.

SOC. But there is another class of arts which achieve their whole purpose through speech and — to put it roughly — require either no action to aid them, or very little; for example, numeration, calculation, geometry, draught-playing, and many other arts: some of these have the speech in about equal proportion to the action, but most have it as the larger part, or absolutely the whole of their operation and effect is by means of speech. It is one of this class of arts that I think you refer to as rhetoric.

GORG. You are right.

SOC. But, mind you, I do not think it is any one of these that you mean to call rhetoric; though, so far as your expression went, you did say that the art which has its effect through speech is rhetoric, and one might retort, if one cared to strain at mere words: So, Gorgias, you call numeration rhetoric! But I do not believe it is either numeration or geometry that you call rhetoric.

GORG. Your belief is correct, Socrates, and your retort just.

SOC. Come now, and do your part in finishing off the answer to my question. Since rhetoric is in fact one of these arts which depend mainly on speech, and there are likewise other arts of the same nature, try if you can tell me with what this rhetoric, which has its effect in speech, is concerned. For instance, suppose some one asked me about one or other of the arts which I was mentioning just now: Socrates, what is the art of numeration? I should tell him, as you did me a moment ago, that it is one of those which have their effect through speech. And suppose he went on to ask: With what is its speech concerned? I should say: With the odd and even numbers, whatever may chance to be the amount of each. And if he asked again: What art is it that you call calculation? I should say that this also is one of those which achieve their whole effect by speech. And if he proceeded to ask: With what is it concerned? I should say — in the manner of those who draft amendments in the Assembly — that "in all else" calculation "corresponds" with numeration, for both are concerned with the same thing, the odd and the even; but that they differ to this extent, that calculation considers the numerical values of odd and even numbers not merely in themselves but in relation to each other. And suppose, on my saying that astronomy also achieves its whole effect by speech, he were to ask me: And the speech of astronomy, with what is it concerned? I should say: With the courses of the stars and sun and moon, and their relative speeds.

GORG.   And you would be right, Socrates.

SOC.   Come then and do your part, Gorgias: rhetoric is one of those arts, is it not, which carry out their work and achieve their effect by speech?

GORG.   That is so.

SOC.   Then tell me what they deal with: what subject is it, of all in the world, that is dealt with by this speech employed by rhetoric?

GORG.   The greatest of human affairs, Socrates, and the best.

SOC.   But that also, Gorgias, is ambiguous, and still by no means clear. I expect you have heard people singing over their cups the old catch, in which the singers enumerate the best things in life, — first health, then beauty, and thirdly, as the author of the catch puts it, wealth got without guile.

GORG.   Yes, I have heard it; but what is the point of your quotation?

SOC.   I mean that, supposing the producers of those blessings which the author of the catch commends — namely, the doctor, the trainer, and the money-getter — were to stand before you this moment, and the doctor first should say: "Gorgias is deceiving you, Socrates; for it is not his art, but mine, that deals with man's greatest good." Then supposing I were to ask him: "And who are you, to say so?" He would probably reply: "A doctor." "Well, what do you mean? That the work of your art is the greatest good?" "What else, Socrates," I expect he would reply, "is health? What greater good is there for men than health?" And supposing the trainer came next and said: "I also should be surprised indeed, Socrates, if Gorgias could show you a greater good in his art than I can in mine." Again I should say to him in his turn: "And who are you, sir? What is your

work?" "A trainer" he would reply, "and my work is making men's bodies
beautiful and strong." After the trainer would come the money-getter,
saying — with, I fancy, a fine contempt for every one: "Pray consider,
Socrates, if you can find a good that is greater than wealth, either on
Gorgias' showing or on that of anyone else at all." "Why then," we should
say to him, "are you a producer of that?" "Yes," he would say. "And who
are you?" "A money-getter." "Well then," we shall say to him, "do you
judge wealth to be the greatest good for men?" "Of course," he will reply.
"But look here," we should say; "our friend Gorgias contends that his own
art is a cause of greater good than yours." Then doubtless his next
question would be: "And what is that good? Let Gorgias answer." Now
come, Gorgias; imagine yourself being questioned by those persons and by
me, and tell us what is this thing that you say is the greatest good for men,
and that you claim to produce.

GORG. A thing, Socrates, which in truth is the greatest good, and a
cause not merely of freedom to mankind at large, but also of dominion
to single persons in their several cities.

SOC. Well, and what do you call it?

GORG. I call it the ability to persuade with speeches either judges in
the law courts or statesmen in the council-chamber or the commons in
the Assembly or an audience at any other meeting that may be held on
public affairs. And I tell you that by virtue of this power you will have the
doctor as your slave, and the trainer as your slave; your money-getter will
turn out to be making money not for himself, but for another, — in fact
for you, who are able to speak and persuade the multitude.

SOC. I think now, Gorgias, you have come very near to showing us
the art of rhetoric as you conceive it, and if I at all take your meaning, you
say that rhetoric is a producer of persuasion, and has therein its whole
business and main consummation. Or can you tell us of any other function
it can have beyond that of effecting persuasion in the minds of an
audience?

GORG. None at all, Socrates; your definition seems to me
satisfactory; that is the main substance of the art.

SOC. Then listen, Gorgias: I, let me assure you, for so I persuade
myself — if ever there was a man who debated with another from a desire
of knowing the truth of the subject discussed, I am such a man; and so, I
trust, are you.

GORG. Well, what then, Socrates?

SOC. I will now tell you. What the real nature of the persuasion is
that you speak of as resulting from rhetoric, and what the matters are with
which persuasion deals, I assure you I do not clearly understand; though I
may have my suspicions as to what I suppose you to mean by it, and with
what things you think it deals. But nevertheless I will ask you what you do
mean by the persuasion that results from rhetoric, and with what matters
you think it deals. Now why is it that, having a suspicion of my own, I am
going to ask you this, instead of stating it myself? It is not on your

account, but with a view to the argument, and to such a progress in it as may best reveal to us the point we are discussing. Just see if you do not think it fair of me to press you with my question: suppose I happened to ask you what Zeuxis was among painters, and you said "a figure painter," would it not be fair of me to ask you what sort of figures he painted, and where?

GORG. Certainly.

SOC. Would this be the reason — that there are also other painters who depict a variety of other figures?

GORG. Yes.

SOC. But if no one besides Zeuxis were a painter, your answer would have been right?

GORG. Yes, of course.

SOC. Come then, tell me now about rhetoric: do you think rhetoric alone effects persuasion, or can other arts do it as well? I mean, for example, when a man teaches anything, does he persuade in his teaching? Or do you think not?

GORG. No, to be sure, Socrates, I think he most certainly does persuade.

SOC. Then let us repeat our question with reference to the same arts that we spoke of just now: does not numeration, or the person skilled in numeration, teach us all that pertains to number?

GORG. Certainly.

SOC. And persuades also?

GORG. Yes.

SOC. So that numeration also is a producer of persuasion?

GORG. Apparently.

SOC. Then if we are asked what kind of persuasion, and dealing with what, we shall reply, I suppose: The instructive kind, which deals with the amount of an odd or an even number; and we shall be able to demonstrate that all the other arts which we mentioned just now are producers of persuasion, and what kind it is, and what it deals with, shall we not?

GORG. Yes.

SOC. Hence rhetoric is not the only producer of persuasion.

GORG. You are right.

SOC. Since then it is not the only one that achieves this effect, but others can also, we should be justified in putting this further question to the speaker, as we did concerning the painter: Then of what kind of persuasion, and of persuasion dealing with what, is rhetoric the art? Or do you not consider that such a further question would be justified?

GORG. Yes, I do.

SOC. Then answer me, Gorgias, since you agree with me on that.

GORG. Well then, I mean that kind of persuasion, Socrates, which you find in the law-courts and in any public gatherings, as in fact I said just now; and it deals with what is just and unjust.

SOC. I, too, I may tell you, had a suspicion that it was this persuasion that you meant, and as dealing with those things, Gorgias; but you must not be surprised if I ask you by-and-by some such question as may seem to be obvious, though I persist in it; for, as I say, I ask my questions with a view to an orderly completion of our argument — I am not aiming at you, but only anxious that we do not fall into a habit of snatching at each other's words with a hasty guess, and that you may complete your own statement in your own way, as the premises may allow.

GORG. And I think you are quite right in doing so, Socrates.

SOC. Come then, let us consider another point. Is there something that you call "having learnt."

GORG. There is.

SOC. And again, "having believed"?

GORG. Yes.

SOC. Then do you think that having learnt and having believed, or learning and belief, are the same thing, or different?

GORG. In my opinion, Socrates, they are different.

SOC. And your opinion is right, as you can prove in this way: if some one asked you — Is there, Gorgias, a false and a true belief? — you would say, Yes, I imagine.

GORG. I should.

SOC. But now, is there a false and a true knowledge?

GORG. Surely not.

SOC. So it is evident again that they are not the same.

GORG. You are right.

SOC. But yet those who have learnt have been persuaded, as well as those who have believed.

GORG. That is so.

SOC. Then would you have us assume two forms of persuasion — one providing belief without knowledge, and the other sure knowledge?

GORG. Certainly.

SOC. Now which kind of persuasion is it that rhetoric creates in law courts or any public meeting on matters of right and wrong? The kind from which we get belief without knowledge, or that from which we get knowledge?

GORG. Obviously, I presume, Socrates, that from which we get belief.

SOC. Thus rhetoric, it seems, is a producer of persuasion for belief, not for instruction in the matter of right and wrong.

GORG. Yes.

SOC. And so the rhetorician's business is not to instruct a law court or a public meeting in matters of right and wrong, but only to make them believe; since, I take it, he could not in a short while instruct such a mass of people in matters so important.

GORG. No, to be sure.

SOC. Come then, let us see what actually is our account of rhetoric: for I confess I am not yet able to distinguish what my own account of it is. When the city holds a meeting to appoint doctors or shipbuilders or any other set of craftsmen, there is no question then, is there, of the rhetorician giving advice? And clearly this is because in each appointment we have to elect the most skillful person. Again, in a case of building walls or constructing harbours or arsenals, our only advisers are the master-builders; or in consulting on the appointment of generals, or on a manoeuvre against the enemy, or on a military occupation, it is the general staff who will then advise us, and not the rhetoricians. Or what do you say, Gorgias, to these instances? For as you claim to be an orator yourself and to make orators of others, it is proper to inquire of you concerning your own craft. And here you must regard me as furthering your own interest: for it is quite likely that some one within these walls has a wish to become your pupil – indeed I fancy I perceive more than one, yes, a number of them, who, perhaps, would be ashamed to press you with questions. So, when you are being pressed with mine, consider that you are being questioned by them as well: "What shall we get, Gorgias, by coming to hear you? On what matters shall we be enabled to give advice to the state? Will it be only on right and wrong, or on those things besides which Socrates was mentioning just now?" So try to give them an answer.

GORG. Well, I will try, Socrates, to reveal to you clearly the whole power of rhetoric: and in fact you have correctly shown the way to it yourself. You know, I suppose, that these great arsenals and walls of Athens, and the construction of your harbours, are due to the advice of Themistocles, and in part to that of Pericles, not to your craftsmen.

SOC. So we are told, Gorgias, of Themistocles; and as to Pericles, I heard him myself when he was advising us about the middle wall.

GORG. So whenever there is an election of such persons as you were referring to, Socrates, you see it is the orators who give the advice and get resolutions carried in these matters.

SOC. That is just what surprises me, Gorgias, and has made me ask you all this time what in the world the power of rhetoric can be. For, viewed in this light, its greatness comes over me as something supernatural.

GORG. Ah yes, if you knew all, Socrates, – how it comprises in itself practically all powers at once! And I will tell you a striking proof of this: many and many a time have I gone with my brother or other doctors to visit one of their patients, and found him unwilling either to take medicine or submit to the surgeon's knife or cautery; and when the doctor failed to persuade him I succeeded, by no other art than that of rhetoric. And I further declare that, if a rhetorician and a doctor were to enter any city you please, and there had to contend in speech before the Assembly or some other meeting as to which of the two should be appointed physician, you would find the physician was nowhere, while the master of speech would be appointed if he wished. And if he had to contend with a member of any other profession whatsoever, the rhetorician would persuade the meeting to appoint him before anyone else in the place: for there is no subject on which the rhetorician could not speak more persuasively than a member of any other profession whatsoever, before a multitude. So great, so strange, is the power of this art. At the same time, Socrates, our use of rhetoric should be like our use of any other sort of exercise. For other exercises are not to be used against all and sundry, just because one has learnt boxing or wrestling or fighting in armour so well as to vanquish friend and foe alike: this gives one no right to strike one's friends, or stab them to death. Nor, in all conscience, if a man took lessons at a wrestling-school, and having got himself into good condition and learnt boxing he proceeded to strike his father and mother, or some other of his relations or friends, should that be a reason for hating athletic trainers and teachers of fighting in armour, and expelling them from our cities. For they imparted their skill with a view to its rightful use against enemies and wrongdoers, in self-defence, not provocation; whereas the others have perverted their strength and art to an improper use. So it is not the teachers who are wicked, nor is the art either guilty or wicked on this account, but rather, to my thinking, those who do not use it properly. Now the same argument applies also to rhetoric: for the orator is able, indeed, to speak against every one and on every question in such a way as to win over the votes of the multitude, practically in any matter he may choose to take up: but he is no whit the more entitled to deprive the doctors of their credit, just because he could do so, or other professionals of theirs; he must use his rhetoric fairly, as in the case of athletic exercise. And, in my opinion, if a man becomes a rhetorician and then uses this power and this art unfairly, we ought not to hate his teacher and cast him out of our cities. For he imparted that skill to be used in all fairness, whilst this man puts it to an opposite use. Thus it is the man who does not use it aright who deserves to be hated and expelled and put to death, and not his teacher.

SOC. I expect, Gorgias, that you as well as I have had no small practice in arguments, and have observed the following fact about them, that it is not easy for people to define to each other the matters which they take in hand to discuss, and to make such exchange of instruction as will fairly bring their debate to an end: no, if they find that some point is in dispute between them, and one of them says that the other is speaking incorrectly or obscurely, they are annoyed and think the remark comes from jealousy of themselves, and in a spirit of contention rather than of inquiry into the matter proposed for discussion. In some cases, indeed, they end by making a most disgraceful scene, with such abusive expressions on each side that the rest of the company are vexed on their own account that they allowed themselves to listen to such fellows. Well, what is my reason for saying this? It is because your present remarks do not seem to me quite in keeping or accord with what you said at first about rhetoric. Now I am afraid to refute you, lest you imagine I am contentiously neglecting the point and its elucidation, and merely attacking you. I therefore, if you are a person of the same sort as myself, should be glad to continue questioning you: if not, I can let it drop. Of what sort am I? One of those who would be glad to be refuted if I say anything untrue, and glad to refute anyone else who might speak untruly; but just as glad, mind you, to be refuted as to refute, since I regard the former as the greater benefit, in proportion as it is a greater benefit for oneself to be delivered from the greatest evil than to deliver some one else. For I consider that a man cannot suffer any evil so great as a false opinion on the subjects of our actual argument. Now if you say that you too are of that sort, let us go on with the conversation; but if you think we had better drop it, let us have done with it at once and make an end of the discussion.

GORG. Nay, I too, Socrates, claim to be of the sort you indicate; though perhaps we should have taken thought also for the wishes of our company. For, let me tell you, some time before you and your friend arrived, I gave the company a performance of some length; and if we now have this conversation I expect we shall seriously protract our sitting. We ought, therefore, to consider their wishes as well, in case we are detaining any of them who may want to do something else.

CHAER. You hear for yourselves, Gorgias and Socrates, the applause by which these gentlemen show their desire to hear anything you may say; for my own part, however, Heaven forbid that I should ever be so busy as to give up a discussion so interesting and so conducted, because I found it more important to attend to something else.

CALL. Yes, by all that's holy, Chaerephon; and let me say, moreover, for myself that among the many discussions which I have attended in my time I doubt if there was one that gave me such delight as this present one. So, for my part, I shall count it a favour even if you choose to continue it all day long.

SOC. Why, Callicles, I assure you there is no hindrance on my side, if Gorgias is willing.

GORG. After that, Socrates, it would be shameful indeed if I were unwilling, when it was I who challenged everybody to ask what questions they pleased. But if our friends here are so minded, go on with the conversation and ask me anything you like . . . .

SOC. Hark you then, Gorgias, to what surprises me in your statements: to be sure, you may possibly be right, and I may take your meaning wrongly. You say you are able to make a rhetorician of any man who chooses to learn from you?

GORG. Yes.

SOC. Now, do you mean, to make him carry conviction to the crowd on all subjects, not by teaching them, but by persuading?

GORG. Certainly I do.

SOC. You were saying just now, you know, that even in the matter of health the orator will be more convincing than the doctor.

GORG. Yes, indeed, I was — meaning, to the crowd.

SOC. And "to the crowd" means "to the ignorant"? For surely, to those who know, he will not be more convincing than the doctor.

GORG. You are right.

SOC. And if he is to be more convincing than the doctor, he thus becomes more convincing than he who knows?

GORG. Certainly.

SOC. Though not himself a doctor, you agree?

GORG. Yes.

SOC. But he who is not a doctor is surely without knowledge of that whereof the doctor has knowledge.

GORG. Clearly.

SOC. So he who does not know will be more convincing to those who do not know than he who knows, supposing the orator to be more convincing than the doctor. Is that, or something else, the consequence?

GORG. In this case it does follow.

SOC. Then the case is the same in all the other arts for the orator and his rhetoric: there is no need to know the truth of the actual matters, but one merely needs to have discovered some device of persuasion which will make one appear to those who do not know to know better than those who know.

GORG. Well, and is it not a great convenience, Socrates, to make oneself a match for the professionals by learning just this single art and omitting all the others?

SOC. Whether the orator is or is not a match for the rest of them by reason of that skill, is a question we shall look into presently, if our argument so requires: for the moment let us consider first whether the rhetorician is in the same relation to what is just and unjust, base and noble, good and bad, as to what is healthful, and to the various objects of all the other arts; he does not know what is really good or bad, noble or base, just or unjust, but he has devised a persuasion to deal with these matters so as to appear to those who, like himself, do not know to know better than he who knows. Or is it necessary to know, and must anyone who intends to learn rhetoric have a previous knowledge of these things when he comes to you? Or if not, are you, as the teacher of rhetoric, to teach the person who comes to you nothing about them — for it is not your business — but only to make him appear in the eyes of the multitude to know things of this sort when he does not know, and to appear to be good when he is not? Or will you be utterly unable to teach him rhetoric unless he previously knows the truth about these matters? Or what is the real state of the case, Gorgias? For Heaven's sake, as you proposed just now, draw aside the veil and tell us what really is the function of rhetoric.

GORG. Why, I suppose, Socrates, if he happens not to know these things he will learn them too from me.

SOC. Stop there: I am glad of that statement. If you make a man a rhetorician he must needs know what is just and unjust either previously or by learning afterwards from you.

GORG. Quite so.

SOC. Well now, a man who has learnt building is a builder, is he not?

GORG. Yes.

SOC. And he who has learnt music, a musician?

GORG. Yes.

SOC. Then he who has learnt medicine is a medical man, and so on with the rest on the same principle; anyone who has learnt a certain art has the qualification acquired by his particular knowledge?

GORG. Certainly.

SOC. And so, on this principle, he who has learnt what is just is just?

GORG. Absolutely, I presume.

SOC. And the just man, I suppose, does what is just.

GORG. Yes.

SOC. Now the just man must *wish* to do what is just?

GORG. Apparently.

SOC. Hence the just man will never wish to act unjustly?

GORG. That must needs be so.

SOC. But it follows from our statements that the rhetorician must be just.

GORG. Yes.

SOC. Hence the rhetorician will never wish to do wrong.

GORG. Apparently not.

SOC. Then do you remember saying a little while ago that we ought not to complain against the trainers or expel them from our cities, if a boxer makes not merely use, but an unfair use, of his boxing? So in just the same way, if an orator uses his rhetoric unfairly, we should not complain against his teacher or banish him from our city, but the man who does the wrong and misuses his rhetoric. Was that said or not?

GORG. It was.

SOC. But now we find that this very person, the rhetorician, could never be guilty of wrongdoing, do we not?

GORG. We do.

SOC. And in our first statements, Gorgias, we said that rhetoric dealt with speech, not on even and odd, but on the just and unjust, did we not?

GORG. Yes.

SOC. Well then, I supposed at the time when you were saying this that rhetoric could never be an unjust thing, since the speeches it made were always about justice; but when a little later you told us that the orator might make even an unjust use of his rhetoric, that indeed surprised me, and thinking the two statements were not in accord I made those proposals, — that if, like myself, you counted it a gain to be refuted, it was worth while to have the discussion, but if not, we had better have done with it. And now that we have come to examine the matter, you see for yourself that we agree once more that it is impossible for the rhetorician to use his rhetoric unjustly or consent to do wrong. Now, to distinguish properly which way the truth of the matter lies will require, by the Dog, Gorgias, no short sitting.

POL. How is this, Socrates? Is that really your opinion of rhetoric, as you now express it? Or, think you, because Gorgias was ashamed not to admit your point that the rhetorician knows what is just and noble and good, and will himself teach these to anyone who comes to him without knowing them; and then from this admission I daresay there followed some inconsistency in the statements made — the result that you are so fond of — when it was yourself who led him into that set of questions![1] For who do you think will deny that he has a knowledge of what is just and can also teach it to others? I call it very bad taste to lead the discussion in such a direction.

SOC. Ah, sweet Polus, of course it is for this very purpose we possess ourselves of companions and sons, that when the advance of years begins to make us stumble, you younger ones may be at hand to set our lives upright again in words as well as deeds. So now if Gorgias and I are stumbling in our words, you are to stand by and set us up again — it is only your duty; and for my part I am willing to revoke at your pleasure anything that you think has been wrongly admitted, if you will kindly observe one condition.

POL. What do you mean by that?

SOC. That you keep a check on that lengthy way of speaking, Polus, which you tried to employ at first.

POL. Why, shall I not be at liberty to say as much as I like?

SOC. It would indeed be a hard fate for you, my excellent friend, if having come to Athens, where there is more freedom of speech than anywhere in Greece, you should be the one person there who could not enjoy it. But as a set-off to that, I ask you if it would not be just as hard on me, while you spoke at length and refused to answer my questions, not to be free to go away and avoid listening to you. No, if you have any concern for the argument that we have carried on, and care to set it on its feet again, revoke whatever you please, as I suggested just now; take your turn in questioning and being questioned, like me and Gorgias; and thus either refute or be refuted. For you claim, I understand, that you yourself know all that Gorgias knows, do you not?

POL. I do.

[1] The defective construction of this sentence is probably intended to mark the agitated manner of Polus in making his protest.

SOC. Then are you with him also in bidding us ask at each point any questions we like of you, as one who knows how to answer?

POL. Certainly I am.

SOC. So now, take whichever course you like: either put questions, or answer them.

POL. Well, I will do as you say. So answer me this, Socrates: since you think that Gorgias is at a loss about rhetoric, what is your own account of it?

SOC. Are you asking what art I call it?

POL. Yes.

SOC. None at all, I consider, Polus, if you would have the honest truth.

POL. But what do you consider rhetoric to be?

SOC. A thing which you say — in the treatise which I read of late — "made art."

POL. What thing do you mean?

SOC. I mean a certain habitude.

POL. Then do you take rhetoric to be a habitude?

SOC. I do, if you have no other suggestion.

POL. Habitude of what?

SOC. Of producing a kind of gratification and pleasure.

POL. Then you take rhetoric to be something fine — an ability to gratify people?

SOC. How now, Polus? Have you as yet heard me tell you what I say it is, that you ask what should follow that — whether I do not take it to be fine?

POL. Why, did I not hear you call it a certain habitude?

SOC. Then please — since you value "gratification" — be so good as to gratify me in a small matter.

POL. I will.

SOC. Ask me now what art I take cookery to be.

POL. Then I ask you, what art is cookery?

SOC. None at all, Polus.

POL. Well, what is it? Tell me.

SOC. Then I reply, a certain habitude.

POL. Of what? Tell me.

SOC. Then I reply, of production of gratification and pleasure, Polus.

POL. So cookery and rhetoric are the same thing?

SOC. Not at all, only parts of the same practice.

POL. What practice do you mean?

SOC. I fear it may be too rude to tell the truth; for I shrink from saying it on Gorgias' account, lest he suppose I am making satirical fun of his own pursuit. Yet indeed I do not know whether this is the rhetoric which Gorgias practises, for from our argument just now we got no very clear view as to how he conceives it; but what I call rhetoric is a part of a

gratifications they gave it, we should have a fine instance of what Anaxagoras described, my dear Polus, — for you are versed in these matters: everything would be jumbled together, without distinction as between medicinal and healthful and tasty concoctions. Well now, you have heard what I state rhetoric to be — the counterpart of cookery in the soul, acting here as that does on the body.

PLATO: PHAEDRUS

Translated by H. N. Fowler

In the Gorgias *Plato had attacked that form of persuasive discourse which developed as "a branch of flattery." In the* Phaedrus, *a complex and brilliant dialogue on rhetoric and love, Plato goes beyond condemnation of a base rhetoric to construct a view of what a noble rhetoric might involve.*

At the opening of the dialogue, Socrates meets Phaedrus on a street in Athens. Phaedrus has just spent the morning listening to the great orator Lysias discoursing on love, praising the merits of the non-lover over those of the lover, and at Socrates' urging, Phaedrus repeats the speech. When Phaedrus has finished, Socrates replies with a better speech on the same theme; then disclaims the speech he has just given and delivers another, even better, praising the madness of love.

The Phaedrus *begins as an attack upon the eloquence of the rhetoricians, but in the* Phaedrus, *unlike the* Gorgias, *Plato also describes a "true rhetoric." The passage reproduced here is from the last section of the dialogue, when Socrates draws forth the rhetorical implications of the earlier speeches.*

258C – 279C

SOCRATES. When an orator or a king is able to rival the greatness of Lycurgus or Solon or Darius and attain immortality as a writer in the state, does he not while living think himself equal to the gods, and has not posterity the same opinion of him, when they see his writings?

PHAEDRUS. Very true.

Reprinted by permission of the publishers and THE LOEB CLASSICAL LIBRARY from H. N. Fowler, translator, Plato, *Phaedrus,* Cambridge, Mass.: Harvard University Press.

SOCRATES. Do you think, then, that any of the statesmen, no matter how ill-disposed toward Lysias, reproaches him for being a writer?

PHAEDRUS. It is not likely, according to what you say; for he would be casting reproach upon that which he himself desires to be.

SOCRATES. Then that is clear to all, that writing speeches is not in itself a disgrace.

PHAEDRUS. How can it be?

SOCRATES. But the disgrace, I fancy, consists in speaking or writing not well, but disgracefully and badly.

PHAEDRUS. Evidently.

SOCRATES. What, then, is the method of writing well or badly? Do we want to question Lysias about this, and anyone else who ever has written or will write anything, whether a public or private document, in verse or in prose, be he poet or ordinary man?

PHAEDRUS. You ask if we want to question them? What else should one live for, so to speak, but for such pleasures? Certainly not for those which cannot be enjoyed without previous pain, which is the case with nearly all bodily pleasures and causes them to be justly called slavish.

SOCRATES. We have plenty of time, apparently; and besides, the locusts seem to be looking down upon us as they sing and talk with each other in the heat. Now if they should see us not conversing at mid-day, but, like most people, dozing, lulled to sleep by their song because of our mental indolence, they would quite justly laugh at us, thinking that some slaves had come to their resort and were slumbering about the fountain at noon like sheep. But if they see us conversing and sailing past them unmoved by the charm of their Siren voices, perhaps they will be pleased and give us the gift which the gods bestowed on them to give to men.

PHAEDRUS. What is this gift? I don't seem to have heard of it.

SOCRATES. It is quite improper for a lover of the Muses never to have heard of such things. The story goes that these locusts were once men, before the birth of the Muses, and when the Muses were born and song appeared, some of the men were so overcome with delight that they sang and sang, forgetting food and drink, until at last unconsciously they died. From them the locust tribe afterwards arose, and they have this gift from the Muses, that from the time of their birth they need no sustenance, but sing continually, without food or drink, until they die, when they go to the Muses and report who honours each of them on earth. They tell Terpsichore of those who have honoured her in dances, and make them dearer to her; they gain the favour of Erato for the poets of love, and that of the other Muses for their votaries, according to their various ways of honouring them; and to Calliope, the eldest of the Muses, and to Urania who is next to her, they make report of those who pass their lives in philosophy and who worship these Muses who are most concerned with heaven and with thought divine and human and whose music is the sweetest. So for many reasons we ought to talk and not sleep in the noontime.

PHAEDRUS. Yes, we ought to talk.

SOCRATES. We should, then, as we were proposing just now, discuss the theory of good (or bad) speaking and writing.

PHAEDRUS. Clearly.

SOCRATES. If a speech is to be good, must not the mind of the speaker know the truth about the matters of which he is to speak?

PHAEDRUS. On that point, Socrates, I have heard that one who is to be an orator does not need to know what is really just, but what would seem just to the multitude who are to pass judgment, and not what is really good or noble, but what will seem to be so; for they say that persuasion comes from what seems to be true, not from the truth.

SOCRATES. "The word," Phaedrus, which the wise "speak must not be rejected," but we must see if they are right; so we must not pass by this which you just said.

PHAEDRUS. You are right.

SOCRATES. Let us then examine it in this way.

PHAEDRUS. How?

SOCRATES. If I should urge you to buy a horse and fight against the invaders, and neither of us knew what a horse was, but I merely knew this about you, that Phaedrus thinks a horse is the one of the tame animals which has the longest ears –

PHAEDRUS. It would be ridiculous, Socrates.

SOCRATES. No, not yet; but if I tried to persuade you in all seriousness, composing a speech in praise of the ass, which I called a horse, and saying that the beast was a most valuable possession at home and in war, that you could use him as a mount in battle, and that he was able to carry baggage and was useful for many other purposes –

PHAEDRUS. Then it would be supremely ridiculous.

SOCRATES. But is it not better to be ridiculous than to be clever and an enemy?

PHAEDRUS. To be sure.

SOCRATES. Then when the orator who does not know what good and evil are undertakes to persuade a state which is equally ignorant, not by praising the "shadow of an ass"[1] under the name of a horse, but by praising evil under the name of good, and having studied the opinions of the multitude persuades them to do evil instead of good, what harvest do you suppose his oratory will reap thereafter from the seed he has sown?

PHAEDRUS. No very good harvest.

SOCRATES. Well, do you think I have reproached the art of speaking too harshly? Perhaps she might say: "Why do you talk such

---

[1] A proverbial expression.

nonsense, you strange men? I do not compel anyone to learn to speak without knowing the truth, but if my advice is of any value, he learns that first and then acquires me. So what I claim is this, that without my help the knowledge of the truth does not give the art of persuasion."

PHAEDRUS. And will she be right in saying this?

SOCRATES. Yes, if the arguments that are coming against her testify that she is an art. For I seem, as it were, to hear some arguments approaching and protesting that she is lying and is not an art, but a craft devoid of art. A real art of speaking, says the Laconian, which does not seize hold of truth, does not exist and never will.

PHAEDRUS. We have need of these arguments, Socrates. Bring them here and examine their words and their meaning.

SOCRATES. Come here, then, noble creatures, and persuade the fair young Phaedrus that unless he pay proper attention to philosophy he will never be able to speak properly about anything. And let Phaedrus answer.

PHAEDRUS. Ask your questions.

SOCRATES. Is not rhetoric in its entire nature an art which leads the soul by means of words, not only in law courts and the various other public assemblages, but in private companies as well? And is it not the same when concerned with small things as with great, and, properly speaking, no more to be esteemed in important than in trifling matters? Is this what you have heard?

PHAEDRUS. No, by Zeus, not that exactly; but the art of speaking and writing is exercised chiefly in lawsuits, and that of speaking also in public assemblies; and I never heard of any further uses.

SOCRATES. Then you have heard only of the treatises on rhetoric by Nestor and Odysseus, which they wrote when they had nothing to do at Troy, and you have not heard of that by Palamedes?

PHAEDRUS. Nor of Nestor's either, unless you are disguising Gorgias under the name of Nestor and Thrasymachus or Theodorus under that of Odysseus.

SOCRATES. Perhaps I am. However, never mind them; but tell me, what do the parties in a lawsuit do in court? Do they not contend in speech, or what shall we say they do?

PHAEDRUS. Exactly that.

SOCRATES. About the just and the unjust?

PHAEDRUS. Yes.

SOCRATES. Then he whose speaking is an art will make the same thing appear to the same persons at one time just and at another, if he wishes, unjust?

PHAEDRUS. Certainly.

SOCRATES. And in political speaking he will make the same things seem to the State at one time good and at another the opposite?

PHAEDRUS. Just so.

SOCRATES. Do we not know that the Eleatie Palamedes (Zeno) has such an art of speaking that the same things appear to his hearers to be alike and unlike, one and many, stationary and in motion?

PHAEDRUS. Certainly.

SOCRATES. Then the art of contention in speech is not confined to courts and political gatherings, but apparently, if it is an art at all, it would be one and the same in all kinds of speaking, the art by which a man will be able to produce a resemblance between all things between which it can be produced, and to bring to the light the resemblances produced and disguised by anyone else.

PHAEDRUS. What do you mean by that?

SOCRATES. I think it will be plain if we examine the matter in this way. Is deception easier when there is much difference between things or when there is little?

PHAEDRUS. When there is little.

SOCRATES. And if you make a transition by small steps from anything to its opposite you will be more likely to escape detection than if you proceed by leaps and bounds.

PHAEDRUS. Of course.

SOCRATES. Then he who is to deceive another, and is not to be deceived himself, must know accurately the similarity and dissimilarity of things.

PHAEDRUS. Yes, he must.

SOCRATES. Now will he be able, not knowing the truth about a given thing, to recognise in other things the great or small degree of likeness to that which he does not know?

PHAEDRUS. It is impossible.

SOCRATES. In the case, then, of those whose opinions are at variance with facts and who are deceived, this error evidently slips in through some resemblances.

PHAEDRUS. It does happen in that way.

SOCRATES. Then he who does not understand the real nature of things will not possess the art of making his hearers pass from one thing to its opposite by leading them through the intervening resemblances, or of avoiding such deception himself?

PHAEDRUS. Never in the world.

SOCRATES. Then, my friend, he who knows not the truth, but pursues opinions, will, it seems, attain an art of speech which is ridiculous, and not an art at all.

PHAEDRUS. Probably.

SOCRATES. Shall we look in the speech of Lysias, which you have with you, and in what I said, for something which we think shows art and the lack of art?

PHAEDRUS. By all means, for now our talk is too abstract, since we lack sufficient examples.

SOCRATES. And by some special good fortune, as it seems, the two discourses contain an example of the way in which one who knows the truth may lead his hearers on with sportive words; and I, Phaedrus, think the divinities of the place are the cause thereof; and perhaps, too, the prophets of the Muses, who are singing above our heads, may have granted this boon to us by inspiration; at any rate, I possess no art of speaking.

PHAEDRUS. So be it; only make your meaning clear.

SOCRATES. Read me the beginning of Lysias' discourse.

PHAEDRUS. You know what my condition is, and you have heard how I think it is to our advantage to arrange these matters. And I claim that I ought not to be refused what I ask because I am not your lover. For lovers repent of —

SOCRATES. Stop. Now we must tell what there is in this that is faulty and lacks art, must we not?

PHAEDRUS. Yes.

SOCRATES. It is clear to everyone that we are in accord about some matters of this kind and at variance about others, is it not?

PHAEDRUS. I think I understand your meaning, but express it still more clearly.

SOCRATES. When one says "iron" or "silver," we all understand the same thing, do we not?

PHAEDRUS. Surely.

SOCRATES. What if he says "justice" or "goodness"? Do we not part company, and disagree with each other and with ourselves?

PHAEDRUS. Certainly.

SOCRATES. Then in some things we agree and in others we do not.

PHAEDRUS. True.

SOCRATES. Then in which of the two are we more easy to deceive, and in which has rhetoric the greater power?

PHAEDRUS. Evidently in the class of doubtful things.

SOCRATES. Then he who is to develop an art of rhetoric must first make a methodical division and acquire a clear impression of each class, that in which people must be in doubt and that in which they are not.

PHAEDRUS. He who has acquired that would have conceived an excellent principle.

SOCRATES. Then I think when he has to do with a particular case, he will not be ignorant, but will know clearly to which of the two classes the thing belongs about which he is to speak.

PHAEDRUS. Of course.

SOCRATES. Well then, to which does Love belong? To the doubtful things or the others?

PHAEDRUS. To the doubtful, surely; if he did not, do you think he would have let you say what you said just now about him, that he is an injury to the beloved and to the lover, and again that he is the greatest of blessings?

SOCRATES. Excellent. But tell me this — for I was in such an ecstasy that I have quite forgotten — whether I defined love in the beginning of my discourse.

PHAEDRUS.   Yes, by Zeus, and wonderfully well.

SOCRATES.   Oh, how much more versed the nymphs, daughters of Achelous, and Pan, son of Hermes, are in the art of speech than Lysias, son of Cephalus! Or am I wrong, and did Lysias also, in the beginning of his discourse on Love, compel us to suppose Love to be some one thing which he chose to consider it, and did he then compose and finish his discourse with that in view? Shall we read the beginning of it again?

PHAEDRUS.   If you like; but what you seek is not in it.

SOCRATES.   Read, that I may hear Lysias himself.

PHAEDRUS.   You know what my condition is, and you have heard how I think it is to our advantage to arrange these matters. And I claim that I ought not to be refused what I ask because I am not your lover. For lovers repent of the kindnesses they have done when their passion ceases.

SOCRATES.   He certainly does not at all seem to do what we demand, for he does not even begin at the beginning, but undertakes to swim on his back up the current of his discourse from its end, and begins with what the lover would say at the end to his beloved. Am I not right, Phaedrus my dear?

PHAEDRUS.   Certainly that of which he speaks is an ending.

SOCRATES.   And how about the rest? Don't you think the parts of the discourse are thrown out helter-skelter? Or does it seem to you that the second topic had to be put second for any cogent reason, or that any of the other things he says are so placed? It seemed to me, who am wholly ignorant, that the writer uttered boldly whatever occurred to him. Do you know any rhetorical reason why he arranged his topics in this order?

PHAEDRUS.   You flatter me in thinking that I can discern his motives so accurately.

SOCRATES.   But I do think you will agree to this, that every discourse must be organised, like a living being, with a body of its own, as it were, so as not to be headless or footless, but to have a middle and members, composed in fitting relation to each other and to the whole.

PHAEDRUS.   Certainly.

SOCRATES.   See then whether this is the case with your friend's discourse, or not. You will find that it is very like the inscription that some say is inscribed on the tomb of Midas the Phrygian.

PHAEDRUS.   What sort of inscription is that, and what is the matter with it?

SOCRATES.   This is it:

A bronze maiden am I; and I am placed upon the tomb of Midas.
So long as water runs and tall trees put forth leaves,
Remaining in this very spot upon a much lamented tomb,

I shall declare to passers by that Midas is buried here;

and you perceive, I fancy, that it makes no difference whether any line of it is put first or last.

PHAEDRUS.   You are making fun of our discourse, Socrates.

SOCRATES.   Then, to spare your feelings, let us say no more of this discourse — and yet I think there were many things in it which would be useful examples to consider, though not exactly to imitate — and let us turn to the other discourses; for there was in them, I think, something which those who wish to investigate rhetoric might well examine.

PHAEDRUS.   What do you mean?

SOCRATES.   The two discourses were opposites; for one maintained that the lover, and the other that the non-lover, should be favoured.

PHAEDRUS.   And they did it right manfully.

SOCRATES.   I thought you were going to speak the truth and say "madly"; however, that is just what I had in mind. We said that love was a kind of madness, did we not?

PHAEDRUS.   Yes.

SOCRATES.   And that there are two kinds of madness, one arising from human diseases, and the other from a divine release from the customary habits.

PHAEDRUS.   Certainly.

SOCRATES.   And we made four divisions of the divine madness, ascribing them to four gods, saying that prophecy was inspired by Apollo, the mystic madness by Dionysus, the poetic by the Muses, and the madness of love, inspired by Aphrodite and Eros, we said was the best. We described the passion of love in some sort of figurative manner, expressing some truth, perhaps, and perhaps being led away in another direction, and after composing a somewhat plausible discourse, we chanted a sportive and mythic hymn in meet and pious strain to the honour of your lord and mine, Phaedrus, Love, the guardian of beautiful boys.

PHAEDRUS.   Yes, and I found it very pleasant to hear.

SOCRATES.   Here let us take up this point and see how the discourse succeeded in passing from blame to praise.

PHAEDRUS.   What do you mean?

SOCRATES.   It seems to me that the discourse was, as a whole, really sportive jest; but in these chance utterances were involved two principles, the essence of which it would be gratifying to learn, if art could teach it.

PHAEDRUS.   What principles?

SOCRATES.   That of perceiving and bringing together in one idea the scattered particulars, that one may make clear by definition the particular thing which he wishes to explain; just as now, in speaking of Love, we said what he is and defined it, whether well or ill. Certainly by this means the discourse acquired clearness and consistency.

PHAEDRUS.   And what is the other principle, Socrates?

SOCRATES. That of dividing things again by classes, where the natural joints are, and not trying to break any part, after the manner of a bad carver. As our two discourses just now assumed one common principle, unreason, and then, just as the body, which is one, is naturally divisible into two, right and left, with parts called by the same names, so our two discourses conceived of madness as naturally one principle within us, and one discourse, cutting off the left-hand part, continued to divide this until it found among its parts a sort of left-handed love, which it very justly reviled, but the other discourse, leading us to the right-hand part of madness, found a love having the same name as the first, but divine, which it held up to view and praised as the author of our greatest blessings.

PHAEDRUS. Very true.

SOCRATES. Now I myself, Phaedrus, am a lover of these processes of division and bringing together, as aids to speech and thought; and if I think any other man is able to see things that can naturally be collected into one and divided into many, him I follow after and "walk in his footsteps as if he were a god." And whether the name I give to those who can do this is right or wrong, God knows, but I have called them hitherto dialecticians. But tell me now what name to give to those who are taught by you and Lysias, or is this that art of speech by means of which Thrasymachus and the rest have become able speakers themselves, and make others so, if they are willing to pay them royal tribute?

PHAEDRUS. They are royal men, but not trained in the matters about which you ask. I think you give this method the right name when you call it dialectic; but it seems to me that rhetoric still escapes us.

SOCRATES. What do you mean? Can there be anything of importance, which is not included in these processes and yet comes under the head of art? Certainly you and I must not neglect it, but must say what it is that remains of rhetoric.

PHAEDRUS. A great many things remain, Socrates, the things that are written in the books on rhetoric.

SOCRATES. Thank you for reminding me. You mean that there must be an introduction first, at the beginning of the discourse; these are the things you mean, are they not? — the niceties of the art.

PHAEDRUS. Yes.

SOCRATES. And the narrative must come second with the testimony after it, and third the proofs, and fourth the probabilities; and confirmation and further confirmation are mentioned, I believe, by the man from Byzantium, that most excellent artist in words.

PHAEDRUS. You mean the worthy Theodorus?

SOCRATES. Of course, And he tells how refutation and further refutation must be accomplished, both in accusation and in defence. Shall we not bring the illustrious Parian, Evenus, into our discussion, who invented covert allusion and indirect praises? And some say that he also wrote indirect censures, composing them in verse as an aid to memory; for he is a clever man. And shall we leave Gorgias and Tisias undisturbed, who saw that probabilities are more to be esteemed than truths, who make small things seem great and great things small by the power of their words, and new things old and old things the reverse, and who invented conciseness of speech and measureless length on all subjects? And once when Prodicus heard these inventions, he laughed, and said that he alone had discovered the art of proper speech, that discourses should be neither long nor short, but of reasonable length.

PHAEDRUS.   O Prodicus! How clever!

SOCRATES.   And shall we not mention Hippias, our friend from Elis? I think he would agree with him.

PHAEDRUS.   Oh yes.

SOCRATES.   And what shall we say of Polus and his shrines of learned speech, such as duplication and sententiousness and figurativeness, and what of the names with which Licymnius presented him to effect beautiful diction?

PHAEDRUS.   Were there not some similar inventions of Protagoras, Socrates?

SOCRATES.   Yes, my boy, correctness of diction, and many other fine things. For tearful speeches, to arouse pity for old age and poverty, I think the precepts of the mighty Chalcedonian hold the palm, and he is also a genius, as he said, at rousing large companies to wrath, and soothing them again by his charms when they are angry, and most powerful in devising and abolishing calumnies on any grounds whatsoever. But all seem to be in agreement concerning the conclusion of discourses, which some call recapitulation, while others give it some other name.

PHAEDRUS.   You mean making a summary of the points of the speech at the end of it, so as to remind the hearers of what has been said?

SOCRATES.   These are the things I mean, these and anything else you can mention concerned with the art of rhetoric.

PHAEDRUS.   There are only little things, not worth mentioning.

SOCRATES.   Never mind the little things; let us bring these other things more under the light and see what force of art they have and when.

PHAEDRUS.   They have a very powerful force, at least in large assemblies.

SOCRATES.   They have; but my friend, see if you agree with me in thinking that their warp has gaps in it.

PHAEDRUS.   Go on and show them.

SOCRATES.   Tell me; if anyone should go to your friend Eryximachus or to his father Acumenus and should say "I know how to apply various drugs to people, so as to make them warm or, if I wish, cold, and I can make them vomit, if I like, or can make their bowels move, and all that sort of thing; and because of this knowledge I claim that I am a physician and can make any other man a physician, to whom I impart the knowledge of these things"; what do you think they would say?

PHAEDRUS. They would ask him, of course, whether he knew also whom he ought to cause to do these things, and when, and how much.

SOCRATES. If then he should say: "No, not at all; but I think that he who has learned these things from me will be able to do by himself the things you ask about?"

PHAEDRUS. They would say, I fancy, that the man was crazy and, because he had read something in a book or had stumbled upon some medicines, imagined that he was a physician when he really had no knowledge of the art.

SOCRATES. And what if someone should go to Sophocles or Euripides and should say that he knew how to make very long speeches about a small matter, and very short ones about a great affair, and pitiful utterances, if he wished, and again terrible and threatening ones, and all that sort of thing, and that he thought by imparting those things he could teach the art of writing tragedies?

PHAEDRUS. They also, I fancy, Socrates, would laugh at him, if he imagined that tragedy was anything else than the proper combination of these details in such a way that they harmonize with each other and with the whole composition.

SOCRATES. But they would not, I suppose, rebuke him harshly, but they would behave as a musician would, if he met a man who thought he understood harmony because he could strike the highest and lowest notes. He would not say roughly, "You wretch, you are mad," but being a musician, he would say in gentler tones, "My friend, he who is to be a harmonist must know these things you mention, but nothing prevents one who is at your stage of knowledge from being quite ignorant of harmony. You know the necessary preliminaries of harmony, but not harmony itself."

PHAEDRUS. Quite correct.

SOCRATES. So Sophocles would say that the man exhibited the preliminaries of tragedy, not tragedy itself, and Acumenus that he knew the preliminaries of medicine, not medicine itself.

PHAEDRUS. Exactly so.

SOCRATES. Well then, if the mellifluous Adrastus or Pericles heard of the excellent accomplishments which we just enumerated, brachylogies and figurative speech and all the other things we said we must bring to the light and examine, do we suppose they would, like you and me, be so illbred as to speak discourteously of those who have written and taught these things as the art of rhetoric? Would they not, since they are wiser than we, censure us also and say, "Phaedrus and Socrates, we ought not to be angry, but lenient, if certain persons who are ignorant of dialectics have been unable to define the nature of rhetoric and on this account have thought, when they possessed the knowledge that is a necessary preliminary to rhetoric, that they had discovered rhetoric, and believe that by teaching these preliminaries to others they have taught them rhetoric completely, and that the persuasive use of these details and the composition of the whole discourse is a small matter which their pupils must supply of themselves in their writings or speeches."

PHAEDRUS. Well, Socrates, it does seem as if that which those men teach and write about as the art of rhetoric were such as you describe. I think you are right. But how and from whom is the truly rhetorical and persuasive art to be acquired?

SOCRATES. Whether one can acquire it, so as to become a perfect orator, Phaedrus, is probably, and perhaps must be, dependent on conditions, like everything else. If you are naturally rhetorical, you will become a notable orator, when to your natural endowments you have added knowledge and practice; at whatever point you are deficient in these, you will be incomplete. But so far as the art is concerned, I do not think the quest of it lies along the path of Lysias and Thrasymachus.

PHAEDRUS. Where then?

SOCRATES. I suppose, my friend, Pericles is the most perfect orator in existence.

PHAEDRUS. Well?

SOCRATES. All great arts demand discussion and high speculation about nature; for this loftiness of mind and effectiveness in all directions seem somehow to come from such pursuits. This was in Pericles added to his great natural abilities; for it was, I think, his falling in with Anaxagoras, who was just such a man, that filled him with high thoughts and taught him the nature of mind and of lack of mind, subjects about which Anaxagoras used chiefly to discourse, and from these speculations he drew and applied to the art of speaking what is of use to it.

PHAEDRUS. What do you mean by that?

SOCRATES. The method of the art of healing is much the same as that of rhetoric.

PHAEDRUS. How so?

SOCRATES. In both cases you must analyse a nature, in one that of the body and in the other that of the soul, if you are to proceed in a scientific manner, not merely by practice and routine, to impart health and strength to the body by prescribing medicine and diet, or by proper discourses and training to give to the soul the desired belief and virtue.

PHAEDRUS. That, Socrates, is probably true.

SOCRATES. Now do you think one can acquire any appreciable knowledge of the nature of the soul without knowing the nature of the whole man?

PHAEDRUS. If Hippocrates the Asclepiad is to be trusted, one cannot know the nature of the body, either, except in that way.

SOCRATES. He is right, my friend; however, we ought not to be content with the authority of Hippocrates, but to see also if our reason agrees with him on examination.

PHAEDRUS. I assent.

SOCRATES. Then see what Hippocrates and true reason say about nature. In considering the nature of anything, must we not consider first, whether that in respect to which we wish to be learned ourselves and to make others learned is simple or multiform, and then, if it is simple, enquire what power of acting it possesses, or of being acted upon, and by what, and if it has many forms, number them, and then see in the case of each form, as we did in the case of the simple nature, what its action is and how it is acted upon and by what?

PHAEDRUS. Very likely, Socrates.

SOCRATES. At any rate, any other mode of procedure would be like the progress of a blind man. Yet surely he who pursues any study scientifically ought not to be comparable to a blind or a deaf man, but evidently the man whose rhetorical teaching is a real art will explain accurately the nature of that to which his words are to be addressed, and that is the soul, is it not?

PHAEDRUS. Of course.

SOCRATES. Then this is the goal of all his effort; he tries to produce conviction in the soul. Is not that so?

PHAEDRUS. Yes.

SOCRATES. So it is clear that Thrasymachus, or anyone else who seriously teaches the art of rhetoric, will first describe the soul with perfect accuracy and make us see whether it is one and all alike, or, like the body, of multiform aspect; for this is what we call explaining its nature.

PHAEDRUS. Certainly.

SOCRATES. And secondly he will say what its action is and toward what it is directed, or how it is acted upon and by what.

PHAEDRUS. To be sure.

SOCRATES. Thirdly, he will classify the speeches and the souls and will adapt each to the other, showing the causes of the effects produced and why one kind of soul is necessarily persuaded by certain classes of speeches, and another is not.

PHAEDRUS. That would, I think, be excellent.

SOCRATES. By no other method of exposition or speech will this, or anything else, ever be written or spoken with real art. But those whom you have heard, who write treatises on the art of speech nowadays, are deceivers and conceal the nature of the soul, though they know it very well. Until they write and speak by this method we cannot believe that they write by the rules of art.

PHAEDRUS. What is this method?

SOCRATES. It is not easy to tell the exact expressions to be used; but I will tell how one must write, if one is to do it, so far as possible, in a truly artistic way.

PHAEDRUS. Speak then.

SOCRATES. Since it is the function of speech to lead souls by persuasion, he who is to be a rhetorician must know the various forms of soul. Now they are so and so many and of such and such kinds, wherefore men also are of different kinds: these we must classify. Then there are also various classes of speeches, to one of which every speech belongs. So men of a certain sort are easily persuaded by speeches of a certain sort for a certain reason to actions or beliefs of a certain sort, and men of another sort cannot be so persuaded. The student of rhetoric must, accordingly, acquire a proper knowledge of these classes and then be able to follow them accurately with his senses when he sees them in the practical affairs of life; otherwise he can never have any profit from the lectures he may have heard. But when he has learned to tell what sort of man is influenced by what sort of speech, and is able, if he comes upon such a man, to recognize him and to convince himself that this is the man and this now actually before him is the nature spoken of in a certain lecture, to which he must now make a practical application of a certain kind of speech in a certain way to persuade his hearer to a certain action or belief — when he has acquired all this, and has added thereto a knowledge of the times for speaking and for keeping silence, and has also distinguished the favourable occasions for brief speech or pitiful speech or intensity and all the classes of speech which he has learned, then, and not till then, will his art be fully and completely finished; and if anyone who omits any of these points in his speaking or writing claims to speak by the rules of art, the one who disbelieves him is the better man. "Now then," perhaps the writer of our treatise will say, "Phaedrus and Socrates, do you agree to all this? Or must the art of speech be described in some other way?"

PHAEDRUS. No other way is possible, Socrates. But it seems a great task to attain to it.

SOCRATES. Very true. Therefore you must examine all that has been said from every point of view, to see if no shorter and easier road to the art appears, that one may not take a long and rough road, when there is a short and smooth one. If you have heard from Lysias or anyone else anything that can help us, try to remember it and tell it.

PHAEDRUS. If it depended on trying, I might, but just now I have nothing to say.

SOCRATES. Then shall I tell something that I have heard some of those say who make these matters their business?

PHAEDRUS. Pray do.

SOCRATES. Even the wolf, you know, Phaedrus, has a right to an advocate, as they say.

PHAEDRUS. Do you be his advocate.

SOCRATES. Very well. They say that there is no need of treating these matters with such gravity and carrying them back so far to first principles with many words; for, as we said in the beginning of this discussion, he who is to be a competent rhetorician need have nothing at all to do, they say, with truth in considering things which are just or good, or men who are so, whether by nature or by education. For in the courts, they say, nobody cares for truth about these matters, but for that which is convincing; and that is probability, so that he who is to be an artist in speech must fix his attention upon probability. For sometimes one must not even tell what was actually done, if it was not likely to be done, but what was probable, whether in accusation or defence; and in brief, a speaker must always aim at probability, paying no attention to truth; for this method, if pursued throughout the whole speech, provides us with the entire art.

PHAEDRUS. You have stated just what those say who pretend to possess the art of speech, Socrates. I remember that we touched upon this matter briefly before, but the professional rhetoricians think it is of great importance.

SOCRATES. Well, there is Tisias whom you have studied carefully; now let Tisias himself tell us if he does not say that probability is that which most people think.

PHAEDRUS. That is just what he says.

SOCRATES. Apparently after he had invented this clever scientific definition, he wrote that if a feeble and brave man assaulted a strong coward, robbed him of his cloak or something, and was brought to trial for it, neither party ought to speak the truth; the coward should say that he had not been assaulted by the brave man alone, whereas the other should prove that only they two were present and should use the well-known argument, "how could a little man like me assault such a man as he is?" The coward will not acknowledge his cowardice, but will perhaps try to invent some other lie, and thus give his opponent a chance to confute him. And in other cases there are other similar rules of art. Is that not so, Phaedrus?

PHAEDRUS. Certainly.

SOCRATES. Oh, a wonderfully hidden art it seems to be which Tisias has brought to light, or some other, whoever he may be and whatever country he is proud to call his own! But, my friend, shall we say in reply to this, or shall we not —

PHAEDRUS. What?

SOCRATES. "Tisias, some time ago, before you came along, we were saying that this probability of yours was accepted by the people because of its likeness to truth; and we just stated that he who knows the truth is always best able to discover likenesses. And so, if you have anything else to say about the art of speech, we will listen to you; but if not, we will put our trust in what we said just now, that unless a man take account of the characters of his hearers and is able to divide things by classes and to comprehend particulars under a general idea, he will never attain the highest human perfection in the art of speech. But this ability he will not gain without much diligent toil, which a wise man ought not to undergo for the sake of speaking and acting before men, but that he may be able to speak and to do everything, so far as possible, in a manner pleasing to the gods. For those who are wiser than we, Tisias, say that a man of sense should surely practise to please not his fellow slaves, except as a secondary consideration, but his good and noble masters. Therefore, if the path is long, be not astonished; for it must be trodden for great ends, not for those you have in mind. Yet your ends also, as our argument says, will be best gained in this way, if one so desires."

PHAEDRUS. I think what you have said is admirable, if one could only do it.

SOCRATES. But it is noble to strive after noble objects, no matter what happens to us.

PHAEDRUS. Certainly.

SOCRATES. We have, then, said enough about the art of speaking and that which is no art.

PHAEDRUS. Assuredly.

SOCRATES. But we have still to speak of propriety and impropriety in writing, how it should be done and how it is improper, have we not?

PHAEDRUS. Yes.

SOCRATES. Do you know how you can act or speak about rhetoric so as to please God best?

PHAEDRUS. Not at all; do you?

SOCRATES. I can tell something I have heard of the ancients; but whether it is true, they only know. But if we ourselves should find it out, should we care any longer for human opinions?

PHAEDRUS. A ridiculous question! But tell me what you say you have heard.

SOCRATES. I heard, then, that at Naucratis, in Egypt, was one of the ancient gods of that country, the one whose sacred bird is called the ibis, and the name of the god himself was Theuth. He it was who invented numbers and arithmetic and geometry and astronomy, also draughts and dice, and, most important of all, letters. Now the king of all Egypt at that time was the god Thamus, who lived in the great city of the upper region, which the Greeks call the Egyptian Thebes, and they call the god himself Ammon. To him came Theuth to show his inventions, saying that they ought to be imparted to the other Egyptians. But Thamus asked what use there was in each, and as Theuth enumerated their uses, expressed praise or blame, according as he approved or disapproved. The story goes that Thamus said many things to Theuth in praise or blame of the various arts, which it would take too long to repeat; but when they came to the letters, "This invention, O king," said Theuth, "will make the Egyptians wiser and will improve their memories; for it is an elixir of memory and wisdom that I have discovered." But Thamus replied, "Most ingenious Theuth, one man has the ability to beget arts, but the ability to judge of their usefulness or harmfulness to their users belongs to another; and now you, who are the father of letters, have been led by your affection to ascribe to them a power the opposite of that which they really possess. For this invention will produce forgetfulness in the minds of those who learn to use it, because they will not practise their memory. Their trust in writing, produced by external characters which are no part of themselves, will discourage the use of their own memory within them. You have invented an elixir not of memory, but of reminding; and you offer your pupils the appearance of wisdom, not true wisdom, for they will read many things without instruction and will therefore seem to know many things, when they are for the most part ignorant and hard to get along with, since they are not wise, but only appear wise."

PHAEDRUS. Socrates, you easily make up stories of Egypt or any country you please.

SOCRATES. They used to say, my friend, that the words of the oak in the holy place of Zeus at Dodona were the first prophetic utterances. The people of that time, not being so wise as you young folks, were content in their simplicity to hear an oak or a rock, provided only it spoke the truth; but to you, perhaps, it makes a difference who the speaker is and where he comes from, for you do not consider only whether his words are true or not.

PHAEDRUS. Your rebuke is just; and I think the Theban is right in what he says about letters.

SOCRATES. He who thinks, then, that he has left behind him any art in writing, and he who receives it in the belief that anything in writing will be clear and certain, would be an utterly simple person, and in truth ignorant of the prophecy of Ammon, if he thinks written words are of any use except to remind him who knows the matter about which they are written.

PHAEDRUS. Very true.

SOCRATES. Writing, Phaedrus, has this strange quality, and is very like painting; for the creatures of painting stand like living beings, but if one asks them a question, they preserve a solemn silence. And so it is with written words; you might think they spoke as if they had intelligence, but if you question them, wishing to know about their sayings, they always say only one and the same thing. And every word, when once it is written, is bandied about alike among those who understand and those who have no interest in it, and it knows not to whom to speak or not to speak; when ill-treated or unjustly reviled it always needs its father to help it; for it has no power to protect or help itself.

PHAEDRUS. You are quite right about that, too.

SOCRATES. Now tell me; is there not another kind of speech, or word, which shows itself to be the legitimate brother of this bastard one, both in the manner of its begetting and in its better and more powerful nature?

PHAEDRUS. What is this word and how is it begotten, as you say?

SOCRATES. The word which is written with intelligence in the mind of the learner, which is able to defend itself and knows to whom it should speak, and before whom to be silent.

PHAEDRUS. You mean the living and breathing word of him who knows, of which the written word may justly be called the image.

SOCRATES. Exactly. Now tell me this. Would a sensible husbandman, who has seeds which he cares for and which he wishes to bear fruit, plant them with serious purpose in the heat of summer in some garden of Adonis, and delight in seeing them appear in beauty in eight days, or would he do that sort of thing, when he did it at all, only in play and for amusement? Would he not, when he was in earnest, follow the rules of husbandry, plant his seeds in fitting ground, and be pleased when those which he had sowed reached their perfection in the eighth month?

PHAEDRUS. Yes, Socrates, he would, as you say, act in that way when in earnest and in the other way only for amusement.

SOCRATES. And shall we suppose that he who has knowledge of the just and the good and beautiful has less sense about his seeds than the husbandman?

PHAEDRUS. By no means.

SOCRATES. Then he will not, when in earnest, write them in ink, sowing them through a pen with words which cannot defend themselves by argument and cannot teach the truth effectually.

PHAEDRUS. No, at least, probably not.

SOCRATES. No. The gardens of letters he will, it seems, plant for amusement, and will write, when he writes, to treasure up reminders for himself, when he comes to the forgetfulness of old age, and for others who follow the same path, and he will be pleased when he sees them putting forth tender leaves. When others engage in other amusements, refreshing themselves with banquets and kindred entertainments, he will pass the time in such pleasures as I have suggested.

PHAEDRUS. A noble pastime, Socrates, and a contrast to those base pleasures, the pastime of the man who can find amusement in discourse, telling stories about justice, and the other subjects of which you speak.

SOCRATES. Yes, Phaedrus, so it is; but, in my opinion, serious discourse about them is far nobler, when one employs the dialectic method and plants and sows in a fitting soul intelligent words which are able to help themselves and him who planted them, which are not fruitless, but yield seed from which there spring up in other minds other words capable of continuing the process for ever, and which make their possessor happy, to the farthest possible limit of human happiness.

PHAEDRUS. Yes, that is far nobler.

SOCRATES. And now, Phaedrus, since we have agreed about these matters, we can decide the others.

PHAEDRUS. What others?

SOCRATES. Those which brought us to this point through our desire to investigate them, for we wished to examine into the reproach against

Lysias as a speech-writer, and also to discuss the speeches themselves and see which were the products of art and which were not. I think we have shown pretty clearly what is and what is not a work of art.

PHAEDRUS. Yes, I thought so, too; but please recall to my mind what was said.

SOCRATES. A man must know the truth about all the particular things of which he speaks or writes, and must be able to define everything separately; then when he has defined them, he must know how to divide them by classes until further division is impossible; and in the same way he must understand the nature of the soul, must find out the class of speech adapted to each nature, and must arrange and adorn his discourse accordingly, offering to the complex soul elaborate and harmonious discourses, and simple talks to the simple soul. Until he has attained to all this, he will not be able to speak by the method of art, so far as speech can be controlled by method, either for purposes of instruction or of persuasion. This has been taught by our whole preceding discussion.

PHAEDRUS. Yes, certainly, that is just about our result.

SOCRATES. How about the question whether it is a fine or a disgraceful thing to be a speaker or writer and under what circumstances the profession might properly be called a disgrace or not? Was that made clear a little while ago when we said –

PHAEDRUS. What?

SOCRATES. That if Lysias or anyone else ever wrote or ever shall write, in private, or in public as lawgiver, a political document, and in writing it believes that it possesses great certainty and clearness, then it is a disgrace to the writer, whether anyone says so, or not. For whether one be awake or asleep, ignorance of right and wrong and good and bad is in truth inevitably a disgrace, even if the whole mob applaud it.

PHAEDRUS. That is true.

SOCRATES. But the man who thinks that in the written word there is necessarily much that is playful, and that no written discourse, whether in metre or in prose, deserves to be treated very seriously (and this applies also to the recitations of the rhapsodes, delivered to sway people's minds, without opportunity for questioning and teaching), but that the best of them really serve only to remind us of what we know; and who thinks that only in words about justice and beauty and goodness spoken by teachers for the sake of instruction and really written in a soul is clearness and perfection and serious value, that such words should be considered the speaker's own legitimate offspring, first the word within himself, if it be found there, and secondly its descendants or brothers which may have sprung up in worthy manner in the souls of others, and who pays no attention to the other words, – that man, Phaedrus, is likely to be such as you and I might pray that we ourselves may become.

PHAEDRUS. By all means that is what I wish and pray for.

SOCRATES. We have amused ourselves with talk about words long enough. Go and tell Lysias that you and I came down to the fountain and sacred place of the nymphs, and heard words which they told us to repeat to Lysias and anyone else who composed speeches, and to Homer or any other who has composed poetry with or without musical accompaniment, and third to Solon and whoever has written political compositions which he calls laws: — If he has composed his writings with knowledge of the truth, and is able to support them by discussion of that which he has written, and has the power to show by his own speech that the written words are of little worth, such a man ought not to derive his title from such writings, but from the serious pursuit which underlies them.

PHAEDRUS. What titles do you grant them then?

SOCRATES. I think, Phaedrus, that the epithet "wise" is too great and befits God alone; but the name "philosopher," that is, "lover of wisdom," or something of the sort would be more fitting and modest for such a man.

PHAEDRUS. And quite appropriate.

SOCRATES. On the other hand, he who has nothing more valuable than the things he has composed or written, turning his words up and down at his leisure, adding this phrase and taking that away, will you not properly address him as poet or writer of speeches or of laws?

PHAEDRUS. Certainly.

SOCRATES. Tell this then to your friend.

PHAEDRUS. But what will you do? For your friend ought not to be passed by.

SOCRATES. What friend?

PHAEDRUS. The fair Isocrates. What message will you give him? What shall we say that he is?

SOCRATES. Isocrates is young yet, Phaedrus; however, I am willing to say what I prophesy for him.

PHAEDRUS. What is it?

SOCRATES. I think he has a nature above the speeches of Lysias and possesses a nobler character; so that I should not be surprised if, as he grows older, he should so excel in his present studies that all who have ever treated of rhetoric shall seem less than children; and I suspect that these studies will not satisfy him, but a more divine impulse will lead him to greater things; for my friend, something of philosophy is inborn in his mind. This is the message that I carry from these deities to my favourite Isocrates, and do you carry the other to Lysias, your favourite.

PHAEDRUS. It shall be done; but now let us go, since the heat has grown gentler.

SOCRETES. Is it not well to pray to the deities here before we go?

PHAEDRUS. Of course.

SOCRATES. O beloved Pan and all ye other gods of this place, grant to me that I be made beautiful in my soul within, and that all external possessions be in harmony with my inner man. May I consider the wise man rich; and may I have such wealth as only the self-restrained man can bear or endure. – Do we need anything more, Phaedrus? For me that prayer is enough.

PHAEDRUS. Let me also share in this prayer; for friends have all things in common.

SOCRATES. Let us go.

ISOCRATES:
AGAINST THE SOPHISTS

Translated by George Norlin

Isocrates, a pupil of Gorgias and Athens' most successful teacher of rhetoric, published early in his career the essay "Against the Sophists," designed to set him apart from the two prevailing modes of education. At the opening of the essay, he attacks as impractical and futile the Eristics, those philosophers who professed to teach wisdom and happiness through disputation about ethical questions. In the section reprinted below, he criticizes the teachers of rhetoric.

Who were the sophists? At various times all the Athenian teachers, even Plato, have been called sophists. Generally, the term referred to a man who took money for teaching, but then as now it also served as an epithet to disparage intellectual or academic rivals, whether philosophers or rhetoricians.

292:9 – 295:22

But it is not these sophists [the Eristics] alone who are open to criticism, but also those who profess to teach political discourse. For the latter have no interest whatever in the truth, but consider that they are masters of an art if they can attract great numbers of students by the smallness of their charges and the magnitude of their professions and get something out of them. For they are themselves so stupid and conceive others to be so dull that, although the speeches which they compose are worse than those which some laymen improvise, nevertheless they promise to make their students such clever orators that they will not overlook any of the possibilities which a subject affords. More than that, they do not attribute any of this power either to the practical experience or to the native ability of the student, but undertake to transmit the science of discourse as simply as they would teach the letters of the alphabet, not having taken trouble to examine into the nature of each kind of knowledge, but thinking that because of the extravagance of their promises they themselves will command admiration and the teaching of discourse will be held in higher esteem – oblivious of the fact that the arts are made great, not by those who are without scruple in boasting about them, but by those who are able to discover all of the resources which each art affords.

For myself, I should have preferred above great riches that philosophy had as much power as these men claim; for, possibly, I should not have been the very last in the profession nor had the least share in its profits. But since it has no such power, I could wish that this prating might cease. For I note that the bad repute which results therefrom does not affect the offenders only, but that all the rest of us who are in the same profession share in the opprobium.

But I marvel when I observe these men setting themselves up as instructors of youth who cannot see that they are applying the analogy of an art with hard and fast rules to a creative process. For, excepting these teachers, who does not know that the art of using letters remains fixed and unchanged, so that we continually and invariably use the same letters for the same purposes, while exactly the reverse is true of the art of discourse? For what has been said by one speaker is not equally useful for the speaker who comes after him; on the contrary, he is accounted most skilled in this art who speaks in a manner worthy of his subject and yet is able to discover in it topics which are nowise the same as those used by others. But the greatest proof of the difference between these two arts is that oratory is good only if it has the qualities of fitness for the occasion, propriety of style, and originality of treatment, while in the case of letters there is no such need whatsoever. So that those who make use of such analogies ought more justly to pay out than to accept fees, since they attempt to teach others when they are themselves in great need of instruction.

However, if it is my duty not only to rebuke others, but also to set forth my own views, I think all intelligent people will agree with me that while many of those who have pursued philosophy have remained in private life, others, on the other hand, who have never taken lessons from any one of the sophists have become able orators and statesmen. For ability, whether in speech or in any other activity, is found in those who are well endowed by nature and have been schooled by practical experience. Formal training makes such men more skillful and more resourceful in discovering the possibilities of a subject; for it teaches them to take from a readier source the topics which they otherwise hit upon in haphazard fashion. But it cannot fully fashion men who are without natural aptitude into good debaters or writers, although it is capable of leading them on to self-improvement and to a greater degree of intelligence on many subjects.

But I desire, now that I have gone this far, to speak more clearly on these matters. For I hold that to obtain a knowledge of the elements out of which we make and compose all discourses is not so very difficult if anyone entrusts himself, not to those who make rash promises, but to those who have some knowledge of these things. But to choose from these elements those which should be employed for each subject, to join them together, to arrange them properly, and also, not to miss what the occasion demands but appropriately to adorn the whole speech with striking thoughts and to clothe it in flowing and melodious phrase — these things, I hold, require much study and are the task of a vigorous and imaginative mind: for this, the student must not only have the requisite aptitude but he must learn the different kinds of discourse and practise himself in their use; and the teacher, for his part, must so expound the principles of the art with the utmost possible exactness as to leave out nothing that can be taught, and, for the rest, he must in himself set such an example of oratory that the students who have taken form under his instruction and are able to pattern after him will, from the outset, show in their speaking a degree of grace and charm which is not found in others. When all of these requisites are found together, then the devotees of philosophy will achieve complete success; but according as any one of the things which I have mentioned is lacking, to this extent must their disciples of necessity fall below the mark.

Now as for the sophists who have lately sprung up and have very recently embraced these pretensions, even though they flourish at the moment, they will all, I am sure, come round to this position. But there remain to be considered those who lived before our time and did not scruple to write the so-called arts of oratory. These must not be dismissed without rebuke, since they professed to teach how to conduct law-suits, picking out the most discredited of terms,[1] which the enemies, not the champions, of this discipline might have been expected to employ — and that too although this facility, in so far as it can be taught, is of no greater aid to forensic than to all other discourse. But they were much worse than those who dabble in disputation; for although the latter expounded such captious theories that were anyone to cleave to them in practice he would at once be in all manner of trouble, they did, at any rate, make professions of virtue and sobriety in their teaching, whereas the former, although exhorting others to study political discourse, neglected all the good things which this study affords, and became nothing more than professors of meddlesomeness and greed.

---

[1] Again and again Isocrates expresses his repugnance to this kind of oratory, and in general it was in bad odour. The precepts of Corax (Crow), for example, were called "the bad eggs of the bad Corax."

And yet those who desire to follow the true precepts of this discipline may, if they will, be helped more speedily towards honesty of character than towards facility in oratory. And let no one suppose that I claim that just living can be taught; for, in a word, I hold that there does not exist an art of the kind which can implant sobriety and justice in depraved natures. Nevertheless, I do think that the study of political discourse can help more than any other thing to stimulate and form such qualities of character.

But in order that I may not appear to be breaking down the pretensions of others while myself making greater claims than are within my powers, I believe that the very arguments by which I myself was convinced will make it clear to others also that these things are true.

ISOCRATES: ANTIDOSIS

Translated by George Norlin

Although he was a master of prose composition, Isocrates lacked the temperament — and the lung-power — to be a great orator. Nonetheless, many of his writings are in the form of orations. The Antidosis, *written when he was eighty-two, is such a composition, and was designed as a defense of his teachings at a hypothetical trial. The trial was fiction, but Isocrates' message was quite serious. It can be read as an extension of "Against the Sophists," the extant fragment of which breaks off before Isocrates spells out his notion of a proper rhetoric. Isocrates taught rhetoric as a practical means of implementing the ideals of pan-Hellenic culture, thus distinguishing himself from the philosophers who preferred abstract speculation, and the rhetoricians who taught rhetoric as a means to personal success.*

253 – 257

We ought. . .to think of the art of discourse just as we think of the other arts, and not to form opposite judgements about similar things, nor show ourselves intolerant toward that power which, of all the faculties which belong to the nature of man, is the source of most of our blessings. For in the other powers which we possess, as I have already said on a former occasion, we are in no respect superior to other living creatures; nay, we are inferior to many in swiftness and in strength and in other resources; but, because there has been implanted in us the power to persuade each other and to make clear to each other whatever we desire, not only have

Reprinted by permission of the publishers and THE LOEB CLASSICAL LIBRARY from George Norlin, Translator, Isocrates, *Antidosis,* Cambridge, Mass.: Harvard University Press.

we escaped the life of wild beasts, but we have come together and founded cities and made laws and invented arts; and, generally speaking, there is no institution devised by man which the power of speech has not helped us to establish. For this it is which has laid down laws concerning things just and unjust, and things honourable and base; and if it were not for these ordinances we should not be able to live with one another. It is by this also that we confute the bad and extol the good. Through this we educate the ignorant and appraise the wise; for the power to speak well is taken as the surest index of a sound understanding, and discourse which is true and lawful and just is the outward image of a good and faithful soul. With this faculty we both contend against others on matters which are open to dispute and seek light for ourselves on things which are unknown; for the same arguments which we use in persuading others when we speak in public, we employ also when we deliberate in our own thoughts; and, while we call eloquent those who are able to speak before a crowd, we regard as sage those who most skillfully debate their problems in their own minds. And, if there is need to speak in brief summary of this power, we shall find that none of the things which are done with intelligence take place without the help of speech, but that in all our actions as well as in all our thoughts speech is our guide, and is most employed by those who have the most wisdom. . . .

274 – 298

I consider that the kind of art which can implant honesty and justice in depraved natures has never existed and does not now exist, and that people who profess that power will grow weary and cease from their vain pretensions before such an education is ever found. But I do hold that people can become better and worthier if they conceive an ambition to speak well, if they become possessed of the desire to be able to persuade their hearers, and, finally, if they set their hearts on seizing their advantage – I do not mean "advantage" in the sense given to that word by the empty-minded, but advantage in the true meaning of that term; and that this is so I think I shall presently make clear.

For, in the first place, when anyone elects to speak or write discourses which are worthy of praise and honour, it is not conceivable that he will support causes which are unjust or petty or devoted to private quarrels, and not rather those which are great and honourable, devoted to the welfare of man and our common good; for if he fails to find causes of this character, he will accomplish nothing to the purpose. In the second place, he will select from all the actions of men which bear upon his subject those examples which are the most illustrious and the most edifying; and, habituating himself to contemplate and appraise such examples, he will feel their influence not only in the preparation of a given discourse but in all the actions of his life. It follows, then, that the power to speak well and think right will reward the man who approaches the art of discourse with love of wisdom and love of honour.

Furthermore, mark you, the man who wishes to persuade people will not be negligent as to the matter of character; no, on the contrary, he will apply himself above all to establish a most honourable name among his fellow-citizens; for who does not know that words carry greater conviction when spoken by men of good repute then when spoken by men who live under a cloud, and that the argument which is made by a man's life is of more weight than that which is furnished by words? Therefore, the stronger a man's desire to persuade his hearers, the more zealously will he strive to be honourable and to have the esteem of his fellow-citizens.

And let no one of you suppose that while all other people realize how much the scales of persuasion incline in favour of one who has the approval of his judges, the devotees of philosophy alone are blind to the power of good will. In fact, they appreciate this even more thoroughly than others, and they know, furthermore, that probabilities and proofs and all forms of persuasion support only the points in a case to which they are severally applied, whereas an honourable reputation not only lends greater persuasiveness to the words of the man who possess it, but adds greater lustre to his deeds, and is, therefore, more zealously to be sought after by men of intelligence than anything else in the world.

I come now to the question of "advantage" – the most difficult of the points I have raised. If any one is under the impression that people who rob others or falsify accounts or do any evil thing get the advantage, he is wrong in his thinking; for none are at a greater disadvantage throughout their lives than such men; none are found in more difficult straits, none live in greater ignominy; and, in a word, none are more miserable than they. No, you ought to believe rather that those are better off now and will receive the advantage in the future at the hands of the gods who are the most righteous and the most faithful in their devotions, and that those receive the better portion at the hands of men who are the most conscientious in their dealings with their associates, whether in their homes or in public life, and are themselves esteemed as the noblest among their fellows.

This is verily the truth, and it is well for us to adopt this way of speaking on the subject, since, as things now are, Athens has in many respects been plunged into such a state of topsy-turvy and confusion that some of our people no longer use words in their proper meaning but wrest them from the most honourable associations and apply them to the basest pursuits. On the one hand, they speak of men who play the buffoon and have a talent for mocking and mimicking as "gifted" – an appellation which should be reserved for men endowed with the highest excellence; while, on the other hand, they think of men who indulge their depraved and criminal instincts and who for small gains acquire a base reputation as "getting the advantage," instead of applying this term to the most righteous and the most upright, that is, to men who take advantage of the good and not the evil things of life. They characterize men who ignore our practical needs and delight in the mental juggling of the ancient sophists as "students of philosophy," but refuse this name to whose who pursue and practise those studies which will enable us to govern wisely both our own households and the commonwealth – which should be the objects of our toil, of our study, and of our every act.

It is from these pursuits that you have for a long time now been driving away our youth, because you accept the words of those who denounce this kind of education. Yes, and you have brought it about that the most promising of our young men are wasting their youth in drinking-bouts, in parties, in soft living and childish folly, to the neglect of all efforts to improve themselves; while those of grosser nature are engaged from morning until night in extremes of dissipation which in former days an honest slave would have despised. You see some of them chilling their wine at the "Nine-fountains"; others, drinking in taverns; others, tossing dice in gambling dens; and many, hanging about the training-schools of the flute-girls.

And as for those who encourage them in these things, no one of those who profess to be concerned for our youth has ever haled them before you for trial, but instead they persecute me, who, whatever else I may deserve, do at any rate deserve thanks for this, that I discourage such habits in my pupils.

But so inimical to all the world is this race of sycophants that when men pay a ransom of a hundred and thirty minae for women who bid fair to help them make away with the rest of their property besides, so far from reproaching them, they actually rejoice in their extravagance; but when men spend any amount, however small, upon their education, they complain that they are being corrupted. Could any charge be more unjust than this against our students? For, while in the prime of vigour, when most men of their age are most inclined to indulge their passions, they have disdained a life of pleasure; when they might have saved expense and lived softly, they have elected to pay out money and submit to toil; and, though hardly emerged from boyhood, they have come to appreciate what most of their elders do not know, namely, that if one is to govern his youth rightly and worthily and make the proper start in life, he must give more heed to himself than to his possessions, he must not hasten and seek to rule over others before he has found a master to direct his own thoughts, and he must not take as great pleasure or pride in other advantages as in the good things which spring up in the soul under a liberal education. I ask you, then, when young men have governed themselves by these principles, ought they not to be praised rather than censured, ought they not to be recognized as the best and the most sober-minded among their fellows?

I marvel at men who felicitate those who are eloquent by nature on being blessed with a noble gift, and yet rail at those who wish to become eloquent, on the ground that they desire an immoral and debasing education. Pray, what that is noble by nature becomes shameful and base when one attains it by effort? We shall find that there is no such thing, but that, on the contrary, we praise, at least in other fields, those who by their own devoted toil are able to acquire some good thing more than we praise those who inherit it from their ancestors. And rightly so; for it is well that in all activities, and most of all in the art of speaking, credit is won, not by gifts of fortune, but by efforts of study. For men who have been gifted with eloquence by nature and by fortune, are governed in what they say by chance, and not by any standard of what is best, whereas those who have gained this power by the study of philosophy and by the exercise of reason never speak without weighing their words, and so are less often in error as to a course of action.

Therefore, it behoves all men to want to have many of their youth engaged in training to become speakers, and you Athenians most of all. For you, yourselves, are pre-eminent and superior to the rest of the world, not in your application to the business of war, nor because you govern yourselves more excellently or preserve the laws handed down to you by your ancestors more faithfully than others, but in those qualities by which the nature of man rises above the other animals, and the race of the Hellenes above the barbarians, namely, in the fact that you have been educated as have been no other people in wisdom and in speech. So, then, nothing more absurd could happen than for you to declare by your votes that students who desire to excel their companions in those very qualities in which you excel mankind, are being corrupted, and to visit any misfortune upon them for availing themselves of an education in which you have become the leaders of the world.

For you must not lose sight of the fact that Athens is looked upon as having become a school for the education of all able orators and teachers of oratory. And naturally so; for people observe that she holds forth the greatest prizes for those who have this ability, that she offers the greatest number and variety of fields of exercise to those who have chosen to enter contests of this character and want to train for them, and that, furthermore, everyone obtains here that practical experience which more than any other thing imparts ability to speak; and, in addition to these advantages, they consider that the catholicity and moderation of our speech, as well as our flexibility of mind and love of letters, contribute in no small degree to the education of the orator. Therefore they suppose, and not without just reason, that all clever speakers are the disciples of Athens.

Beware, then, lest it make you utterly ridiculous to pronounce a disparaging judgement upon the reputation which you have among the Hellenes even more than I have among you. Manifestly, by such an unjust verdict, you would be passing sentence upon yourselves. It would be as if the Lacedacmonians were to attempt to penalize men for training themselves in preparation for war, or as if the Thessalians saw fit to punish men for practising the art of horsemanship. Take care, therefore, not to do yourself this wrong and not to lend support to the slanders of the enemies of Athens rather than to the eulogies of her friends.

ARISTOTLE: THE RHETORIC

Translated by Richard Claverhouse Jebb

In every rediscovery of rhetoric — and there have been many — one work seems to stand as either guiding light or point of departure. Aristotle's Rhetoric, *written in the late fourth century B.C., has, since its composition, provided the conceptual framework for the study of rhetoric. Even those who have sought alternative theories are identified primarily by their rejection of Aristotle or "neo-Aristotelianism." Complex, lucid, seminal, Aristotle's work has had both beneficial and harmful influences on the study of rhetoric. On the one hand, it supplies the basis for opening up the compositional and theoretical possibilities in a rhetorical situation; on the other, it is so persuasive that is has closed many theorists into an ingrown and mechanical system. Aristotle himself has avoided the dilemma by creating a work at once systematic and open-ended. The following selection, from the beginning of* The Rhetoric, *sets forth the premises upon which Aristotle bases his theory of rhetoric, a theory which can help the speaker to discern "in every case the available means of persuasion," and which can guide the theorist in a general investigation of rhetorical interaction.*

1354A — 1359A

RHETORIC is the counterpart of Dialectic, — since both are concerned with things of which the cognizance is, in a manner, common to all men and belongs to no definite science. Hence all men in a manner use both; for all men to some extent make the effort of examining and of submitting

Reprinted from Richard Claverhouse Jebb, translator, Aristotle, *The Rhetoric of Aristotle*, Cambridge, England: At the University Press.

to inquiry, of defending or accusing. People in general do these things either quite at random, or merely with a knack which comes from the acquired habit. Since both ways are possible, clearly it must be possible to reduce them to method; for it is possible to consider the cause why the practised or the spontaneous speaker hits his mark; and such an inquiry, all would allow, is the function of an art.

Now hitherto the writers of treatises on Rhetoric have constructed only a small part of that art; for proofs form the only artistic element, all else being mere appendage. These writers, however, say nothing about enthymemes, which are the body of proof, but busy themselves chiefly with irrelevant matters. The exciting of prejudice, of pity, of anger, and such like emotions of the soul, has nothing to do with the fact, but has regard to the judge. So that if trials were universally managed, as they are at present managed in some at least of the cities, and for the most part in the best governed, such people would have nothing to say. All the world over, men either admit that the laws ought so to forbid irrelevant speaking, or actually have laws which forbid it, as is the case in the procedure of the Areiopagos; a wise provision. For it is a mistake to warp the judge by moving him to anger or envy or pity; it is as if a man, who was going to use a rule, should make it crooked. Further, it is clear that the litigant's part is simply to prove that the fact is or is not, has occurred or has not occurred. Whether it is great or small, just or unjust, in any respects which the lawgiver has not defined, is a question, of course, on which the judge must decide for himself, instead of being instructed upon it by the litigant. Now it is most desirable that well-drawn laws should, as far as possible, define everything themselves, leaving as few points as possible to the discretion of the judges; first, because it is easier to get a small than a large number of men qualified by their intelligence to make laws and try causes; next, because legislative acts are done after mature deliberation, whereas judgments are given off-hand, so that it is hard for the judge to satisfy the demands of justice and expediency.

Most important of all, the decision of the lawgiver concerns no special case, but is prospective and general; when we come to the ekklesiast and the dikast, they have to decide actual and definite cases; and they are often so entangled with likings and hatreds and private interests, that they are not capable of adequately considering the truth, but have their judgment clouded by private pleasure or pain. On all other points, then, we say, the judge ought to be given as little discretionary power as possible; but the question whether a thing has or has not happened, will or will not be, is or is not, must perforce be left in his hands; these things the lawgiver cannot forsee. If, then, this is so, it is manifest that irrelevant matter is treated by all those technical writers who define the other points, — as what the proem, the narrative and each of the other parts should contain; for they busy themselves here solely with creating a certain mind in the judge, – but teach nothing about artificial proof, that is, about the way in which one is to become a master of enthymemes.

It is for this reason that, though the same method applies to public and to forensic speaking, and though the Deliberative branch is nobler and worthier of a citizen than that which deals with private contracts, they ignore the former, and invariably aim at systematizing the art of litigation. In public speaking it is less worth while to talk about things beside the subject. Deliberative oratory is less knavish than Forensic, and embraces larger interests. In a public debate, the judge judges in his own cause, so that nothing more is needful than to prove that the case stands as the adviser says. In forensic speaking this is not enough; it is important to win over the hearer. The judge's award concerns other men's affairs; and if he views these in reference to his own interest, and listens in a partial spirit, he indulges the litigant instead of deciding the cause. Hence it is that in many places, as we said before, the law forbids irrelevant pleading: in the public assembly, the judges themselves take care of that.

It is manifest that the artistic Rhetoric is concerned with proofs. The rhetorical proof is a sort of demonstration, for we entertain the strongest persuasion of a thing when we conceive that it has been demonstrated. A rhetorical demonstration is an enthymeme, – this being, generally speaking, the most authoritative of proofs. The enthymeme again is a sort of syllogism, and every kind of syllogism alike comes under the observation of Dialectic, either generally or in one of its departments. Hence it is clear that he who is best able to investigate the elements and the genesis of the syllogism will also be the most expert with the enthymeme, when he has further mastered its subject-matter and its differences from the logical syllogism. Truth and the likeness of truth come under the observation of the same faculty. (It may be added that men are adequately gifted for the quest of truth and generally succeed in finding it.) Hence the same sort of man who can guess about truth, must be able to guess about probabilities.

It is plain, then, that the mass of technical writers deal with irrelevant matter; it is plain, too, why they have leaned by choice towards forensic speaking.

Rhetoric is useful, first, because truth and justice are naturally stronger than their opposites; so that, when awards are not given duly, truth and justice must have been worsted by their own fault. This is worth correcting. Again, supposing we had the most exact knowledge, there are some people whom it would not be easy to persuade with its help; for scientific exposition is in the nature of teaching, and teaching is out of the question; we must give our proofs and tell our story in popular terms, – as we said in the *Topics* with reference to controversy with the many. Further, – one should be able to persuade, just as to reason strictly, on both sides of a question; not with a view to using the twofold power – one must not be the advocate of evil – but in order, first, that we may know the whole state of the case; secondly, that, if anyone else argues dishonestly, we on our part may be able to refute him. Dialectic and Rhetoric, alone among all arts, draw indifferently an affirmative or a negative conclusion: both these arts alike are impartial. The conditions of the subject-matter, however, are not the same; that which is true and better being naturally, as a rule, more easy to demonstrate and more convincing. Besides it would be absurd that, while incapacity for physical self-defence is a reproach, incapacity for mental defence should be none; mental effort being more distinctive of man than bodily effort. If it is objected that an abuser of the rhetorical faculty can do great mischief, this, at any rate, applies to all good things except virtue, and especially to the most useful things, as strength, health, wealth, generalship. By the right use of these things a man may do the greatest good, and by the unjust use, the greatest mischief.

It appears, then, that Rhetoric is not concerned with any single or definite class of subjects but is parallel to Dialectic: it appears, too, that it is useful; and that its function is not to persuade, but to discover the available means of persuasion in each case, according to the analogy of all other arts. The function of the medical art is not to cure, but to make such progress towards a cure as the case admits; since it is possible to treat judiciously even those who can never enjoy health. Further it is clear that it belongs to the same art to observe the persuasive and the apparent persuasive, as, in the case of Dialectic, to observe the real and the apparent syllogism. For the essence of Sophistry is not in the faculty but in the moral purpose: only, in the case of Rhetoric, a man is to be called a rhetorician with respect to his faculty, without distinction of his moral purpose; in the case of Dialectic, a man is 'sophist' in respect to his moral purpose, but of his faculty.

Let us now attempt to speak of the method itself – the mode, and the means, by which we are to succeed in attaining our objects. By way of beginning we will once more define the art, and then proceed.

Let Rhetoric be defined, then, as the faculty of discerning in every case the available means of persuasion. This is the function of no other art. Each of the other arts is instructive or persuasive about its proper subject-matter; as the medical art about things wholesome or unwholesome, – geometry, about the properties of magnitudes, arithmetic, about numbers, – and so with the rest of the arts and sciences. But Rhetoric appears to have the power of discerning the persuasive in regard (one may say) to any given subject; and therefore we describe it as having the quality of Art in reference to no special or definite class of subjects.

Proofs are either artificial or inartificial. By 'inartificial' I mean such things as have not been supplied by our own agency, but were already in existence, – such as witnesses, depositions under torture, contracts, and the like: by 'artificial' I mean such things as may be furnished by our method and by our own agency; so that, of these, the 'inartificial' have only to be used; the 'artificial' have to be invented.

Of proofs provided by the speech there are three kinds; one kind depending on the character of the speaker; another, on disposing the hearer in a certain way; a third, a demonstration or apparent demonstration in the speech itself.

Ethical proof is wrought when the speech is so spoken as to make the speaker credible; for we trust good men more and sooner, as a rule, about everything; while, about things which do not admit of precision, but only of guess-work, we trust them absolutely. Now this trust, too, ought to be produced by means of the speech, – not by a previous conviction that the speaker is this or that sort of man. It is not true, as some of the technical writers assume in their systems, that the moral worth of the speaker contributes nothing to his persuasiveness; nay, it might be said that almost the most authoritative of proofs is that supplied by character.

The hearers themselves become the instruments of proof when emotion is stirred in them by the speech; for we give our judgments in different ways under the influence of pain and of joy, of liking and of hatred; and this, I repeat, is the one point with which the technical writers of the day attempt to deal. This province shall be examined in detail when we come to speak of the emotions.

Proof is wrought through the speech itself when we have demonstrated a truth or an apparent truth by the means of persuasion available in a given case.

These being the instruments of our proofs, it is clear that they may be mastered by a man who can reason; who can analyse the several types of Character and the Virtues, and thirdly, the Emotions – the nature and quality of each emotion, the sources and modes of its production. It results that Rhetoric is, as it were, an offshoot of Dialectic and of that Ethical science which may fairly be called Politics. Hence it is that Rhetoric and its professors slip into the garb of Political Science – either through want of education, or from pretentiousness, or from other human causes. Rhetoric is a branch or an image of Dialectic, as we said at the beginning. Neither of them is a science relating to the nature of any definite subject-matter. They are certain faculties of providing arguments.

Enough has perhaps been said about the faculty of Dialectic and of Rhetoric and about their relation to each other. With regard to those proofs which are wrought by demonstration, real or apparent, just as in Dialectic there is Induction on the one hand, and Syllogism or apparent Syllogism on the other, so it is in Rhetoric. The Example is an Induction. The Enthymeme is a Syllogism; the Apparent Enthymeme is an Apparent Syllogism. I call the Enthymeme a Rhetorical Syllogism and the Example a

Rhetorical Induction. All men effect their proofs by demonstration, either with examples or with enthymemes; there is no third way. Hence, since universally it is necessary to demonstrate anything whatever either by syllogism or by induction (and this we see from the *Analytics*), it follows that Induction and Syllogism must be identical respectively with Example and Enthymeme. The difference between Example and Enthymeme is manifest from the *Topics*. There, in reference to syllogism and induction, it has already been said that the proving of a proposition by a number of like instances, is, in Dialectic, Induction — answering to the Example in Rhetoric; and that, when certain things exist, and something else comes to pass through them, distinct from them but due to their existing, either as an universal or as an ordinary result, this is called in Dialectic, a Syllogism, as in Rhetoric it is called an Enthymeme. It is clear that the Rhetorical branch of Dialectic commands both these weapons. What has been said in the *Methodica* holds good here also; some rhetorical discourses rely on Example, some on Enthymeme; and so, likewise, some rhetoricians prefer the one and some the other. Arguments from Example are not the less persuasive; but arguments in the form of Enthymeme are the more applauded. The reason of this, and the way to use either, will be explained by and by. Now let us define the things themselves more clearly.

First, the notion of persuasion is relative; some things being at once persuasive and credible in themselves, other things because they are supposed to be demonstrated by persons who are so. Again, no art considers the particular; thus the medical art considers, not what is wholesome for Sokrates or Kallias, but what is so for a certain sort of man or of certain class. This is characteristic of an Art, whereas particulars are infinite and cannot be known. Hence Rhetoric, too, will consider, not what is probable to the individual, as to Sokrates or Hippias, but what is probable to a given class, just as Dialectic does. Dialectic does not reason for *any* premisses — dotards have notions of their own — but from premisses which require discussion. So does Rhetoric reason only upon recognised subjects of debate. Its concern is with subjects on which we deliberate, not having reduced them to systems; and with hearers who cannot grasp the unity of an argument which has many stages, or follow a long chain of reasoning. We debate about things which seem capable of being either thus or thus. Matters which admit of no ambiguity, past, present, or future, are debated by no one, on that supposition: it is useless.

Now, one may construct a syllogism and draw a conclusion either from facts already reduced to syllogisms or from facts which have not been proved syllogistically, but which need such proof, because they are not probable. The former of these processes is necessarily difficult to follow owing to its length; — the umpire being assumed to be a plain man. Reasonings of the latter kind are not persuasive, because drawn from premisses which are not admitted or probable. Hence both the enthymeme and the example must deal with things which are (as a rule) contingent — the example, as a kind of induction, the enthymeme as a syllogism, and as a syllogism of few elements, — often, of fewer than the normal syllogism. Thus, if one of these elements is something notorious, it need not even be stated, as the hearer himself supplies it. For instance, to prove that Dorieus has been victor in a contest, for which the prize is a crown, it is enough to say that he has been victor in the Olympic games. It is needless to add that in the Olympic contests the prize is a crown; every one is aware of that.

The premisses of rhetorical syllogisms seldom belong to the class of necessary facts. The subject-matter of judgments and deliberations is usually contingent; for it is about their actions that men debate and take thought; but actions are all contingent, no one of them, one may say, being necessary. And results which are merely usual and contingent must be deduced from premisses of the same kind, as necessary results from necessary premisses: — this, too, has been shown in the *Analytics*. It follows that the propositions from which enthymemes are taken will be sometimes necessarily true, but more often contingently true. Now the materials of the enthymeme are Probabilities and Signs. It follows that Probabilities and Signs must answer to the Contingent and the Necessary truths.

The Probable is that which usually happens; (with a limitation, however, which is sometimes forgotten — namely that the thing *may* happen otherwise:) the Probable being related to that in respect of which it is probable as Universal to Particular.

One kind of Sign is as Particular to Universal; the other, as Universal to Particular. The Infallible Sign is called *tekmêrion;* the Fallible Sign has no distinctive name. By Infallible Signs I mean those which supply a strict Syllogism. Hence it is that this sort of Sign is called *tekmêrion,* for when people think that what they have said is irrefutable, then they think that they are bringing a *tekmêrion* (a *conclusive* proof) — as if the matter had been demonstrated and *concluded* (πεπερασμένον); for *tekmar* and *peras* mean the same thing *('limit')* in the old language.

The Sign which is as a Particular to a Universal would be illustrated by saying, 'Wise men are just; *for* Sokrates was wise and just.' This is a Sign, indeed, but it can be refuted, even though the statement be a fact; for it does not make a syllogism. On the other hand, if one said — 'Here is a sign that he is ill — he is feverish'; or, 'she is a mother, for she has milk,' this is a strict proof. This is the only conclusive sign (or *tekmêrion*); for this alone, if the fact be true, is irrefutable. Another Sign, which is as Universal to Particular, would be exemplified by saying — 'This is a sign that he has a fever, he breathes quick.' But this, too, even though it be true, is refutable. A man may breathe hard without having a fever.

The nature of the Probable, of a Sign and of a conclusive Sign, and the nature of the difference between them have been explained sufficiently for our present purpose. In the *Analytics* a fuller account of them has been given, and of the reason why some of them are inconclusive, while others are strictly logical. It has been said that an Example is an Induction, and the matters with which it is concerned have been stated. It is neither as part to whole nor as whole to part nor as whole to whole, but as part to part, as like to like. When both things come under the same class, but one is better known than the other, that better-known one is an Example. For instance, it is argued that Dionysios aims at a tyranny in asking for a body-guard; for Peisistratos formerly, when he had such a design, asked for a guard, and, having got it, became tyrant; – as did Theagenes at Megara; and so all the other cases known to the speaker become Examples in reference to Dionysios – as to whom they do not yet know that this was his motive for the request. All these cases come under the same general principle, that a man who aims at a tyranny asks for a body-guard.

Such, then, are the sources from which the professedly demonstrative proofs are drawn. In regard to enthymemes, there is an important distinction which has been almost universally ignored; a distinction which applies equally to the syllogisms employed by Dialectic. Some enthymemes belong properly to Rhetoric, as some syllogisms belong properly to Dialectic; other enthymemes are peculiar to other arts and faculties, either existent or still to be formulated. Hence, though the speaker does not perceive it, the more he handles his subject with technical appropriateness, the more he is passing out of the province of Dialectic and Rhetoric. My meaning will be plainer when expressed more fully. Dialectical and Rhetorical syllogisms deal properly with the so-called topics (or common-places), by which I mean here the *Universal* topics applicable to Justice, Physics, Politics, and a variety of other subjects of all sorts. Take the topic of More or Less. This topic will not help us to make a syllogism or an enthymeme about Justice rather than about Physics or anything else, different though these things are in kind.

Particular Common-places are those arising from the propositions relative to the several species and classes of things. Thus there are propositions about Physics from which it is impossible to make a syllogism or an enthymeme about Ethics, – and others again, about Ethics from which one cannot reason upon Physics; and so in each case. The Universal Common-places will not make a man intelligent about any special class of things; since they have no special subject-matter. As to the Particular Common-places, the more carefully a speaker picks his propositions, the nearer he will be unconsciously coming to a science distinct from Dialectic and Rhetoric; for, if he lights upon special first principles, this will be no longer Dialectic or Rhetoric, but that science of which he has the first principles. Most enthymemes are based upon these Particular or Special Common-places; – fewer upon the Universal. As in the *Topics,* then, so here we must distinguish, in regard to enthymemes, the Special Topics and the Universal Topics from which they are to be taken. By Special Topics I mean the propositions peculiar to any given subject; by Universal Topics, those which are common to all. We will begin with the Special Topics. But first of all we must determine how many branches of Rhetoric there are, in order that, having done this, we may ascertain separately the elements and the propositions of each.

The species of Rhetoric are three in number, for the hearers of speeches belong to that number of classes. The speech has three elements — the speaker, the subject, and the person addressed; and the end proposed has reference to this last, that is, to the hearer. Now the hearer must be either spectator or judge; and, if judge, then of the past or of the future. The judge of things future is (for instance) the ekklesiast; the judge of things past, the dikast; the other hearer is a spectator of the faculty. It follows that there must be three kinds of rhetorical speeches, the deliberative, the forensic, the epideictic.

Now the elements of counsel are exhortation and dissuasion; since both private advisers and speakers in the public interest always either exhort or dissuade. The elements of litigation are accusation and defence; since the parties to a suit must be occupied with one or the other of these. The elements of an epideictic speech are praise and blame. The times which belong to these classes severally are: — to the deliberative speaker, the future; for he offers advice, exhorting or dissuading, about things to be; — to the litigant, the past; for the subjects of accusation on the one hand and defence on the other are always things past; — to the epideictic speaker, properly the present; for all men praise or blame in accordance with existing conditions, though they often avail themselves also of reminiscences from the past and conjectures about the future.

For these three classes there are three distinct ends, namely: — for the counsellor, utility or harm (since the exhorter advises a thing as being better, and the dissuader opposes it as being worse), and it is in reference to this topic that he uses the subsidiary topics of justice and injustice, honour and shame; — for litigants, justice and injustice, — and these, again, use subsidiary topics in reference to this one; — for those who praise or blame, the honourable and the shameful; and these, too, refer their other topics to this standard.

That the end of each class is such as has been stated is shown by this fact, that the other points are sometimes not contested by the speakers. For instance, the litigant will sometimes not dispute that a thing has happened or that he has done harm; but that he is guilty of an injustice, he will never admit; else there would be no need of a lawsuit. Similarly, speakers in debate often give up all other points, but will not allow that they are advising an inexpedient course, or dissuading from one which is advantageous; while, as to showing that it is no injustice to enslave a neighbouring and perhaps unoffending community, they often give themselves no anxiety. In the same way panegyrists and censurers do not consider whether such an one's acts were expedient or harmful; but often make it a ground of positive praise that, regardless of his own advantage, he did something or other noble. For instance they praise Achilles for coming to the rescue of his friend Patroklos, when he knew that he must die, though he might have lived. Now for Achilles such a death was nobler; but life was expedient.

It appears from what has been said that we must first ascertain the propositions bearing upon these topics. Now signs, fallible or infallible, and probabilities are the propositions of Rhetoric; for as, universally, a syllogism is formed of propositions, so the enthymeme is a syllogism formed of the above-named propositions.

And as there can be no performance, past or future, of impossible things, but only of possible; and since things, which have not occurred, cannot have been done, and things, which are not to be, cannot be about to be done; — it is necessary alike for the Deliberative, for the Forensic, and for the Epideictic speaker to have propositions about the Possible and the Impossible, and on the question whether a thing has or has not happened, is or is not to be. Besides, since all men in praising or blaming, in exhorting or dissuading, in accusing or defending try to prove, not merely the above facts, but also that the good or evil, the honour or disgrace, the justice or injustice is great or small, whether they are taken absolutely or in comparison with each other, it is plain that it will be necessary to have propositions about greatness or smallness, and about greater or less, both universally and in particular cases; as on the question which is the greater or less good, the greater or less act of injustice — and so with the rest.

These, then, are the subjects in which it is necessary to ascertain the available propositions.

RHETORICA AD ALEXANDRUM

Translated by H. Rackham

Rhetorica Ad Alexandrum, *probably written near the beginning of the third century B.C., by an unknown author (perhaps Anaximenes), is the major extant example of the earlier practical handbooks of sophistic rhetoric. George Kennedy writes: "If one looks back over the first hundred and fifty years of rhetorical theory, Aristotle's* Rhetoric *seems to tower above all the remains, for it is infinitely more imaginative and richer than the* Rhetorica Ad Alexandrum *and undoubtedly more so than any lost handbook of the age."*[1] *Contrasting the two works, H. Rackham says of the* Ad Alexandrum: *"It merely considers the problem of how to carry conviction with an audience, and gives none of the warnings against the abuse of oratory nor any of the background of logic, psychology and ethics that render Aristotle's* Rhetoric *a philosophical work. In fact, it represents the sophistic school of rhetoric that Aristotle opposed."*[2]

While similarities exist between the two works, such as their structural parallel, which would not have been prevalent before the fourth century B.C., conflict does exist between Ad Alexandrum *and Aristotle's treatment of the traditional three kinds of rhetoric. Although* Ad Alexandrum *accepts them, the author further breaks them down into seven species, which are discussed in the sections printed below. While Aristotle builds a philosophical base for his discussion of each kind of*

Reprinted by permission of the publishers and THE LOEB CLASSICAL LIBRARY from H. Rackham, translator, *Rhetorica Ad Alexandrum,* Cambridge, Mass.: Harvard University Press.

[1] George Kennedy, *The Art of Persuasion in Greece* (Princeton, N. J., 1963), p. 123.

[2] Introduction, *Rhetorica Ad Alexandrum,* Translated by H. Rackham (Cambridge, Mass., 1957), p. 258.

oratory, Ad Alexandrum *seems only to offer a series of commonplaces which the orator might learn and apply in any speech. The reader is given, somewhat clumsily, rules without any understanding of their importance or their reason for success.*

I, 1421B:5 — VI, 1427B:35

Public speeches are of three kinds, parliamentary, ceremonial and forensic. Of these there are seven species, exhortation, dissuasion, eulogy, vituperation, accusation, defence, and investigation — either by itself or in relation to another species. This list enumerates the species to which public speeches belong; and we shall employ them in parliamentary debates, in arguing legal cases about contracts, and in private intercourse. We may be able to discuss them most readily if we take the species seriatim and enumerate their qualities, their uses and their arrangement.

First let us discuss exhortation and dissuasion, as these are among the forms most employed in private conversation and in public deliberation.

Speaking generally, exhortation is an attempt to urge people to some line of speech or action, and dissuasion is an attempt to hinder people from some line of speech or action. These being their definitions, one delivering an exhortation must prove that the courses to which he exhorts are just, lawful, expedient, honourable, pleasant and easily practicable; or failing this, in case the courses he is urging are disagreeable, he must show that they are feasible, and also that their adoption is unavoidable. One dissuading must apply hindrance by the opposite means: he must show that the action proposed is not just, not lawful, not expedient, not honourable, not pleasant and not practicable; or failing this, that it is laborious and not necessary. All courses of action admit of both these descriptions, so that no one having one or other of these sets of fundamental qualities available need be at a loss for something to say.

These, then, are the lines of argument at which those exhorting or dissuading ought to aim. I will try to define the nature of each, and to show from what sources we can obtain a good supply of them for our speeches.

What is just is the unwritten custom of the whole or the greatest part of mankind, distinguishing honourable actions from base ones. The former are to honour one's parents, do good to one's friends and repay favours to one's benefactors; for these and similar rules are not enjoined on men by written laws but are observed by unwritten custom and universal practice. These then are the just things.

Law is the common agreement of the state enjoining in writing how men are to act in various matters.

What is expedient is the preservation of existing good things, or the acquisition of goods that we do not possess, or the rejection of existing evils, or the prevention of harmful things expected to occur. Things expedient for individuals you will classify under body, mind and external possessions. Expedient for the body are strength, beauty, health; for the mind, courage, wisdom, justice; expedient external possessions are friends, wealth, property; and their opposites are inexpedient. Expedient for a state are such things as concord, military strength, property and a plentiful revenue, good and numerous allies. And briefly, we consider all things that resemble these expedient, and things opposite to these inexpedient.

Honourable things are those from which some distinction or some distinguished honour will accrue to the agents, pleasant things are those that cause delight, easy ones those accomplished with very little time and labour and expense, practicable all those that are able to be done, necessary those the performance of which does not rest with ourselves but which are as they are in consequence, as it were, of divine or human compulsion.

Such is the nature of the just, the lawful, the expedient, the honourable, the pleasant, the easy, the practicable and the necessary. We shall find plenty to say about them by using these conceptions in themselves as stated above, and also their analogies and their opposites and the previous judgements of them made by the gods or by men of repute or by judges or by our opponents.

The nature of justice we have, then, already explained. The argument from analogy to the just is as follows: 'As we deem it just to obey our parents, in the same way it behoves our sons to copy the conduct of their fathers,' and 'As it is just to do good in return to those who do us good, so it is just not to do harm to those who do us no evil.' This is the way in which we must take the analogous to the just; and we must illustrate the actual example given from its opposites: 'As it is just to punish those who do us harm, so it is also proper to do good in return to those who do us good.' The judgement of men of repute as to what is just you will take thus: 'We are not alone in hating and doing harm to our enemies, but Athens and Sparta also judge it to be just to punish one's enemies.' This is how you will pursue the topic of the just, taking it in several forms.

The nature of legality we have previously defined; but when it serves our purpose we must bring in the person of the legislator and the terms of the law, and next the argument from analogy to the written law. This may be as follows: 'As the lawgiver has punished thieves with the severest penalties, so also deceivers ought to be severely punished, because they are thieves who steal our minds'; and 'Even as the lawgiver has made the next of kin the heirs of those who die childless, so in the present case I ought to have the disposal of the freedman's estate, because as those who gave him his freedom are dead and gone, it is just that I myself being their next of kin should have control of their freedman.' This is how the topic of analogy to the legal is taken. That of its opposite is taken as follows: 'If the law prohibits the distribution of public property, it is clear that the lawgiver judged all persons who take a share in it to be guilty of an offence.' 'If the laws enjoin that those who direct the affairs of the community honourably and justly are to be honoured, it is clear that they deem those who destroy public property deserving of punishment.' This is the way in which what is legal is illustrated from its opposites. It is illustrated from previous judgements thus: 'Not only do I myself assert that this was the intention of the lawgiver in enacting this law, but also on a former occasion when Lysitheides put forward considerations very similar to those now advanced by me the court voted in favour of this interpretation of the law.' This is how we shall pursue the topic of legality, exhibiting it in several forms.

The nature of expediency has been defined in what came before; and we must include in our speeches with topics previously mentioned any argument from expediency also that may be available, and pursue the same method as that which we followed in dealing with legality and justice, displaying the expedient also in many forms. The argument from analogy to the expedient may be as follows: 'As it is expedient in war to post the bravest men in the front line, so it is profitable in the constitution of states for the wisest and most just to rank above the multitude'; and 'As it is expedient for people in health to be on their guard against contracting disease, so also it is expedient for states enjoying a period of concord to take precautions against the rise of faction.' This is the mode of treatment which you will pursue in multiplying cases of analogy to the expedient. You will demonstrate the expedient from cases of the opposite thus: 'If it is profitable to honour virtuous citizens, it would be expedient to punish vicious ones'; 'If you think it inexpedient for us to go to war with Thebes single-handed, it would be expedient for us to make an alliance with Sparta before going to war with Thebes.' This is how you will demonstrate the expedient from cases of the opposite. The proper way to take the opinion of judges of repute is as follows: 'When Sparta had defeated Athens in war she decided that it would be expedient for herself not to enslave the city; and again when Athens in cooperation with Thebes had it in her power to destroy Sparta, she decided that it would be expedient for her to let it survive.'

You will have plenty to say on the topics of justice, legality and expediency by pursuing them in this manner. Develop those of honour, facility, pleasure, practicability and necessity in a similar way. These rules will give us plenty to say on these topics.

Next let us determine the number and nature of the subjects about which and the considerations on which we deliberate in council-chambers and in parliaments. If we clearly understand the various classes of these, the business in hand at each debate will itself supply us with arguments specially adapted to it, while we shall readily be able to produce general ideas applicable to the particular matter in hand if we have been familiar with them long before. For these reasons, therefore, we must classify the matters that universally form the subject of our deliberations in common. To speak summarily therefore, the subjects about which we shall make public speeches are seven in number: our deliberations and speeches in council and in parliament must necessarily deal with either religious ritual, or legislation, or the form of the constitution, or alliances and treaties with other states, or way, or peace, or finance. These, then, being the subjects of our deliberations in council and of our speeches in parliament, let us examine each of them, and consider the ways in which we can deal with them when making a speech.

In speaking about rites of religion, three lines can be taken: either we shall say that we ought to maintain the established ritual as it is, or that we ought to alter it to a more splendid form, or alter it to a more modest form. When we are saying that the established ritual ought to be maintained, we shall draw arguments from considerations of right by saying that in all countries it is deemed wrong to depart from the ancestral customs, that all the oracles enjoin on mankind the performance of their sacrifices in the ancestral manner, and that it is the religious observances of the original founders of cities and builders of the gods' temples that it behoves us most to conserve. Arguing from expediency, we shall say that the performance of the sacrifices in the ancestral manner will be advantageous either for individual citizens or for the community on the ground of economy, and that it will profit the citizens in respect of courage because if they are escorted in religious processions by heavy infantry, cavalry and light-armed troops the pride that they will take in this will make them more courageous. We can urge it on the ground of honour if it has resulted in the festivals being celebrated with so much splendour; on the ground of pleasure if a certain elaboration has been introduced into the sacrifices of the gods merely as a spectacle; on the ground of practicability if there has been neither deficiency nor extravagance in the celebrations. These are the lines we must pursue when we are advocating the established order, basing our considerations on the arguments already stated or arguments similar to them, and on such explanation of our case as is feasible.

When we are advocating the alteration of the sacrificial rites in the direction of greater splendour, we shall find plausible arguments for changing the ancestral institutions in saying (1) that to add to what exists already is not to destroy but to amplify the established order; (2) that in all probability even the gods show more benevolence towards those who pay them more honour; (3) that even our forefathers used not to conduct the sacrifices always on the same lines, but regulated their religious observances both private and public with an eye to the occasions and to the prosperity of their circumstances; (4) that this is the manner in which we administer both our states and our private households in all the rest of our affairs as well; (5) and also specify any benefit of distinction or pleasure that will accrue to the state if these recommendations are carried out, developing the subject in the manner explained in the former cases. When, on the other hand, we are advocating a reduction to a more modest form, we must first (1) direct our remarks to the condition of the times and show how the public are less prosperous now than they were previously; then argue (2) that probably it is not the cost of the sacrifices but the piety of those who offer them that give pleasure to the gods; (3) that people who do a thing that is beyond their capacity are judged by both gods and men to be guilty of great folly; (4) that questions of public expenditure turn not only on the human factor but also on the good or bad state of finance. These, then, and similar lines of argument will be available to support our proposals with regard to sacrifices. Let us now define what is the best form of sacrifice, in order that we may know how to frame proposals and pass laws for its regulation. The best of all sacrifical ceremonies is one organized in a manner that is pious towards the gods, moderate in expense, of military benefit, and brilliant as a spectacle. It will show piety to the gods if the ancestral ritual is preserved; it will be moderate in expense if not all the offerings carried in procession are used up; brilliant as a spectacle if lavish use is made of gold and things of that sort which are not used up in the celebration; of military advantage if cavalry and infantry in full array march in the procession.

These considerations will provide us with the finest ways of organizing the ceremonies of religion; and what has been said before will inform us of the lines that may be followed in public speeches about the various forms of religious celebration.

Let us next in a similar manner discuss the subject of law and the constitution of the state. Laws may be briefly described as common agreements of a state, defining and prescribing in writing various rules of conduct.

In democracies legislation should make the general run of minor offices elected by lot (for that prevents party faction) but the most important offices elected by the vote of the community; under this system the people having sovereign power to bestow the honours on whom they choose will not be jealous of those who obtain them, while the men of distinction will the more cultivate nobility of character, knowing that it will be advantageous for them to stand in good repute with their fellow-citizens. This is how the election of officials should be regulated by law in a democracy. A detailed discussion of the rest of the administration would be a laborious task; but to speak summarily, precautions must be taken to make the laws deter the multitude from plotting against the owners of landed estates and engender in the wealthy an ambition to spend money on the public services. This the law might effect if some offices were reserved for the propertied classes, as a return for what they spent on public objects, and if among the poorer people the laws paid more respect to the tillers of the soil and the sailor class than to the city rabble, in order that the wealthy may be willing to undertake public services and the multitude may devote itself to industry and not to cadging. In addition to this there should be strict laws laid down prohibiting the distribution of public lands and the confiscation of property on the decease of the owners, and severe penalties should be imposed on those who transgress these enactments. A public burial-ground in a fine situation outside the city should be assigned to those who fall in war, and their sons should receive public maintenance till they come of age. Such should be the nature of the legal system enacted in a democracy.

In the case of oligarchies, the laws should assign the offices on an equal footing to all those sharing in citizenship. Election to most of the offices should be by lot, but for the most important it should be by vote, under oath, with a secret ballot and very strict regulations. The penalties enacted for those attempting to insult any of the citizens should in an oligarchy be very heavy, as the multitude resents insolent treatment more than it is annoyed by exclusion from office. Also differences between the citizens should be settled as quickly as possible and not allowed to drag on; and the mob should not be brought together from the country to the city, because such gatherings lead to the masses making common cause and over-throwing the oligarchies.

And, speaking generally, the laws in a democracy should hinder the many from plotting designs upon the property of the wealthy, and in an oligarchy they should deter those who have a share in the government from treating the weaker men with insolence and toadying to their fellow-citizens. These considerations will inform you of the objects at which the laws and framework of the constitution of the state should aim.

One who wishes to advocate a law has to prove that it will be equal for the citizens, consistent with the other laws, and advantageous for the state, best of all as promoting concord, or failing that, as contributing to the noble qualities of the citizens or to the public revenues or to the good repute of the commonwealth or the power of the state or something else of the kind. In speaking against a proposal the points to consider are, first, is the law not impartial? next, will it be really at variance with the other laws and not in agreement with them? and in addition, instead of promoting any of the objects stated, will it on the contrary be detrimental to them?

This will supply us with plenty of material for making proposals and speeches about laws and the constitution of the commonwealth.

We will proceed to the consideration of alliances and covenants with other states. Covenants must necessarily be framed in accordance with regulations and common agreements; and it is necessary to secure allies on occasions when people by themselves are weak or when a war is expected, or to make an alliance with one nation because it is thought that this will deter another nation from war. These and a number of additional similar reasons are the grounds for making allies; and when one wishes to support the formation of an alliance it is necessary to show that the situation is of this nature, and to prove if possible that the contracting nation is reliable in character, and has done the state some service previously, and is very powerful and a near neighbour, or failing this, you must collect together whichever of these advantages do exist. When you are opposing the alliance you can show first that it is not necessary to make it now, secondly that the proposed allies are not really reliable, thirdly that they have treated us badly before, or if not, that they are remote in locality and not really able to come to our assistance on the suitable occasions. From these and similar considerations we shall be well supplied with arguments to use in opposing and in advocating alliances.

Again, let us in the same manner pick out the most important considerations on the question of peace and war. The following are the arguments for making war on somebody: that we have been wronged in the past, and now that opportunity offers ought to punish the wrongdoers; or, that we are being wronged now, and ought to go to war in our own defence − or in defence of our kinsmen or of our benefactors; or, that our allies are being wronged and we ought to go to their help; or, that it is to the advantage of the state in respect of glory or wealth or power or the like. When we are exhorting people to go to war we should bring together as many of these arguments as possible, and afterwards show that most of the factors on which success in war depends are on the side of those whom we are addressing. Success is always due either to the favour of the gods which we call good fortune, or to man-power and efficiency, or financial resources, or wise generalship, or to having good allies, or to natural advantages of locality. When exhorting people to war we shall select and put forward those among these and similar topics that are most relevant to the situation, belittling the resources of the adversaries and magnifying and amplifying our own.

If, on the other hand, we are trying to prevent a war that is impending, we must first employ arguments to prove either that no grievance exists at all or that the grievances are small and negligible; next we must prove that it is not expedient to go to war, by enumerating the misfortunes that befall mankind in war, and in addition we must show that the factors conducive to victory in war (which are those that were enumerated just above) are more to be found on the side of the enemy. These are the considerations to be employed to avert a war that is impending. When we are trying to stop a war that has already begun, if those whom we are advising are getting the upper hand, the first thing to say is that sensible people should not wait till they have a fall but should make peace while they have the upper hand, and next that it is the nature of war to ruin many even of those who are successful in it, whereas it is the nature of peace to save the vanquished while allowing the victors to enjoy the prizes for which they went to war; and we must point out how many and how incalculable are the changes of fortune that occur in war. Such are the considerations to be employed in exhorting to peace those who are gaining the upper hand in a war. Those who have encountered a reverse we must urge to make peace on the ground of what has actually happened to them, and on the ground that they ought to learn from their misfortunes not to be exasperated with their wrongful aggressors, and because of the dangers that have already resulted from not making peace, and because it would be better to sacrifice a portion of their possessions to the stronger power than to be vanquished in war and lose their lives as well as their property. And briefly, we have to realize that it is the way of all mankind to bring their wars with one another to an end either when they think that their adversaries' claims are just, or when they quarrel with their allies or grow tired of the war or afraid of the enemy, or when internal faction breaks out among them.

Consequently if you collect those among all of these and similar points that are most closely related to the facts, you will not be at a loss for appropriate matter for a speech about war and peace.

It still remains for us to discuss finance. The first thing to be considered is whether any part of the national property has been neglected, and is neither producing revenue nor set apart for the service of religion. I refer, for example, to neglect of some public places the sale or lease of which to private citizens might bring revenue to the state; for that is a very common source of income. If nothing of this sort is available, it is necessary to have a system of taxation based on property qualifications, or for the poor to be under the duty of rendering bodily service in emergencies while the rich furnish money and the craftsmen arms. To put it briefly, when introducing financial proposals one must say that they are fair to the citizens, permanent and productive, and that the plans of the opposition have the opposite qualities.

What has been said has shown us the subjects that we shall employ in parliamentary speeches, and the portions of those subjects that we shall use in composing speeches of exhortation and of dissuasion. Next let us put forward for our consideration the eulogistic and vituperative species of oratory.

The eulogistic species of oratory consists, to put it briefly, in the amplification of creditable purposes and actions and speeches and the attribution of qualities that do not exist, while the vituperative species is the opposite, the minimization of creditable qualities and the amplification of discreditable ones. Praiseworthy things are those that are just, lawful, expedient, noble, pleasant and easy to accomplish (the exact nature of these qualities and where to find materials for enlarging on them has been stated in an earlier passage). When eulogizing one must show in one's speech that one of these things belongs to the person in question or to his actions, as directly effected by him or produced through his agency or incidentally resulting from his action or done as a means to it or involving it as an indispensable condition of its performance; and similarly in vituperating one must show that the qualities opposite to these belong to the person vituperated. Instances of incidental result are bodily health resulting from devotion to athletics, loss of health as a result of a neglect of exercise, increased intellectual ability resulting from the pursuit of philosophy, destitution resulting from neglect of one's affairs. Examples of things done as a means are when men endure many toils and dangers for the sake of receiving a wreath of honour from their compatriots, or neglect everyone else for the sake of gratifying the persons they are in love with. Examples of indispensable conditions are a supply of sailors as indispensable for a naval victory and the act of drinking as indispensable for intoxication. By pursuing such topics in the same manner as those discussed before you will have a good supply of matter for eulogy and vituperation.

To put it briefly, you will be able to amplify and minimize all such topics by pursuing the following method. First you must show, as I lately explained, that the actions of the person in question have produced many bad, or good, results. This is one method of amplification. A second method is to introduce a previous judgement – a favourable one if you are praising, an unfavourable one if you are blaming – and then set your own statement beside it and compare them with one another, enlarging on the strongest points of your own case and the weakest ones of the other and so making your own case appear a strong one. A third way is to set in comparison with the thing you are saying the smallest of the things that fall into the same class, for thus your case will appear magnified, just as men of medium height appear taller when standing by the side of men shorter than themselves. Also the following way of amplifying will be available in all cases. Supposing a given thing has been judged a great good, if you mention something that is its opposite, it will appear a great evil; and similarly supposing something is considered a great evil, if you mention its opposite, it will appear a great good. Another possible way of magnifying good or bad actions is if you prove that the agent acted intentionally, arguing that he had long premeditated doing the acts, that he repeatedly set about doing them, that he went on doing them a long time, that no one else had attempted them before, that he did them in conjunction with persons whom no one else had acted with or in succession to persons whom no one else had followed, that he was acting willingly, that he was acting deliberately, that we should all be happy, or unfortunate, if we all acted like him. One must also argue one's case by employing comparison, and amplify it by building up one point on another, as follows: 'It is probable that anybody who looks after his friends, also honours his own parents; and anybody who honours his parents will also wish to benefit his own country.' And in brief, if you prove a man responsible for many things, whether good or bad, they will bulk large in appearance. You must also consider whether the matter bulks larger when divided up into parts or when stated as a whole, and state it in whichever way it makes a bigger show. By pursuing these methods in amplifications you will be able to make them most numerous and most effective.

To minimize either good points or bad ones by your speeches you will pursue the opposite method to that which we have described in the case of magnifying — best of all, if you prove the person not to be responsible at all, or failing that, only responsible for the fewest and smallest things possible.

These rules instruct us how we are to amplify or minimize whatever matters we are bringing forward for eulogy or vituperation. The materials for amplification are useful in the other species of oratory as well, but it is in eulogy and vituperation that they are most efficacious. The above remarks will make us adequately equipped in regard to them.

Let us next in a similar manner define the elements composing and the proper mode of employing the species of oratory used in accusation and defence — the oratory connected with forensic practice. To put it briefly, the oratory of accusation is the recital of errors and offences, and that of defence the refutation of errors and offences of which a man is accused or suspected. These being the functions of each of these species, the line to take in accusing is to say, in a case where your accusation refers to wickedness, that the actions of your adversaries are actually dishonest and illegal and detrimental to the mass of the citizens, and when it refers to folly, that they are detrimental to the agent himself, disgraceful, unpleasant and impracticable. These and similar accusations are the line of attack against persons guilty of wickedness or folly. But accusers must also be careful to notice what are the kinds of offences for which there are punishments fixed by law and which are the offences in regard to which the penalties are decided by the jury. In cases where the law has determined the penalty, the accuser must direct his attention solely to proving that the act has been committed. When the jury assess, he must amplify the offences and the errors of his opponents, and if possible prove that the defendant committed the offence of his own free will, and not from a merely casual intention, but with a very great amount of preparation; or if it is not possible to prove this, but you think the other side will try to prove that the accused made a mistake in some way, or that although intending to act honourably in the matter he failed by bad luck, you must dissipate compassion by telling your audience that men have no business to act first and afterwards say they have made a mistake, but that they ought to look before they leap; and next, that even if the defendant really did make a mistake or have bad luck, it is more proper for him to be punished for his failures and mistakes than a person who has committed neither; moreover, the lawgiver did not let off people who make mistakes but made them liable to justice, or else everybody would be making mistakes. Also say that if they listen to a man who puts up a defence of that sort, they will have many people doing wrong on purpose, as if they bring it off they will be able to do whatever they like, and if they fail they will escape being punished by saying that it was an accident. This is the sort of argument which accusers must employ to dissipate compassion; and, as has been said before, they must employ amplification to show that their opponents' actions have been attended by many bad consequences.

These, then, are the divisions composing the species of oratory used in accusation.

The defence species comprises three methods. Defendant must either prove that he did none of the things he is charged with; or if he is forced to admit them, he must try to show that what he did was lawful and just and noble and to the public advantage; or if he cannot prove this, he must attempt to gain forgiveness by representing his acts as an error or misfortune, and by showing that only small mischief has resulted from them. You must distinguish between injustice, error, and misfortune: define injustice as the deliberate commission of evil, and say that for offences of that sort the severest penalties should be inflicted; declare that a harmful action done unwittingly is an error; and class a failure to carry out some honourable intention, if it is not due to oneself but to other people or to luck, as misfortune. Also say that unjust conduct is peculiar to wicked people, but that error and misfortune in one's actions is not peculiar to yourself alone but is common to all mankind, including the members of the jury. You must claim to receive compassion for being forced to plead guilty to a charge of that sort, making out that error and misfortune are shared by your hearers. A defendant must have in view all the offences for which the laws have fixed the punishments and for which the jury assesses the penalties; and in a case where the law fixes the punishments he should show that he did not commit the act at all or that his conduct was lawful and right, whereas when the jury has been made the assessor of the penalty, he should not in the same way deny having committed the act, but try to show that he did his adversary little damage and that that was involuntary.

These and similar arguments will supply us with plenty of material in accusations and defences. It still remains for us to discuss the species of oratory employed in investigation.

Investigation may be summarily defined as the exhibition of certain intentions or actions or words as inconsistent with one another or with the rest of someone's conduct. The investigator must try to find some point in which either the speech that he is investigating is self-contradictory or the actions or the intentions of the person under investigation run counter to one another. This is the procedure – to consider whether perhaps in the past after having first been a friend of somebody he afterwards became his enemy and then became the same man's friend again; or committed some other inconsistent action indicating depravity; or is likely in the future, should opportunities befall him, to act in a manner contrary to his previous conduct. Similarly observe also whether something that he says when speaking now is contrary to what he has said before; and likewise also whether he has ever adopted a policy contrary to his previous professions, or would do so if opportunities offered. And on similar lines you should also take the features in the career of the person under investigation inconsistent with his other habits of conduct that are estimable. By thus pursuing the investigational species of oratory there is no method of investigation that you will leave out.

All the species of oratory have now been distinguished. They are to be employed both separately, when suitable, and jointly, with a combination of their qualities — for though they have very considerable differences, yet in their practical application they overlap. In fact the same is true of them as of the various species of human beings; these also are partly alike and partly different in their appearance and in their perceptions.

"THE RHETORIC OF PHILODEMUS"

A Paraphrased Translation by Harry M. Hubbell

Among the excavations at Herculaneum in the eighteenth century, many charred papyri were found which constituted an extensive private library of philosophical works, belonging perhaps to Philodemus, a Greek contemporary of Cicero who lived at Rome. Unfortunately, Hubbell comments: "The expectations aroused in the scholarly world by the discovery of these papyri have been realized only to a small degree. For instead of finding the lost works of some master of Greek literature, it was seen that the library was composed of philosophical works, almost entirely of the Epicurean school; nor were the volumes written by the greatest of the Epicureans, but mainly by Philodemus, at best an authority of the second rank."[1] *Because of a controversy among first century B.C. Epicureans concerning the utility of rhetoric, Zeno of Sidon and Philodemus argued that a certain kind of rhetoric, which they labeled "sophistic," was an art and that other Epicureans were distorting the original concepts of their founder Epicurus as set forth in his own treatise* On Rhetoric. *Hubbell writes: "The Epicureans as a whole rejected all rhetoric as useless; Zeno and Philodemus held that the epideictic branch of rhetoric was a proper subject for study because that alone could be reduced to rule, whereas the parts involving persuasion depend on the speaker's ability to catch the proper flavor. The rhetorical works of Philodemus are an exposition of this doctrine."*[2] *George Kennedy calls the treatise important as a "reconstruction of the dispute between rhetoric*

Reprinted from "The Rhetoric of Philodemus," *Transactions of The Connecticut Academy of Arts and Letters,* with translation and commentary by Harry M. Hubbell, 23 (Sept., 1920), pp. 243-382.

[1] Harry M. Hubbell, *op. cit.,* pp. 247-248.

[2] Hubbell, *op. cit.,* p. 251.

and philosophy which broke out in the second century [B.C.] "[1] *Hubbell indicates that while his translation is precisely literal where possible, the fragmentary nature of the papyrus has forced him to approximate and conjecture on details in many cases. Of Philodemus' seven books, the first discusses the nature of "art"; the second questions whether rhetoric is an art, criticizes the arguments for and against, and presents Philodemus' view that "sophistic" rhetoric is an art but other branches are not; the third book, largely lost, asserts that the sophistical school does not produce statesmen and in fact often is harmful; the fourth book criticizes in detail the claims of rhetoric (apparently as presented in an unnamed rhetorical manual) and denies the sophistical schools' ability to teach a beautiful style; the fifth book discusses the disadvantages of rhetoric and contrasts the wretched life of the rhetor with the happy life of the philosopher; the sixth book attacks the philosophical schools which advocated the study of rhetoric; and the seventh book criticizes the Stoic attitude toward rhetoric and Aristotle's rhetorical principles, ending with a final comparison between rhetoric and philosophy. The excerpts presented below include all of Book I, and a section from Book V.*

I

Some sciences depend entirely on natural ability and need but little practice; some accomplish their purpose of and by themselves, granted that the workman has the natural endowment common to all the human race; no practice is necessary; some do not need natural ability but only practice.

In the case of some arts, their purpose can be accomplished partially and reasonably well by those who have not studied the principles of the art; in other cases only the person technically trained can succeed.

Some say that an art must have definite rules, e. g. grammaticé, others that an art is merely wisdom or skill ($\sigma o \phi \iota a$), others require that it have a definite purpose, e. g. Plato; others demand that it shall tend to improve life.

Those who define art fall into the error of expecting that one definition will cover all arts (*or rather* that all arts fulfil equally all the requirements of the definition), in order to obtain what they call the union of arts ($\sigma \acute{\upsilon} \nu \delta \epsilon \sigma \mu o \varsigma$). Then when they find an art which has some characteristic not shared by the others, as is frequently the case, they exclude it from the position of an art.

In the sciences there is frequently an interchange of function: two sciences produce the same result. But this does not prove that they are not arts. It is not unheard-of for the same result to be accomplished by two

[1] George Kennedy, *The Art of Persuasion in Greece* (Princeton, N. J., 1963), p. 301.

arts, and perhaps this is the best way of distinguishing the merely useful from the necessary art.

Objections can be made to most if not all of the argument here mentioned. The worst class of arguments are those which act as boomerangs and demolish the position of the disputant. As far as these arguments are concerned no one can object to the opponents' saying that there are perfect artists and imperfect ones as well. It is unfair to blame the perfect artist for the failures of his imperfect colleague. But that is what the present critics are doing. The end of rhetoric is to persuade in a speech; consequently it is idle to mention other means of persuasion, such as beauty. If laymen sometimes persuade by means of a speech it does not follow that they persuade better or more frequently than the trained rhetor.

Apart from the aforementioned obscurities you will find that many of the arguments overstep the bounds of the facts under discussion and are built up on double meanings of words. Many of the arguments do not differ in validity, but by a variety of examples display the fertility of the inventors. Then, too, in these arguments there is a great deal of bare assertion, entirely unsupported by argument (ἀκάτάσκευον κατασκνή= constructive argument).

The following error is found in almost all the arguments: they assume from the lack of technical treatises at a given time or place that no art then existed. But it is hardly to be expected that we can find technical works in a period in which the art of writing had not been invented.

Most, if not all, the arguments do not prove what they claim to prove even if the premises be granted. For if the art of music does not produce the ability to read and write, it may still be the art of other things. Similarly if they assume that sophistic rhetoric does not produce political science or practical rhetorical ability, they are right, but that does not preclude the possibility that sophistic is an art.

"Just as dialectic is an art, but accomplishes nothing unless combined with ethics or physics, so rhetoric is an art, but accomplishes nothing unless combined with politics." There are many other errors in the arguments, but we do not intend to take them up in detail.

Those Epicureans are to be censured who assume that sophistic is not an art, and thus run counter to the teachings of Epicurus, Metrodorus and Hermarchus, as we shall show later. Such Epicureans are almost guilty of parricide.

Section I-1: Refutation of arguments against rhetoric.

The arguments are quoted in direct form without introduction, and are followed by a brief criticism. The first is fragmentary but may be reconstructed as follows:

"The Spartans and Romans expelled rhetors." This does not prove that it is not an art, for states have expelled physicians, musicians and even philosophers.

The [next] argument . . . is missing, but must have run somewhat as follows: "An art always produces a beneficial result."

But the captain sometimes loses his ship, the physician kills his patient. We must either deny that navigation and medicine are arts, or abandon the demand that all arts must always be beneficial. "Different arts do not attain the same end, but grammarians and dialectians attain the end of rhetoric." Others do persuade, but the end of rhetoric is not to persuade but to persuade in a rhetorical speech. The philosopher persuades by force of logic, Phryne by her beauty; neither persuades rhetorically.

"An untrained person should not be able to excel one who has been trained in an art, but in rhetoric this sometimes occurs." The untrained man may excel the trained man at times in a conjectural art ($\sigma\tau o\chi\alpha\sigma\tau\iota\kappa\dot{\eta}$), but never in an exact science. But if the layman without experience be compared with a man trained in the schools the comparison does not justify the conclusion that sophistic and politics are not arts.

"In other arts the rules are true, in rhetoric they are false." (The reply is fragmentary but seems to mean): The same statement might be made about philosophy or medicine. In those some lay down principles which are not true, but the error of some individuals does not prove that the whole subject is not an art if properly treated.

(a) "The artist does not deny that he is an artist, but the rhetor does." The major premise is false. Some artists do deny that they have an art.

"And yet if the meanest artists do not deny that they have an art we should not expect the sophists to deny it." But as a matter of fact philosophers, geometricians, poets and physicians sometimes do deny it, thinking thereby to allay the suspicions of those who expect to be deceived.

"They deny that they possess the so-called sophistic rhetoric, and say that it is not a separate kind of rhetoric. However they do lay claim to the possession of experience in practical affairs reduced to a system, and ability to discuss these matters, and boast of it; a good example is Demosthenes." It is a disgrace for them to be ashamed of their art. However as sophistic offers no system for public speaking, how can it produce public speakers?

"Therefore it is plain that some criticize the art as having no characteristic which distinguishes it from other arts." In the case of other arts, too, which are really or apparently harmful, some criticize the teachers not for what they profess to know, but for what they do not even desire to accomplish.

"Every artist professes to accomplish a result, the rhetor does not profess to persuade," By no means all artists profess to accomplish the end of their art at all times. All who deal with conjectural arts, as, for example, physicians and pilots, sometimes fail in their purpose. The rhetor does profess to accomplish his purpose, which is not to persuade always, but to persuade better than one who has not been trained.

(Fragmentary and obscure.) "Every artist claims the province of the art as his own peculiar field (i. e. as belonging to the trained man and him alone); but the earliest speakers possessed the power of rhetoric before the art of rhetoric was formulated." On this principle we have to reject the art of medicine because men healed before Asclepius.

"A rhetor never charges others with lack of art, but with being in a state of mind which prevents them from seeing the connection of events." Therefore we must say that rhetoric is not a matter of practice or experience. For they would have claimed the results of practice for themselves.

"Men spoke better before manuals of rhetoric were written than they have since." The facts are granted, but inasmuch as rhetoric is not entirely subject to the rules of art, but demands much practice and natural ability, it is not surprising if they were once better rhetors than now, just as there were better philosophers. By this reasoning we should have to deny the position of an art to medicine and poetics. Then too, one might claim that there are good rhetors now. However sophists did not flourish before the technical treatises, but the arts were introduced by the statesmen, not by those who had made no study of the subject; and there are other arts about which nothing has been written as is the case in many parts of the barbarian world.

Section I-2: Refutation of arguments in favor of rhetoric.

Having now discussed the arguments against rhetoric's being an art we shall now take up the arguments in its favor.

General criticism of these arguments.

They assert that it is an art without establishing the preliminary principles on which their statement rests.

They fail to see that not only is art required for some purposes, but practice is required for others, and think that the same training is adequate for sophistic and politics, whereas there is no art of the latter.

If they apply the term "art" to the state of mind adapted for making rhetorical speeches, how can this be the property of only a few?

Let us take up the arguments one at a time.

"If the rhetors did not use a method we would not find many paying money for their courses." This argument rests on the supposition that rhetoric is an art of politics. This is contradicted by Epicurus in his treatise Π ερί τῆς ρητορικῆς in which he says: "Those who study in the rhetorical schools are deceived. They are charmed by the tricks of style, and pay no attention to the thought, believing that if they can learn to speak in this style they will succeed in the assembly and court of law. But then they find that this style is wholly unfitted for practical speaking they realize that they have lost their money." In this respect rhetoric may fittingly be compared to the art of prophecy. "Not a few who were unable to speak in public have gained ability by studying in the rhetorical schools." But some come out of the schools worse than when they went in. And if some improve, it may be from other causes which we shall discuss elsewhere; and we shall also discuss elsewhere why they frequent the schools. This improvement does not demonstrate that rhetoric is an art for it is possible for speakers to improve by practice and experience.

[If it were not an art] "the majority of the students would not become good, but inefficient." Yet we see at times some without art producing more and better speakers than those who possess accurate knowledge; this proves that it is not an art. Some leave the study of sophistic to the child, and afterward give the youth the benefit of association with those who have had practical experience in the assembly and courts. Then if they succeed they are said to have studied with sophists, and the sophists get the credit for giving them the training which they have received from another source.

"Lawyers and statesmen send their sons to the sophists to pursue those studies which gave them their ability." In the first place some insist that they wasted the time which they spent in study with the sophists, and send their sons to their own teacher — the people. However if they do send them to the sophists it is because they do not want their sons to be deprived of any possible advantage to be obtained at the rhetorical schools, but they do not expect the school to produce a trained statesman. Some send their sons to the rhetoricians merely for a liberal education, putting rhetoric on a par with other studies.

"As in music and grammar so in rhetoric there is a transmission of knowledge from teacher to pupil, and the training is not without method." There may be a transmission of knowledge which is not connected with an art but acquired by experience and observation. The statement that "the training is not without method" is mere assertion without any argument to support it. If the statement means that sophistic is an art of practical speaking it is entirely wrong. (Lacuna.) In publishing technical works they are like the Chaldaens and prophets who give out dreams to deceive the people, and are themselves deceived. If we grant anything we grant that sophistic is an art; but not even those who teach it believe that it is an art of politics.

[If there were no art of rhetoric] "none of those who speak powerfully and intelligently would speak artistically." We may turn the argument around and say that if some speak artistically before the court or the assembly the graduates of the school do not share any of their good qualities. However we may be accused of using language loosely and failing to distinguish between what comes with art and what without. For we use the word "artistic" in our everyday speech in a loose way, e. g. one plays games artistically.

"On seeing a beautiful statue you would say without argument that it was the product of art; you will pass the same judgment after investigating the acts of statesmen." One might acknowledge that the works of the panegyrists are the products of art. But inasmuch as the acts of a statesman deal with a subject which cannot be reduced to the rules of art how can they reveal that they are the products of art.

"If it were not an art those who have studied it would not practice proof (or demonstration)." Not only is one who has not studied an art unable to do the work of an art, but one who has not practiced and observed cannot reap the benefits. By studying what pleases the crowd and practicing, one can become skilled in politics. This is a strong proof that sophistic is not the art of politics.[1] If it is, let him who has studied the technical treatises go before the people and speak!

Section I-3: Criticism of the views of Epicureans on rhetoric.

The Epicureans who claim that rhetoric is an art of *writing* speeches and delivering epideictic orations make the error of applying the term *rhetoric* to what should properly be called *sophistic*. Those who admit that sophistic is an art, but deny that there is an art of forensic and deliberative oratory because sophistic is not the art of these branches, have failed to prove that there is no art of forensic and deliberative oratory. There may be a method of these branches; but all they have shown is that some do succeed by means of natural ability and experience without the aid of rhetoric. Nor have they established beyond a doubt, as they should, that sophistic is the art of epideictic. The treatise on rhetoric ascribed to Polyaenus we have already shown to be spurious.

[1] Here Philodemus seems to be attacking "sophistic" which he elsewhere admits as an art. The inconsistency is only apparent, however, as will be plain if we examine closely the meaning of "sophistic" as defined by Philodemus. The "sophists" are in his language the professional teachers of rhetoric, and sophistic is the subject taught in these schools. This subject matter is called "rhetoric" by those who teach it, and it is claimed that it trains for deliberative and forensic oratory, and therefore is an art. This Philodemus denies. The ability to persuade in a speech whether in law court or in public assembly, he says, is the result of natural endowment and facility acquired by practice; it must be acquired by each individual and cannot be set down in the form of rules and imparted from teacher to pupil; hence it cannot be called an art. In so far, then, as the professors of rhetoric attempt to teach the principles of public speaking and the laws of politics with a view to producing statesmen, they fail, for sophistic is not an art of politics. Later he sets the limits of sophistic – it is the art of epideixis and nothing more.

Those who say it is an art, but requires ability and practice, not to acquire it but to attain the end completely, have utterly failed. They have not made the division between the different parts of rhetoric (i. e. sophistic and practical rhetoric) which was made by Epicurus and his immediate successors. Epicurus demonstrated that sophistic is an art of writing speeches and delivering epideictic orations but is not the art of forensic or deliberative oratory; accordingly they say that sophistic is an art; his successors likewise have said that there is no art of politics. They certainly leave no place for any science of politics.

Moreover their statement that ability and practice are needed to learn the art of sophistic is false, or we must make the same statement about philosophy. Their illustration from the art of grammar turns against them. For natural ability is required for rhetoric just as much as it is as a foundation for grammar. In the case of grammar natural ability and practice are required in order to acquire the knowledge of the subject, not to attain the end. Consequently if rhetoric is similar to grammar we must admit that ability and practice are needed to acquire rhetoric. When they say that ability is required for delineation, for making suitable gestures, etc., and experience is needed to judge the proper occasion for speaking, what have they left for art? They ought to show what *is* needed to acquire the art if ability and practice are not needed.

Those are wrong who claim that rhetoric is not an art on the assumption that an art must have method and a transmission of definite knowledge, if on the other hand they allow medicine which is conjectural to be an art.

Their expression εἴ τις προείληφε assumes that one can define art as one chooses.

While criticizing those who do not make proper divisions, they fail to differentiate between the several parts of rhetoric.

Politics is an art according to their grouping of the sciences and this is false. For it has no method, nor is it even a conjectural art. This can be proven by passages from Epicurus and Metrodorus. (Some of which are quoted.)

It is stupid to say that the rhetors have *observed* the elements which generally persuade, and have reduced them to a system, and that we persuade by use of prooemium and narrative and the other parts of an oration.

A fourth class present arguments which are a combination of the last two, and are open to the same objections. Their definition of art is "a state of training acquired as a result of observation by which the proposed end is obtained generally and with reasonable probability." This removes the distinctive characteristic of an art which is its method and general principles applying to the individual cases. The practical skill acquired by observation is not called an art by the Greeks except that sometimes in a loose use of language people call a clever woodchopper an artist. If we call observation and practice art we should include under the term all human activity.

They say that politics is not an art, and yet they claim that rhetoric i. e. πολιτικὴ ῥητορική is helpful in practical life. How can rhetoric be called an art when it does not help the artist but sometimes makes him inferior to the layman. Dialectic and Sophistic may be arts by their definition, but in differentiating between them and rhetoric they prove that rhetoric has no method. The other differences which they point out all go to show that rhetoric is not an art. These points of difference are seen when it contributes anything it is something insignificant and accidental; (2) it is not necessary, a layman can do as well as an artist; (3) its principles are easily acquired; (4) it depends largely on practice and memory. In short rhetoric has no method.

Bromius in his discussion of the arts passes over sophistical rhetoric on the ground that it is not regarded as an art either by people in general or by Epicurus. The only art that he will allow in this connection is politics. How can he do this when sophistic *is* an art and is so considered by the leaders of our school? If he considers sophistic to be no art why does he not prove his statement? How can he make the claim that the good statesman has calculated the means of arousing the emotions, and of persuasion, and uses these continually? Any success which the speakers attain they attain because of practice, but they do not succeed universally. Furthermore, his statement that the technical treatises of the rhetoricians are not entirely barren is in direct contradiction to the teachings of Epicurus who says that all such treatises are useless for producing the political faculty.

Section II: Philodemus' theories about rhetoric.

We shall now present our own views under the following heads:

(a) Definition of art according to usage.
(b) Epicurean doctrine declares that sophistic rhetoric is an art.
(c) Sophistic is an art of epideixis and writing of speeches, but not of forensic and deliberative oratory.
(d) Politics depends on investigation and practice, but has none of the essentials of an art.

Section II-a: Definition of 'art.'

An art, as the term is commonly used, is a state or condition resulting from the observation of certain common and elementary principles, which apply to the majority of cases, accomplishing such a result as cannot be attained by one who has not studied it, and doing this regularly and certainly and not by conjecture. For the moment we may leave out of the discussion whether or not a looser use of the word sanctions the inclusion under the heading 'art' of all occupations depending wholly on practice. The definition applies both to the exact sciences like grammar and music which have certain definite rules, and to the conjectural which are in possession of certain common elements affecting individual cases, although these common elements may not have been completely mastered, and the result may not be accomplished always but only more frequently than by those who do not possess the art.

(There follows a passage which cannot be restored.)

If rhetoric has no method it is not an art. We apply the terms 'experience,' 'observation,' 'practice' when one has failures as well as successes; but we never call this art, for the essence of art is to accomplish the result always.

[Another lacuna; apparently, A dancer] has observed the proper way of producing a beautiful effect, i. e. how to stand, how to walk, etc., but he has no method or elementary principles to impart as has the musician. The same statement applies to acrobats. If we class these occupations as arts we shall include practically everything. To sum up; these which we now say are arts we say have a certain character which is possessed by grammar and sculpture; and those which we deny are arts lack this character and are characterized by observation. On the basis of this definition we declare sophistic to be an art and politics not.

*V**

Philosophy is more profitable than epideictic rhetoric especially if one practice rhetoric in the fashion of the sophists. . . .

The philosopher has many τόποι concerning practical justice and other virtues about which he is confident; the busybody (i. e. the rhetorician) is quite the opposite. Nor is one who does not appear before kings and popular assemblies forced to play second part to the rich, as do rhetors who are compelled to employ flattery all their lives.

The instruction given by the sophists is not only stupid but shameless, and lacking in refinement and reason.

(Fragments IV—VIII and col. II are hopeless.)

He makes an incredible statement when he claims that one skilled in such subjects (viz. philosophy) could not be of noble character, and that such studies bring no one happiness, and that no one except a madman would be interested in them. For apart from the knowledge an educated man ought to have, he should obey the laws, realizing that they apply to him. . . .

[*Book V consists of three groups of fragments. The following fragments make up the third group — Eds.]

If the goodwill of one's country is esteemed the fairest crown of victory, the defeated also ought to fare well. A common country should bestow benefits in common. But as we see in one country a rhetor neglected rather than crowned, and in another country one is banished, tortured and insulted, let us without claiming a share in the ability to manage a city by persuasion, be content [to live the quiet life of a philosopher].

Very few if any of the [tyrants] have been overthrown by their mercenaries, whereas many statesmen have been rejected by their fellow citizens, and slaughtered like cattle, nay they are worse off than cattle, for the butcher does not hate the cattle, but the tortures of the dying statesmen are made more poignant by hatred.

It is claimed for rhetoric that it protects property like a strong tower. First if we are not rich we do not need rhetoric. Secondly it is much better to lose one's wealth if one can not keep it otherwise, than to spend one's life in rhetoric.

But Cephenides (Drone) the rich man is a prey to slaves and prophets as well as to sycophants.

. . . they are unable to make the multitude friendly to them, as the crowd of politicans can.

The philosophers are not vexed if people, like foolish sheep or cattle, attend to an inferior, but are satisfied that what they say, particularly about the attitude of the common people, shall please the few; and in action they are most blameless, nor do they as slaves of all, try to rule everything for themselves. For they do not expect to satisfy their wants at the expense of the public. But those philosophers who envy other's property while they pretend to need nothing, and are detected being coy, these men the people despise, but consider them less wretched than the rhetors, because so many obtain the same result that the rhetors obtain.

It is numbered among the glories of rhetoric that it can "sail the deep seas" while those who speak briefly are rejected like small boats unable to sail far from shore, because they accomplish nothing brilliant. If by "sail the deep seas" they mean "make long speeches," then rhetoric is a crazy profession. If by "sail deep seas" they mean treat at length a subject needing detailed treatment, and arrogate to themselves alone this power, not even then are they in their right minds; for the philosophers, or any one else with sense can treat a subject in this manner. However if they examine a subject minutely by their "deep sea" method, then the rhetors are mistaken in thinking they speak only about large subjects. . . .*1.26.* They borrow the dialectic method from the philosophers, and pride themselves on something which they reject as a principle.

For the method of question and answer is necessary not only in philosophy and education, but often in the ordinary intercourse of life. The method of joint inquiry frequently demands this style. Moreover this method is adopted by the rhetor in the assembly as well as in the court of justice. "Rhetoric enables a man to be a guard of metics, a friend of citizens and a protector of those of lesser rank." Therefore one could not say that a rich man does not possess happiness unless he knows rhetoric, but that he is much better off without it. For he ought not to fortify himself, but to free himself from paying ransom to speechwriters.

Consequently though both methods are useful, they neglect one of them. Those who say that the rhetors use the method of question and answer in its highest degree cannot prove that this method is peculiar to them, nor that they rather than the philosophers wrote technical works about it. Neither the modern sophists in their teaching, nor the ancients in their published works attained such distinction in dialectic as have the philosophers.

They say that the rhetor does not seek pleasure from such foolish subjects as geometry, but producing arts and sciences of daily life, he directs men to that path which leads to the city and place of assembly, which they themselves follow. It is ridiculous for them to say that geometry produces pleasure and glory. Certainly we do not claim to devote our whole life to it. . . . The philosopher is versed in the characters and methods of living which result in faction and exile, through a knowledge of which it is possible most correctly to govern the city and the assembly. The sophists have unawares, made a simile which applies to themselves; for it is their profession which does not enter into the civil life and the assembly, and is of no help to human life. So it is reasonable that some do not care at all for what they say, but refuse to accept rhetoric and sophistic and politics even cursorily, considering one foolish, the other most inimical to peace of mind.

If the remarks following directly after these were intended to apply to the dialecticians — they are no concern of ours; if they apply to us they are mere chatter, because when we claim to speak accurately as the rhetors cannot because their speeches are composed of probabilities, they proceed to say that spider webs are finer than cloth but less useful; similarly the finespun subtleties of the philosophers are useless for practical purposes because no one in deliberating uses syllogisms, but probabilities. So that if we use syllogisms, what appeared advantageous at one time would not remain so; whence there is no one possibility which will be advantageous if brought to pass, but the only thing left is to guess on a basis of probability. . . . After assuming that speeches can be made according to strict logic, they proceed to use in both deliberative and forensic oratory, nothing but probabilities, and often the less probable rather than the more; besides they seek broad effect rather than accuracy and systematic treatment, as is natural since they have no *method,* but depend entirely on observation, and quickly discard their observations because of the changes of the populace which are quicker than those of the Euripus. But the philosophers do not restrict themselves to rigidly logical argument. . . .

The nature of justice and injustice — that one is always advantageous and the other never, can be settled entirely by strict logic. Anyone who applies guesswork to such subjects is simply foolish. Then their talk about spider webs, bits and saws for cutting millet seeds is nonsense. . . . It is clearly proven that the art of the rhetor is of no assistance for a life of happiness.

[The sophist says] it is better to estimate roughly on large subjects than to treat accurately of some small subject of no importance. Perhaps we can add to the accomplishments of rhetoric that it can talk in a general way about subjects of no importance.

The comparison of great and small subjects is kept up at the end of the column in the reference to fishing for tunnies and sprats.

. . . to one who wonders why they can see clearly into a dark and difficult subject, and are unable to see what is in plain sight of all, they apply the figure of the owl. Such remarks as they made about oaths and counsels, not only no philosopher but not even a man of ordinary taste would. . . . The doctrines of the philosophers are not too finespun for practical life, and the doctrines of the rhetors are not suitable, so that having demonstrated that the doctrines of the politicians are like one or the other — they compare us to owls.

Their next statement is that there is no distinction between justice and injustice except that commonly accepted by the people, and that those who assume a different standard are like those who seek to substitute a coinage of their own for that established by the state; the new coinage is useless, for it will not pass current and the maker's life would not be safe.

By rhetoric neither [is accomplished] as it seems, but political science is not investigated or taught by the rhetoricians, either exclusively or to a higher degree than by others.

The philosophers of our school agree with οἱ πολλοί on a question of what is just and good, differing from them only in this that they arrive at their conclusions by logic as well as by feeling, and never forget these conclusions, but always compare the chief good with things indifferent. They do differ from οἱ πολλοί about the means to attain happiness, and do not think that offices, power, conquests and the like are proper means to the end. Similarly the principles derived by them from "notions" we judge to be just and noble; but we differ from the common opinion as to what corresponds to the "notion." (I. e. what produces the end — pleasure — which is perceived by all.)

Not only *some* philosophers differ from the popular ideas of right and wrong, but *all* statesmen do. For in their period of office they are wholly concerned to change popular opinion on questions of right and justice and advantage. If this is so, how do we resemble those who scorn current coinage, and seek for substitutes? Apart from the fact that we do not despise theories based on "notions," how could we be said to be acting in this way if we assume the true principles of right and wrong? For some of these are helpful to them as well as to us whether they grant it or not; others are really established customs, and will not allow themselves to be used unless we assume them in keeping with the former principles. For if they do not have the true idea of hot and cold, it is not our authority which they oppose. It is possible for a fate to befall them like that of those who differ (with their states) about coinage — and how can their search be called useless if there is really anything better — if the cities will not accept the innovations, and the inventor's life is not safe. For it makes no difference to those truly well if others will not adopt hygienic measures, nor to those who avoid fire or snow, if others refuse to acknowledge the natural qualities residing in them. It is astounding for them to say that the natural means of safety will not protect them.

Some things are just or unjust by nature and never change, others vary according to locality and condition. Laws which are not of this nature, but are established for various reasons ought to be obeyed, or if the philosophers do not think that they can live well under these laws they ought to leave the country. They can be social to a high degree by observing those principles which make for likeness and not for difference; we can do this without being observed as well as with publicity; with pleasure and not under compulsion; steadily and not in an uncertain fashion.

If rhetoric imparts an experience of these things, so that it is the only road to the happy life, yet it does not lead to courts and assemblies, where there are more wrecks than ever at Cape Caphereus.

[Rhetoricians say that this art makes men good] for one will wish to seem prudent and just in order to obtain favors from the people.

[It is strange that one would not endure to be taught virtue] whereas if he were sick he would endure being forced to undergo treatment. But their interjection of the argument that virtue cannot be taught is untimely. For Socrates showed that political virtue cannot be taught, proving his case by the inability of Themistocles, Aristides and Pericles to train their sons to be their equals. By the same means one could prove that sophistic rhetoric cannot be taught. *1.30.* But "rhetoric would be able to benefit a man who by its help can persuade the people that he is of high character." Quite the contrary; even if a man be virtuous otherwise, he is considered a scoundrel because he is a rhetor. They say that we ought to believe that there is something better than truth which does not persuade, on the testimony of Euripides who says; "Mortals' coin is not only shining silver but virtue" (i. e. virtue in the commonly accepted sense). At any rate they purchase many things by character, as well as by money. But why should a philosopher pay attention to Euripides, especially since he has no proof ... ? Some say they pursue virtue not expecting to receive anything from it; others desire safety for the sake of happiness.

"Suppose a virtuous man made the object of a slanderous attack, and unable to persuade the jury of his innocence; he would be punished, not pitied and honored." Certainly. But worst of all is not to recognize exalted virtue, but to consider it wickedness. According to the argument of the rhetors one ought to study the reputable rather than the monstrous – and that when the greatest statesmen bring to the bema things which should be associated only with the vilest of men. The so-called virtuous men when they are called to account before the people refuse to stand trial. They think they are to suffer a treatment much worse than that accorded to the sick, much less acquire virtue, just as if virtue were not a real good, or there were no real cure which the people apply when they judge a man in the wrong.

"Furthermore it has been said that we (i. e. the rhetoricians) fight not against external enemies at whose hand it is honorable to die, but against internal enemies at whose hands it is disgraceful to die; that we have nothing to do with virtue – for that did not save Socrates; – nor with medicine – *that* saves men from disease, not from prison; nor with any other profession than rhetoric which helps those who strive not only for their lives but to obtain money, and to prevent disfranchisement and exile."

However we shall repel our enemies with their own weapons. Virtue did not help Socrates because when he was led to court it was lacking in some people. Medicine and other professions help even in prison. If a philosopher falls a victim to such a death, it is not a disgrace to him but to those who kill him. However he does not live in fear of meeting such a fate. For the supersititions of the common people do not disturb one who is persuaded that he shall have no existence after death.

If for these reasons persuasion was reasonably considered a good by them, she would have been deified by philosophy. The fact that through it no little harm is done is not true of philosophical persuasion, but of rhetorical which Pisistratus used; wherefore it does not belong to the category of the greatest goods as they perversely say, nor to the special categories of power and wealth. If one does not use these well, he would receive much harm. Philosophy shows us how to find and use everything necessary for a happy life.

CICERO: DE ORATORE

Translated by E. W. Sutton and H. Rackham

H. Rackham calls De Oratore, *written by Cicero in 55 B.C. when he was driven from public affairs, "indeed worthy of the greatest of Roman orators, who regards oratory as of supreme practical importance in the guidance of affairs, and who resolves, while his mind is still vigorous and powerful, to devote his enforced leisure to placing on record the fruits of his experience, for the instruction of future statesmen."*[1] *In a letter to Lentulus in 54 B.C., Cicero writes that he has composed a dialogue on oratory in three books which "embrace the theories of rhetoric held by the ancients, including those of Aristotle and Isocrates." Critics Blass, Jebb, and Hubbell all assert the strong Isocratean influences found in Cicero's* De Oratore, *especially when Cicero emphasizes the widest possible range for the orator's activity; when he calls the orator the source from whom flows all the forces for civilization and government; and when he suggests that the orator is also the best available statesman and moral guide.*[2] *William Sattler suggests that Cicero was familiar with at least ten of Plato's dialogues, including the* Gorgias *and the* Phaedrus, *which he used heavily. Because of his high regard for Isocrates, Cicero employs Plato's praise of him in the* Phaedrus *to substantiate his idea of the orator-philosopher-statesman.*[3] *Aristotle's influence on Cicero is seen*

Reprinted by permission of the publishers and THE LOEB CLASSICAL LIBRARY from E. W. Sutton and H. Rackham, translators, Cicero, *De Oratore,* Cambridge, Mass.: Harvard University Press.

[1] Introduction, Cicero, *De Oratore,* Translated by E. W. Sutton and completed, with an introduction by H. Rackham (Cambridge, Mass., 1949), p. xi.

[2] See especially, Harry M. Hubbell, *The Influence of Isocrates on Cicero, Dionysius, and Aristides* (New Haven, 1914).

[3] For Platonic influences on Cicero, see, William M. Sattler, "Some Platonic Influences in the Rhetorical Works of Cicero," *Quarterly Journal of Speech,* 35 (1949), pp. 104-109.

through his use in De Oratore *of the Aristotelian dialogue form instead of the Platonic form and by his similar treatment of logical and emotional proofs as an important part of invention.*[1]

De Oratore *recalls an imagined discussion which occurred in 91 B.C., during Cicero's youth. Although he introduces several characters, including himself, the two principals are Lucius Licinius Crassus and Marcus Antonius. Crassus was Rome's leading orator before Cicero and also had served as Cicero's tutor. Antonius, three years Crassus' senior, was also noted as a superior orator during the time of Cicero's youth. In the sections of Book I given below, Crassus (representing Cicero's views) and Antonius, with Scaevola, Sulpicius and Cotta, begin to discuss the nature and functions of rhetoric.*

VIII, 29 — XXIII, 109

In that place, as Cotta was fond of relating, Crassus introduced a conversation on the pursuit of oratory, with a view to relieving all minds from the discourse of the day before. He began by saying that Sulpicius and Cotta seemed not to need exhortation from him but rather commendation, seeing that thus early they had acquired such skill as not merely to be ranked above their equals in age, but to be comparable with their elders. "Moreover," he continued, "there is to my mind no more excellent thing than the power, by means of oratory, to get a hold on assemblies of men, win their good will, direct their inclinations wherever the speaker wishes, or divert them from whatever he wishes. In every free nation, and most of all in communities which have attained the enjoyment of peace and tranquility, this one art has always flourished above the rest and ever reigned supreme. For what is so marvellous as that, out of the innumerable company of mankind, a single being should arise, who either alone or with a few others can make effective a faculty bestowed by nature upon every man? Or what so pleasing to the understanding and the ear as a speech adorned and polished with wise reflections and dignified language? Or what achievement so mighty and glorious as that the impulses of the crowd, the consciences of the judges, the austerity of the Senate, should suffer transformation through the eloquence of one man? What function again is so kingly, so worthy of the free, so generous, as to bring help to the suppliant, to raise up those that are cast down, to bestow security, to set free from peril, to maintain men in their civil rights? What

---

[1] See Frederich Solmsen, "Aristotle and Cicero on the Orator's Playing upon Feelings," *Classical Philology,* 33 (1938), pp. 39–404, and his "The Aristotelian Tradition in Ancient Rhetoric," *American Journal of Philology,* 62 (1941), pp. 35–50 and 169–190. For possible Stoic influences, see George St. Stock, *Stoicism* (London, 1908).

too is so indispensable as to have always in your grasp weapons wherewith you can defend yourself, or challenge the wicked man, or when provoked take your revenge?

"Nay more (not to have you for ever contemplating public affairs, the bench, the platform, and the Senate-house), what in hours of ease can be a pleasanter thing or one more characteristic of culture, than discourse that is graceful and nowhere uninstructed? For the one point in which we have our very greatest advantage over the brute creation is that we hold converse one with another, and can reproduce our thought in word. Who therefore would not rightly admire this faculty, and deem it his duty to exert himself to the utmost in this field, that by so doing he may surpass men themselves in that particular respect wherein chiefly men are superior to animals? To come, however, at length to the highest achievements of eloquence, what other power could have been strong enough either to gather scattered humanity into one place, or to lead it out of its brutish existence in the wilderness up to our present condition of civilization as men and as citizens, or, after the establishment of social communities, to give shape to laws, tribunals, and civic rights? And not to pursue any further instances — wellnigh countless as they are — I will conclude the whole matter in a few words, for my assertion is this: that the wise control of the complete orator is that which chiefly upholds not only his own dignity, but the safety of countless individuals and of the entire State. Go forward therefore, my young friends, in your present course, and bend your energies to that study which engages you, that so it may be in your power to become a glory to yourselves, a source of service to your friends, and profitable members of the Republic."

Thereupon Scaevola observed, in his courteous way, "On his other points I am in agreement with Crassus (that I may not disparage the art or the renown of my father-in-law Gaius Laelius, or of my son-in-law here), but the two following, Crassus, I am afraid I cannot grant you: first your statement that the orators were they who in the beginning established social communities, and who not seldom have preserved the same intact, secondly your pronouncement that, even if we take no account of the forum, of popular assemblies, of the courts of justice, or of the Senate-house, the orator is still complete over the whole range of speech and culture. For who is going to grant you, that in shutting themselves up in walled cities, human beings, who had been scattered originally over mountain and forest, were not so much convinced by the reasoning of the wise as snared by the speeches of the eloquent, or again that the other beneficial arrangements involved in the establishment or the preservation of States were not shaped by the wise and valiant but by men of eloquence and fine diction? Or do you perhaps think that it was by eloquence, and not rather by good counsel and singular wisdom, that the great Romulus gathered together his shepherds and refugees, or brought about marriages with the Sabines, or curbed the might of the neighbouring tribes? Is there a trace of eloquence to be discerned in Numa Pompilius? Is there a trace in Servius Tullius? Or in the other kings who have contributed so much that is excellent to the building-up of the State? Then even after the kings had been driven forth (and we note that such expulsion had itself been accomplished by the mind of Lucius Brutus and not by his tongue), do we not see how all that followed was full of planning and empty of talking? For my part, indeed, should I care to use examples from our own and other communities, I could cite more instances of damage done, than of aid given to the cause of the State by men of first-rate eloquence, but putting all else aside, of all men to whom I have listened except you two, Crassus, it seems to me that the most eloquent were Tiberius and Gaius Sempronius, whose father, a man of discretion and character, but no speaker whatever, was many a time and most particularly when Censor the salvation of the commonwealth. Yet it was not any studied flow of speech, but a nod and a word of his that transferred the freedmen into the city tribes;   and had he not done so, we should long ago have lost the constitution which, as it is, we preserve only with difficulty. His sons, on the other hand, who were accomplished speakers and equipped for oratory with every advantage of nature or training, after they had taken over a State that was flourishing exceedingly because of their father's counsels and their ancestors' military achievements, wrecked the commonwealth by the use of this eloquence to which, according to you, civil communities still look for their chief guidance.

"What of our ancient ordinances and the customs of our forefathers? What of augury, over which you and I, Crassus, preside, greatly to the welfare of the Republic? What of our religious rites and ceremonies? What of those rules of private law, which have long made their home in our family, though we have no reputation for eloquence? Were these things contrived or investigated or in any way taken in hand by the tribe of orators? Indeed I remember that Servius Galba, a man who spoke as a god, and Marcus Aemilius Porcina and Gaius Carbo himself, whom you crushed in your early manhood, were all of them ignorant of the statutes, all at a complete loss among the institutions of our ancestors, all uninstructed in the law of the Romans; and except yourself, Crassus, who rather from your own love of study, than because to do so was any peculiar duty of the eloquent, have learned the Roman system from our family, this generation of ours is unversed in law to a degree that sometimes makes one blush.

"But as for the claim you made at the close of your speech, and made as though in your own right — that whatever the topic under discussion, the orator could deal with it in complete fullness — this, had we not been here in your own domain, I would not have borne with, and I should be at the head of a multitude who would either fight you by injunction, or summon you to make joint seizure by rule of court, for so wantonly making forcible entry upon other people's possessions.

"For, to begin with, all the disciples of Pythagoras and Democritus would bring statutory process against you, and the rest of the physicists would assert their claims in court, elegant and impressive speakers with whom you could not strive and save your stake. Besides this, schools of philosophers, back to great Socrates their fountain-head, would beset you: they would demonstrate that you have learned nothing concerning the good in life, or of the evil, nothing as to the emotions of the mind or of human conduct, nothing of the true theory of living, that you have made no research at all and are wholly without understanding respecting these things; and after this general assault upon you each sect would launch its particular action against you in detail. The Academy would be at your heels, compelling you to deny in terms your own allegation, whatever it might have been. Then our own friends the Stoics would hold you entangled in the toils of their wranglings and questionings. The Peripatetics again would prove that it is to them that men should resort for even those very aids and trappings of eloquence which you deem to be the special aids of orators, and would show you that on these subjects of yours Aristotle and Theophrastus wrote not only better but also much more than all the teachers of rhetoric put together. I say nothing of the mathematicians, men of letters or devotees of the Muses, with whose arts this rhetorical faculty of yours is not in the remotest degree allied. And so, Crassus, I do not think you should make professions so extensive and so numerous. What you are able to guarantee is a thing great enough, namely, that in the courts whatever case you present should appear to be the better and more plausible, that in assemblies and in the Senate your oratory should have most weight in carrying the vote, and lastly, that to the intelligent you should seem to speak eloquently and to the ignorant truthfully as well. If you can achieve anything more than this, therein you will seem to me not an orator but a Crassus, who is making use of some talent that is peculiarly his own and not common to orators in general."

Then Crassus replied, "I know very well, Scaevola, that these views of yours are often put forward and discussed among the Greeks. For I listened to their most eminent men, on my arrival in Athens as a quaestor from Macedonia, at a time when the Academy was at its best, as was then asserted, with Charmadas, Clitomachus and Aeschines to uphold it. There was also Metrodorus, who, together with the others, had been a really diligent disciple of the illustrious Carneades himself, a speaker who, for spirited and copious oratory, surpassed, it was said, all other men. Mnesarchus too was in his prime, a pupil of your great Panactius, and Diodorus, who studied under Critolaus the Peripatetic. There were many others besides, of distinguished fame as philosophers, by all of whom, with one voice as it were, I perceived that the orator was driven from the helm of State, shut out from all learning and knowledge of more important things, and thrust down and locked up exclusively in law-courts and petty little assemblies, as if in a pounding-mill. But I was neither in agreement with these men, nor with the author and originator of such discussions, who spoke with far more weight and eloquence than all of them — I mean Plato — whose *Gorgias* I read with close attention under Charmadas during those days at Athens, and what impressed me most deeply about Plato in that book was, that it was when making fun of orators that he himself seemed to me to be the consummate orator. In fact controversy about a word has long tormented those Greeklings, fonder as they are of argument than of truth. For, if anyone lays it down that an orator is a man whose sole power is that of speaking copiously before the Praetor or at a trial, or in the public assembly or the Senate-house, none the less even to an orator thus limited such critic must grant and allow a number of attributes, inasmuch as without extensive handling of all public business, without a mastery of ordinances, customs and general law, without a knowledge of human nature and character, he cannot engage, with the requisite cleverness and skill, even in these restricted activities. But to a man who has learned these things, without which no one can properly ensure even those primary essentials of advocacy, can there by anything lacking that belongs to the knowledge of the highest matters? If, on the other hand, you would narrow the idea of oratory to nothing but the speaking in ordered fashion, gracefully and copiously, how, I ask, could your orator attain even so much, if he were to lack that knowledge whereof you people deny him the possession? For excellence in speaking cannot be made manifest unless the speaker fully comprehends the matter he speaks about. It follows that, if the famous natural philosopher Democritus spoke with elegance, as he is reported and appears to me to have spoken, those notable subjects of his discourse belonged to the natural philosopher, but his actual elegance of diction must be put down to the orator. And if Plato spoke with the voice of a god of things very far away from political debate, as I allow that he did, if again Aristotle and Theophrastus and Carneades, on the themes which they treated, were eloquent and displayed charm of style and literary form, then, granting that the topics of their discourse may be found in certain other fields of research, yet their actual style is the peculiar product of this pursuit which we are now discussing and investigating, and of no other. For we see that sundry authorities dealt with these same subjects in spiritless and feeble fashion, Chrysippus for instance, reputed as he is to have been the most acute of disputants, and not to have failed to meet the requirements of philosophy just because he had not acquired this gift of eloquence from an alien art.

"What then is the difference, or by what means will you discriminate between the rich and copious diction of those speakers whom I have mentioned, and the feebleness of such as do not adopt this variety and elegance of language? The sole distinction will surely be that the good speakers bring, as their peculiar possession, a style that is harmonious, graceful, and marked by a certain artistry and polish. Yet this style, if the underlying subject-matter be not comprehended and mastered by the speaker, must inevitably be of no account or even become the sport of universal derision. For what so effectually proclaims the madman as the hollow thundering of words — be they never so choice and resplendent — which have no thought or knowledge behind them? Therefore whatever the theme, from whatever art or whatever branch of knowledge it be taken, the orator, just as if he had got up the case for a client, will state it better and more gracefully than the actual discoverer and the specialist. For if anyone is going to affirm that there are certain ideas and subjects which specially belong to orators, and certain matters whereof the knowledge is railed-off behind the barriers of the Courts, while I will admit that these oratorical activities of ours are exercised within this area with less intermission than elsewhere, nevertheless among these very topics there are points in abundance which even the so-called professors of rhetoric neither teach nor understand. Who indeed does not know that the orator's virtue is pre-eminently manifested either in rousing men's hearts to anger, hatred, or indignation, or in recalling them from these same passions to mildness and mercy? Wherefore the speaker will not be able to achieve what he wants by his words, unless he has gained profound insight into the characters of men, and the whole range of human nature, and those motives whereby our souls are spurred on or turned back. And all this is considered to be the special province of philosophers, nor will the orator, if he take my advice, resist their claim; but when he has granted their knowledge of these things, since they have devoted all their labour to that alone, still he will assert his own claim to the oratorical treatment of them, which without that knowledge of theirs is nothing at all. For this is the essential concern of the orator, as I have often said before, — a style that is dignified and graceful and in conformity with the general modes of thought and judgement.

"And while I acknowledge that Aristotle and Theophrastus have written about all these things, yet consider, Scaevola, whether it is not wholly in my favour, that, whereas I do not borrow from them the things that they share with the orator, they on their part grant that their discussions on these subjects are the orator's own, and accordingly they entitle and designate all their other treatises by some name taken from their distinctive art, but these particular books as dealing with Rhetoric. And indeed when, while a man is speaking — as often happens — such commonplaces have cropped up as demand some mention of the immortal gods, of dutifulness, harmony, or friendship, of the rights shared by citizens, by men in general, and by nations, of fair-dealing moderation or greatness of soul, or virute of any and every kind, all the academies and schools of philosophy will, I do believe, raise the cry that all these matters are their exclusive province, and in no way whatever the concern of the orator. But when I have allowed that they may debate these subjects in their holes and corners, to pass an idle hour, it is to the orator none the less that I shall entrust and assign the task of developing with complete charm and cogency the same themes which they discuss in a sort of thin and bloodless style. These points I used to argue at Athens with the philosophers in person, under pressure from our friend Marcus Marcellus, who is now Aedile of the Chair, and assuredly, if he were not at this moment producing the Games, would be taking part in our present colloquy; indeed even in those days of his early youth his devotion to these studies was marvellous.

"But now as regards the institution of laws, as regards war and peace, allies and public dues, and the legal rights assigned to classes of citizens according to variations of rank and age, let the Greeks say, if they please, that Lycurgus and Solon (although I hold that they should be rated as eloquent) were better informed than Hyperides or Demosthenes, who were really accomplished and highly polished orators; or let our own folk prefer in this regard the Ten Commissioners — who wrote out the Twelve Tables and were necessarily men of practical wisdom — to Servius Galba and your father-in-law Gaius Laelius, whose outstanding renown for eloquence is established. For never will I say that there are not certain arts belonging exclusively to those who have employed all their energies in the mastery and exercise thereof, but my assertion will be that the complete and finished orator is he who on any matter whatever can speak with fullness and variety.

' Indeed in handling those causes which everybody acknowledges to be within the exclusive sphere of oratory, there is not seldom something to be brought forth and employed, not from practice in public speaking — the only thing you allow the orator — but from some more abstruse branch of knowledge. I ask, for instance, whether an advocate can either assail or defend a commander-in-chief without experience of the art of war, or sometimes too without knowledge of the various regions of land or sea? Whether he can address the popular assembly in favour of the passing or rejection of legislative proposals, or the Senate concerning any of the departments of State administration, if he lack consummate knowledge — practical as well as theoretical — of political science? Whether a speech can be directed to inflaming or even repressing feeling and passion — a faculty of the first importance to the orator — unless the speaker has made a most careful search into all those theories respecting the natural characters and the habits of conduct of mankind, which are unfolded by the philosophers?

"And I rather think I shall come short of convincing you on my next point — at all events I will not hesitate to speak my mind: your natural science itself, your mathematics, and other studies which just now you reckoned as belonging peculiarly to the rest of the arts, do indeed pertain to the knowledge of their professors, yet if anyone should wish by speaking to put these same arts in their full light, it is to oratorical skill that he must run for help. If, again, it is established that Philo, that master-builder who constructed an arsenal for the Athenians, described the plan of his work very eloquently to the people, his eloquence must be ascribed not to his architectural, but rather to his oratorical ability. So too, if Marcus Antonius here had had to speak on behalf of Hermodorus upon the construction of dockyards, having got up his case from his client, he would then have discoursed gracefully and copiously of an art to which he was not a stranger. Asclepiades also, he with whom we have been familiar both as physician and as friend, at the time when he was surpassing the rest of his profession in eloquence, was exhibiting, in such graceful speaking, the skill of an orator, not that of a physician. In fact that favourite assertion of Socrates — that every man was eloquent enough upon a subject that he knew — has in it some plausibility but no truth: it is nearer the truth to say that neither can anyone be eloquent upon a subject that is unknown to him, nor, if he knows it perfectly and yet does not know how to shape and polish his style, can he speak fluently even upon that which he does know.

"Accordingly, should anyone wish to define in a comprehensive manner the complete and special meaning of the word, he will be an orator, in my opinion worthy of so dignified a title, who, whatever the topic that crops up to be unfolded in discourse, will speak thereon with knowledge, method, charm and retentive memory, combining with these qualifications a certain distinction of bearing. If however someone considers my expression 'whatever the topic' to be altogether too extensive, he may clip and prune it to his individual taste, but to this much I shall hold fast — though the orator be ignorant of what is to be found in all the other arts and branches of study, and know only what is dealt with in debate and the practice of public-speaking; none the less, if he should have to discourse even on these other subjects, then after learning the technicalities of each from those who know the same, the orator will speak about them far better than even the men who are masters of these arts. For example, should our friend Sulpicius here have to speak upon the art of war, he will inquire of our relative Gaius Marius, and when he has received his teachings, will deliver himself in such fashion as to seem even to Gaius Marius to be almost better informed on the subject than Garius Marius himself; while if his topic is to be the law of private rights, he will consult yourself and, notwithstanding your consummate learning and skill in these very things which you have taught him, he will surpass you in the art of exposition. If again some matter should confront him wherein he must speak of human nature, human vices or the passions, of moderation or self-control, of sorrow or death, then perhaps if he thinks fit — although an orator must have knowledge of such things — he will have taken counsel with Sextus Pompeius, a man accomplished in moral science; so much he will assuredly achieve, that whatever his subject and whoever his instructor, on that subject he will express himself far more gracefully than his master himself. Nevertheless, if he will listen to me, since philosophy is divided into three branches, which respectively deal with the mysteries of nature, with the subtleties of dialectic, and with human life and conduct, let us quit claim to the first two, by way of concession to our indolence, but unless we keep our hold on the third, which has ever been the orator's province, we shall leave the orator no sphere wherein to attain greatness. For which reason this division of philosophy, concerned with human life and manners, must all of it be mastered by the orator; as for the other matters, even though he has not studied them, he will still be able, whenever the necessity arises, to beautify them by his eloquence, if only they are brought to his notice and described to him.

"Indeed if it is agreed in learned circles that a man who knew no astronomy — Aratus to wit — has sung of the heavenly spaces and the stars in verse of consummate finish and excellence, and that another who was a complete stranger to country life, Nicander of Colophon, has written with distinction on rural affairs, using something of a poet's skill and not that of a farmer, what reason is there why an orator should not discourse most eloquently concerning those subjects which he has conned for a specific argument and occasion? The truth is that the poet is a very near kinsman of the orator, rather more heavily fettered as regards rhythm, but with ampler freedom in his choice of words, while in the use of many sorts of ornament he is his ally and almost his counterpart; in one respect at all events something like identity exists, since he sets no boundaries or limits to his claims, such as would prevent him from ranging whither he will with the same freedom and licence as the other. For with regard to your remark, Scaevola, that, had you not been in my domain, you would not have endured my assertion that the orator must be accomplished in every kind of discourse and in every department of culture, I should certainly never have made that assertion, did I consider myself to be the man I am endeavouring to portray. But, as was often said by Gaius Lucilius — who was not altogether pleased with you, and for that very reason less intimate with myself than he wished, but for all that an instructed critic and thorough gentleman of the city — my opinion is this, that no one should be numbered with the orators who is not accomplished in all those arts that befit the well-bred; for though we do not actually parade these in our discourse, it is none the less made clear to demonstration whether we are strangers to them or have learned to know them. Just as ball-players do not in their game itself employ the characteristic dexterity of the gymnasium, and yet their very movements show whether they have had such training or know nothing of that art; and, just as, in the case of those who are portraying anything, even though at the moment they are making no use of the painter's art, there is none the less no difficulty in seeing whether or not they know how to paint; even so is it with these same speeches in the Courts, the popular assembly and the Senate-house — granting that the other arts may not be specially brought into play, still it is made easily discernible whether the speaker has merely floundered about in this declamatory business or whether, before approaching his task of oratory, he has been trained in all the liberal arts."

At this point Scaevola smilingly declared: "Crassus, I will strive with you no longer. For, in this very speech you have made against me, you have by some trick so managed matters as both to grant me what I said did not belong to the orator, and then somehow or another to wrest away these things again and hand them over to the orator as his absolute property. And as regards these subjects, when on my arrival in Rhodes as praetor I discussed with Apolonius, that supreme master of this science of rhetoric, the things that I had learned from Panaetius, he as usual jeered at philosophy and expressed contempt for it and talked at large in a vein more graceful than serious; whereas your argument has been of such a kind that you not only refrained from despising any of the arts or sciences, but described them all as the attendants and handmaids of oratory. And for my own part, if ever any one man should have mastered all of them, and that same man should have united with them this added power of perfectly graceful expression, I cannot deny that he would be a remarkable kind of man and worthy of admiration; but if such a one there should be, or indeed ever has been, or really ever could be, assuredly you would be that one man, who both in my opinion and in that of everyone else, have left all other orators − if they will pardon my saying so − almost without glory. But if you yourself, while lacking nothing of the knowledge that has to do with law-court speaking and politics, have nevertheless not mastered the further learning which you associate with the orator, let us see whether you may not be attributing to him more than the real facts of the case allow."

Here Crassus interposed: "Remember that I have not been speaking of my own skill, but of that of an orator. For what have men like myself either learned or had any chance of knowing, who entered upon practice before ever we reached the study of theory, whom our professional activities in public speaking, in the pursuit of office, in politics, and about the affairs of our friends, wore out ere we could form any conception of the importance of these other matters? But if you find such excellence in me who, if perhaps − as you hold − I have not been completely wanting in ability, have assuredly been wanting in learning and leisure and (to tell the truth) in the requisite enthusiasm for instruction as well, what think you would be the quality and stature of an orator in whom all that I have not attained should be combined with ability such as my own or greater?"

Thereupon Antonius observed: "Crassus, to my mind you establish your case, and I do not doubt that, if a man has grasped the principles and nature of every subject and of every art, he will in consequence be far better equipped as a speaker. But in the first place such knowledge is hard to win, especially in the life we lead, and amid the engagements that are ours, and then again there is the danger of our being led away from our traditional practice of speaking in a style acceptable to the commonalty and suited to advocacy. For it seems to me that the eloquence of these men, to whom you referred just now, is of an entirely different kind, albeit they speak gracefully and cogently, either upon natural philosophy or upon the affairs of mankind: theirs is a polished and flowery sort of diction, redolent rather of the training-school and its suppling-oil than of our political hurly-burly and of the Bar. For – when I think of it – although it was late in life and only lightly that I came into touch with Greek literature, still, when on my journey to Cilicia as proconsul I reached Athens, I tarried there for several days by reason of the difficulty in putting to sea: at any rate, as I had about me daily the most learned men, pretty nearly the same as those whom you have lately mentioned, a rumour having somehow spread among them that I, just like yourself, was usually engaged in the more important causes, every one of them in his turn contributed what he could to a discussion on the function and method of an orator.

"Some of them were for maintaining, as did your authority Mnesarchus[1] himself, that those whom we called orators were nothing but a sort of artisans with ready and practised tongues, whereas no one was an orator save the wise man only, and that eloquence itself, being, as it was, the science of speaking well, was one type of virtue, and he who possessed a single virtue possessed all of them, and the virtues were of the same rank and equal one with another, from which it followed that the man of eloquence had every virtue and was a wise man. But this was a thorny and dry sort of language, and entirely out of harmony with anything we thought. Charmadas, however, would speak far more copiously upon the same topics, not that he intended thereby to reveal his own opinion, – it being accepted tradition of the Academy always and against all comers to be of the opposition in debate – just then, however, he was pointing out that those who were styled rhetoricians and propounded rules of eloquence, had no clear comprehension of anything, and that no man could attain skill in speaking unless he had studied the discoveries of the philosophers.

"Certain Athenians, accomplished speakers and experienced in politics and at the Bar, argued on the other side, among them too being that Menedemus, who was lately in Rome as my guest; and when he asserted that there was a special sort of wisdom, which had to do with investigating the principles of founding and governing political communities, this roused up a man of quick temper[2] and full to overflowing of learning of every kind and a really incredible diversity and multiplicity of facts. For he proceeded to inform us that every part of this same wisdom had to be sought from philosophy, nor were those institutions in a State which dealt with the immortal gods, the training of youth, justice, endurance, self-control, or moderation in all things, or the other principles without which States could not exist or at any rate be well-conditioned, to be met

---

[1] Mnesarchus represents the Stoics, whose fundamental doctrine of the unity and coequality of all virtues implies that the philosopher alone can be an orator.

[2] Charmadas of the Academy.

with anywhere in the paltry treatises of rhetoricians. Whereas, if those
teachers of rhetoric embraced within their art so vast a multitude of the
noblest themes, how was it, he inquired, that their books were stuffed full
of maxims relating to prefaces, perorations and similar trumpery — for so
did he describe them — while concerning the organization of States, or the
drafting of laws, or on the topics of fair-dealing, justice, loyalty, or the
subduing of the passions or the building of human character, not a syllable
was to be found in their pages? But as for their actual rules he would scoff
at them by showing that not only were their authors devoid of that
wisdom which they arrogated to themselves, but they were ignorant even
of the true principles and methods of eloquence. For he was of opinion
that the main object of the orator was that he should both appear himself,
to those before whom he was pleading, to be such a man as he would
desire to seem (an end to be attained by a reputable mode of life, as to
which those teachers of rhetoric had left no hint among their instructions),
and that the hearts of his hearers should be touched in such fashion as the
orator would have them touched (another purpose only to be achieved by
a speaker who had investigated all the ways wherein, and all the
allurements and kind of diction whereby, the judgement of men might be
inclined to this side or to that); but according to him such knowledge lay
thrust away and buried deep in the very heart of philosophy, and those
rhetoricians had not so much as tasted it with the tip of the tongue. These
assertions Menedemus would strive to disprove by quoting instances rather
than by arguments, for, while reciting from his ready recollection many
magnificant passages from the speeches of Demosthenes, he would
demonstrate how that orator, when by his eloquence he was compelling
the passions of the judges or of the people to take any direction he chose,
knew well enough by what means to attain results which Charmadas would
say that no one could compass without the aid of philosophy.

"To this Charmadas replied that he did not deny to Demosthenes the
possession of consummate wisdom and the highest power of eloquence,
but whether Demosthenes owed this ability to natural talent or, as was
generally agreed, had been a devoted disciple of Plato, the present question
was not what Demosthenes could do, but what those rhetoricians were
teaching. More than once too he was carried so far away by his discourse
as to argue that there was no such thing as an art of eloquence; and after
showing this by arguments — because, as he said, we were born with an
aptitude alike for coaxing and unctuously stealing into favour with those
from whom a boon had to be sought, and for daunting our antagonists by
threats, for setting forth how a deed was done, and establishing our own
charges and disproving the allegations of the other side, and for making, in
the closing words of a speech, some use of protest and lamentation (in
which operations he declared that every resource of the orator was
brought into play), and because habit and practice sharpened the edge of
discernment and quickened the fluency of delivery, then he would also

support his case by an abundance of instances. For in the first place (he would say) not a single writer on rhetoric — it looked as if of set purpose — had been even moderately eloquent, and he searched all the way back to the days of one Corax and a certain Tisias who, he stated, were acknowledged to have been the founders and first practitioners of this art, while on the other hand he would cite a countless host of very eloquent men who had never learned these rules or been at all anxious to make their acquaintance; and among these — whether in jest or because he thought so and had even so heard — he went on to mention me in the list, as one who had never studied those matters and yet (according to him) had some ability in oratory. To one of these points of his — that I had never learned anything — I readily agreed, but as to the other I considered that he was either making game of me or was even himself mistaken. He said, however, that there was no 'art' which did not consist in the knowledge and clear perception of facts, all tending to a single conclusion and incapable of misleading; but everything with which orators dealt was doubtful and uncertain, since all the talking was done by men who had no real grasp of their subject, and all the listening by hearers who were not to have knowledge conveyed to them, but some short-lived opinion that was either untrue or at least not clear. In a word, he then looked like persuading me that no craft of oratory existed, and that no one could speak with address or copiously unless he had mastered the philosophical teachings of the most learned men. And in these discussions Charmadas was wont to speak with warm admiration of your talents, Crassus, explaining that he found in me a very ready listener, in yourself a most doughty antagonist.

"And so, won over by these same views, I actually wrote down in a little pamphlet — which slipped abroad without my knowledge or consent and got into the hands of the public — the statement that I had known sundry accomplished speakers, but no one so far who was eloquent, inasmuch as I held anyone to be an accomplished speaker who could deliver his thought with the necessary point and clearness before an everyday audience, and in accord with what I might call the mental outlook of the average human being, whereas I allowed the possession of eloquence to that man only who was able, in a style more admirable and more splendid, to amplify and adorn any subject he chose, and whose mind and memory encompassed all the sources of everything that concerned oratory. If this is a hard matter for ourselves, because, before we have entered on the required study, we are overwhelmed by the hunt for office and the business of the Bar, none the less let it be accepted as attainable in fact and in the nature of things. For personally, so far as I can form a prediction, and judging from the vast supply of talent which I see existent among our fellow-citizens, I do not despair of its coming to pass that some day some one, keener in study than we are or ever have been, endowed with ampler leisure and earlier opportunity for learning, and

exhibiting closer application and more intensive industry, who shall have
given himself up to listening, reading and writing, will stand forth as an
orator such as we are seeking, who may rightly be called not merely
accomplished but actually eloquent; and after all, to my mind either
Crassus is such a man already, or, should some one of equal natural ability
have heard, read and written more than Crassus, he will only be able to
improve to some slight extent upon him."

At this point, "We never looked for it," exclaimed Sulpicius, "but it
has fallen out, Crassus, just as both I and Cotta earnestly hoped, I mean
that you two should slip into this particular conversation. For on our way
hither we were thinking that it would be delightful enough if, while you
and Antonius were talking about anything else, we might still manage to
catch from your discourse something worth remembering; but that you
should enter at large upon so real and wellnigh exhaustive a discussion of
this whole matter – be it practice, art or natural talent – seemed to us a
thing we could hardly hope for. The fact is that I, who from my earliest
manhood was aglow with enthusiasm for you both, and a positive devotion
to Crassus – seeing that on no occasion did I leave his side – could never
get a word out of him respecting the nature and theory of eloquence,
although I pleaded in person, besides making frequent trial of him through
the agency of Drusus, whereas on this subject you, Antonius, – and what I
shall say is true – have never failed me at all in my probings or
interrogatories, and have many a time explained to me what rules you
were wont to observe in practical oratory. Now then that each of you has
opened up a way of reaching these very objects of our quest, and since it
was Crassus who led off in this discussion, grant us the favour of
recounting with exactness of detail, your respective opinions upon every
branch of oratory. If we do win this boon from you both, I shall be deeply
grateful, Crassus, to this school in your Tusculan villa, and shall rank these
semi-rural training-quarters of yours far above the illustrious Academy and
the Lyceum."

Thereupon the other rejoined, "Nay, Sulpicius, but let us rather ask
Antonius, who both has the ability to do what you demand, and, as I
understand you to say, has been in the habit of so doing. For as for me,
you yourself have just told us how I have invariably run away from all
discussions of this sort, and time and again have refused compliance with
your desire and indeed your importunity. This I used to do, not from
arrogance or churlishness, nor because I was unwilling to gratify your
entirely legitimate and admirable keenness – the more so as I had
recognized that you were above all other men eminently endowed by
nature and adapted for oratory – but in solemn truth it was from want of
familiarity with arguments of that kind, and awkwardness in handling
those theories set forth in what claims to be an art."

Cotta then observed, "Since we have secured what seemed most difficult − that you, Crassus, should say anything at all about these matters − as for what remains, it will now be our own fault if we let you go without explaining to us all that we have been inquiring about." "Limiting the inquiry, I imagine," answered Crassus, "to those subjects which, as the phrase goes in accepting an inheritance, are within my knowledge and power." "By all means," returned Cotta, "for what is beyond your own power or knowledge, who among us is so shameless as to claim to be within his own?" "In that case," replied Crassus, "provided that I may disclaim powers which I do not possess, and admit ignorance of what I do not know, − put what questions to me you please." "Well then," said Sulpicius, "what we ask you to tell us first is your opinion of the view Antonius advanced just now − whether you hold that there is any such thing as an 'art' of oratory?" "How now?" exclaimed Crassus, "Do you think I am some idle talkative Greekling, who is also perhaps full of learning and erudition, that you propound me a petty question on which to talk as I will? For when was it, think you, that I troubled myself about these matters or reflected upon them, and did not rather always laugh to scorn the effrontery of those persons who, from their chairs in the schools, would call upon any man in the crowded assemblage to propound any question that he might have to put? It is related that Gorgias of Leontini was the author of this practice, who was thought to be undertaking and professing something very magnificent when he advertised himself as ready for any topic whatever on which anyone might have a fancy to hear him. Later, however, they began to do this everywhere, and are doing it to this day, with the result of there being no theme so vast, so unforeseen, or so novel, that they do not claim to be prepared to say about it all that there is to be said. But had I supposed that you, Cotta, or you, Sulpicius, wished to listen to anything of the kind, I would have brought some Greek or other here to amuse you with discussions of that sort; and even now this can easily be managed. For staying with Marcus Piso (a young man, but already given up to this pursuit, possessing talent of the highest order and deeply devoted to myself) there is Staseas the Peripatetic, a man whom I know well enough, and who, as I understand to be agreed among experts, is quite supreme in that department of his."

"Staseas! what Staseas? what Peripatetic are you talking to me about?" said Mucius. "It is for you, Crassus, to comply with the wishes of young men, who do not want the everyday chatter of some unpractised Greek, or old sing-songs out of the schools, but something from the wisest and most eloquent man in the world, and one who, not in the pages of pamphlets, but in the most momentous causes, and that too in this seat of imperial power and splendour, holds the first place for judgment and eloquence; they are anxious to learn the opinion of the man whose footsteps they long to follow. Moreover, just as I have always accounted you the ideal orator, even so I have never ascribed to you higher praise for eloquence than for kindliness, which quality it becomes you on the present occasion to exercise to the very utmost, and not to run away from the discussion into which two young men of eminent ability are desirous of your entering."

"For my part," answered the other, "I am anxious to humour your friends, and I shall make no difficulty about saying, in my brief fashion, what I think upon each point. And to that first question – since I do not think it dutiful, Scaevola, for me to disregard your claims – I answer, 'I think there is either no art of speaking at all or a very thin one,' all the quarrelling in learned circles being really based upon a dispute about a word. For if, as Antonius just now explained, an art is defined as consisting in things thoroughly examined and clearly apprehended, and which are also outside the control of mere opinion, and within the grasp of exact knowledge, then to me there seems to be no such thing as an art of oratory. For all the kinds of language we ourselves use in public speaking are changeable matter, and adapted to the general understanding of the crowd. If however the actual things noticed in the practice and conduct of speaking have been heeded and recorded by men of skill and experience, if they have been defined in terms, illuminated by classification, and distributed under subdivisions – and I see that it has been possible to do this – I do not understand why this should not be regarded as an art, perhaps not in that precise sense of the term, but at any rate according to the other and popular estimate. But whether this be an art, or only something like an art, assuredly it is not to be disdained . . . .

PETRONIUS:
"AMONG THE RHETORICIANS"

Translated by William Arrowsmith

In the extant portions of Petronius' Satyricon, the first surviving novel of a picaresque kind, written about 66 A.D., a Greek freedman Encolpius visits the seaports of southern Italy where he is presented "with a devastating picture of much that was indecent, depraved, and vulgar in the contemporary underworld."[1] In "Among the Rhetoricians," printed below in its entirety, Encolpius, representing Petronius, attacks Agamemnon, a rhetorician, calling the art of declamation the root of the evil surrounding rhetoric, and contrasting the low state of rhetoric and general moral decay in mid-first century A.D. with the talented rhetoric of the periods of Sophocles, Euripides, Plato, and Demosthenes. Agamemnon's weak reply allows Encolpius to have the last word in his attack against rhetoric.

[1] "But look here," I protested, "aren't you professors hounded by just these same Furies of inflated language and pompous heroics? How else can you account for all that wretched rant:

> Nay, but gentle sirs, mark ye well these wounds I suffered in the struggle to preserve our common liberties. 'Twas on thy behalf I made the supreme sacrifice of this eye. Vouchsafe me, therefore, a helping hand. Guide me to my children, for my withers are unwrung and support my frame no more. . .

And so on.

[1] J. W. Atkins, *Literary Criticism in Antiquity: Volume II, Graeco-Roman* (Cambridge, England, 1934), p. 160.

"No one would mind this claptrap if only it put our students on the road to real eloquence. But what with all these sham heroics and this stilted bombast you stuff their heads with, by the time your students set foot in court, they talk as though they were living in another world. No, I tell you, we don't educate our children at school; we stultify them and then send them out into the world half-baked. Any why? Because we keep them utterly ignorant of real life. The common experience is something they never see or hear. All they know is pirates trooping up the beach in chains, tyrants scribbling edicts compelling sons to chop off their fathers' heads or oracles condemning three virgins — but the more the merrier — to be slaughtered to stop some plague. Action or language, it's all the same: great sticky honeyballs of phrases, every sentence looking as though it had been plopped and rolled in poppyseed and sesame. [2] A boy gorged on a diet like this can no more acquire real taste than a cook can stop stinking. What's more, if you'll pardon my bluntness, it was you rhetoricians who more than anyone else strangled true eloquence. By reducing everything to sound, you concocted this bloated puffpaste of pretty drivel whose only real purpose is the pleasure of punning and the thrill of ambiguity. Result? Language lost its sinew, its nerve. Eloquence died.

"But in those great days when Sophocles and Euripides invariably found the exact word, talent had not yet been cramped into the mold of these set-speeches of yours. Long before you academic pedants smothered genius with your arrogance, Pindar and the nine lyric poets were still so modest that they declined even to attempt the grand Homeric manner. Nor are my objections based on poetry alone. What about Plato or Demosthenes? I never heard it said of them that they ever submitted to your sort of formal training. No, great language is chaste language — if you'll let me use a word like 'chaste' in this connection — not turgidity and worked-up purple patches. It soars to life through a natural, simple loveliness. But then, in our own time, that huge flatulent rhetoric of yours moved from Asia to Athens. Like a baleful star, it blighted the minds of the young; their talents shriveled at the very moment when they might have taken wing and gone on to greatness. And once the standards of good speech were corrupted, eloquence stopped dead or stuttered into silence. Who, I ask you, has achieved real greatness of style since Thucydides and Hyperides? Poetry herself is sick, her natural glow of color leached away. All the literary arts, in fact, cloyed with this diet of bombast, have stunted or died, incapable of whitening naturally into an honest old age. And in painting you see the same decay: on the very day when Egyptian arrogance dared to reduce it to a set of sterile formulas, that great art died."

[3] Agamemnon, however, refused to let me rant on an instant longer than it had taken him to sweat out his declamation in the classroom.

"Young man," he broke in, "I see that you are a speaker of unusual taste and, what is even rarer, an admirer of common sense. So I shan't put you off with the usual hocus-pocus of the profession. But in all justice allow me to observe that we teachers should not be saddled with the blame for this bombast of which you complain. After all, if the patients are lunatics, surely a little professional lunacy is almost mandatory in the doctor who deals with them. And unless we professors spout the sort of twaddle our students admire, we run the risk of being, in Cicero's phrase, 'left alone at our lecterns.' Let me offer you by way of analogy those professional sponges in the comic plays who scrounge their suppers by flattering the rich. Like us, they must devote their entire attention to one end – the satisfaction of their audience; for unless their little springes con their listeners' ears, they stand to lose their quarry. We are, that is, rather in the position of a fisherman: unless he baits his hook with the sort of tidbit the little fishes like, he is doomed to spend eternity sitting on his rock without a chance of a bite.

[4] "So what should the verdict be? In my opinion, those parents who refuse to impose a stern discipline upon their sons must bear the blame. As with everything else, even their children are sacrificed on the altar of their ambition. Then, in their haste and greed to reap a harvest, they shove these callow, newborn babies into the public arena, and eloquence – that same eloquence which they profess to honor as the crown of a liberal education – is chopped down in size to fit a fetus. *If* however, our students' lessons could be graded by order of difficulty; *if* the minds of the young could be molded and shaped by long years of intimacy with the minds of great thinkers; *if* these crude attempts to form a style could be ruthlessly chastened and these budding talents steeped in the study of great models, then, and only then, might our great lost art of oratory recover her old magnificence. But what do we find instead? The schoolrooms packed with children wasting their time and playing at learning; our recent graduates disgracing themselves in public life and, what is worst of all, the very things that they mislearned when young, they are reluctant to confess in old age. And lest you think I despise the simplicity and spontaneity of old Lucilius, let me extemporize my sentiments in verse:

[5] ADVICE TO A YOUNG POET

If greatness, poet, is your goal,
the craft begins with self-control.
For poems are of the poet part,
and what he is decides his art.
With character true poems begin.
Poet, learn your discipline.

Avoid ambition as the blight
of talent. If the rich invite
you out to dine, be proud; decline.
Don't snuff your genius in your wine
nor pin your Muse to clique or claque.
Avoid the postures of the hack.

TACITUS: DIALOGUS

Translated by William Peterson

Tacitus, whom Herbert W. Benario called Rome's greatest historian, wrote his Dialogue *on Orators probably between 102 and 107 A.D., after which he withdrew from his role as an orator in favor of the study of history. Benario writes:*

> The *Dialogue* is based on Ciceronian antecedents and is Ciceronian in style and vocabulary; sentences are long and periodic rather than short, brusque, and lapidary. . . .
> But why is the style so different from all else by Tacitus? The ability and capacity to write in various styles, almost, as it were, to change clothes, were the marks of the trained rhetorician, who realized that different genres of literature required different garbs. In a genre in which Cicero was the acknowledged master, nothing was more appropriate than the Ciceronian garb.[1]

The excerpt below is from a speech by Messalla. He reminisces about the old days, lamenting that the modern schools of rhetoric are ruining young orators. When Maternus, later in the dialogue, indicates his decision to leave the law courts for the pursuit of poetry, he must have exemplified Tacitus' determination to leave the field of oratory because he felt it no longer was worthy of his talents.

"Well then, in the good old days the young man who was destined for the oratory of the bar, after receiving the rudiments of a sound training at

Reprinted by permission of the publishers and THE LOEB CLASSICAL LIBRARY from William Peterson, translator, Tacitus, *Dialogus*, Cambridge, Mass.: Harvard University Press.

[1]Introduction, *Agricola, Germany, Dialogue on Orators*. Translated with an introduction and notes by Herbert W. Benario (Indianapolis, 1967), pp. xv–xvi.

home, and storing his mind with liberal culture, was taken by his father, or his relations, and placed under the care of some orator who held a leading position at Rome. The youth had to get the habit of following his patron about, of escorting him in public, of supporting him at all his appearances as a speaker, whether in the law courts or on the platform, hearing also his word-combats at first hand, standing by him in his duellings, and learning, as it were, to fight in the fighting-line. It was a method that secured at once for the young students a considerable amount of experience, great self-possession, and a goodly store of sound judgment: for they carried on their studies in the light of open day, and amid the very shock of battle, under conditions in which any stupid or ill-advised statement brings prompt retribution in the shape of the judge's disapproval, taunting criticism from your opponent — yes, and from your own supporters expressions of dissatisfaction. So it was a genuine and unadulterated eloquence that they were initiated in from the very first; and though they attached themselves to a single speaker, yet they got to know all the contemporary members of the bar in a great variety of both civil and criminal cases. Moreover a public meeting gave them the opportunity of noting marked divergences of taste, so that they could easily detect what commended itself in the case of each individual speaker, and what on the other hand failed to please. In this way they could command, firstly, a teacher, and him the best and choicest of his kind, one who could show forth the true features of eloquence, and not a weak imitation; secondly, opponents and antagonists, who fought with swords, not with wooden foils; and thirdly, an audience always numerous and always different composed of friendly and unfriendly critics, who would not let any points escape them, whether good or bad. For the oratorical renown that is great and lasting is built up, as you know, quite as much among the opposition benches as on those of one's own side; indeed, its growth in that quarter is sturdier, and takes root more firmly. Yes, under such instructors, the young man who is the subject of this discourse, the pupil of real orators, the listener in the forum, the close attendant on the law courts, trained to his work in the school of other people's efforts, who got to know his law by hearing it cited every day, who became familiar with the faces on the bench, who made the practice of public meetings a subject of constant contemplation, and who had many opportunities of studying the vagaries of the popular taste, — such a youth, whether he undertook to appear as prosecutor or for the defence, was competent right away to deal with any kind of case, alone and unaided. Lucius Crassus was only eighteen when he impeached Gaius Carbo, Caesar twenty when he undertook the prosecution of Dolabella, Asinius Pollio twenty-one when he attacked Gaius Cato, and Calvus not much older when he prosecuted Vatinius. The speeches they delivered on those occasions are read to this day with admiration.

"But nowadays our boys are escorted to the schools of the so-called 'professors of rhetoric,' – persons who came on the scene just before the time of Cicero but failed to find favour with our forefathers, as is obvious from the fact that the censors Crassus and Domitius ordered them to shut down what Cicero calls their 'school of shamelessness.' They are escorted, as I was saying, to these schools, of which it would be hard to say what is most prejudicial to their intellectual growth, the place itself, or their fellow-scholars, or the studies they pursue. The place has nothing about it that commands respect, – no one enters it who is not as ignorant as the rest; there is no profit in the society of the scholars, since they are all either boys or young men who are equally devoid of any feeling of responsibility whether they take the floor or provide an audience; and the exercises in which they engage largely defeat their own objects. You are of course aware that there are two kinds of subject-matter handled by these professors, the deliberative and the disputatious. Now while, as regards the former, it is entrusted to mere boys, as being obviously of less importance and not making such demands on the judgment, the more mature scholars are asked to deal with the latter, – but, good heavens! what poor quality is shown in their themes, and how unnaturally they are made up! Then in addition to the subject-matter that is so remote from real life, there is the bombastic style in which it is presented. And so it comes that themes like these: 'the reward of the king-killer,' or 'the outraged maid's alternatives,' or 'a remedy for the plague,' or 'the incestuous mother,' and all the other topics that are treated every day in the school, but seldom or never in actual practice, are set forth in magniloquent phraseology; but when the speaker comes before a real tribunal . . .

". . . to have regard to the subject in hand. With him it was an impossibility to give forth any utterance that was trivial or commonplace. Great oratory is like a flame: it needs fuel to feed it, movement to fan it, and it brightens as it burns.

"At Rome too the eloquence of our forefathers owed its development to the same conditions. For although the orators of to-day have also succeeded in obtaining all the influence that it would be proper to allow them under settled, peaceable, and prosperous political conditions, yet their predecessors in those days of unrest and unrestraint thought they could accomplish more when, in the general ferment and without the strong hand of a single ruler, a speaker's political wisdom was measured by his power of carrying conviction to the unstable populace. This was the source of the constant succession of measures put forward by champions of the people's rights, of the harangues of state officials who almost spent the night on the hustings, of the impeachments of powerful criminals and hereditary feuds between whole families, of schisms among the aristocracy and never-ending struggles between the senate and the commons. All this tore the commonwealth in pieces, but it provided a sphere for the oratory of those days and heaped on it what one saw were vast rewards. The more influence a man could wield by his powers of speech, the more readily did he attain to high office, the further did he, when in office, outstrip his colleagues in the race for precedence, the more did he gain favour with the great, authority with the senate, and name and fame with the common people. These were the men who had whole nations of foreigners under their protection, several at a time; the men to whom state officials presented their humble duty on the eve of their departure to take up the government of a province, and to whom they paid their respects on their return; the men who, without any effort on their own part, seemed to have praetorships and consulates at their beck and call; the men who even when out of office were in power, seeing that by their advice and authority they could bend both the senate and the people to their will. With them moreover it was a conviction that without eloquence it was impossible for any one either to attain to a position of distinction and prominence in the community, or to maintain it: and no wonder they cherished this conviction, when they were called on to appear in public even when they would rather not, when it was not enough to move a brief resolution in the senate, unless one made good one's opinion in an able speech, when persons who had in some way or other incurred odium, or else were definitely charged with some offence, had to put in an appearance in person, when moreover evidence in criminal trials had to be given not indirectly or by affidavit, but personally and by word of mouth. So it was that eloquence not only led to great rewards, but was also a sheer necessity; and just as it was considered great and glorious to have the reputation of being a good speaker, so, on the other hand, it was accounted discreditable to be inarticulate and incapable of utterance.

QUINTILIAN: INSTITUTIO ORATORIA

Translated by H. E. Butler

Quintilian's Institutes of Oratory *were written about 95 A.D. during the period when the Emperor Domitian daily condemned many Roman citizens to death for the slightest suspicion of disrespect for the emperor and banished all philosophers from Rome for fear that they would turn the people against him. Before his assassination in 96 A.D., the Emperor even designated himself the* censor perpetuus, *the censor of public morals. As Quintilian's patron, Domitian entrusted the rhetorical education of his two grand nephews to his care. However, between the time that Quintilian mentioned this charge in Book III of his* Institutes *and the time that Book XII was completed, both nephews had been driven into exile by their uncle. It is natural that the* Institutes *which emphasize throughout that "the orator must above all things study morality," has been subject to much criticism as an insincere document. F. H. Colson calls it a treatise on "Lying as a Fine Art for Those Fully Conscious of Their Own Rectitude."[1] Of Domitian's appointment of Quintilian as teacher of his grand nephews, John Quincy Adams writes:*

He appears to have been too much elated by the honor of this appointment; and, in the effusions of his gratitude or of his servility, prostitutes his eloquence in strains of adulation to the emperor, which cannot wipe off a stain from the infamy of Domitian, but which shed some portion of it upon his panegyrist. For the manners of the age, and the nature of the government, some allowance must be made; and, if any thing could be wanting to complete our abhorrence of arbitrary power, it would be sufficient to behold a

Reprinted by permission of the publishers and THE LOEB CLASSICAL LIBRARY from H. E. Butler, translator, Quintilian, *Institutio Oratoria*, Cambridge, Mass.: Harvard University Press.

[1] F. H. Colson, Introduction, *M Fabii Quintiliani Institutionis Oratoriae Liber I* Cambridge, England, 1924), p. xxviii.

man of Quinctilian's genius and industry prostrate in the dust before a being, like Domitian. In the midst of this degradation, it is however some consolation to observe gleams of unquenchable virtue, still piercing through the gloom.[1]

Despite the problem of Quintilian's relation to Domitian, his influence has been significant, especially in developing the theory that a good orator must be a good man. Donald Lemen Clark suggests that an adequate knowledge of rhetorical education among the Greeks and Romans could be based on Quintilian alone because he came at the end of the great classical period of rhetorical development and summed it all up.[2] St. Jerome and St. Augustine both used materials from the Institutes. *The fifth century Roman rhetorician Jules Victor absorbed so much of Quintilian that some modern editors have used his* Ars Rhetorica *to correct the text of the* Institutes *itself.[3] Charles H. Haskins, in* The Renaissance of the Twelfth Century, *suggests that Quintilian's precepts were considered most important in twelfth century French education. After Poggio Bracciolino's discovery of a complete text of the* Institutes *in 1416, it became an important influence in the classical revival, being used in the doctrines of many Renaissance writers and educators. Since the first printing of the complete text in 1470, the* Institutes *of Oratory has undergone 19 complete editions and single books have been edited many more times.[4]*

"Quintilian attacks the question whether rhetoric is useful. He admits that it can be misused, like other good things, but this is no reason for thinking it an evil thing. There is, however, no real problem for those who accept Quintilian's definition; if the orator is a good man, there can be no doubt about the usefulness of oratory.[5] It seems clear that for the modern speaker or writer, Quintilian's major contribution is his emphasis on the worth of the individual communicator and the ethical standards which he needs to adopt.

[1]John Quincy Adams, *Lectures on Rhetoric and Oratory*, With a new introduction by J. Jeffery Auer and Jerald L. Banninga, 2 vols. (New York, 1962), I, 153-154.

[2]Donald Lemen Clark, *Rhetoric in Greco-Roman Education* (New York, 1957), p. 14.

[3]James J. Murphy, Introduction, Quintilian, *On the Early Education of the Citizen-Orator.* Translated by John Selby Watson, Edited by James J. Murphy (Indianapolis, 1965), p. xxi. For a 41 page study of Quintilian's influence, see Colson, *op. cit.,* xliii-lxxxix.

[4]James Murphy, *op. cit.,* p. xxvii.

[5]Donald Lemen Clark, pp. 115-116.

I, 1 – III, 12

The orator then, whom I am concerned to form, shall be the orator as defined by Marcus Cato, "a good man, skilled in speaking." But above all he must possess the quality which Cato places first and which is in the very nature of things the greatest and most important, that is, he must be a good man. This is essential not merely on account of the fact that, if the powers of eloquence serve only to lend arms to crime, there can be nothing more pernicious than eloquence to public and private welfare alike, while I myself, who have laboured to the best of my ability to contribute something of value to oratory, shall have rendered the worst of services to mankind, if I forge these weapons not for a soldier, but for a robber. But why speak of myself? Nature herself will have proved not a mother, but a stepmother with regard to what we deem her greatest gift to man, the gift that distinguishes us from other living things, if she devised the power of speech to be the accomplice of crime, the foe to innocency and the enemy of truth. For it had been better for men to be born dumb and devoid of reason than to turn the gifts of providence to their mutual destruction. But this conviction of mine goes further. For I do not merely assert that the ideal orator should be a good man, but I affirm that no man can be an orator unless he is a good man. For it is impossible to regard those men as gifted with intelligence who on being offered the choice between the two paths of virtue and of vice choose the latter, nor can we allow them prudence, when by the unforseen issue of their own actions they render themselves liable not merely to the heaviest penalties of the laws, but to the inevitable torment of an evil conscience. But if the view that a bad man is necessarily a fool is not merely held by philosophers, but is the universal belief of ordinary men, the fool will most assuredly never become an orator. To this must be added the fact that the mind will not find leisure even for the study of the noblest of tasks, unless it first be free from vice. The reasons for this are, first, that vileness and virtue cannot jointly inhabit in the selfsame heart and that it is as impossible for one and the same mind to harbour good and evil thoughts as it is for one man to be at once both good and evil: and secondly, that if the intelligence is to be concentrated on such a vast subject as eloquence it must be free from all other distractions, among which must be included even those preoccupations which are free from blame. For it is only when it is free and self-possessed, with nothing to divert it or lure it elsewhere, that it will fix its attention solely on that goal, the attainment of which is the object of its preparations. If on the other hand inordinate care for the development of our estates, excess of anxiety over household affairs, passionate devotion to hunting or the sacrifice of whole days to the shows of the theatre, rob our studies of much of the time that is their due (for every moment that is given to other things involves a loss of time for study), what, think you, will be the results of desire, avarice, and envy, which waken such violent thoughts within our souls that they disturb our very slumbers and our dreams? There is nothing so preoccupied, so distracted, so rent and torn by so many and such varied passions as an evil mind. For when it cherishes some dark design, it is tormented with hope, care and anguish of spirit, and even when it has accomplished its criminal purpose, it is racked by anxiety, remorse and the fear of all manner of punishments. Amid such passions as these what room is there for literature or any virtuous pursuit? You might as well look for fruit in land that is choked with thorns and brambles. Well then, I ask you, is not simplicity of life essential if we are to be able to endure the toil entailed by study? What can we hope to get from lust or luxury? Is not the desire to win praise one of the strongest stimulants to a passion for literature? But does that mean that we are to suppose that praise is an object of concern to bad men? Surely every one of my readers must by now have realised that oratory is in the main concerned with the treatment of what is just and honourable? Can a bad and unjust man speak on such themes as the dignity of the subject demands? Nay, even if we exclude the most important aspects of the question now before us, and make the impossible concession that the best and worst of men may have the same talent, industry and learning, we are still confronted by the question as to which of the two is entitled to be called the better orator. The answer is surely clear enough: it will be he who is the better man. Consequently, the bad man and the perfect orator can never be identical. For nothing is perfect, if there exists something else that is better. However, as I do not wish to appear to adopt the practice dear to the Socratics of framing answers to my own questions, let me assume the existence of a man so obstinately blind to the truth as to venture to maintain that a bad man equipped with the same talents, industry and learning will be not a whit inferior to the good man as an orator; and let me show that he too is mad. There is one point at any rate which no one will question, namely, that the aim of every speech is to convince the judge that the case which it puts forward is true and honourable. Well then, which will do this best, the good man or the bad? The good man will without doubt more often say what is true and honourable. But even supposing that his duty should, as I shall show may sometimes happen, lead him to make statements which are false, his words are still certain to carry greater weight with his audience. On the other hand bad men, in their contempt for public opinion and their ignorance of what is right, sometimes drop their mask unawares, and are impudent in the statement of their case and shameless in their assertions. Further, in their attempt to achieve the impossible they display an unseemly persistency and unavailing energy. For in lawsuits no less than in the ordinary paths of life, they cherish depraved expectations. But it often happens that even when they tell the truth they fail to win belief, and the mere fact that such a man is its advocate is regarded as an indication of the badness of the case.

I must now proceed to deal with the objections which common opinion is practically unanimous in bringing against this view. Was not Demosthenes an orator? And yet we are told that he was a bad man. Was not Cicero an orator? And yet there are many who have found fault with his character as well. What am I to answer? My reply will be highly unpopular and I must first attempt to conciliate my audience. I do not consider that Demosthenes deserves the serious reflexions that have been made upon his character to such an extent that I am bound to believe all the charges amassed against him by his enemies; for my reading tells me that his public policy was of the noblest and his end most glorious. Again, I cannot see that the aims of Cicero were in any portion of his career other than such as may become an excellent citizen. As evidence I would cite the fact that his behaviour as counsul was magnificent and his administration of his province a model of integrity, while he refused to become one of the twenty commissioners, and in the grievous civil wars which afflicted his generation beyond all others, neither hope nor fear ever deterred him from giving his support to the better party, that is to say, to the interests of the common weal. Some, it is true, regard him as lacking in courage. The best answer to these critics is to be found in his own words, to the effect that he was timid not in confronting peril, but in anticipating it. And this he proved also by the manner of his death, in meeting which he displayed a singular fortitude. But even if these two men lacked the perfection of virtue, I will reply to those who ask if they were orators, in the manner in which the Stoics would reply, if asked whether Zeno, Cleanthes or Chrysippus himself were wise men. I shall say that they were great men deserving our veneration, but that they did not attain to that which is the highest perfection of man's nature. For did not Pythagoras desire that he should not be called a wise man, like the sages who preceded him, but rather a student of wisdom? But for my own part, conforming to the language of every day, I have said time and again, and shall continue to say, that Cicero was a perfect orator, just as in ordinary speech we call our friends good and sensible men, although neither of these titles can really be given to any save to him that has attained to perfect wisdom. But if I am called upon to speak strictly and in accordance with the most rigid laws of truth, I shall proclaim that I seek to find that same perfect orator whom Cicero also sought to discover. For while I admit that he stood on the loftiest pinnacle of eloquence, and can discover scarcely a single deficiency in him, although I might perhaps discover certain superfluities which I think he would have pruned away (for the general view of the learned is that he possessed many virtues and a few faults, and he himself states that he has succeeded in suppressing much of his youthful exuberance), none the less, in view of the fact that, although he had by no means a low opinion of himself, he never claimed to be the perfect sage, and, had he been granted longer life and less troubled conditions for the composition of his works, would doubtless have spoken better still, I shall not lay myself open to the charge of ungenerous criticism, if I say that I believe that he failed actually to achieve that perfection to the attainment of which none have approached more nearly, and indeed had I felt otherwise in this connexion, I might have defended my point with greater boldness and freedom.[1] Marcus Antonius declared that he had seen no man who was genuinely eloquent (and to be eloquent is a far less achievement than to be an orator), while Cicero himself has failed to find his orator in actual life and merely imagines and strives to depict the ideal. Shall I then be afraid to say that in the eternity of time that is yet to be, something more perfect may be found than has yet existed? I say nothing of those critics who will not allow sufficient credit even for eloquence to Cicero and Demosthenes, although Cicero himself does not regard Demosthenes as flawless, but asserts that he sometimes nods, while even Cicero fails to satisfy Brutus and Calvus (at any rate they criticised his style to his face), or to win the complete approval of either of the Asinii, who in various passages attack the faults of his oratory in language which is positively hostile.

However, let us fly in the face of nature and assume that a bad man has been discovered who is endowed with the highest eloquence. I shall none the less deny that he is an orator. For I should not allow that every man who has shown himself ready with his hands was necessarily a brave man, because true courage cannot be conceived of without the accompaniment of virtue. Surely the advocate who is called to defend the accused requires to be a man of honour, honour which greed cannot corrupt, influence seduce, or fear dismay. Shall we then dignify the traitor, the deserter, the turncoat with the sacred name of orator? But if the quality which is usually termed goodness is to be found even in quite ordinary advocates, why should not the orator, who has not yet existed, but may still be born, be no less perfect in character than in excellence of speech? It is no hack-advocate, no hireling pleader, nor yet, to use no harsher term, a serviceable attorney of the class generally known as *causidici,* that I am seeking to form, but rather a man who to extraordinary natural gifts has added a thorough mastery of all the fairest branches of knowledge, a man sent by heaven to be the blessings of mankind, one to whom all history can find no parallel, uniquely perfect in every detail and utterly noble alike in thought and speech. How small a portion of all these abilities will be required for the defence of the innocent, the repression of crime or the support of truth against falsehood in suits involving questions of money? It is true that our supreme orator will bear his part in such tasks, but his powers will be displayed with brighter splendour in greater matters than these, when he is called upon to

---

[1] Quintilian's reverence for Cicero is such that he feels hampered in maintaining his thesis.

direct the counsels of the senate and guide the people from the paths of error to better things. Was not this the man conceived by Virgil and described as quelling a riot when torches and stones have begun to fly:

> "Then, if before their eyes some statesman grave
> Stand forth, with virtue and high service crowned,
> Straight are they dumb and stand intent to hear."

Here then we have one who is before all else a good man, and it is only after this that the poet adds that he is skilled in speaking:

> "His words their minds control, their passions soothe."

Again, will not this same man, whom we are striving to form, if in time of war he be called upon to inspire his soldiers with courage for the fray, draw for his eloquence on the innermost precepts of philosophy? For how can men who stand upon the verge of battle banish all the crowding fears of hardship, pain and death from their minds, unless those fears be replaced by the sense of the duty that they owe their country, by courage and the lively image of a soldier's honour? And assuredly the man who will best inspire such feelings in others is he who has first inspired them in himself. For however we strive to conceal it, insincerity will always betray itself, and there was never in any man so great eloquence as would not begin to stumble and hesitate so soon as his words ran counter to his inmost thoughts. Now a bad man cannot help speaking things other than he feels. On the other hand, the good will never be at a loss for honourable words or fail to find matter full of virtue for utterance, since among his virtues practical wisdom will be one. And even though his imagination lacks artifice to lend it charm, its own nature will be ornament enough, for if honour dictate the words, we shall find eloquence there as well. Therefore, let those that are young, or rather let all of us, whatever our age, since it is never too late to resolve to follow what is right, strive with all our hearts and devote all our efforts to the pursuit of virtue and eloquence; and perchance it may be granted to us to attain to the perfection that we seek. For since nature does not forbid the attainment of either, why should not someone succeed in attaining both together? And why should not each of us hope to be that happy man? But if our powers are inadequate to such achievement, we shall still be the better for the double effort in proportion to the distance which we have advanced toward either goal. At any rate let us banish from our hearts the delusion that eloquence, the fairest of all things, can be combined with vice. The power of speaking is even to be accounted an evil when it is found in evil men; for it makes its possessors yet worse than they were before.

I think I hear certain persons (for there will always be some who had rather be eloquent than good) asking, "Why then is there so much art in connexion with eloquence? Why have you talked so much of 'glosses,' the methods of defence to be employed in difficult cases, and sometimes even of actual confession of guilt, unless it is the case that the power and force of speech at times triumphs over truth itself? For a good man will only plead good cases, and those might safely be left to truth to support without the aid of learning," Now, though my reply to these critics will in the first place be a defence of my own work, it will also explain what I consider to be the duty of a good man on occasions when circumstances have caused him to undertake the defence of the guilty. For it is by no means useless to consider how at times we should speak in defence of falsehood or even of injustice, if only for this reason, that such an investigation will enable us to detect and defeat them with the greater ease, just as the physician who has a thorough knowledge of all that can injure the health will be all the more skilful in the prescription of remedies. For the Academicians, although they will argue on either side of a question, do not thereby commit themselves to taking one of these two views as their guide in life to the exclusion of the other, while the famous Carneades, who is said to have spoken at Rome in the presence of Cato the Censor, and to have argued against justice with no less vigour than he had argued for justice on the preceding day, was not himself an unjust man. But the nature of virtue is revealed by vice, its opposite, justice becomes yet more manifest from the contemplation of injustice, and there are many other things that are proved by their contraries. Consequently the schemes of his adversaries should be no less well known to the orator than those of the enemy to a commander in the field. But it is even true, although at first sight it seems hard to believe, that there may be sound reason why at times a good man who is appearing for the defence should attempt to conceal the truth from the judge. If any of my readers is surprised at my making such a statement (although this opinion is not of my own invention, but is derived from those whom antiquity regarded as the greatest teachers of wisdom), I would have him reflect that there are many things which are made honourable or the reverse not by the nature of the facts, but by the causes from which they spring. For if to slay a man is often a virtue and to put one's own children to death is at times the noblest of deeds, and if it is permissible in the public interest to do deeds yet more horrible to relate than these, we should assuredly take into consideration not solely and simply what is the nature of the case which the good man undertakes to defend, but what is his reason and what his purpose in so doing. And first of all everyone must allow, what even the sternest of the Stoics admit, that the good man will sometimes tell a lie, and further that he will sometimes do so for comparatively trivial reasons; for example we tell countless lies to sick children for their good and make many promises to them which we do not intend to perform. And there is clearly far more justification for lying when it is a question of diverting an assassin from his victim or deceiving an enemy to save our country.

Consequently a practice which is at times reprehensible even in slaves, may on other occasions be praiseworthy even in a wise man. If this be granted, I can see that there will be many possible emergencies such as to justify an orator in undertaking cases of a kind which, in the absence of any honourable reason, he would have refused to touch. In saying this I do not mean that we should be ready under any circumstances to defend our father, brother or friend when in peril (since I hold that we should be guided by stricter rules in such matters), although such contingencies may well cause us no little perplexity, when we have to decide between the rival claims of justice and natural affection. But let us put the problem beyond all question of doubt. Suppose a man to have plotted against a tyrant and to be accused of having done so. Which of the two will the orator, as defined by us, desire to save? And if he undertakes the defence of the accused, will he not employ falsehood with no less readiness than the advocate who is defending a bad case before a jury? Again, suppose that the judge is likely to condemn acts which were rightly done, unless we can convince him that they were never done. Is not this another case where the orator will not shrink even from lies, if so he may save one who is not merely innocent, but a praiseworthy citizen? Again, suppose that we realise that certain acts are just in themselves, though prejudicial to the state under existing circumstances. Shall we not then employ methods of speaking which, despite the excellence of their intention, bear a close resemblance to fraud. Further, no one will hesitate for a moment to hold the view that it is in the interests of the commonwealth that guilty persons should be acquitted rather than punished, if it be possible thereby to convert them to a better state of mind, a possibility which is generally conceded. If then it is clear to an orator that a man who is guilty of the offences laid to his charge will become a good man, will he not strive to secure his acquittal? Imagine for example that a skilful commander, without whose aid the state cannot hope to crush its enemies, is labouring under a charge which is obviously true: will not the common interest irresistibly summon our orator to defend him? We know at any rate that Fabricius publicly voted for and secured the election to the consulate of Cornelius Rufinus, despite the fact that he was a bad citizen and his personal enemy, merely because he knew that he was a capable general and the state was threatened with war. And when certain persons expressed their surprise at his conduct, he replied that he had rather be robbed by a fellow-citizen than be sold as a slave by the enemy. Well then, had Fabricius been an orator, would he not have defended Rufinus against a charge of peculation, even though his guilt were as clear as day? I might produce many other similar examples, but one of them taken at random is enough. For my purpose is not to assert that such tasks will often be incumbent on the orator whom I desire to form, but merely to show that, in the event of his being compelled to take such action, it will not invalidate our definition of an orator as a "good man, skilled in speaking."

And it is necessary also both to teach and learn how to establish difficult cases by proof. For often even the best cases have a resemblance to bad and, the charges which tell heavily against an innocent person frequently have a strong resemblance to the truth. Consequently, the same methods of defence have to be employed that would be used if he were guilty. Further, there are countless elements which are common to both good cases and bad, such as oral and documentary evidence, suspicions and opinions, all of which have to be established or disposed of in the same way, whether they be true or merely resemble the truth. Therefore, while maintaining his integrity of purpose, the orator will modify his pleading to suit the circumstances.

II. Since then the orator is a good man, and such goodness cannot be conceived as existing apart from virtue, virtue, despite the fact that it is in part derived from certain natural impulses, will require to be perfected by instruction. The orator must above all things devote his attention to the formation of moral character and must acquire a complete knowledge of all that is just and honourable. For without this knowledge no one can be either a good man or skilled in speaking, unless indeed we agree with those who regard morality as intuitive and as owing nothing to instruction: indeed they go so far as to acknowledge that handicrafts, not excluding even those which are most despised among them, can only be acquired by the result of teaching, whereas virtue, which of all gifts to man is that which makes him most near akin to the immortal gods, comes to him without search or effort, as a natural concomitant of birth. But can the man who does not know what abstinence is, claim to be truly abstinent? or brave, if he has never purged his soul of the fears of pain, death and superstition? or just, if he has never, in language approaching that of philosophy, discussed the nature of virtue and justice, or of the laws that have been given to mankind by nature or established among individual peoples and nations? What a contempt it argues for such themes to regard them as being so easy of comprehension! However, I pass this by; for I am sure that no one with the least smattering of literary culture will have the slightest hesitation in agreeing with me. I will proceed to my next point, that no one will achieve sufficient skill even in speaking, unless he makes a thorough study of all the workings of nature and forms his character on the precepts of philosophy and the dictates of reason. For it is with good cause that Lucius Crassus, in the third book of the *de Oratore*, affirms that all that is said concerning equity, justice, truth and the good, and their opposites, forms part of the studies of an orator, and that the philosophers, when they exert their powers of speaking to defend these virtues, are using the weapons of rhetoric, not their own. But he also confesses that the knowledge of these subjects must be sought from the philosophers for the reason that, in his opinion, philosophy has more effective possession of them. And it is for the same reason that Cicero in several of his books and letters proclaims that eloquence has its fountain-head in the most secret springs of wisdom, and that consequently for a considerable time the instructors of morals and of eloquence were identical. Accordingly this exhortation of mine must not be taken to mean that I wish the orator to be a philosopher, since there is no other way of life that is further removed from the duties of a statesman and the tasks of an orator. For what philosopher has ever been a frequent speaker in the courts or won renown in public assemblies? Nay, what philosopher has ever taken a prominent part in the government of the state, which forms the most frequent theme of their instructions? None the less I desire that he, whose character I am seeking to mould, should be a "wise man" in the Roman sense, that is, one who reveals himself as a true statesman, not in the discussions of the study, but in the actual practice and experience of life. But inasmuch as the study of philosophy has been deserted by those who have turned to the pursuit of eloquence, and since philosophy no longer moves in its true sphere of action and in the broad daylight of the forum, but has retired first to porches and gymnasia and finally to the gatherings of the schools, all that is essential for an orator, and yet is not taught by the professors of eloquence, must undoubtedly be sought from those persons in whose possession it has remained. The authors who have discoursed on the nature of virtue must be read through and through, that the life of the orator may be wedded to the knowledge of things human and divine. But how much greater and fairer would such subjects appear if those who taught them were also those who could give them most eloquent expression! O that the day may dawn when the perfect orator of our heart's desire shall claim for his own possession that science that has lost the affection of mankind through the arrogance of its claims and the vices of some that have brought disgrace upon its virtues, and shall restore it to its place in the domain of eloquence, as though he had been victorious in a trial for the restoration of stolen goods! And since philosophy falls into three divisions, physics, ethics and dialectic, which, I ask you, of these departments is not closely connected with the task of the orator?

Let us reverse the order just given and deal first with the third department which is entirely concerned with words. If it be true that to know the properties of each word, to clear away ambiguities, to unravel perplexities, to distinguish between truth and falsehood, to prove or to refute as may be desired, all form part of the functions of an orator, who is there that can doubt the truth of my contention? I grant that we shall not have to employ dialectic with such minute attention to detail when we are pleading in the courts as when we are engaged in philosophical debate, since the orator's duty is not merely to instruct, but also to move and delight his audience; and to succeed in doing this he needs a strength, impetuosity and grace as well. For oratory is like a river: the current is stronger when it flows within deep banks and with a mighty flood, than when the waters are shallow and broken by the pebbles that bar their way.

And just as the trainers of the wrestling school do not impart the various *throws* to their pupils that those who have learnt them may make use of all of them in actual wrestling matches (for weight and strength and wind count for more than these), but that they may have a store from which to draw one or two of such tricks, as occasion may offer; even so the science of dialectic, or if you prefer it of disputation, while it is often useful in definition, inference, differentiation, resolution of ambiguity, distinction and classification, as also in luring on or entangling our opponents, yet if it claim to assume the entire direction of the struggles of the forum, will merely stand in the way of arts superior to itself and by its very subtlety will exhaust the strength that has been pared down to suit its limitations. As a result you will find that certain persons who show astonishing skill in philosophical debate, as soon as they quit the sphere of their quibbles, are as helpless in any case that demands more serious pleading as those small animals which, though nimble enough in a confined space, are easily captured in an open field.

Proceeding to moral philosophy or ethics, we may note that it at any rate is entirely suited to the orator. For vast as is the variety of cases (since in them, as I have pointed out in previous books, we seek to discover certain points by conjecture, reach our conclusions in others by means of definition, dispose of others on legal grounds or by raising the question of competence, while other points are established by syllogism and others involve contradictions or are diversely interpreted owing to some ambiguity of language), there is scarcely a single one which does not at some point or another involve the discussion of equity and virtue, while there are also, as everyone knows, not a few which turn entirely on questions of quality. Again in deliberative assemblies how can we advise a policy without raising the question of what is honourable? Nay, even the third department of oratory, which is concerned with the tasks of praise and denunciation, must without a doubt deal with questions of right and wrong. For the orator will assuredly have much to say on such topics as justice, fortitude, abstinence, self-control and piety. But the good man, who has come to the knowledge of these things not by mere hearsay, as though they were just words and names for his tongue to employ, but has grasped the meaning of virtue and acquired a true feeling for it, will never be perplexed when he has to think out a problem, but will speak out truly what he knows. Since, however, *general* questions are always more important than special (for the particular is contained in the universal, while the universal is never to be regarded as something superimposed on the particular), everyone will readily admit that the studies of which we are speaking are pre-eminently concerned with general questions. Further, since there are numerous points which require to be determined by appropriate and concise definitions (hence the *definitive basis* of cases), it is surely desirable that the orator should be instructed in such things by those who have devoted special attention to the subject. Again, does not every question of law turn either on the precise meaning of words, the discussion of equity, or conjecture as to the intention — subjects which in part encroach on the domain of dialectic and in part on that of ethics? Consequently all oratory involves a natural admixture of all these philosophic elements — at least, that is to say, all oratory that is worthy of the name. For mere garrulity that is ignorant of all such learning must needs go astray, since its guides are either non-existent or false.

Physics[1] on the other hand is far richer than the other branches of philosophy, if viewed from the standpoint of providing exercise in speaking, in proportion as a loftier inspiration is required to speak of things divine than of things human; and further it includes within its scope the whole of ethics, which as we have shown are essential to the very existence of oratory. For, if the world is governed by providence, it will certainly be the duty of all good men to bear their part in the administration of the state. If the origin of our souls be divine, we must win our way towards virtue and abjure the service of the lusts of our earthly body. Are not these themes which the orator will frequently be called upon to handle? Again there are questions concerned with auguries and oracles or any other religious topic (all of them subjects that have often given rise to the most important debates in the senate) on which the orator will have to discourse, if he is also to be the statesman we would have him be. And finally, how can we conceive of any real eloquence at all proceeding from a man who is ignorant of all that is best in the world? If our reason did not make these facts obvious, we should still be led by historical examples to believe their truth. For Pericles, whose eloquence, despite the fact that it has left no visible record for posterity, was none the less, if we may believe the historians and that free-speaking tribe, the old comic poets, endowed with almost incredible force, is known to have been a pupil of the physicist Anaxagoras, while Demosthenes, greatest of all the orators of Greece, sat at the feet of Plato. As for Cicero, he has often proclaimed the fact that he owed less to the schools of rhetoric than to the walks of Academe: nor would he ever have developed such amazing fertility of talent, had he bounded his genius by the limits of the forum and not by the frontiers of nature herself.

But this leads me to another question as to which school of philosophy is like to prove of most service to oratory, although there are only a few that can be said to contend for this honour. For in the first place Epicurus banishes us from his presence without more ado, since he bids all his followers to fly from learning in the swiftest ship that they can find. Nor would Aristippus, who regards the highest good as consisting in physical pleasure, be likely to exhort us to the toils entailed by our study. And what part can Pyrrho have in the work that is before us? For he will have doubts as to whether there exist judges to address, accused to defend, or a

---

[1] I.e. natural philosophy in the widest sense.

senate where he can be called upon to speak his opinion. Some authorities hold that the Academy will be the most useful school, on the ground that its habit of disputing on both sides of a question approaches most nearly to the actual practice of the courts. And by way of proof they add the fact that this school has produced speakers highly renowned for their eloquence. The Peripatetics also make it their boast that they have a form of study which is near akin to oratory. For it was with them in the main that originated the practice of declaiming on general questions by way of exercise. The Stoics, though driven to admit that generally speaking, their teachers have been deficient both in fullness and charm of eloquence, still contend that no men can prove more acutely or draw conclusions with greater subtlety than themselves. But all these arguments take place within their own circle, for, as though they were tied by some solemn oath or held fast in the bonds of some superstitious belief, they consider that it is a crime to abandon a conviction once formed. On the other hand, there is no need for an orator to swear allegiance to any one philosophic code. For he has a greater and nobler aim, to which he directs all his efforts with as much zeal as if he were a candidate for office, since he is to be made perfect not only in the glory of a virtuous life, but in that of eloquence as well. He will consequently select as his models of eloquence all the greatest masters of oratory, and will choose the noblest precepts and the most direct road to virtue as the means for the formation of an upright character. He will neglect no form of exercise, but will devote special attention to those which are of the highest and fairest nature. For what subject can be found more fully adapted to a rich and weighty eloquence than the topics of virtue, politics, providence, the origin of the soul and friendship? The themes which tend to elevate mind and language alike are questions such as what things are truly good, what means there are of assuaging fear, restraining the passions and lifting us and the soul that came from heaven clear of the delusions of the common herd.

But it is desirable that we should not restrict our study to the precepts of philosophy alone. It is still more important that we should know and ponder continually all the noblest sayings and deeds that have been handed down to us from ancient times. And assuredly we shall nowhere find a larger or more remarkable store of these than in the records of our own country. Who will teach courage, justice, loyalty, self-control, simplicity, and contempt of grief and pain better than men like Fabricius, Curius, Regulus, Decius, Mucius and countless others? For if the Greeks bear away the palm for moral precepts, Rome can produce more striking examples of moral performance, which is a far greater thing. But the man who does not believe that it is enough to fix his eyes merely on his own age and his own transitory life, but regards the space allotted for an honourable life and the course in which glory's race is run as conditioned solely by the memory of posterity, will not rest content with a mere knowledge of the events of history. No, it is from the thought of posterity that he must inspire his soul with justice and derive that freedom of spirit which it is his duty to display when he pleads in the courts or gives counsel in the senate. No man will ever be the consummate orator of whom we are in quest unless he has both the knowledge and the courage to speak in accordance with the promptings of honour.

III. Our orator will also require a knowledge of civil law and of the custom and religion of the state in whose life he is to bear his part. For how will he be able to advise either in public or in private, if he is ignorant of all the main elements that go to make the state? How can he truthfully call himself an advocate if he has to go to others to acquire that knowledge which is all-important in the courts? He will be little better than if he were a reciter of the poets. For he will be a mere transmitter of the instructions that others have given him, it will be on the authority of others that he propounds what he asks the judge to believe, and he whose duty it is to succour the litigant will himself be in need of succour. It is true that at times this may be effected with but little inconvenience, if what he advances for the edification of the judge has been taught him and composed in the seclusion of his study and learnt by heart there like other elements of the case. But what will he do, when he is confronted by unexpected problems such as frequently arise in the actual course of pleading? Will he not disgrace himself by looking round and asking the junior counsel who sit on the benches behind him for advice? Can he hope to get a thorough grasp of such information at the very moment when he is required to produce it in his speech? Can he make his assertions with confidence or speak with native simplicity as though his arguments were his own? Grant that he may do so in his actual speech. But what will he do in a debate, when he has continually to meet fresh points raised by his opponent and is given no time to learn up his case? What will he do, if he has no legal expert to advise him or if his prompter through insufficient knowledge of the subject provides him with information that is false? It is the most serious drawback of such ignorance, that he will always believe that his adviser knows what he is talking about. I am not ignorant of the generally prevailing custom, nor have I forgotten those who sit by our store-chests and provide weapons for the pleader: I know too that the Greeks did likewise: hence the name of *pragmaticas* which was bestowed on such persons. But I am speaking of an orator, who owes it as a duty to his case to serve it not merely by the loudness of his voice, but by all other means that may be of assistance to it. Consequently I do not wish my orator to be helpless, if it so chance that he puts in an appearance for the preliminary proceedings to which the hour before the commencement of the trial is allotted, or to be unskilful in the preparation and production of evidence. For who, sooner than himself, should prepare the points which he wishes to be brought out when he is pleading? You might as well suppose that the qualifications of a successful general consist merely in courage and energy in the field of battle and skill in meeting all the demands of actual conflict, while suffering him to be ignorant of the methods of levying troops, mustering and equipping his forces, arranging for supplies or selecting a suitable position for his camp, despite the fact that preparation for war is an essential preliminary for its successful conduct. And yet such a general would bear a very close resemblance to the advocate who leaves much of the detail that is necessary for success to the care of others, more especially in view of the fact that this, the most necessary element in the management of a case, is not as difficult as it may perhaps seem to outside observers. For every point of law, which is certain, is based either on written law or accepted custom: if, on the other hand, the point is doubtful, it must be examined in the light of equity. Laws which are either written or founded on accepted custom present no difficulty, since they call merely for knowledge and make no demand on the imagination. On the other hand, the points explained in the rulings of the legal experts turn either on the interpretation of words or on the distinction between right and wrong. To understand the meaning of each word is either common to all sensible men or the special possession of the orator, while the demands of equity are known to every good man. Now I regard the orator above all as being a man of virtue and good sense, who will not be seriously troubled, after having devoted himself to the study of that which is excellent by nature, if some legal expert disagrees with him; for even they are allowed to disagree among themselves. But if he further wishes to know the views of everyone, he will require to read, and reading is the least laborious of all the tasks that fall to the student's lot. Moreover, if the class of legal experts is as a rule drawn from those who, in despair of making successful pleaders, have taken refuge with the law, how easy it must be for an orator to know what those succeed in learning, who by their own confession are incapable of becoming orators! But Marcus Cato was at once a great orator and an expert lawyer, while Scaevola and Servius Sulpicius were universally allowed to be eloquent as well. And Cicero not merely possessed a sufficient supply of legal knowledge to serve his needs when pleading, but actually began to write on the subject, so that it is clear that an orator has not merely time to learn, but even to teach the law.

Let no one, however, regard the advice I have given as to the attention due to the development of character and the study of the law as being impugned by the fact that we are familiar with many who, because they were weary of the toil entailed on those who seek to scale the heights of eloquence, have betaken themselves to the study of law as a refuge for their indolence. Some of these transfer their attention to the praetor's edicts or the civil law, and have preferred to become specialists in *formulae,* or legalists, as Cicero calls them, on the pretext of choosing a more useful branch of study, whereas their real motive was its comparative easiness. Others are the victims of a more arrogant form of sloth; they assume a stern air and let their beards grow, and, as though despising the precepts of oratory, sit for a while in the schools of the philosophers, that, by an assumption of a severe mien before the public gaze and by an affected contempt of others they may assert their moral superiority, while leading a life of debauchery at home. For philosophy may be counterfeited, but eloquence never.

ST. AUGUSTINE:
ON CHRISTIAN DOCTRINE

Translated by D. W. Robertson, Jr.

Charles Sears Baldwin writes: "A clean break is made by St. Augustine. The fourth book of his De Doctrina Christiana *has historical significance in the early years of the fifth century out of all proportion to its size; for it begins rhetoric anew. It not only ignores sophistic; it goes back over centuries of the lore of personal triumph to the ancient idea of moving men to truth; and it gives to the vital counsels of Cicero a new emphasis for the urgent tasks of preaching the word of God."*[1] *Augustine provides a fitting transition between the classical period of literature and the medieval and renaissance emphasis on rhetoric and poetic. James J. Murphy suggests that: "The basic issue was whether the Church should adopt in toto the contemporary culture which Rome had taken over from Greece. The fate of rhetoric, as a part of the Greco-Roman culture, was involved not only in the debate over the larger issue, but in more limited controversies about its own merits. Indeed, the contrast between* Verbum *(Word of God) and* verbum *(word of man) was stressed from the very beginnings of the Church, long before the broader cultural issue was joined."*[2] *Augustine defends his position in the debate by this analogy:*

Medicines for the body which are administered to men by men do not help them unless health is conferred by God, who can cure without them; yet they are nevertheless applied even though they are useless without His aid. And if they are applied courteously, they

[1] *Medieval Rhetoric and Poetic* (Gloucester, Mass., 1959), p. 51.

[2] James J. Murphy, "Saint Augustine and the Debate about a Christian Rhetoric," *Readings in Rhetoric.* Compiled and edited by Lionel Crocker and Paul A. Carmack (Springfield, Ill., 1965), p. 205.

are considered to be among works of mercy or kindness. In the same way, the benefits of teaching profit the mind when they are applied by men, when assistance is granted by God, who could have given the gospel to man even though it came not from men nor through a man.

He who seeks to teach in speech what is good, spurning none of these three things, that is, to teach, to delight, and to persuade, should pray and strive that he be heard intelligently, willingly, and obediently. When he does this well and properly, he can justly be called eloquent, even though he fails to win the assent of his audience.[1]

Included below are Sections 1 to 5, 12, and part of 13 from Book IV of De Doctrina Christiana *which contains much of the substance for Augustine's argument for a Christian rhetoric based on the precepts of Roman eloquence.*

I – V

This work of ours entitled *On Christian Doctrine* was at the beginning divided into two parts. For after the Prologue in which I replied to those who would criticize it, I wrote, "There are two things necessary to the treatment of the Scriptures: a way of discovering those things which are to be understood, and a way of teaching what we have learned. We shall speak first of discovery and second of teaching." Since we have already said much concerning discovery and devoted three books to that one part, with the help of God we shall say a few things concerning teaching, so that, if possible, we shall conclude everything with one book and thus complete the whole work in four books.

But first in these preliminary remarks I must thwart the expectation of those readers who think that I shall give the rules of rhetoric here which I learned and taught in the secular schools. And I admonish them not to expect such rules from me, not that they have no utility, but because, if they have any, it should be sought elsewhere if perhaps some good man has the opportunity to learn them. But he should not expect these rules from me, either in this work or in any other.

For since by means of the art of rhetoric both truth and falsehood are urged, who would dare to say that truth should stand in the person of its defenders unarmed against lying, so that they who wish to urge falsehoods may know how to make their listeners benevolent, or attentive, or docile

[1] St. Augustine, *op. cit.*, pp. 142-143.

in their presentation, while the defenders of truth are ignorant of that art? Should they speak briefly, clearly, and plausibly while the defenders of truth speak so that they tire their listeners, make themselves difficult to understand and what they have to say dubious? Should they oppose the truth with fallacious arguments and assert falsehoods, while the defenders of truth have no ability either to defend the truth or to oppose the false? Should they, urging the minds of their listeners into error, ardently exhort them, moving them by speech so that they terrify, sadden, and exhilarate them, while the defenders of truth are sluggish, cold, and somnolent? Who is so foolish as to think this to be wisdom? While the faculty of eloquence, which is of great value in urging either evil or justice, is in itself indifferent, why should it not be obtained for the uses of the good in the service of truth if the evil usurp it for the winning of perverse and vain causes in defense of iniquity and error?

But whatever observations and rules concerning this matter there may be, in accordance with which one acquires through exercise and habit a most skillful use of vocabulary and plentiful verbal ornaments, are established by what is called eloquence or oratory. Those who are able to do so quickly, having set aside an appropriate period of time, should learn them at a proper and convenient age outside of these writings of mine. For the masters of Roman eloquence themselves did not hesitate to say that, unless one can learn this art quickly, he can hardly learn it at all. Why should we inquire whether this is true? For even if these rules can sometimes be learned by those who are slow, we do not hold them to be of such importance that we would wish mature and grave men to spend their time learning them. It is enough that they be the concern of youths; nor should they concern all of those whom we wish to educate for the utility of the Church, but only those who are not pursuing some more urgent study, or one which obviously ought to take precedence over this one. For those with acute and eager minds more readily learn eloquence by reading and hearing the eloquent than by following the rules of eloquence. There is no lack of ecclesiastical literature, including that outside of the canon established in a place of secure authority, which, if read by a capable man, even though he is interested more in what is said than in the eloquence with which it is said, will imbue him with that eloquence while he is studying. And he will learn eloquence especially if he gains practice by writing, dictating, or speaking what he has learned according to the rule of piety and faith. But if capacity of this kind to learn eloquence is lacking, the rules of rhetoric will not be understood, nor will it help any if they are in some small measure understood after great labor. Even those who have learned these rules and speak fluently and eloquently cannot be aware of the fact that they are applying them while they are speaking unless they are discussing the rules themselves; indeed, I think that there is hardly a single eloquent man who can both speak well and think of the rules of eloquence while he is speaking. And we should beware lest what should be said escape us while we are thinking of the artistry of the discourse. Moreover, in the speeches and sayings of the eloquent, the precepts of eloquence are found to have been fulfilled, although the speakers did not think of them in order to be eloquent or while they were being eloquent, and they were eloquent whether they had learned the rules or never come in contact with them. They fulfilled them because they were eloquent; they did not apply them that they might be eloquent.

Therefore, since infants are not taught to speak except by learning the expressions of speakers, why can men not be made eloquent, not by teaching them the rules of eloquence, but by having them read and hear the expressions of the eloquent and imitate them in so far as they are able to follow them? Have we not seen examples of this being done? For we know many men ignorant of the rules of eloquence who are more eloquent than many who have learned them; but we know of no one who is eloquent without having read or heard the disputations and sayings of the eloquent. For boys do not need the art of grammar which teaches correct speech if they have the opportunity to grow up and live among men who speak correctly. Without knowing any of the names of the errors, they criticize and avoid anything erroneous they hear spoken on the basis of their own habits of speech, just as city dwellers, even if they are illiterate, criticize the speech of rustics.

Thus the expositor and teacher of the Divine Scripture, the defender of right faith and the enemy of error, should both teach the good and extirpate the evil. And in this labor of words, he should conciliate those who are opposed, arouse those who are remiss, and teach those ignorant of his subject what is occurring and what they should expect. But when he has either found his listeners to be benevolent, attentive, and docile, or has caused them to be so, other aims are to be carried out as the cause requires. If those who hear are to be taught, exposition must be composed, if it is needed, that they may become acquainted with the subject at hand. In order that those things which are doubtful may be made certain, they must be reasoned out with the use of evidence. But if those who hear are to be moved rather than taught, so that they may not be sluggish in putting what they know into practice and so that they may fully accept those things which they acknowledge to be true, there is need for greater powers of speaking. Here entreaties and reproofs, exhortations and rebukes, and whatever other devices are necessary to move minds must be used.

And almost all men who make use of eloquence do not cease to do all of those things which I have mentioned.

But since some do these things dully, unevenly, and coldly, while others do them acutely, ornately, and vehemently, he should approach this work about which we are speaking who can dispute or speak wisely, even though he cannot do so eloquently, so that he may be of benefit to his hearers, even though he benefits them less than he would if he could also speak eloquently. But he who is foolish and abounds in eloquence is the more to be avoided the more he delights his auditor with those things to which it is useless to listen so that he thinks that because he hears a thing said eloquently it is true. This lesson, moreover, did not escape those who thought to teach the art of rhetoric. They granted that "wisdom without eloquence is of small benefit to states; but eloquence without wisdom is often extremely injurious and profits no one." If those who taught the rules of eloquence, in the very books in which they did so, were forced by the power of truth to confess this, being ignorant of that true wisdom which descends supernal from the Father of Lights, how much more ought we, who are the sons and ministers of this wisdom, to think in no other way? For a man speaks more or less wisely to the extent that he has become more or less proficient in the Holy Scriptures. I do not speak of the man who has read widely and memorized much, but of the man who has well understood and has diligently sought out the sense of the Scriptures. For there are those who read them and neglect them, who read that they may remember but neglect them in that they fail to understand them. Those are undoubtedly to be preferred who remember the words less well, but who look into the heart of the Scriptures with the eye of their own hearts. But better than either of these is he who can quote them when he wishes and understands them properly.

For one who wishes to speak wisely, therefore, even though he cannot speak eloquently, it is above all necessary to remember the words of Scripture. The poorer he sees himself to be in his own speech, the more he should make use of Scripture so that what he says in his own words he may support with the words of Scripture. In this way he who is inferior in his own words may grow in a certain sense through the testimony of the great. He shall give delight with his proofs when he cannot give delight with his own words. Indeed, he who wishes to speak not only wisely but also eloquently, since he can be of more worth if he can do both, should more eagerly engage in reading or hearing the works of the eloquent and in imitating them in practice than in setting himself to learn from the masters of the art of rhetoric. But those to be read or heard should be those truly recommended not only for their eloquence but also for the fact that they have written or spoken wisely. For he who speaks eloquently is heard with pleasure; he who speaks wisely is heard with profit. Hence the Scripture does not say, "the multitude of the eloquent, " but "the multitude of the wise is the welfare of the whole world." Just as things which are both bitter and healthful are frequently to be taken, so also a pernicious sweetness is always to be avoided. But what is better than a wholesome sweetness or a sweet wholesomeness? The more eagerly the sweetness is desired, the more readily the wholesomeness becomes profitable. There are men of the Church who treat the Scriptures not only wisely but eloquently. And there is not enough time for reading them, rather than that they could ever fail those who are studious and have leisure to read them. . .

XII – XIII

Therefore a certain eloquent man [Cicero] said, and said truly, that he who is eloquent should speak in such a way that he teaches, delights, and moves. Then he added, "To teach is a necessity, to please is a sweetness, to persuade is a victory." Of the three, that which is given first place, that is, the necessity of teaching, resides in the things which we have to say, the other two in the manner in which we say it. Thus he who speaks when he would teach cannot think that he has said what he wished to say to the person he wishes to teach so long as that person does not understand him. For even though he has said something which he himself understands, he is not yet to be thought of as having spoken to the person who does not understand him; on the other hand, if he is understood, he has spoken, no matter how he has spoken. But if he desires also to delight or to move the person to whom he speaks he will not do it simply by speaking in any way at all; but the manner in which he speaks determines whether he does so. Just as the listener is to be delighted if he is to be retained as a listener, so also he is to be persuaded if he is to be moved to act. And just as he is delighted if you speak sweetly, so is he persuaded if he loves what you promise, fears what you threaten, hates what you condemn, embraces what you commend, sorrows at what you maintain to be sorrowful; rejoices when you announce something delightful, takes pity on those whom you place before him in speaking as being pitiful, flees those whom you, moving fear, warn are to be avoided; and is moved by whatever else may be done through grand eloquence toward moving the minds of listeners, not that they may know what is to be done, but that they may do what they already know should be done.

But if they still do not know this, instruction should come before persuasion. And perhaps when the necessary things are learned, they may be so moved by a knowledge of them that it is not necessary to move them further by greater powers of eloquence. But when it is necessary, it is to be done, and it is necessary when they know what should be done but do not do it. And for this reason teaching is a necessity. But men may act and still not act in accordance with what they know. But who would tell them to do something in accordance with what they do not know? And therefore persuasion is not a necessity because it need not always be applied if the listener consents through teaching and even through delight also. But it is also true that persuasion is victory, for people may be taught and pleased and still not consent. And of what use are the first two if the third does not follow? But delight is not a necessity either. Sometimes, when the truth is demonstrated in speaking, an action which pertains to the function of teaching, eloquence is neither brought into play nor is any attention paid to whether the matter or the discourse is pleasing, yet the matter itself is pleasing when it is revealed simply because it is true. Whence many are delighted simply by the exposure and refutation of falsehoods. These do not delight because they are falsehoods; but since it is true that they are false, the very language in which this is demonstrated to be true delights.

Because of those whose fastidiousness is not pleased by truth if it is stated in any other way except in that way in which the words are also pleasing, delight has no small place in the art of eloquence. But when this has been added it is not sufficient for the obdurate who have profited neither from understanding what was said nor from delighting in the manner in which it was taught. How do these help a man who both confesses the truth and praises the eloquence but still does not give his assent, on account of which alone the speaker, when he urges something, pays careful attention to the things which he is saying? When such things are taught that it is sufficient to know or to believe them, they require no more consent than an acknowledgment that they are true. But when that which is taught must be put into practice and is taught for that reason, the truth of what is said is acknowledged in vain and the eloquence of the discourse pleases in vain unless that which is learned is implemented in action. It is necessary therefore for the ecclesiastical orator, when he urges that something be done, not only to teach that he may instruct and to please that he may hold attention, but also to persuade that he may be victorious. For it now remains for that man, in whom the demonstration of truth, even when suavity of diction was added, did not move to consent, to be persuaded by the heights of eloquence.

UNIT TWO: INVENTION

QUINTILIAN: INSTITUTIO ORATORIA

Translated by H. E. Butler

Invention, the first canon of rhetoric, concerns itself with the content of discourses. It begins with study and analysis of the situation giving rise to the composition, and then leads to the discovery, selection, development, and adaptation of materials to fulfill the rhetor's purpose.

The section reprinted here from Quintilian's Institutes of Oratory *deals with the first phase of the inventive process by describing how to locate the issue, which Quintilian calls the* basis *of the question. Other writers and translators have called this the doctrine of* stasis or status, *which is defined as "the location or center of an argument,"[1] or "the conjoining of two conflicting statements, thus forming the centre of the argument and determining the character of the case."[2]*

III, v, 1 − 5

Every speech. . . consists at once of that which is expressed and that which expresses, that is to say of matter and words. Skill in speaking is perfected by nature, art and practice, to which some add a fourth department, namely imitation, which I however prefer to include under art. There are also three aims which the orator must always have in view; he must instruct, move and charm his hearers. This is a clearer division than that made by those who divide the task of oratory into that which relates to

Reprinted by permission of the publishers and THE LOEB CLASSICAL LIBRARY from H. E. Butler, Translator, Quintilian, *Institutio Oratoria*, Cambridge, Mass.: Harvard University Press.

[1] Lester Thonssen and A. Craig Baird, *Speech Criticism* (New York, 1948), p. 93.

[2] Harry Caplan, translator, *Rhetorica ad Herennium* (Cambridge, Mass., 1954), p. 18, note.

things and that which concerns the emotions, since both of these will not always be present in the subjects which we shall have to treat. For some themes are far from calling for any appeal to the emotions, which, although room cannot always be found for them, produce a most powerful effect wherever they do succeed in forcing their way. The best authorities hold that there are some things in oratory which require proof and others which do not, a view with which I agree. Some on the other hand, as for instance Celsus, think that the orator will not speak on any subject unless there is some question involved in it; but the majority of writers on rhetoric are against him, as is also the threefold division of oratory, unless indeed to praise what is allowed to be honourable and to denounce what is admittedly disgraceful are no part of an orator's duty.

It is, however, universally agreed that all questions must be concerned either with something that is written or something that is not. Those concerned with what is written are questions of law, those which concern what is not written are questions of fact. Hermagoras calls the latter *rational* questions, the former *legal* questions, for so we may translate λογικόν and νομικόν· Those who hold that every question concerns either things or words, mean much the same. . . .

III, vi, 80 – 104

There are three things on which enquiry is made in every case: we ask *whether a thing is, what it is,* and *of what kind it is.* Nature herself imposes this upon us. For first of all there must be some subject for the question, since we cannot possibly determine *what a thing is,* or *of what kind it is,* until we have first ascertained *whether it is,* and therefore the first question raised is *whether it is.* But even when it is clear that a thing *is,* it is not immediately obvious *what it is.* And when we have decided what it is, there remains the question of its *quality.* These three points once ascertained, there is no further question to ask. These heads cover both *definite* and *indefinite questions.* One or more of them is discussed in every demonstrative, deliberative or forensic theme. These heads again cover all cases in the courts, whether we regard them from the point of view of *rational* or *legal questions.* For no legal problem can be settled save by the aid of *definition, quality* and *conjecture.* Those, however, who are engaged in instructing the ignorant will find it useful at first to adopt a slightly less rigid method: the road will not be absolutely straight to begin with, but it will be more open and will provide easier going. I would have them therefore learn above all things that there are four different methods which may be employed in every case, and he who is going to plead should study them as first essentials. For, to begin with the defendant, far the strongest method of self-defence is, if possible, to deny the charge. The second best is when it is possible to reply that the particular act with which you are charged was never committed. The third and most honourable is to maintain that the act was justifiable. If none of these lines of defence are feasible, there remains the last and only hope of safety: if it is impossible either to deny the charge or justify the act, we must evade the charge with the aid of some point of law, making it appear that the action has been brought against us illegally. Hence arise those questions of *legal action* or *competence*. For there are some things, which, although not laudable in themselves, are yet permitted by law; witness the passage in the Twelve Tables authorising creditors to divide up a debtor's body amongst themselves, a law which is repudiated by public custom. There are also certain things which although equitable are prohibited by law (witness the restrictions placed on testamentary disposition). The accuser likewise has four things which he must keep in mind: he must prove that something was done, that a particular act was done, that it was wrongly done, and that he brings his charge according to law. Thus every cause will turn on the same sorts of questions, though the parts of plaintiff and defendant will sometimes be interchanged: for instance in the case of a claim for a reward, it will be the plaintiff's task to show that what was done was right.

These four schemes or forms of action which I then called *general bases* fall into two classes as I have shown, namely, the *rational* and the *legal.* The *rational* is the simpler, as it involves nothing more than the consideration of the nature of things. In this connection, therefore, a mere mention of *conjecture, definition* and *quality* will suffice. *Legal questions* necessarily have a larger number of species, since there are many laws and a variety of forms. In the case of one law we rely on the letter, in others on the spirit. Some laws we force to serve our turn, when we can find no law to support our case, others we compare with one another, and on others we put some novel interpretation. Thus from these three *bases* we get three resemblances of *bases*: sometimes simple, sometimes complex, but all having a character of their own, as, for instance, when questions of the *letter of the law* and its *intention* are involved, for these clearly come under *conjecture* or *quality*; or again where the syllogism is involved, for this is specially connected with *quality*; or where contradictory laws are involved, for these are on the same footing as the *letter of the law and intention*; or yet again in cases of *ambiguity,* which is always resolved by *conjecture.* *Definition* also belongs to both classes of question, namely those concerned with the consideration of *facts* and those concerned with the *letter of the law.* All these questions, although they come under the three *bases,* yet since, as I have mentioned, they have certain characteristic features of their own, require to be pointed out to learners; and we must allow them to be called *legal bases or questions* or *minor heads*, as long as it is clearly understood that none of them involve any other *questions* than the three I have mentioned. As regards questions of *quantity, number, relation*, and, as some have thought, *comparison,* the case is different. For these have no connexion with the complexities of the law, but are concerned with reason only. Consequently they must always be regarded as coming under *conjecture* or *quality,* as, for instance, when we ask with what purpose, or at what time, or place something was done.

But I will speak of individual questions when I come to handle the rules for *division*. This much is agreed to by all writers, that one *cause* possesses one *basis,* but that as regards secondary questions related to the main issue of the trial, there may frequently be a number in one single cause. I also think there is at times some doubt as to which *basis* should be adopted, when many different lines of defence are brought to meet a single charge; and, just as in regard to the complexion to be given to the statement of the facts of the case, that complexion is said to be the best which the speaker can best maintain, so in the present connexion I may say that the best *basis* to choose is that which will permit the orator to develop a maximum of force. It is for this reason that we find Cicero and Brutus taking up different lines in defence of Milo. Cicero says that Clodius was justifiably killed because he sought to waylay Milo, but that Milo had not designed to kill him; while Brutus, who wrote his speech merely as a rhetorical exercise, also exults that Milo has killed a bad citizen. In complicated causes, however, two or three *bases* may be found, or different *bases*: for instance a man may plead that he did not do one thing, and that he was justified in doing another, or to take another similar class of case, a man may deny two of the charges. The same thing occurs when there is a question about some one thing which is claimed by a number of persons who may all of them rely on the same kind of plea (for instance, on the right of the next of kin), or may put in different claims, one urging that the property was left him by will, another that he is next of kin. Now whenever a different defence has to be made against different claimants, there must be different *bases*, as for example the well-known controversial theme: "Wills that are made in accordance with law shall be valid. When parents die intestate, their children shall be the heirs. A disinherited son shall receive none of his father's property. A bastard, if born before a legitimate son, shall be treated as legitimate, but if born after a legitimate son shall be treated merely as a citizen. It shall be lawful to give a son in adoption. Every son given in adoption shall have the right to re-enter his own family if his natural father has died childless. A father of two legitimate sons gave one in adoption, disinherited the other, and acknowledged a bastard, who was born to him later. Finally after making the disinherited son his heir he died. All three sons lay claim to the property." *Nothus* is the Greek word for a bastard; Latin, as Cato emphasized in one of his speeches, has no word of its own and therefore borrows the foreign term. But I am straying from the point. The son who was made heir by the will finds his way barred by the law "A disinherited son shall receive none of his father's property." The *basis* is one resting on the *letter of the law* and *intention*, and the problem is whether he can inherit by any means at all? can he do so in accordance with the intention of his father? or in virtue of the fact that he was made heir by the will? The problem confronting the bastard is twofold, since he was born after the two legitimate sons and was not born before a legitimate son. The first problem involves a syllogism: are those sons who have been cast out from their own family to be regarded as though they had never been born? The second is concerned with the letter of the law and intention. For it is admitted that he was not born before any legitimate son, but he will defend his claim by appealing to the intention of the law, which he will maintain to imply that the bastard, born when there was no legitimate son in the family, should rank as legitimate. He will dismiss the letter of the law, pointing out that in any case the position of a bastard is not prejudiced by the fact that no legitimate son was born after him, and arguing as follows: — "Suppose that the only son is a bastard, what will his position be? Merely that of a citizen? and yet he was not born after any legitimate son. Or will he rank as a son in all respects? But he was not born before the legitimate sons. As it is impossible to stand by the letter of the law we must stand by its intentions." It need disturb no one that one law should originate two *bases*. The law is twofold, and therefore has the force of two laws. To the son who desires to re-enter the family, the disinherited's first reply is, "Even though you are allowed to re-enter the family, I am still the heir." The *basis* will be the same as in the claim put forward by the disinherited son, since the question at issue is whether a disinherited son can inherit. Both the disinherited and the bastard will object, "You cannot re-enter the family, for our father did not die childless." But in this connexion each will rely on his own particular question. For the disinherited son will say that even a disinherited man does not cease to be a son, and will derive an argument from that very law which denies his claim to the inheritance; namely that it was unnecessary for a disinherited son to be excluded from possession of his father's property if he had ceased to be one of the family; but now, since in virtue of his rights as son he would have been his father's heir if he had died intestate, the law is brought to bar his claim; and yet the law does not deprive him of his position as son, but only of his position as heir. Here the *basis* is *definitive*, as turning on the definition of a son. Again the bastard in his turn will urge that his father did not die childless, employing the same arguments that he had used in putting forward his claim that he ranked as a son; unless indeed he too has recourse to definition, and raises the question whether even bastards are not sons. Thus in one case we shall have either two special *legal bases*, namely the *letter of the law* and *intention*, with the *syllogism* and also *definition*, or those three which are really the only *bases* strictly so called, *conjecture* as regards the *letter of the law and intention, quality* in the *syllogism,* and *definition*, which needs no explanation.

Further every kind of case will contain a *cause,* a *point for the decision of the judge,* and a *central argument.* For nothing can be said which does not contain a reason, something to which the decision of the judge is directed, and finally something which, more than aught else, contains the substance of the matter at issue.

ARISTOTLE: THE RHETORIC

Translated by Richard Claverhouse Jebb

In the following selection, Aristotle considers the forces of ethos *and* pathos. Ethos *stems from the speaker's character as perceived by the audience;* pathos *stems from the emotional forces generated when the speaker adapts to and agitates audience predispositions. Following his definitions of these "psychological" proofs, Aristotle analyzes the various emotions which the speaker must exhibit or induce. We present here the section on friendship and hatred. Note that the discussion of these emotions is important at many stages of the process of discerning the available means of persuasion. The speaker must be able to convince his audience of his friendship for them, and to induce their friendship for him. He may need to create hatred for an opponent, or friendship for his client. Or, seen from another perspective, he may need to convince a group of jurors that a defendent he is prosecuting might have been motivated in an alleged crime by hatred. Or, he might set forth friendship as a good toward which his policies will lead the audience. In all of these ways, a knowledge of human nature can guide the rhetor's process of discovery, when analyzing both the audience and the case at hand.*

II, i, 1 (1377a) — 9 (1378a)

This, then, is an account of the premises to be used in exhorting or dissuading, praising or blaming, accusing or defending, and of the popular notions and propositions available for producing belief in each case; since the enthymemes concern these and come from these, if we take each branch of Rhetoric by itself. And since Rhetoric has a view to judgment,

Reprinted from Richard Claverhouse Jebb, translator, Aristotle, *The Rhetoric of Aristotle,* Cambridge, England: At the University Press.

for, both in debates and in lawsuits, there is judging, the speaker must not only see that the speech shall prove its point, or persuade, but must also develop a certain character in himself and in the judge, as it matters much for persuasiveness, — most of all in debate, but secondarily in lawsuits too — that the speaker should appear a certain sort of person, and that the judges should conceive him to be disposed towards them in a certain way; — further, that the judges themselves should be in a certain mood. The apparent character of the speaker tells more in debate, the mood of the hearer in lawsuits. Men have not the same views when they are friendly and when they hate, when they are angry or placid, but views either wholly different or different in a large measure. The friendly man regards the object of his judgment as either no wrong-doer or a doer of small wrong: the hater takes the opposite view. The man who desires and is hopeful (supposing the thing in prospect to be pleasant), thinks that it will be, and that it will be good; the man who is indifferent, or who feels a difficulty, thinks the opposite.

The speakers themselves are made trustworthy by three things; for there are three things, besides demonstrations, which make us believe. These are, intelligence, virtue and good-will. Men are false in their statements, and their counsels, from all or one of the following causes. Either through folly, they have not right opinions; or having right opinions, they say through knavery what they do not think; or they are sensible and honest, but not well-disposed; whence they may happen not to advise the best course, although they see it. Besides these cases there is no other. It follows that the man who is thought to have all the three qualities must win the belief of the hearers. Now the means of appearing intelligent and good are to be got from the analysis of the virtues; for the same means will enable one to give such a character either to another person or to himself. Good-will and friendliness have now to be discussed under the head of the Affections. The Affections are those things, being attended by pleasure or pain, by which men are altered in regard to their judgments; — as anger, pity, fear, and the like, with their opposites. In respect to each, three points are to be determined; in respect to anger, for instance, in what state men are prone to anger, — with whom they are wont to be angry, — and at what things: for, supposing we knew one or two, but not all, of these things, it would be impossible to excite anger; and so in the other cases. As then, in the former part of the subject, we sketched the available propositions, so we propose to do here also, applying an analysis of the same kind. . .

II, iv, 1 (1381a) – 32 (1382a)

Let us now state the objects and the causes of men's friendship and hatred, — after first defining friendship and friendliness. Friendship, then, may be defined as wishing for a person those things which one thinks good, – wishing them for his sake, not for one's own, – and tending, in so far as one can, to effect these things. A friend is one who likes, and is liked in return; and men think themselves friends, when they think that they are thus related to each other. This granted, it follows that a friend is one who rejoices in our good and grieves for our pain, and this purely on our account. All men rejoice at the occurrence of what they wish, and grieve at the reverse; so that the feelings of pain or pleasure point to the wish. They are friends, then, for whom the same things are good and evil, and who are friends and enemies of the same people; for they must needs have the same wishes; and so, one who wishes for another just what he wishes for himself, appears to be that person's friend. Men like, too, those who have done good to themselves, or to those for whom they care; – whether such benefits were great, or zealously done, or done at such or such a moment, and for the recipient's sake.

We like also those who, we think, wish to do us good. We like our friends' friends, and those who like the persons whom we like; and those who are liked by those that are liked by ourselves; and those who are the enemies of our enemies – who hate the persons whom we hate – who are hated by the objects of our hatred; for all these consider the same things to be good as ourselves, so that they must wish our good, – and this, we saw, is the part of a friend. Also, we like those who are apt to benefit us pecuniarily, or in regard to the protection of life; hence we honour the generous and brave, and the just. Such we conceive to be those, who do not live on others; and such are they, who live by labour, – chief among these, agriculturists, and chief among the agriculturists, the small farmers. We like temperate men, too, because they are not unjust; and men who are no meddlers, for the same reason. We like those whose friends we wish to be, if they show themselves willing; and such are the morally good and those held in repute either by all or by the best or by those whom we ourselves admire, or by those who admire us. Again, we like those who are pleasant to live with and to pass one's time with – such being the good-tempered, – those who do not tend to expose our mistakes, – those who are not disputatious or quarrelsome; for all such are combative, and combatants seem to wish against us. Men are liked, too, who have tact in giving and taking badinage; for the good-humoured butt, as well as the judicious joker, has the same drift as his neighbour. We like those who praise the good things which we possess, especially those which we fear we do *not* possess. We like those who are cleanly in their person, their dress, their whole life. We like those who do not reproach us with our mistakes, or their benefits; for both tend to put us in the wrong. We like those who do not bear a grudge, who do not hoard their grievances, but are ready to make up a quarrel; for we think that they will be to ourselves such as we conceive that they are to the rest of the world. We like those who are not evil-speakers, and who know, not the bad, but the good, in their neighbours and in us; for this is the part of the good man. We like those who do not strain against the angry or the eager; for such are combative. We like those who have some earnest feeling towards us, as admiration, a belief that we are good, or a delight in us; especially when this is felt about the things, for which we ourselves most wish to be admired, or to be thought good or pleasant. We like those who resemble us and have the same pursuits, provided that they do not thwart us, and that our livelihood does not come from the same source; for then it becomes a case of 'potter against potter'. We like those who desire the same things, — provided it is possible for us to enjoy them at the same time: if not, the last case is repeated. We like those to whom we are so related that, while we do not despise them, we do not feel shame with them as to appearances; and those before whom we *are* ashamed of the things really shameful. We like those with whom we vie, and those by whom we wish to be emulated, not envied; to these we are, or wish to be, friends. We like those, with whom we work for good, supposing that we ourselves are not to have greater ills. We are friends to those who show kindness equally to the absent and to the present; hence all men like those who are thus true to the dead. And, generally, we like those who are strongly attached to their friends, and do not leave them in the lurch: for, of good men, we most like those who are good at liking. We like those, too, who do not sham to us; and such are they who speak even of their own weaknesses. For, as has been said, we feel no shame with friends about appearances. If, then, one who feels such shame is not a friend, he who does not feel it, resembles a friend. We like those who are not formidable, and with whom we feel confidence; for no one likes him whom he dreads. The several species of friendship are — Companionship, Intimacy, Kinship and the rest. Among the *things* which cause friendship are graciousness — doing a thing unasked — and doing without publishing it; for so it seems to be done simply for our own sake.

Enmity and Hatred of course may be illustrated by the opposite considerations. Among things which cause Enmity are anger — spiting — slander. Now anger arises from things which concern ourselves; but Enmity may exist without this personal concernment; since, if we conceive a person to be such or such, we hate him. Anger is always concerned with particulars, as with Kallias or Sokrates; Hatred is directed also against classes; for everyone hates a thief and an informer. Anger can be cured by time; Hatred is incurable. Anger is an aiming at pain; Hatred, at evil; for the angry man wishes the other to feel; the hater does not care. Now, painful things are all to be felt; but the worst evils are the least to be felt, — Injustice and Folly; for the presence of the vice gives no pain. Anger is attended with pain, hatred is not; for the angry man is pained, but not the hater. The angry man is capable of pity, when much has happened, — the hater, never; for the one wishes the object of his wrath to suffer in return, — the other wishes him not to be.

Hence, then, clearly we can prove that people *are* enemies or friends; or, if they are not, make them such; or, if they pretend, refute them; or, if they contend with us through anger or through enmity, bring them into whichever mood we choose.

ARISTOTLE: THE RHETORIC

Translated by Richard Claverhouse Jebb

*One of Aristotle's most important contributions to rhetorical theory was
his development of the role of reason in public discourse, chiefly through
the concepts of the enthymeme and the topics. At least three different
kinds of topics are described in* The Rhetoric. *Special topics are derived
from the subject matter of various fields of knowledge, such as politics or
physics; the universal, common, or general topics are "commonplaces" in
which arguments suitable to any subject matter may be located, such as
possibility and impossibility, the past, the future, and the greatness or
smallness of things; finally, there are special* forms *or lines of argument
which the speaker can use when constructing enthymemes. The
enthymeme, or rhetorical syllogism, is a form of deductive reasoning
adapted to the unique conditions of public discourse – the uncertainty of
facts and premises relating to public issues, the fallibility of general
audiences, and the situational difficulties attending the act of oral
communication. The following selection, from Book II of* The Rhetoric,
*contains Aristotle's description of universal topics and elementary lines of
argument, as well as his account of induction (example) and deduction
(enthymeme) in rhetoric. Together, the selection provides a good
introduction to* logos: *the rational process by which speakers conform
their goals to the facts of the external world and to an audience's view of
that world.*

II, xviii, 1 (1392) – xxiii, 30 (1400b)

The use of all persuasive speech has a view to a decision; for there is no
further need of speaking about things which we know and have decided.

Reprinted from Richard Claverhouse Jebb, translator, Aristotle, *The Rhetoric of
Aristotle,* Cambridge, England: At the University Press.

154

This is no less the case when the speaker aims at encouraging or dissuading one man only, as those who seek to admonish or to persuade may do. *That one* man is no less a judge; for he, whom we have to persuade, is, speaking generally, a judge. And it is so equally, whether we are speaking against a real adversary or against an imaginary case; since here we have to use our speech for the overthrow of arguments opposed to us, and to these arguments we address ourselves as to a living opponent. The same thing holds good of epideictic speaking: the speech is framed with reference to the spectator considered as a judge. As a rule, however, he alone is a judge in the simple sense, who decides a question in some issue of civil life; for there is a question of fact both in regard to the matter of a lawsuit and in regard to the subject of a debate. The characters of the several polities have already been treated under the head of Deliberative Rhetoric. We may be considered, then, to have defined the way and the means of making our speech reflect a character.

And since each species of Rhetoric has, as we saw, a distinct end; since, in regard to all of these, we have now got those popular principles and premisses from which men take their proofs in debate, in display, in forensic argument; since, further, we have defined the available means of making speeches ethical; – it remains for us to discuss the *general* appliances. All men are compelled in speaking to apply the topic of Possible and Impossible; and to try to show, either that a thing will be, or that it has been. Further, the topic of Size is common to all speeches; all men use depreciation and amplification in debate, in praising or blaming, in accusing or defending. When these topics have been defined, we must try to say what we have to say of Enthymemes generally, and of Examples, in order that, by the addition of what is still wanting, we may fulfil our original purpose. Of the general commonplaces, that of Amplification is, as has been said, most popular to Epideictic speaking; that of the Past to Forensic, for the decision concerns past facts; that of the Possible and Future to Deliberative.

First, then, let us speak of the Possible and Impossible. Now if, of two opposites, one can exist or come into existence, the other also would seem to be possible. For instance, if a man can be healed, he can also fall sick: for the potentiality of opposites, as such, is one. And, if of two like things one is possible, the other is. And, if the harder is possible, the easier is so. And, if the good and beautiful form of a thing can come into being, the thing generally can come into being; for it is harder for a fine house, than for a house, to exist. And, if there can be a beginning of anything, there can be an end; for no impossibility comes or begins to come into existence. Thus it neither happens, nor could begin to happen, that the diagonal of a square is commensurate with its side. And, if the end of a thing is possible, the beginning is so; for all things come from a beginning.

And, if that which is later in existing, or in being born, can arise, that which is earlier can; for instance, if a man can come into existence, a boy can; for boyhood is the earlier stage – and, if a boy, then a man; for boyhood is the beginning. Those things, too, are possible, of which the love or desire is natural; for no one, as a rule, is enamoured or desirous of impossibilities. Those things, of which there are sciences and arts, can exist and come into existence. Things are possible, again, which have the beginning of birth in things which we can compel or persuade; such being those powers of which we are the superiors or the masters or the friends. When the parts of a thing are possible, the whole is so; and, when the whole is possible, the parts are so – as a rule. Thus, if the various parts of a shoe, the toe-piece, the strap, the side-leather, are possible, shoes are possible; and, if shoes are possible, the toe-piece, the strap, and the side-leather are possible, and, if the genus belongs to the number of possibilities, the species does; and *vice versa*; thus, if a sailing vessel can exist, a trireme can, and *vice versa* of two things naturally interdependent, one is possible, the other is so; as, if double is possible, half is so; and *vice versa*. And, if a thing can come to pass without art of preparation, much more can it do so with them; whence Agathon's saying –

'Some things we have to effect by art; others come to us by necessity or chance.'

If a thing is possible for the worse and weaker and more foolish, it is more so for their opposites; as Isokrates said that it was strange if Euthynos had learned this, and *he* should not be able to discover it. The topics for Impossibility are of course to be found in the opposites of these.

The question of Past Fact may be treated on these principles. First, if the less natural thing has happened, the more natural thing must have happened too. Again, if the usually later thing has happened, the earlier has happened; for instance, if he has forgotten a thing, he also learned it once. If he could and would, he has done the thing: for all men do what they would and can; there is nothing in the way. Again, if there was no external hindrance and he was angry; or, if he had the power and the *desire*, he has done the thing; for, as a rule, men do, if they can, the things for which they have an appetite, – bad men, through intemperance; good men, because they desire good things, Or, if he was going to do the thing, (you can say that he has done it); for it is *probable* that one, who intended an action, did it. A thing *has* happened, if those things have happened, of which it was the natural sequel or motive; thus, if it has lightened, it has thundered; – if he attempted the action, he did it. Or, if, again, those things have happened, to which it was the natural antecedent or means; thus, if it has thundered, it has lightened; or if he *did* the act, he made the attempt. In all such cases, the conclusion may be either necessarily or only generally true. The topics for the *negation* of Past Fact will obviously be found in the opposites of these.

The way to treat Fact Future appears from the same consideration. That *will* be, for which there is the power and the wish; or, which desire or anger, coupled with power, prompts. Hence, too, if there is the impulse or the intention to do a thing, it *will* be; for, as a rule, things which are about to happen, come to pass rather than things which are *not* so. A thing *will* be, if its natural antecedents have already come to pass; thus, if it is cloudy, it is likely to rain. Or, if the means to an end have come into being, the end is likely to be; thus, if there is a foundation-stone, there will be a house.

As to the Greatness and Smallness of things, greater and less, and generally great things and small, all is clear from what has been already said by us. Under the Deliberative brand of Rhetoric we have discussed the relative greatness of goods, and the abstract greater and less. Now, as in each kind of speaking the proposed end is a good, — namely, the Expedient, the Honourable, or the Just, — it follows that all speakers must derive their topics of amplification from these goods. It is waste of words to inquire further about *abstract* greatness and pre-eminence; for particulars are more momentous in practice than universals.

Enough, then, of the Possible and Impossible; Fact Past, Fact Future, the negation of these; and further of the Greatness or Smallness of things.

It remains to speak of the Proofs common to all Rhetoric, as we have spoken of their particular elements. The common proofs are generically two — Example and Enthymeme; for the maxim is part of an Enthymeme. First then, we will speak of the Example; for the Example is like Induction, and Induction is the primary process.

There are two kinds of Example. One kind consists in the use of historical parallel, another in the use of artificial parallel. Artificial parallel takes the form either of comparison or of fable, like AEsop's or the Libyan fables. It would be using historical parallel, if one were to say that we must arm against the Great King and not let him subdue Egypt; for, in a former instance, Darius did not come over till he had got Egypt, but, having got it, he came; and Xerxes, again, did not attack us till he had got it, but, having got it, he came; and so this man[1] too, if he gets it, will come over — therefore he must not be allowed to get it. 'Comparison' means such illustrations as those of Sokrates — saying, for instance, that magistrates ought not to be appointed by lot, for it is like appointing athletes, not by athletic power, but by lot, or as if the appointment of a pilot from among the crew were to go, not by skill, but by lot. Instances of fables are that of Stesichoros about Phalaris, and that of AEsop on behalf of the demagogue.

[1] Artaxerxes III (Ochus), 361-338 [B.C.]

When the people of Himera had made Phalaris their military dictator, and were going to give him a body-guard, Stesichoros told them, among other things, a story about a horse, who had a meadow all to himself, until a deer came and began to spoil his pasturage. When the horse, wishing to be avenged on the deer, asked a certain man whether this could be done with his help, 'Yes,' said the man, 'if you are bitted, and I mount you armed with javelins.' The horse agreed, and was mounted; but, instead of being avenged, he was himself enslaved to the man. 'So in your own case,' said Stesichoros − 'take care that, in your desire to chastise your enemies, you do not fare like the horse. You have the bit in your mouths already; if you give him a guard, and allow him to mount, you will be finally enslaved to Phalaris.'

AEsop, defending at Samos a demagogue who was being tried for his life, said that a fox, trying to cross a river, was once swept into a crevice in the rocks, and, not being able to get out, suffered miseries for a long while, being covered with dog-fleas. A hedgehog in his wanderings seeing the fox, took pity on her, and asked whether he should remove the fleas. The fox objected; and, on the hedgehog asking why, said − 'These are sated, and draw little blood; but if you take them away, others will come with an appetite, and drain what blood is left to me.' 'Now you, too, Samians, will take no more hurt from this man; for he is rich; but if you kill him, others will come poor, and will fritter and waste your public wealth.'

Fables suit public speaking, and have this advantage, that, while it is hard to find historical parallels, it is comparatively easy to find fables in point; in fact, one must contrive them, as one contrives comparisons, if one can discover an analogy, which literary knowledge will make easy. The fabulous parallels are more easy to provide, but the historical parallels are more useful for the purpose of debate; since, as a rule, the future is like the past.

When we have no Enthymemes, Examples must be used as demonstrations (for they are the means of proof); when we have, as testimonies; − using them as epilogue to the Enthymemes: for, when the Examples are put *first,* they seem like an induction, but induction is not appropriate to Rhetoric except in a few cases; whereas, if they are *subjoined,* they seem like testimonies; and, in all cases, a witness is persuasive. Hence, if you put the Examples first, you must use many; if at the end, even one is enough; for even one witness is useful, if good.

It has now been explained how many kinds of example there are, and how and when they should be used. As to the citation of Maxims; when a maxim has been defined, it will best appear, in regard to what subjects, and at what times, and by whom, maxims may fitly be used in speaking. A maxim is a statement, not about a particular fact, as about the character of Iphikrates, but general; not about all things, as about 'straight' being the opposite of 'curved,' but about those things which are the objects of action, and which it is desirable or undesirable to do. So, since the Enthymeme is that syllogism which concerns such things, maxims may be said to be the conclusions and the premisses of Enthymemes without the syllogism: — as

'No man of good sense should have his children brought up over-wise':

this is a maxim; when the cause, the *wherefore,* is added, it is the complete enthymeme, as: —

'for, besides the general charge of sloth, they reap jealous dislike from their fellow citizens.'

Again: —

'There is no man who is wholly prosperous': —

and

'There is no man who is free' —

are maxims; but, when placed beside the sequel, they are enthymemes:

'For he is the slave of money or of chance.'

If, then, a maxim is what has been said, it follows that there are four kinds of maxims. The maxim either will, or will not, have a reason subjoined. Those maxims which need demonstration are such as state something unexpected or disputed; those which state nothing unexpected, have no reason added. Of the latter class, some will not need the added reason, because they are familiar beforehand; as —

'It is an excellent thing for a man to be healthy, to *our* thinking' —

for most people think so. Others do not need the added reason, because they are plain at the first glance, as —

'A lover is ever kindly.'

Of the maxims which have a reason added, some are imperfect enthymemes; as —

'No man of good sense,' &c.;

others are in the nature, but not in the form, of enthymemes; and these are the most popular. They are those in which the reason for the statement is *implied*; as

'Do not, being a mortal, cherish immortal anger.'

To say that it is not right to cherish anger is a maxim: the added words, 'being a mortal,' are the wherefore. Similarly —

'The mortal should have mortal, not immortal thoughts.'

It is clear, then, from what has been said, how many kinds of maxim there are, and in what case each kind is suitable. When the statement is a disputed, or a startling one, the maxim should have its reason added. We may put this reason first, making a maxim of the conclusion: — as — 'For my part, as it is not desirable to be envied or to be inactive, I hold that it is better not to be educated.' Or this maxim may be stated first, and the former clause added. When the statement is not startling, but merely not self-evident, the reason ought to be added in as terse a form as possible. Laconic or enigmatic sayings also suit cases of this kind: as the saying of Stesichoros to the Locrians, that it is better not to be insolent, lest the grasshoppers should have to sing on the ground. The use of maxims is suitable to elderly men, and in regard to subjects with which one is conversant; for sententiousness, like story-telling, is unbecoming in a younger man; while, in regard to subjects with which one is not conversant, it is stupid and shows want of culture. It is token enough of this that rustics are the greatest coiners of maxims, and the readiest to set forth their views.

Spurious generalization is most convenient in expressing bitter complaint or indignation; and here, either at the outset, or when the fact has been proved. Even trite and common maxims should be used, if they can serve; since, just because they are common, they seem right, on the supposition that all the world is agreed about them. Thus, one who calls his men into danger before they have sacrificed, may quote —

'The one best omen is to fight for one's country';

or, if he calls on them to face danger when they are the weaker —

'The war-god is for both sides.'

Or, if he is urging them to destroy their enemies' children, though these are doing no wrong —

'He is a fool, who slays the father, and leaves the children.'

Some proverbs, again, are also maxims; — as the proverb 'an Attic neighbour.' [1] Our maxims ought sometimes to controvert sayings which have become public property (as 'know thyself,' — 'Do nothing excessively'), if thus our character will appear better, or if our maxim expresses passion. It would express passion if, for instance, an angry speaker were to say — 'The saying that it is well to "know thyself," is a lie. If this man had known himself, he would never have presumed to be general.' This would make our character more attractive — 'We ought not, as some say, to love in the expectation of hating — rather we should hate in the expectation of loving.' One should make one's moral predilections plain by the very statement of the maxim; or, failing this, one should add one's reason [2], — as by saying — 'We ought to love, not, as some say, but in the expectation of loving always; for the other sort of love is insidious.' Else thus: — 'But I do not like the saying; for the genuine friend ought to love in the expectation of loving always.' 'Nor do I like the saying, Do nothing excessively. Bad men should be hated excessively.'

One great help, which maxims lend in speaking, arises from the vulgarity [3] of the hearers. They are delighted when a general statement of the speaker hits those opinions which they hold in a particular case. My meaning will be clearer when put as follows — and at the same time we shall be set on the track of the best maxims. A maxim is, as has been said, a general statement, and men are pleased when a sentiment, which they already entertain on special grounds, is stated in general terms. Thus, if a man is afflicted with bad neighbours or bad children, he will give ear to the statement, that nothing is so trying as neighbourhood, nothing so foolish as begetting children. Hence, we must guess what sort of prepossessions they have, and how they came by them; then we must express, in general terms, these views on these subjects. This, then, is one of the advantages of using maxims. It has another still greater: — it gives a moral character to our speech. Speeches have a moral character, when they show a moral purpose. All maxims do effect this, since the man who uses a maxim makes a general declaration of his moral predilections; so that, if the maxims are good, they give the appearance of a good character to him who uses them.

In regard to maxims, then — their nature, their kinds, the way to use them and the advantages they yield — this account may suffice.

Let us now speak of Enthymemes — first, generally, of the way to look for them — then, of their topics; for these two parts of the subject are distinct.

It has been said already that the enthymeme is a syllogism, and in

[1] Quoted by Zenobios II 28. The Corinthian envoy in Thucydides (I 70) describes it as the national character of the Athenians 'neither to remain in peace themselves, nor to suffer others to do so.'

[2] *i.e.* you must add the reason *why you disapprove of the received maxim;* xiii 4.

[3] *i.e.* their love of the commonplace.

what sense it is a syllogism, and how it differs from the dialectical syllogism. We must not draw conclusions from far back, and we must not take everything in. If we do the former, the length of the chain causes perplexity; if the latter, our statement of what is obvious is mere garrulity. This is the reason why the uneducated are more persuasive than the educated for popular audiences, — as the poets say of the uneducated, that 'they have a finer charm for the ear of the crowd.' Educated men state general principles and draw general conclusions; uneducated men draw conclusions, which lie close at hand, from facts within their own experience. We must not argue, then, from all opinions, but from those of the sort defined, — as from those of the judges, or those of persons in whom they believe; it must be clear, too, that these opinions are universally or generally entertained. And we must reason, not exclusively from necessary premises, but also from merely probable premises.

Now, first of all, we must grasp the necessity of knowing all or some of the special facts belonging to the subject on which we are to speak and reason, — whether the subject of the reasoning be political or of any other kind; for, if you know none of these facts, you will have no premises. How, for instance, could we advise the Athenians on the question of going to war, unless we knew the nature of their power, — whether it is a naval force or a land force, or both, — and its amount; then, what their revenues are, and who are their friends or enemies; further, what wars they have waged, and how; and so forth. How could we praise them, if we were not prepared with the seafight at Salamis, or the battle of Marathon, or the services rendered to the Herakleidae, and such things; — since all men found their praise on the glories, real or seeming, of its object? Similarly, they rest their censure on the opposite things, considering what dishonour attaches or seems to attach to the censured — as that they brought the Greeks under the yoke, or enslaved those who had bravely fought with them against the barbarians — the men of AEgina and Potidaea — and so on; or, if there has been any like mistake on their part. In the same way, accusers and defenders have in their view the special conditions of the case. It makes no difference whether our subject is the Athenians or the Lacedaemonians, or a man or a god. Suppose we are advising Achilles, praising or blaming, accusing or defending him; we must take those things which are, or seem, peculiar to him, in order that our praise or blame may be set out from his particular honours or dishonours, our accusation or defence from his injustice or justice, our advice from his interests or dangers. And so in regard to any subject whatever. Thus, the question whether Justice is or is not a good must be argued from the attributes of Justice and of the Good.

So, since we always effect our proof by these means, whether our reasoning process is comparatively strict, or rather lax; since, that is, we do not take our premises from things in general, but from things peculiar to our special subject — and it is plain that the properly logical proof can be wrought in no other way — it is plainly necessary, as we showed in the *Topics,* to have (first of all) a selection of premises about the possible and the most convenient subjects; secondly, to deal with sudden contingencies on the same plan — that is, by referring, not to indefinite generalities, but to the special subject-matter of our speech, — bringing into the sphere of our argument as many facts as possible, which have the closest bearing on the subject; for, the larger our knowledge of its particular conditions, the easier will be the proof; and, the closer we keep to the subject, the more appropriate and the less general will be our topics. By 'general' topics I mean, for instance, praising Achilles for being a man and a hero and having gone against Troy — these things being true of many other persons, so that such a speaker praises Achilles no more than he praises Diomede. By 'special' topics I mean things which are attributes of Achilles and of no one else — as having slain Hektor, bravest of the Trojans, and Kyknos, the invulnerable, who hindered all the Greeks from landing — or because he was the youngest man of the expedition, and bound by no oath — and so forth.

This, then, is one principle, and the first, on which our enthymemes are to be chosen — in reference to their special materials. Now let us speak of their elementary forms. By the 'elementary form' of an enthymeme I mean the *place* (or class) to which it belongs. There are two kinds of enthymemes. One kind is Demonstrative (affirmatively or negatively); the other kind is Refutative: — the distinction being the same as in Dialectic between Refutation and Syllogism. The Demonstrative Syllogism consists in drawing a conclusion from consistent propositions; the Refutative, in drawing a conclusion from conflicting propositions. Now it may be said that we are in possession of our topics in regard to the several special subjects, which are useful or necessary. We have chosen our propositions in regard to each; so that we have already ascertained the topics from which enthymemes are to be drawn about Good or Evil, Honourable or Shameful, Just or Unjust; likewise about characters, feelings, moral states. But further, and from another point of view, let us get commonplaces for enthymemes in general. We will point out, side by side, the Refutative and the Demonstrative topics; and the topics of what appear to be enthymemes, but are not so, since they are not syllogisms. When these matters have been explained, we will determine the several modes of destroying or attacking enthymemes.

I. One topic of Demonstrative Enthymemes is from opposites. We must see whether the opposite holds good of the opposite, for the purpose of refutation, if the argument is not on our side; — or, for the purpose of establishing the point, if it is so. Thus 'It is good to be temperate; for it is harmful to be intemperate.' Or, to take the instance in the *Messêniakos* — 'If war is the cause of the present evils, we must correct them by means of peace.'

'If it is not just to wax wroth with unwitting wrong-doers, neither are thanks due to him who does a good deed because he must.'

'But, if there is such a thing in the world as specious lying, thou mayest be sure of the opposite — that there is much truth, which does not win men's trust.'

2. Another topic is supplied by the various inflexions of the stem. What can or cannot be said of one form, can or cannot be said of another. Thus — 'The just is not always good; else *justly* would be always *well*; but the fact is that it is not desirable to be put to death justly.'

3. Another topic is from Relative Terms. If it can be said of the one person that he *acted* well or justly, it can be said of the other that he has *suffered* well or justly; or, if the command was right, the execution of the command has been right. Thus Diomedon, the farmer of taxes, said of the taxes — 'If it is no shame for you to sell, it is no shame for us to buy.' And, if 'well' or 'justly' can be predicated of the sufferer, it can be predicated of the doer. This argument, however, may be used fallaciously: for, granting that the man has deserved his fate, it does not follow that he deserved it from you. Hence we ought to consider separately the fitness of the suffering for the sufferer, and the fitness of the deed for the doer, and then turn the argument in whichever way is convenient: — for sometimes there is a discrepancy, and (the justice of the suffering) does not hinder (the deed from being wrong). Thus, in the *Alkmaeon* of Theodektes:

'But did no one in the world hate thy mother?'

Alkmaeon answers —

'Nay, one should take the question in two parts.'

And when Alphesiboea asks 'how?', he rejoins —

'They doomed her to death, but spared my life.'

Take, again, the lawsuit about Demosthenes and the slayers of Nikânor: — since they were judged to have slain him justly, he was held to have deserved his death. Or the case of the man who was killed at Thebes[1] — in which the accused asks that it may be decided whether that man deserved to die, — meaning that it cannot be wrong to have slain a man who deserved death.

4. Another topic is that of Degree; as — 'If the very gods are not all-knowing, men are not likely to be so'; for this means that, if a

---

[1] Euphron, tyrant of Sikyon till about 364 B.C.

condition is not present, where it would be *more* natural, of course it is not present, where it would be *less* so. The inference that a man strikes his neighbours, seeing that he strikes his father, comes from this argument — that, if the rarer thing exists, the more frequent thing exists also; for people strike their fathers more rarely than they strike their neighbours. The argument, then, may stand thus. Or it may be argued that, if a thing does not exist, where it is more frequent, it does not exist where it is rarer; or that, if it exists where it is rarer, it exists where it is more frequent — according as it may be needful to prove that it does or that it does not exist. Again, this topic may be used in a case of parity: — hence the lines —

'Thy father is to be pitied for having lost his children; and is not OEneus to be pitied for having lost his famous son?'

So it may be argued that, if Theseus did no wrong, neither did Paris; or that, if the Tyndaridae did none, neither did Paris; or that, if Hektor killed Patroklos, Paris killed Achilles; or that, if other artists are not contemptible, neither are philosophers; or that, if generals are not contemptible, because in many cases they are put to death, neither are sophists; or, 'if a private person ought to respect the opinion of Athens, Athens ought to respect that of Greece.'

5. Another topic is from considerations of time. Thus Iphikrates said in his speech against Harmodios — 'If, before doing the deed, I had claimed the statue on condition of doing it, you would have given it: now that I have done the deed, will you not give it? You are ready to promise rewards, when you expect a benefit; — do not withdraw them, when you have reaped it. Again, the argument about the Thebans allowing Philip to pass through into Attica: — 'If he had asked this before he came to the help of Phocis, they would have promised it. It is absurd, then, if they are to refuse him a passage because he waived the point and trusted them.'

6. Another topic is taken from things said (by the adversary), applied to our own case as compared with his. The ways of doing this are various — as in the *Teucer*. Iphikrates used this against Aristophon, — asking whether Aristophon would betray the ships for money? — and, when he said 'No,' rejoining — 'So you, being Aristophon, would not betray them; would I, being Iphikrates?' It is necessary that the adversary should be more liable to the suspicion of crime; else, the effect will be ludicrous — as if one were to say this in answer to the accusations of Aristeides. The argument is meant to create distrust of the accusers; for, as a rule, the accuser is by way of being better than the defendant: this assumption, then, should always be confuted. Generally speaking, a man is absurd when he upbraids others with what he himself does, or would do; or when he exhorts others to do what he himself does not, or is incapable of doing.

7. Another topic is from Definition. Thus — 'What is the supernatural? Is it a god or the work of a god? He, however, who thinks that there is the

work of a god, must needs think that there are gods.' Or, take the saying of Iphikrates, that the best man is the noblest, for Harmodios and Aristogeiton had nothing noble about them, until they had done a noble deed; — and that he himself is more nearly akin to them: — 'At all events my deeds are more nearly akin than yours to the deeds of Harmodios and Aristogeiton. Another example is the remark in the *Alexandros*: — 'all will allow that men of unruly life are not contented with the enjoyment of one love.' Or the reason which Sokrates gives for not going to Archelaos: — 'It is an insolence not to be able to make an equal return for benefits, just as it is to requite them with evil'. In all these cases the speaker defines and ascertains the meaning of a term with a view to reasoning on his subject.

8. Another commonplace is from the various senses of a word — of which 'rightly' was our example in the *Topics.*

9. Another is from Division: as 'All men do wrong from one of three motives — on account of *this,* or *this,* or *this*; here two of the motives are out of the question, and the accusers themselves do not impute the third.'

10. Another topic is from Induction: as, from the case of the woman of Peparêthos[1], it might be argued that women always discern the truth about their own children. Thus in an instance at Athens, when the orator Mantias was at law with his son, the mother settled the point for him; in another instance at Thebes, the woman of Dodona declared Ismênias to be father of the son whom Stilbôn was disputing with him, and on this ground the Thebans held Thettaliskos to be the son of Ismênias. Take, again, the example in the *Law* of Theodektês: 'If men do not entrust their own horses to those who have taken bad care of other people's, neither will they entrust their own ships to those who have upset the ships of others. If it is so, then, in all cases, we ought not to use for our own protection those who have ill-guarded the safety of others.' Or, take the saying of Alkidamas, that 'all men honour the wise: — at least the Parians have paid honour to Archilochos, though he was a reviler; the Chians to Homer, though he was not their fellow-citizen; the Mytileneans to Sappho, though a woman, — the Lacedaemonians even raised Cheilon to their Senate, though they are anything but fond of letters; the Italiots honoured Pythagoras; the Lampsakenes gave burial, and still pay honours, to Anaxagoras, though an alien...<They who use the laws of philosophers always prosper> for the Athenians prospered by the use of Solon's laws, and the Lacedaemonians by using those of Lykurgos; and, at Thebes, no sooner did philosophers become the leading men, than the State prospered.'

11. Another topic is taken from a decision on the same point, or on a like point, or on the opposite point — especially if it has been the decision

---

[1] This passage is paraphrased by Eustath. on *Od.* i 215, 'A woman of Peparêthos, by her deposition that a boy was her own son, solved the contention about him,' *i.e.* the mother, who had not seen her son for a long time, was able, by memory or insight, to bring some evidence which settled the point (R.C.J.).

of all men at all times; or else of a majority of mankind, – or of wise or good men, most or all, – or of our own judges, or of them to whom they listen; or of those whose decision, being that of the masters of the situation, it is impossible to reverse, or discreditable to reverse, as that of the gods, or our father or our teachers, – as Autoklês said of Mixidêmidês, that it was strange, if trial before the Areiopagos was good enough for the 'Awful Goddesses, but not good enough for Mixidêmidês. Or, take Sappho's saying that death is an evil – for the gods have so judged, or they would die. Or the remark of Aristippos, in answer to a saying of Plato's, which he thought rather compromising – 'Well, at least our friend' (meaning Sokrates) 'said nothing of the kind.' Again, Agêsipolis asked the god at Delphi (after first consulting the oracle at Olympia), whether *he* took the same view as his father – implying that it would be indecent to contradict his father. And thus Isokrates represented Helen as good, since Theseus chose her; Paris as good, seeing that the goddesses preferred him; Evagoras, again, he says, is good, inasmuch as Konon after his misfortune passed by all others and came to Evagoras.

12. Another topic consists in taking separately the parts of a subject: as in the *Topics* – what sort of motion is the soul? It must be *this* kind or *this* kind. The *Sokrates* of Theodektes affords an example – 'Against what temple has he sinned? What gods, acknowledged by the city, has he failed to honour?'

13. Since it happens, in most cases, that the same thing has the same result, good or bad, another topic consists in arguing from the Consequence, – whether in exhorting or dissuading, accusing or defending, praising or blaming. Thus: – 'Culture has the bad consequence of exciting envy, and the good consequence of making one wise.' Therefore 'we ought not to cultivate ourselves, for it is not well to be envied.' Or rather – 'we *ought* to cultivate ourselves, for it is well to be wise.' The Art of Kallippos[1] is simply this topic, with the addition of the topic of Possibility and the rest, as described above (c. xix).

14. It is another topic, when we have either to exhort or dissuade in reference to two opposite things, and have to use the method just stated in regard to both. There is this difference that, in the former case, any two things are contrasted; here, the things contrasted are opposites. For instance, the priestess urged her son *not* to speak in public; 'for,' she said, 'if you speak justly, you will be hated by men; if unjustly, by the gods.' Or, '*No* – you *ought* to speak in public, for if you speak justly, the gods will love you; if unjustly, men.' This is the same thing as the saying about buying the salt along with the marsh[2]; and in this consists the 'retortion'

---

[1] § 21; one of the early writers on the Art of Rhetoric, possibly the person described as one of the first pupils of Isokrates in *Antid.* § 93.

[2] *i.e.* 'The unprofitable and unwholesome marsh with the profitable salt inseparably connected with it' (Cope); a proverb not found elsewhere.

of the dilemma — when each of two opposite things has both a good and a bad consequence, opposite respectively to each other.

15. As men do not approve the same things in public and in their secret thoughts, but in public must approve just and honourable things, while, from their private point of view, they are apt to prefer their own advantage, another topic consists in trying to infer either of these sentiments from the other. This is the most effective sort of paradox.

16. Another topic is taken from the symmetry of results. Thus Iphikrates, when they were trying to make his son take a public service, because though he was under age, he was a big boy, said that, 'if they count big boys as men, they must enact that little men are boys.' And Theodektes in his *Law*: 'You make citizens of mercenaries, such as Strabax and Charidêmos, for their merit; will you not make exiles of those, who have done fatal mischief with the mercenaries?'

17. Another topic consists in arguing identity of cause from identity of effect. Thus, Xenophanes said that those who allege the gods to have come into existence are as impious as those who allege that they are dead; for, either way, it results that at one time the gods were not. And, universally, any given result may be treated as constant: — 'You are about to decide the fate, not of Isokrates, but of the pursuit of Philosophy.' Or, it may be argued, that 'to give earth and water' means slavery — 'to share in the Common Peace' means obeying orders. (We must take whichever view may serve.)

18. Another topic is taken from the fact that men do not always make the same choice at a later as at an earlier time, but may reverse it. This enthymeme gives an example — 'It is strange if, when we were in exile, we fought to return, and, having returned, are to go into exile to avoid fighting. In the one case, they chose to keep their homes at the cost of fighting: — in the other, they choose *not* to fight at the cost of losing their homes.

19. Another topic consists in treating the conceivable as the actual reason for a thing existing or having come to pass. Suppose, for example, that one has given something to another for the purpose of paining him by withdrawing it: — whence the saying —

'The god bestows large blessings on many men, not in kindness, but that the troubles which they find may be more signal.'

Or the passage from Antiphon's *Meleager*: —

'Not that they may slay the beast, but that they may witness the bravery of Meleager to Greece.'

Or the remark in the *Ajax* of Theodektes, that Diomedes chose Odysseus, not in order to honour him, but in order that his own follower might be a lesser man; for this motive is possible.

20. Another topic is common to the lawcourts and to debate — viz. to consider the inducements and drawbacks, the reasons for doing or avoiding an action; for these are the conditions which, according as they are present or absent, make an action desirable or undesirable: the former, if, for example, it is possible, easy, advantageous to the doer or his friends, hurtful and damaging to his enemies, — or if the penalty for the act is comparatively small. The grounds of suasion are these — the grounds of dissuasion are the opposite. The same motives form grounds of accusation or defence: — the deterring motives, of defence; the inciting motives, of accusation. This topic represents the whole Art of Pamphilos and of Kallippos.

21. Another topic concerns things which appear to have happened, but which are incredible. We may say, that men would not have fancied them, if they had not been true or nearly true. Or we may say, that this makes it *more* certain; for the things in which men believe are either facts or probabilities; if then it be incredible and not probable, it must be true; because its probability and plausibility are not the reason for this belief about it. Thus Androkles the Pitthean said in arraigning the law, when they interrupted his speech — 'The laws need a law to correct them, just as fish need salt — improbable and surprising as it is that creatures reared in brine should need salt — just as dried olives need olive-oil — though it is incredible that olive-oil should be needed by the sources of its own being.'

22. Another topic, useful for Refutation, consists in taking account of any inconsistency in the series of dates or acts or statements, and this in three separate ways. First, in the case of the adversary — as: — 'He says that he loves you, but he conspired with the Thirty.' Secondly, in our own case; — 'And he says that I am litigious, but cannot prove that I have ever been engaged in a single lawsuit.' Thirdly, in our case, as compared with that of the adversary: — '*He* has never lent anything, but *I* have ransomed many of you.'

23. Another topic, useful for persons and causes discredited, or seemingly discredited, by a prejudice, is to give the reason of the paradox; for then there is something which accounts for the prejudice. Thus a woman, who had palmed off her son on another woman, was suspected from embracing him of being the youth's paramour; but, when the cause was stated, the prejudice was dispelled. Thus, again, in the *Ajax* of Theodektes, Odyesseus tells Ajax *why* he is not thought braver than Ajax, though he is really so.

24. Another topic consists in arguing, from the presence or absence of the Cause, the existence or non-existence of the Effect; for Cause and Effect go together, and nothing is without a cause. Thus, when Thrasybulos charged Leôdamas with having been recorded as infamous on the acropolis, and having erased the record in the time of the Thirty, Leôdamas said in his defence — 'It is impossible; the Thirty would have trusted me the more for my enmity with the people being registered.'

25. There is another topic, when it was or is possible to devise a better course than the speaker is recommending or taking, or has taken. Clearly, if the course is not this better course, he has not taken it; for no one willingly and wittingly chooses the worse. (This however is a fallacy; for the better plan often becomes clear after the event, though it was doubtful before it.)

26. When an intended action is contrary to some former action, another topic consists in viewing them together. Thus, when the people of Elea asked Xenophanes whether they should sacrifice to Leukothea and wail for her, his advice was — 'If you consider her a goddess, do not wail: if a woman, do not sacrifice.'

27. Another topic consists in founding accusation or defence upon mistakes. Thus, in the *Medea* of Karkinos, the accusers contend that she has slain her children — at any rate, they are not to be found; — for Medea had made the mistake of sending her children away. She says, in her defence, that she would have slain, *not* the children, but Jason; for, supposing her capable of the other murder, it would have been a blunder for her not to have done *this*. This special topic of enthymeme constitutes the whole of the Art in use before Theodoros.

28. Another topic is from a play on names. Thus Sophokles —

'Steel, truly, like the name thou bearest.' [1]

This is commonly used in praises of the gods. Thus, too, Konon punned on the name of Thrasybulos; Hêrodikos on the names of Thrasymachos and Pôlos, and said of Draco the lawgiver that his laws are 'not the laws of a man but of a dragon — they are so cruel.' And thus in Euripides, Hecuba says of 'Aphrodite (the Foam-born),'

'Well may her name be the beginning of folly.'

And Chaerêmôn —

'Pentheus, with name prophetic of his doom.'

The Refutative Enthymemes seem more brilliant than the Demonstrative, because the refutative enthymeme is the bringing together of opposites in a small compass; and, when two things are put side by side, they are plainer to the hearer. But, of all syllogisms, whether refutative or demonstrative, those are most applauded, of which we foresee the conclusion from the beginning — and this, not because they are superficial; for we are at the same time pleased with our own quickness: — or those, with which we can just keep up, as soon as they are started.

---

[1] Frag. 597, Nauck, ed. 2. The line refers to the cruelty of Sidêrô (the wife of Salmôneus) to her step-daughter Tyro.

CICERO: DE ORATORE

Translated by E. W. Sutton and H. Rackham

Cicero's De Oratore *contains a discussion of ethical and emotional proof from the point of view of theorist and master practitioner that contrasts with Aristotle's more philosophical view.*

II, xliii, 182 — liii, 216

"A potent factor in success, then, is for the characters, principles, conduct and course of life, both of those who are to plead cases and of their clients, to be approved, and conversely those of their opponents condemned; and for the feelings of the tribunal to be won over, as far as possible, to goodwill towards the advocate and the advocate's client as well. Now feelings are won over by a man's merit, achievements or reputable life, qualifications easier to embellish, if only they are real, than to fabricate where nonexistent. But attributes useful in an advocate are a mild tone, a countenance expressive of modesty, gentle language, and the faculty of seeming to be dealing reluctantly and under compulsion with something you are really anxious to prove. It is very helpful to display the tokens of good-nature, kindness, calmness, loyalty and a disposition that is pleasing and not grasping or covetous, and all the qualities belonging to men who are upright, unassuming and not given to haste, stubbornness, strife or harshness, are powerful in winning goodwill, while the want of them estranges it from such as do not possess them; accordingly the very opposites of these qualities must be ascribed to our opponents. But all this kind of advocacy will be best in those cases wherein the arbitrator's feelings are not likely to be kindled by what I may call the ardent and

Reprinted by permission of the publishers and THE LOEB CLASSICAL LIBRARY from E. W. Sutton and H. Rackham, translators, Cicero, *De Oratore*, Cambridge, Mass.: Harvard University Press.

impassioned onset. For vigorous language is not always wanted, but often such as is calm, gentle, mild: this is the kind that most commends the parties. By 'parties' I mean not only persons impeached, but all whose interests are being determined, for that was how people used the term in the old days. And so to paint their characters in words, as being upright, stainless, conscientious, modest and long-suffering under injustice, has a really wonderful effect; and this topic, whether in opening, or in stating the case, or in winding-up, is so compelling, when agreeably and feelingly handled, as often to be worth more than the merits of the case. Moreover so much is done by good taste and style in speaking, that the speech seems to depict the speaker's character. For by means of particular types of thought and diction, and the employment besides of a delivery that is unruffled and eloquent of good-nature, the speakers are made to appear upright, well-bred and virtuous men.

"But closely associated with this is that dissimilar style of speaking which, in quite another way, excites and urges the feelings of the tribunal towards hatred or love, ill-will or well-wishing, fear or hope, desire or aversion, joy or sorrow, compassion or the wish to punish, or by it they are prompted to whatever emotions are nearly allied and similar to these passions of the soul, and to such as these.

"Another desirable thing for the advocate is that the members of the tribunal, of their own accord, should carry within them to Court some mental emotion that is in harmony with what the advocate's interest will suggest. For, as the saying goes, it is easier to spur the willing horse than to start the lazy one. But if no such emotion be present, or recognizable, he will be like a careful physician who, before he attempts to administer a remedy to his patient, must investigate not only the malady of the man he wishes to cure, but also his habits when in health, and his physical constitution.

"This indeed is the reason why, when setting about a hazardous and important case, in order to explore the feelings of the tribunal, I engage wholehcartedly in a consideration so careful, that I scent out with all possible keenness their thoughts, judgements, anticipations and wishes, and the direction in which they seem likely to be led away most easily by eloquence. If they surrender to me, and as I said before, of their own accord lean towards and are prone to take the course in which I am urging them on, I accept their bounty and set sail for that quarter which promises something of a breeze. If however an arbitrator is neutral and free from predisposition, my task is harder, since everything has to be called forth by my speech, with no help from the listener's character. But so potent is that Eloquence, rightly styled, by an excellent poet, 'soulbending sovereign of all things,' that she can not only support the sinking and bend the upstanding, but, like a good and brave commander, can even make prisoner a resisting antagonist.

"These are the details for which Crassus was playfully importuning me just now, when he said that I always handled them ideally, and he praised what he called the brilliant treatment of them in the cases of Manius Aquilius, Gaius Norbanus and sundry others. Now I give you my word, Crassus, that I always tremble when these things are handled by yourself in Court: such is the mental power, such the passion, so profound the indignation, ever manifest in your glance, features, gesture, even in that wagging finger of yours; so mighty is the flow of your most impressive and happy diction, so sound, true and original your sentiments, and so innocent of colouring-matter or paltry dye, that to me you seem to be not merely inflaming the arbitrator, but actually on fire yourself.

"Moreover it is impossible for the listener to feel indignation, hatred or ill-will, to be terrified of anything, or reduced to tears of compassion, unless all those emotions, which the advocate would inspire in the arbitrator, are visibly stamped or rather branded on the advocate himself. Now if some feigned indignation had to be depicted, and that same kind of oratory afforded only what was counterfeit and produced by mimicry, some loftier art would perhaps be called for. As things stand, Crassus, I do not know how it may be with yourself or the rest, but in my own case there is no reason why I should lie to men of consummate experience, who are also my best friends: I give you my word that I never tried, by means of a speech, to arouse either indignation or compassion, either ill-will or hatred, in the minds of a tribunal, without being really stirred myself, as I worked upon their minds, by the very feelings to which I was seeking to prompt them. For it is not easy to succeed in making an arbitrator angry with the right party, if you yourself seem to treat the affair with indifference; or in making him hate the right party, unless he first sees you on fire with hatred yourself; nor will he be prompted to compassion, unless you have shown him the tokens of your own grief by word, sentiment, tone of voice, look and even by loud lamentation. For just as there is no substance so ready to take fire, as to be capable of generating flame without the application of a spark, so also there is no mind so ready to absorb an orator's influence, as to be inflammable when the assailing speaker is not himself aglow with passion.

"Again, lest haply it should seem a mighty miracle, for a man so often to be roused to wrath, indignation and every inward emotion — and that too about other people's business — the power of those reflections and commonplaces, discussed and handled in a speech, is great enough to dispense with all make-believe and trickery: for the very quality of the diction, employed to stir the feelings of others, stirs the speaker himself even more deeply than any of his hearers. And, not to have us astonished at this happening in litigation, or before arbitrators, or in the impeachments of our friends, or among a crowd of people, or in political life, or public debate, when not only our talent is under criticism (no great matter, though even this should not be overlooked, when you have claimed a proficiency attained by few), but other and far more important attributes are on trial, I mean our loyalty, sense of duty and carefulness, under whose influence, even when defending complete strangers, we still cannot regard them as strangers, if we would be accounted good men ourselves. However, as I said, not to have this seem a marvel among us, what can be so unreal as poetry, the theatre or stage-plays? And yet, in that sort of things, I myself have often been a spectator when the actor-man's eyes seemed to me to be blazing behind his mask, as he spoke those solemn lines,

> Darest thou part from thy brother, or Salamis enter without him,
> Dreading the mien of thy sire not at all?

Never did he utter that word 'mien,' without my beholding an infuriated Telamon maddened by grief for his son. Whenever too he lowered his voice to a plaintive tone, in the passage,

> Aged and childless,
> Didst tear and bereave and didst quench me, forgetting the death of
>   thy brother,
> Forgetting his tiny son, though entrusted to thee as a guardian?

I thought I heard sobs of mourning in his voice. Now if that player, though acting it daily, could never act that scene without emotion, do you really think that Pacuvius, when he wrote it, was in a calm and careless frame of mind? That could never be. For I have often heard that — as they say Democritus and Plato have left on record — no man can be a good poet who is not on fire with passion, and inspired by something very like frenzy.

"Do not suppose then that I myself, though not concerned to portray and reproduce in language the bygone misfortunes and legendary griefs of heroes, and though presenting my own personality and not representing another's, did without profound emotion the things I did when closing that famous case, in which my task was to maintain Manius Aquilius in his civic rights. For here was a man whom I remembered as having been consul, commander-in-chief, honoured by the Senate, and mounting in procession to the Capitol; on seeing him cast down, crippled, sorrowing and brought to the risk of all he held dear, I was myself overcome by compassion before I tried to excite it in others. Assuredly I felt that the Court was deeply affected when I called forward my unhappy old client, in his garb of woe, and when I did those things approved by yourself, Crassus — not by way of technique, as to which I know not what to say, but under stress of deep emotion and indignation — I mean my tearing open his tunic and exposing his scars. While Gaius Marius, from his seat in court, was strongly reinforcing, by his weeping, the pathos of my appeal, and I, repeatedly naming him, was committing his colleague to his care, and calling upon him to speak himself in support of the common interests of commanders-in-chief, all this lamentation, as well as my invocation of every god and man, every citizen and ally, was accompanied by tears and vast indignation on my own part; had my personal indignation been missing from all the talking I did on that occasion, my address, so far from inspiring compassion, would positively have deserved ridicule. And so I am telling you this, Sulpicius, as naturally such a kindly and accomplished teacher would do, in order to help you to be wrathful, indignant and tearful in your speech-making.

"But why indeed should I teach this to you, who, in prosecuting my comrade and quaestor, had kindled such a blaze, not by eloquence only, but far more by vehemence, indignation and fiery enthusiasm, that I hardly ventured to draw near and put it out? For all the advantages in that case had been yours: you were citing to the Court the violence, the flight, the stone-throwing and the tribunes' ruthlessness that marked the disastrous and lamentable affair of Caepio; then too it was established that Marcus Aemilius, chief of Senate and chief of State, had been struck by a stone, while it was undeniable that Lucius Cotta and Titus Didius, on trying to veto a resolution, had been forcibly driven from sanctuary.

"In the result, while you, only a stripling, were thought to be conducting this public prosecution with consummate distinction, I, a past censor, was thought to be acting not quite honourably in bearing to defend a factious citizen, who moreover had been merciless to a past consul in distress. Citizens of the best repute formed the tribunal; men of respectability crowded the Court; so that I had difficulty in winning a grudging sort of acceptance of my plea that at any rate my client was my old quaestor. In these circumstances how can I say I used any particular technique? What I did I will relate, if you think fit, you will give my line of defence some place or other in your system.

"I classified all the types of civil discord, their weaknesses and dangers, and that part of my speech I derived from all the vicissitudes in the history of our own community, winding up with the assertion that civil discords, though always troublesome, had yet sometimes been justifiable and well-nigh unavoidable. Next I discussed the considerations lately recalled by Crassus; how that neither the expulsion of kings from this State, nor the establishment of tribunes of the commons, nor the frequent restriction of the consuls' power by decrees of the commons, nor the bestowal upon the Roman People of the right of appeal, that famous buttress of the State and defence of freedom, could any of them have been effected without aristocratic opposition; and that, if those particular civil discords had been beneficial to our community, the mere fact of a popular movement having been caused must not instantly be counted against Gaius Norbanus for heinous wickedness and indeed a capital offence. That if rightfulness had ever been conceded to an incitement of the Roman People to sedition, – a concession which I was showing to have been frequent –, there had never been a juster cause than this one. After that I altered my course and turned my entire speech into a denunciation of the running-away of Caepio and a lament for the destruction of his army: in this way, besides chafing anew by my words the sores of people mourning for their own folk, I was kindling the feelings of the Roman Knights, who constituted the Court I was addressing, into fresh hatred of Quintus Caepio, from whom they had been estranged already over the composition of the criminal Courts.

"But when I felt I had a firm hold on the Court and on my line of defence, and I had won the goodwill of the public, whose claims I had upheld even when involved with civil discord, and I had turned all hearts on the tribunal in favour of my cause, by reason either of the national disaster, or of yearning grief for kindred, or of private hatred of Caepio, then I began to blend with this impetuous and violent type of oratory that other mild and gentle type, which I have already discussed, pleading that I was fighting for my comrade, who by ancestral tradition should stand in a filial relation to myself, and also (I might say) for my own fair fame and general welfare; no happening could more deeply disgrace my reputation, or cause me more bitter sorrow, than for it to be thought that I, so often the saviour of complete strangers to myself, provided only they were my fellow-citizens, had been unable to aid my own comrade. I begged the Court, should they see me affected by justifiable and loyal grief, to excuse this in consideration of my years, official career and achievements, particularly if, in the course of other trials, they had observed that I always made my petitions on behalf of friends in jeopardy, never for myself. Thus all through that speech for the defence, and indeed the trial itself, it was in the fewest possible words that I glanced over and lightly touched the matters which seemed dependent upon scientific treatment, I mean my discussion of the Statute of Appuleius, and my exposition of the nature of treason. By means of these two modes of speech, the one inflammatory, the other eulogistic, and neither of them much elaborated by rules of art, I so managed the whole of that case as to seem most passionate when reviving hatred of Caepio, and mildest when describing my conduct towards my own connexions. So, Sulpicius, it was rather by working upon, than by informing, the minds of the tribunal, that I beat your prosecution on that occasion."

Here Sulpicius observed, "Upon my word, Antonius, your account of those matters is true, for never did I see anything slip through the fingers in the way that verdict slipped that day through mine. For when (as you told us) I had left you with a conflagration rather than a case to dispose of, – ye Gods! – what an opening you made! How nervous, how irresolute you seemed! How stammering and halting was your delivery! How you clung at the outset to the solitary excuse everyone was making for you – that you were defending your own familiar friend and quaestor! So, in the first place, did you prepare the way towards getting a hearing! Then, just as I was deciding that you had merely succeeded in making people think intimate relationship a possible excuse for your defending a wicked citizen, — lo and behold! — so far unsuspected by other people, but already to my own serious alarm, you began to wriggle imperceptibly into your famous defence, of no factious Norbanus, but of an incensed Roman People, whose wrath, you urged, was not wrongful, but just and well-deserved. After that what point against Caepio did you miss? How you leavened every word with hatred, malice and pathos! And all this not only in your speech for the defence, but also in your handling of Scaurus and the rest of my witnesses, whose evidence you rebutted by no disproof, but by fleeing for refuge to that same national outbreak. When just now you were reminding us of these things, I certainly felt no need of any maxims, for that actual reproduction, in your own words, of your methods of defence is to my mind the most instructive of teaching."

"For all that," answered Antonius, "we will, if you please, go on to set forth the principles we generally adopt in speaking, and the points we chiefly keep in view: for a long career and experience in the most weighty affairs have taught us, by this time, to hold fast to the ways of stirring the feelings of mankind.

"My own practice is to begin by reflecting whether the case calls for such treatment; for these rhetorical fireworks should not be used in petty matters, or with men of such temper that our eloquence can achieve nothing in the way of influencing their minds, unless we would be deemed fit objects of ridicule, or even of disgust, as indulging in heroics over trifles, or setting out to uproot the immovable. Now, since the emotions which eloquence has to excite in the minds of the tribunal, or whatever other audience we may be addressing, are most commonly love, hate, wrath, jealousy, compassion, hope, joy, fear or vexation, we observe that love is won if you are thought to be upholding the interests of your audience, or to be working for good men, or at any rate for such as that audience deems good and useful. For this last impression more readily wins love, and the protection of the righteous esteem; and the holding-out of a hope of advantage to come is more effective than the recital of past benefit. You must struggle to reveal the presence, in the cause you are upholding, of some merit or usefulness, and to make it plain that the man, for whom you are to win this love, in no respect consulted his own interests and did nothing at all from personal motives. For men's private gains breed jealousy, while their zeal for others' service is applauded.

"And here we must be watchful, not to seem to extol unduly the merits and renown — jealousy's favourite target — of those whom we would have beloved for their good works. Then too, from these same commonplaces, we shall learn as well to instigate hatred of others as to turn it away from ourselves and our clients: and these same general heads are to be employed in kindling and also in assuaging wrath. For, if you glorify the doing of something ruinous or unprofitable to your particular audience, hate is engendered: while, if it be something done against good men in general, or those to whom the particular doer should never have done it, or against the State, no such bitter hate is excited, but a disgust closely resembling ill-will or hate. Fear again is struck from either the perils of individuals or those shared by all: that of private origin goes deeper, but universal fear also is to be traced to a similar source.

"The treatment of hope, joy and vexation is similar to this, and identical in each case, but I rather think that the emotion of jealousy is by far the fiercest of all, and needs as much energy for its repression as for its stimulation. Now people are especially jealous of their equals, or of those once beneath them, when they feel themselves left behind and fret at the others' upward flight; but jealousy of their betters also is often furious, and all the more so if these conduct themselves insufferably, and overstep their rightful claims on the strength of pre-eminent rank or prosperity; if these advantages are to be made fuel for jealousy, it should before all be pointed out that they were not the fruit of merit; next that they even came by vice and wrongdoing, finally that the man's deserts, though creditable and impressive enough, are still exceeded by his arrogance and disdain. To quench jealousy, on the other hand, it is proper to emphasize the points that those advantages were the fruit of great exertion and great risks, and were not turned to his own profit but to that of other people; and that, as for any renown he himself may seem to have won, though no unfair recompense for his risk, he nevertheless finds no pleasure therein, but casts it aside and disclaims it altogether: and we must by all means make sure (since most people are jealous, and this failing is remarkably general and widespread, while jealousy is attracted by surpassingly brilliant prosperity) that the belief in such prosperity shall be weakened, and that what was supposed to be outstanding prosperity shall be seen to be thoroughly blended with labour and sorrow. Lastly compassion is awakened if the hearer can be brought to apply to his own adversities, whether endured or only apprehended, the lamentations uttered over someone else, or if, in his contemplation of another's case, he many a time goes back to his own experience. Thus, while particular occasions of human distress are deeply felt, if described in moving terms, the dejection and ruin of the righteous are especially lamentable. And, just as that other kind of style, which by bearing witness to the speaker's integrity is to preserve the semblance of a man of worth, should be mild and gentle (as I have repeatedly said already), so this kind, assumed by the speaker in order to transform men's feelings or influence them in any desired way, should be spirited and emotional.

"But these two styles, which we require to be respectively mild and emotional, have something in common, making them hard to keep apart. For from that mildness, which wins us the goodwill of our hearers, some inflow must reach this fiercest of passions, wherewith we inflame the same people, and again, out of this passion some little energy must often be kindled within that mildness: nor is any style better blended than that wherein the harshness of strife is tempered by the personal urbanity of the advocate, while his easy-going mildness is fortified by some admixture of serious strife.

"Now in both styles of speaking, the one demanding passion and strife, and the other adapted to recommendation of the speaker's life and manners, the opening of a speech is unhurried, and none the less its closing should also be lingering and long drawnout. For you must not bound all of a sudden into that emotional style, since it is wholly alien to the merits of the case, and people long to hear first just what is peculiarly within their own cognizance, while, once you have assumed that style, you must not be in a hurry to change it. For you could not awaken compassion, jealousy or wrath at the very instant of your onset, in the way that a proof is seized upon as soon as propounded, and a second and third called for. This is because the hearer's mentality corroborates the proof, and no sooner is it uttered than it is sticking in his memory, whereas that passionate style searches out an arbitrator's emotional side rather than his understanding, and that side can only be reached by diction that is rich, diversified and copious, with animated delivery to match. Thus concise or quiet speakers may inform an arbitrator, but cannot excite him, on which excitement everything depends.

"By this time it is plain that the power to argue both sides of every question is abundantly furnished from the same commonplaces. But your opponents' proof must be countered, either by contradicting the arguments chosen to establish it, or by showing that their desired conclusion is not supported by their premisses and does not follow therefrom; or, if you do not so rebut it, you must adduce on the opposite side some proof of greater or equal cogency. Lastly appeals, whether mild or passionate, and whether for winning favour or stirring the feelings, must be swept aside by exciting the opposite impressions, so that goodwill may be done away with by hate, and compassion by jealousy.

ST. AUGUSTINE:
ON CHRISTIAN DOCTRINE

Translated by D. W. Robertson, Jr.

With the beginning of the Christian era, the classical doctrine of inventio *needed rethinking. Now the homiletician had to decide what he was responsible for and what God would supply, whether as a preacher and teacher he was an interpreter or a creator of ideas. Augustine's reformulation of classical doctrine to meet the needs of a preacher who had at hand, if he could only read it correctly, the certainty of the word of God, in distinction to the probabilities available to earlier Greek and Roman rhetors, marks a major change in the relation of the speaker or writer to his materials. The following selections are from Books I and III of Augustine's* On Christian Doctrine.

I, i

There are two things necessary to the treatment of the Scriptures: a way of discovering those things which are to be understood, and a way of teaching what we have learned. We shall speak first of discovery and second of teaching. This is a great and arduous work, and since it is difficult to sustain, I fear some temerity in undertaking it. It would be thus indeed if I relied on myself alone, but now while the hope of completing such a work lies in Him from whom I have received much concerning these things in thought, it is not to be feared that He will cease giving me more when I have begun to use what He has already given me. Everything which does not decrease on being given away is not properly owned when it is owned and not given. For He says, "He that hath, to him shall be given." Therefore He will give to those that have, that is, to those benevolently using that which they have received He will increase and heap up what He gives. There were at one time five loaves and at another time seven before they began to be given to the needy; and when this began to be done, baskets and hampers were filled, although thousands of men were fed. Just as the loaves increased when they were broken, the Lord has granted those things necessary to the beginning of this work, and when they begin to be given out they will be multiplied by His inspiration, so that in this task of mine I shall not only suffer no proverty of ideas but shall rejoice in wonderful abundance.

I, vi — vii

Have we spoken or announced anything worthy of God? Rather I feel that I have done nothing but wish to speak: if I have spoken, I have not said what I wished to say. Whence do I know this, except because God is ineffable? If what I said were ineffable, it would not be said. And for this reason God should not be said to be ineffable, for when this is said something is said. And a contradiction in terms is created, since if that is ineffable which cannot be spoken, then that is not ineffable which can be called ineffable. This contradiction is to be passed over in silence rather than resolved verbally. For God, although nothing worthy may be spoken of Him, has accepted the tribute of the human voice and wished us to take joy in praising Him with our words. In this way he is called *Deus*. Although He is not recognized in the noise of these two syllables, all those who know the Latin language, when this sound reaches their ears, are moved to think of a certain most excellent immortal nature.

For when the one God of gods is thought of, even by those who recognize, invoke, and worship other gods either in Heaven or on earth, He is thought of in such a way that the thought seeks to attain something than which there is nothing better or more sublime. Since men are moved by diverse goods, some by those which appeal to the bodily senses, some by those which pertain to the understanding of the mind, those who are given to the bodily senses think the God of gods to be either the sky, or that which they see shining most brightly in the sky, or the world itself. Or, if they seek to go beyond the world, they imagine something luminous or infinite, or with a vain notion shape it in that form which seems best to them, perhaps thinking of the form of the human body if they place that above others. If they do not think of a God of gods but rather of innumerable gods of equal rank, they shape them in their minds according to that bodily shape which they think excellent. Those, however, who seek to know what God is through the understanding place Him above all things mutable, either visible and corporal or intelligible and spiritual. All men struggle emulously for the excellence of God, and no one can be found who believes God to be something to which there is a superior. Thus all agree that God is that thing which they place above all other things.

I, xiii

How did He come except that "the Word was made flesh, and dwelt among us"? It is as when we speak. In order that what we are thinking may reach the mind of the listener through the fleshly ears, that which we have in mind is expressed in words and is called speech. But our thought is not transformed into sounds: it remains entire in itself and assumes the form of words by means of which it may reach the ears without suffering any deterioration in itself. In the same way the Word of God was made flesh without change that He might dwell among us.

I, xxv — xxvi

Thus man should be instructed concerning the way of loving, that is, concerning the way of loving himself profitably. To doubt that he loves himself and desires to improve himself is madness. But he must be instructed how he should love his body so that he may care for it in an ordinate and prudent way. That he loves his body and wishes to have it safe and whole is equally obvious. But a man can love more than the health and soundness of his body. For many have been found willingly to undergo pains and loss of members so that something else which they loved more might be pursued. Yet a man need not be told that he should not love the health and safety of his body because he loves something else more. For the miser, although he loves money, still buys himself bread. And when he does this he spends money which he loves greatly and wishes to increase, but he esteems more the health of his body which is sustained by bread. It would be superfluous to dispute further about such a transparent matter, but the error of the impious often forces us to do this.

Therefore, since there was no need for a precept that anyone love himself and his own body, because we love that which we are and that which is below us and pertains to us in accordance with a constant law of nature which is also effective among beasts — for beasts also love themselves and their bodies — there remained a necessity only that we receive precepts concerning that which is equal to us and that which is above us. "Thou shalt love," He said, "the Lord they God with thy whole heart, and with thy whole soul, and with thy whole mind," and "Thou shalt love thy neighbor as thyself. On these two commandments dependeth the whole law and the prophets." "Now the end of the commandment is charity," and this is twofold: a love of God and a love of our neighbor. Thus if you think of yourself as a whole embracing both a soul and a body and your neighbor also as a whole embracing both a soul and a body — for the soul and the body constitute a man — nothing which is to be loved is omitted from these two precepts. For when love of God is placed first and the character of that love is seen to be described so that all other loves must flow into it, it may seem that nothing has been said about the love of yourself. But when it is said, "Thou shalt love thy neighbor as thyself" at the same time, it is clear that love for yourself is not omitted.

I, xxxv − xl

The sum of all we have said since we began to speak of things thus comes to this: it is to be understood that the plenitude and the end of the Law and of all the sacred Scriptures is the love of a Being which is to be enjoyed and of a being that can share that enjoyment with us, since there is no need for a precept that anyone should love himself. That we might know this and have the means to implement it, the whole temporal dispensation was made by divine Providence for our salvation. We should use it, not with an abiding but with a transitory love and delight like that in a road or in vehicles or in other instruments, or, if it may be expressed more accurately, so that we love those things by which we are carried along for the sake of that toward which we are carried.

Whoever, therefore, thinks that he understands the divine Scriptures or any part of them so that it does not build the double love of God and of our neighbor does not understand it at all. Whoever finds a lesson there useful to the building of charity, even though he has not said what the author may be shown to have intended in that place, has not been deceived, nor is he lying in any way. Lying involves the will to speak falsely; thus we find many who wish to lie, but no one who wishes to be deceived. Since a man lies knowingly but suffers deception unwittingly, it is obvious that in a given instance a man who is deceived is better than a man who lies, because it is better to suffer iniquity than to perform it. Everyone who lies commits iniquity, and if anyone thinks a lie may sometimes be useful, he must think that iniquity is sometimes useful also. But no one who lies keeps faith concerning that about which he lies. For he wishes that the person to whom he lies should have that faith in him which he does not himself keep when he lies. But every violator of faith is iniquitous. Either iniquity is sometimes useful, which is impossible, or a lie is always useless.

But anyone who understands in the Scriptures something other than that intended by them is deceived, although they do not lie. However, as I began to explain, if he is deceived in an interpretation which builds up charity, which is the end of the commandments, he is deceived in the same way as a man who leaves a road by mistake but passes through a field to the same place toward which the road itself leads. But he is to be corrected and shown that it is more useful not to leave the road, lest the habit of deviating force him to take a crossroad or a perverse way.

In asserting rashly that which the author before him did not intend, he may find many other passages which he cannot reconcile with his interpretation. If he acknowledges these to be true and certain, his first interpretation cannot be true, and under these conditions it happens, I know not why, that, loving his own interpretation, he begins to become angrier with the Scriptures than he is with himself. And if he thirsts persistently for the error, he will be overcome by it. "For we walk by faith and not by sight," and faith will stagger if the authority of the Divine Scriptures wavers. Indeed, if faith staggers, charity itself languishes. And if anyone should fall from faith, it follows that he falls also from charity, for a man cannot love that which he does not believe to exist. On the other hand, a man who both believes and loves, by doing well and by obeying the rules of good customs, may bring it about that he may hope to arrive at that which he loves. Thus there are these three things for which all knowledge and prophecy struggle: faith, hope, and charity.

But the vision we shall see will replace faith, and that blessedness to which we are to come will replace hope; and when these things are falling away, charity will be increased even more. If we love in faith what we have not seen, how much more will we love it when we begin to see it? And if we love in hope what we have not attained, how much more will we love it when we have attained it? Between temporal and eternal things there is this difference: a temporal thing is loved more before we have it, and it begins to grow worthless when we gain it, for it does not satisfy the soul, whose true and certain rest is eternity; but the eternal is more ardently loved when it is acquired than when it is merely desired. It is possible for no one desiring it to expect it to be more valuable than it actually is so that he may find it less worthy than he expected it to be. However highly anyone approaching it may value it, he will find it more valuable when he attains it.

Thus a man supported by faith, hope, and charity, with an unshaken hold upon them, does not need the Scriptures except for the instruction of others. And many live by these three things in solitude without books. Whence in these persons I think the saying is already exemplified, "whether prophecies shall be made void, or tongues shall cease, or knowledge shall be destroyed." In them, as if by instruments of faith, hope, and charity, such an erudition has been erected that, holding fast to that which is perfect, they do not seek that which is only partially so — perfect, that is, in so far as perfection is possible in this life. For in comparison with the life to come, the life of no just and holy man is perfect here. Hence "there remain," he says, "faith, hope, and charity, these three: but the greatest of these is charity." And when anyone shall reach the eternal, two of these having fallen away, charity will remain more certain and more vigorous.

Therefore, when anyone knows the end of the commandments to be charity "from a pure heart, and a good conscience, and an unfeigned faith," and has related all of his understanding of the Divine Scriptures to these three, he may approach the treatment of these books with security. For when he says "charity" he adds "from a pure heart," so that nothing else would be loved except that which should be loved. And he joins with this "a good conscience" for the sake of hope, for he in whom there is the smallest taint of bad conscience despairs of attaining that which he believes in and loves. Third, he says "an unfeigned faith." If our faith involves no lie, then we do not love that which is not to be loved, and living justly, we hope for that which will in no way deceive our hope.

With this I have said as much as I wished to say concerning faith at the present time, since in other books either by others or by myself much has already been said. Then may this be the limit to this book. In the remainder we shall discuss signs, in so far as God has granted us ability.

III, i

A man fearing God diligently seeks His will in the Holy Scriptures. And lest he should love controversy, he is made gentle in piety. He is prepared with a knowledge of languages lest he be impeded by unknown words and locutions. He is also prepared with an acquaintance with certain necessary things lest he be unaware of their force and nature when they are used for purposes of similitudes. He is assisted by the accuracy of texts which expert diligence in emendation has procured. Thus instructed, he may turn his attention to the investigation and solution of the ambiguities of the Scriptures. That he may not be deceived by ambiguous signs we shall offer some instruction. It may be, however, that he will deride those ways which we wish to point out as puerile either because of the greatness of his acumen or the brilliance of his illumination. Nevertheless, as I set out to say, he who has a mind to be instructed by us, in so far as he may be instructed by us, will know that the ambiguity of Scripture arises either from words used literally or figuratively, both of which types we have discussed in the second book.

III, x

To this warning that we must beware not to take figurative or transferred expressions as though they were literal, a further warning must be added lest we wish to take literal expressions as though they were figurative. Therefore a method of determining whether a locution is literal or figurative must be established. And generally this method consists in this: that whatever appears in the divine Word that does not literally pertain to virtuous behavior or to the truth of faith you must take to be figurative. Virtuous behavior pertains to the love of God and of one's neighbor; the truth of faith pertains to a knowledge of God and of one's neighbor. For the hope of everyone lies in his own conscience in so far as he knows himself to be becoming more proficient in the love of God and of his neighbor. Concerning these things we have spoken in the first book.

But since humanity is inclined to estimate sins, not on the basis of the importance of the passion involved in them, but rather on the basis of their own customs, so that they consider a man to be culpable in accordance with the way men are reprimanded and condemned ordinarily in their own place and time, and, at the same time, consider them to be virtuous and praiseworthy in so far as the customs of those among whom they live would so incline them, it so happens that if Scripture commends something despised by the customs of the listeners, or condemns what those customs do not condemn, they take the Scriptural locution as figurative if they accept it as an authority. But Scripture teaches nothing but charity, nor condemns anything except cupidity, and in this way shapes the minds of men. Again, if the minds of men are subject to some erroneous opinion, they think that whatever Scripture says contrary to that opinion is figurative. But it asserts nothing except the catholic faith as it pertains to things past, future, and present. It is a history of past things, an announcement of future things, and an explanation of present things, but all these things are of value in nourishing and supporting charity and in conquering and extirpating cupidity.

I call "charity" the motion of the soul toward the enjoyment of God for His own sake, and the enjoyment of one's self and of one's neighbor for the sake of God: but "cupidity" is a motion of the soul toward the enjoyment of one's self, one's neighbor, or any corporal thing for the sake of something other than God. That which uncontrolled cupidity does to corrupt the soul and its body is called a "vice"; what it does in such a way that someone else is harmed is called a "crime." And these are the two classes of all sins, but vices occur first. When vices have emptied the soul and led it to a kind of extreme hunger, it leaps into crimes by means of which impediments to the vices may be removed or the vices themselves sustained. On the other hand, what charity does to the charitable person is called "utility"; what it does to benefit one's neighbor is called "beneficence." And here utility occurs first, for no one may benefit

another with that which he does not have himself. The more the reign of
cupidity is destroyed, the more charity is increased.

III, xii

Those things which seem almost shameful to the inexperienced, whether
simply spoken or actually performed either by the person of God or by
men whose sanctity is commended to us, are all figurative, and their
secrets are to be removed as kernels from the husk as nourishment for
charity. Whoever uses transitory things in a more restricted way than is
customary among those with whom he lives is either superstitious or
temperate. But whoever so uses them that he exceeds the measure
established by the custom of the good men among his neighbors either
signifies something or is vicious. In all instances of this kind it is not the
use of the things but the desire of the user which is culpable. Thus no
reasonable person would believe under any circumstances that the feet of
the Lord were anointed with precious ointment by the woman in the
manner of lecherous and dissolute men whose banquets we despise. For
the good odor is good fame which anyone in the works of a good life will
have when he follows in the footsteps of Christ, as if anointing His feet
with a most precious odor. In this way what is frequently shameful in
other persons is in a divine or prophetic person the sign of some great
truth. Certainly union with a prostitute is one thing when morals are
corrupted and quite another thing in the prophecy of the prophet Osee. If,
moreover, it is shameful to strip the body of clothing at the banquets of
the drunken and lascivious, it is not on this account shameful to be naked
in the baths.

Careful attention is therefore to be paid to what is proper to places,
times, and persons lest we condemn the shameful too hastily. It may be
that a wise man may use the most precious food without any vice of ardor
or voraciousness, but a fool may glow with the most filthy flame of
gluttony before the vilest food. Any healthy man would rather eat fish as
the Lord did than lentils after the manner of Esau the grandson of
Abraham, or barley in the fashion of oxen. But because they eat coarser
food it does not follow that certain beasts are more continent than we are.
For in all things of this kind we are to be commended or reprimanded, not
because of the nature of the things which we use, but because of the
motive in using them and the way in which they are desired . . . .

III, xv

Thus when the tyranny of cupidity has been overthrown, charity reigns
with its most just laws of love for God for the sake of God and of one's

self and of one's neighbor for the sake of God. Therefore in the consideration of figurative expressions a rule such as this will serve, that what is read should be subjected to diligent scrutiny until an interpretation contributing to the reign of charity is produced. If this result appears literally in the text, the expression being considered is not figurative.

III, xvii

It often happens that a person who is, or thinks he is, in a higher grade of spiritual life thinks that those things which are taught for those in lower grades are figurative. For example, if he embraces the celibate life and has made himself a eunuch for the Kingdom of Heaven, he thinks it necessary to take anything the sacred books admonish concerning the love and rule of a wife as figurative rather than literal. And if anyone has sought to keep his virgin unmarried, he wishes to take as figurative that passage which says, "Marry thy daughter, and thou shalt do a great work." Therefore this should be added to the rules necessary for understanding the Scriptures: some things are taught for everyone in general; others are directed toward particular classes of people, in order that the medicine of instruction may be applicable not only to the general state of health but also to the special infirmities of each member. For what cannot be elevated to a higher class must be cared for in its own class.

UNIT THREE: ARRANGEMENT

ARISTOTLE: THE RHETORIC

Translated by Richard Claverhouse Jebb

In the Phaedrus, *Socrates argues: "Every discourse must be organized, like a living being, with a body of its own, as it were, so as not to be headless or footless, but to have a middle and members, composed in fitting relation to each other and to the whole." In contrast to this functional approach to arrangement advocated by Plato and Aristotle, sophistic rhetorics of the period such as* Rhetorica ad Alexandrum *stressed a very mechanical arrangement of seven or more parts of a speech designed for the oratory of the law courts.*

Aristotle, in his classic statement about arrangement, here attacks the absurdities of the then current, stereotyped division.

III, xiii, 1 − 5

It remains to speak of Arrangement. The speech has two parts: − it is necessary to *state* the matter which is our subject, and to *prove* it. We cannot, then, have a statement without a demonstration, or a demonstration without a previous statement; for the demonstrator must demonstrate something, and the expositor set a thing forth, in order to prove it. One of these processes is Statement, the other Proof: − just as one might divide Dialectic into Problem and Demonstration. The division now in use is absurd. 'Narrative' belongs, I presume, to Forensic speaking only. In Epideiktic or in Deliberative rhetoric, how can we have Narrative in their sense, or Refutation of the adversary, or Epilogue to the argument? Again, 'Proem,' 'Contrast,' 'Review,' have a place in Deliberative speaking, *only* where there is a personal controversy.

Reprinted from Richard Claverhouse Jebb, translator, Aristotle, *The Rhetoric of Aristotle,* Cambridge, England: At the University Press.

Accusation and Defence, also, are often present in such a speech, but not *qua* Deliberative speech. The Epilogue, again, is not essential even to a Forensic speech — as, when the speech is short, or the matter easy to remember; for the advantage of Epilogue is abridgment. The *necessary* parts of the speech, then, are Statement and Proof. These are proper to all. The greatest number that can be allowed is four — Proem, Statement, Proof, Epilogue. 'Refutation' comes under the head of Proof; 'Contrast' is a way of amplifying one's own argument, and is therefore a part of Proof, since he who does this, is demonstrating something. This is not true of the Proem, nor, again, of the Epilogue, which merely refreshes the memory. If, then, we are to follow Theodoros in taking into our division such terms as the above, we shall have 'Narrative Proper' distinguished from 'Supplementary' or 'Preliminary Narrative' — 'Refutation' from 'Supplementary Refutation.' Now a new term should be brought in, *only* where there is a distinct kind of thing to differentiate; otherwise, it is empty and nonsensical, like the terms used by Likymnios in his Art — 'Speeding on' — 'Aberration' — 'Ramifications.'

RHETORICA AD HERENNIUM

Translated by Harry Caplan

In his article, "Cicero's Rhetoric in the Middle Ages," James J. Murphy concludes:

> Cicero had a well-deserved medieval reputation as "master of eloquence." It must be kept in mind, however, that this reputation is based largely upon a book he wrote at the age of nineteen — the *De Inventione* — and upon the highly schematized *Rhetorica Ad Herennium* which was generally attributed to him. Both these books are products of late Hellenistic codifications of rhetorical doctrine which were introduced into Roman education around 100 B.C.[1]

Written by an unknown author, at an uncertain date, with an unknown original title, and perhaps only the revised notes of a student, the Rhetorica Ad Herennium *nevertheless is the oldest Latin rhetoric extant. Caplan calls it a "technical manual, systematic and formal in arrangement; its exposition is bald, but in the greatest part clear and precise."[2] Still, "the fact that the treatise appeared, from Jerome's time as a work by Cicero gave it a prestige which it enjoyed for over a thousand years."[3] Caplan concludes: "For us, however, it has literary importance because it is our only complete representative of the system it teaches. We may further readily admit that the work lacks the larger philosophical insight of*

Reprinted by permission of the publishers and THE LOEB CLASSICAL LIBRARY from Harry Caplan, translator, [Cicero], *Rhetorica Ad Herennium*, Cambridge, Mass.: Harvard University Press.

[1] James J. Murphy, "Cicero's Rhetoric in the Middle Ages," *Quarterly Journal of Speech*, 53 (Dec., 1967), p. 341.

[2] Harry Caplan, *op. cit.*, Introduction, p. vi.

[3] *Ibid.*, pp. vii-viii.

Aristotle's Rhetoric, *but that is not to deny its excellence as a practical treatise of the kind doubtless used by Roman orators. It is, moreover, itself not without usefulness for the modern student of the art.* "[1]

In contrast to Aristotle's four-part division of a speech, Ad Herennium includes six. *Unlike the Peripatetic model,* Ad Herennium *totally subjects disposition to invention, thus making it very narrow and somewhat uninteresting in scope. The six parts of the discourse are described below in part of Book I, section iii, and a broader discussion of these parts is presented from Book III, section ix.*

I, iii, 4

Invention is used for the six parts of a discourse: the Introduction, Statement of Facts, Division, Proof, Refutation, and Conclusion. The Introduction is the beginning of the discourse, and by it the hearer's mind is prepared for attention. The Narration or Statement of Facts sets forth the events that have occurred or might have occurred. By means of the Division we make clear what matters are agreed upon and what are contested, and announce what points we intend to take up. Proof is the presentation of our arguments, together with their corroboration. Refutation is the destruction of our adversaries' arguments. The Conclusion is the end of the discourse, formed in accordance with the principles of the art. . . .

III, ix, 16 – 18

Since it is through the Arrangement that we set in order the topics we have invented so that there may be a definite place for each in the delivery, we must see what kind of method one should follow in the process of arranging. The kinds of Arrangement are two: one arising from the principles of rhetoric, the other accommodated to particular circumstances.

Our Arrangement will be based on the principles of rhetoric when we observe the instructions that I have set forth in Book I — to use the Introduction, Statement of Facts, Division, Proof, Refutation, and Conclusion, and in speaking to follow the order enjoined above. It is likewise on the principles of the art that we shall be basing our Arrangement, not only of the whole case throughout the discourse, but also of the individual arguments, according to Proposition, Reason, Proof of the Reason, Embellishment, and Résumé, as I have explained in Book II. This Arrangement, then, is twofold — one for the whole speech, and the

[1] *Ibid.,* p. xxxiv.

other for the individual arguments – and is based upon the principles of rhetoric.

But there is also another Arrangement, which, when we must depart from the order imposed by the rules of the art, is accommodated to circumstance in accordance with the speaker's judgement; for example, if we should begin our speech with the Statement of Facts, or with some very strong argument, or the reading of some documents; or if straightway after the Introduction we should use the Proof and then the Statement of Facts; or if we should make some other change of this kind in the order. But none of these changes ought to be made except when our cause demands them. For if the ears of the audience seem to have been deafened and their attention wearied by the wordiness of our adversaries, we can advantageously omit the Introduction, and begin the speech with either the Statement of Facts or some strong argument. Then, if it is advantageous – for it is not always necessary – one may recur to the idea intended for the Introduction. If our cause seems to present so great a difficulty that no one can listen to the Introduction with patience, we shall begin with the Statement of Facts and then recur to the idea intended for the Introduction. If the Statement of Facts is not quite plausible, we shall begin with some strong argument. It is often necessary to employ such changes and transpositions when the cause itself obliges us to modify with art the Arrangement prescribed by the rules of the art.

In the Proof and Refutation of arguments it is appropriate to adopt an Arrangement of the following sort: (1) the strongest arguments should be placed at the beginning and at the end of the pleading; (2) those of medium force, and also those that are neither useless to the discourse nor essential to the proof, which are weak if presented separately and individually, but become strong and plausible when conjoined with the others, should be placed in the middle. For immediately after the facts have been stated the hearer waits to see whether the cause can by some means be proved, and that is why we ought straightway to present some strong argument. (3) And as for the rest, since what has been said last is easily committed to memory, it is useful, when ceasing to speak, to leave some very strong argument fresh in the hearer's mind. This arrangement of topics in speaking, like the arraying of soldiers in battle, can readily bring victory.

CICERO: DE INVENTIONE

Translated by H. M. Hubbell

Cicero discusses the parts of a speech both in De Inventione *and perhaps better in* De Partitione Oratoria. De Partitione Oratoria *was written near the end of Cicero's life, in about 46 B.C., for his son who was then 19. De* Inventione *was an incomplete work, written about the time Cicero was himself 19, and later disclaimed as those essays "of a youthful schoolboy." Nonetheless, both are highly technical and* De Inventione, *together with the* Ad Herennium, *gained Cicero wide acclaim throughout the middle ages, while neither Aristotle's* Rhetoric *nor Cicero's more mature efforts were even known. Since* De Inventione *was influential and* De Partitione Oratoria *was not, sections from the former have been chosen for inclusion here. Because of the extensive and lengthy treatment which Cicero gives every division of the speech, only brief excerpts are offered to show the germ of his thought in relation to each of the seven parts. Like* Ad Herennium, *Cicero links* dispositio *so closely to* inventio, *that it is difficult to tell where one begins and the other ends.*

I, xiv, 19 – xv, 21

Then, after all these points about the case have been discovered, the separate divisions of the whole case must be considered. For it does not follow that everything which is to be said first must be studied first; for the reason that, if you wish the first part of the speech to have a close agreement and connexion with the main statement of the case, you must derive it from the matters which are to be discussed afterward. Therefore when the point for decision and the arguments which must be devised for

Reprinted by permission of the publishers and THE LOEB CLASSICAL LIBRARY from H. M. Hubbell, translator, Cicero, *De Inventione*, Cambridge, Mass.: Harvard University Press.

the purpose of reaching a decision have been diligently discovered by the rules of art, and studied with careful thought, then, and not till then, the other parts of the oration are to be arranged in proper order. These seem to me to be just six in number: exordium, narrative, partition, confirmation, refutation, peroration.

Now since the exordium has to come first, we shall likewise give first the rule for a systematic treatment of the exordium. An exordium is a passage which brings the mind of the auditor into a proper condition to receive the rest of the speech. This will be accomplished if he becomes well-disposed, attentive, and receptive. Therefore one who wishes his speech to have a good exordium must make a careful study beforehand of the kind of case which he has to present. There are five kinds of cases: honourable, difficult, mean, ambiguous, obscure. An honourable case is one which wins favour in the mind of the auditor at once without any speech of ours: the difficult is one which has alienated the sympathy of those who are about to listen to the speech. The mean is one which the auditor makes light of and thinks unworthy of serious attention; the ambiguous is one in which the point for decision is doubtful, or the case is partly honourable and partly discreditable so that it engenders both goodwill and ill-will; the obscure case is one in which either the auditors are slow of wit, or the case involves matters which are rather difficult to grasp. Hence, since the kinds of cases are so diverse, it is necessary to construct the exordium on a different plan in each kind of case. The exordium is, then, divided into two species, *introduction* and *insinuation*. An introduction is an address which directly and in plain language makes the auditor well-disposed, receptive, and attentive. Insinuation is an address which by dissimulation and indirection unobtrusively steals into the mind of the auditor.

In the difficult case, if the auditors are not completely hostile, it will be permissible to try to win their good-will by an introduction; if they are violently opposed it will be necessary to have recourse to the insinuation. For if amity and good-will are sought from auditors who are in a rage, not only is the desired result not obtained, but their hatred is increased and fanned into a flame. In the mean case, on the other hand, it is necessary to make the audience attentive in order to remove their disdain. If an ambiguous case has a doubtful point for the judge's decision, the exordium must begin with a discussion of this very point. But if the case is partly honourable and partly discreditable, it will be proper to try to win good-will so that the case may seem to be transferred to the honourable class. When, however, the case is really in the honourable class, it will be possible either to pass over the introduction or, if it is convenient, we shall begin with the narrative or with a law or some very strong argument which supports our plea: if, on the contrary, it is desirable to use the introduction, we must use the topics designed to produce good-will, that the advantage which already exists may be increased. . . .

I, xviii, 25 — xix, 27

This is about all that it seemed necessary to say concerning the introduction and the insinuation separately: now it seems desirable to state some brief rules which will apply to both alike.

The *exordium* ought to be sententious to a marked degree and of a high seriousness, and, to put it generally, should contain everything which contributes to dignity, because the best thing to do is that which especially commends the speaker to his audience. It should contain very little brilliance, vivacity, or finish of style, because these give rise to a suspicion of preparation and excessive ingenuity. As a result of this most of all the speech loses conviction and the speaker, authority.

The following are surely the most obvious faults of *exordia,* which are by all means to be avoided: it should not be general, common, interchangeable, tedious, unconnected, out of place, or contrary to the fundamental principles. A *general* exordium is one which can be tacked to many cases, so as to seem to suit them all. A *common* exordium is one equally applicable to both sides of the case. The *interchangeable* can with slight changes be used by the opponent in a speech on the other side. The *tedious* exordium is one which is spun out beyond all need with a superabundance of words or ideas. The *unconnected* is one which is not derived from the circumstances of the case nor closely knit with the rest of the speech, as a limb to a body. It is *out of place* if it produces a result different from what the nature of the case requires: for example, if it makes the audience receptive when the case calls for good-will, or uses an introduction when the situation demands an insinuation. It is contrary to fundamental principles when it achieves none of the purposes for which rules are given about exordia, that is, when it renders the audience neither well-disposed, nor attentive, nor receptive, or produces the opposite result; and nothing surely can be worse than that. This is enough to say about the exordium.

The *narrative* is an exposition of events that have occurred or are supposed to have occurred. There are three kinds: one which contains just the case and the whole reason for the dispute; a second in which a digression is made beyond the strict limits of the case for the purpose of attacking somebody, or of making a comparison, or of amusing the audience in a way not incongruous with the business in hand, or for amplification. The third kind is wholly unconnected with public issues, which is recited or written solely for amusement but at the same time provides valuable training. It is subdivided into two classes: one concerned with events, the other principally with persons. That which consists of an exposition of events has three forms: *fabula, historia, argumentum. Fabula* is the term applied to a narrative in which the events are not true and have no verisimilitude, for example:

"Huge winged dragons yoked to a car."

Historia is an account of actual occurrences remote from the recollection of our own age, as:

"War on men of Carthage Appius decreed."

Argumentum is a fictitious narrative which nevertheless could have occurred. An example may be quoted from Terence:

"For after he had left the school of youth."

But the form of narrative which is concerned with persons is of such a sort that in it can be seen not only events but also the conversation and mental attitude of the characters. For example: "He comes to me perpetually, crying, 'What are you about, Micio? Why are you bringing the boy to ruin on our hands? Why this licence? Why these drinking parties? Why do you pile him up the guineas for such a life and let him spend so much at the tailor's? It's extremely silly of you.' He himself is extremely hard, past right and sense." This form of narrative should possess great vivacity, resulting from fluctuations of fortune, contrast of characters, severity, gentleness, hope, fear, suspicion, desire, dissimulation, delusion, pity, sudden change of fortune, unexpected disaster, sudden pleasure, a happy ending to the story. But these embellishments will be drawn from what will be said later about the rules of style . . . .

I, xxi, 30 − xxii, 32

The narrative will be plausible if it seems to embody characteristics which are accustomed to appear in real life; if the proper qualities of the character are maintained, if reasons for their actions are plain, if there seems to have been ability to do the deed, if it can be shown that the time was opportune, the space sufficient and the place suitable for the events about to be narrated; if the story fits in with the nature of the actors in it, the habits of ordinary people and the beliefs of the audience. Verisimilitude can be secured by following these principles.

In addition to observing these precepts, one must also be on guard not to insert a narrative when it will be a hindrance or of no advantage, and also not to have it out of place or in a manner other than that which the case requires. A narrative can be a hindrance when a presentation of the events alone and by themselves gives great offence, which it will be necessary to mitigate in arguing and pleading the case. When this situation arises, it will be necessary to distribute the narrative piecemeal throughout the speech and to add an explanation directly after each section so that the remedy may heal the wound and the defence may immediately lessen the animosity. A narrative is of no advantage when the facts have been explained by the opponents and it is of no importance to us to tell the story again or in a different way. The narrative is also useless when the audience has grasped the facts so thoroughly that it is of no advantage to us to instruct them in a different fashion. In such a case one must dispense with narrative altogether. The narrative is out of place when it is not set in that part of the speech which the situation demands; this topic we shall take up when we discuss arrangement, for it affects the arrangement. The narrative is not presented in the manner required by the case when a point which helps the opponent is explained clearly and elegantly, or a point which helps the speaker is presented obscurely and carelessly. Therefore, to avoid this fault, the speaker must bend everything to the advantage of his case, by passing over all things that make against it which can be passed over, by touching lightly on what must be mentioned, and by telling his own side of the story carefully and clearly.

Sufficient has, I think, been said about narrative; let us now pass to the *partition*.

In an argument a partition correctly made renders the whole speech clear and perspicuous. It takes two forms, both of which greatly contribute to clarifying the case and determining the nature of the controversy. One form shows in what we agree with our opponents and what is left in dispute; as a result of this some definite problem is set for the auditor on which he ought to have his attention fixed. In the second form the matters which we intend to discuss are briefly set forth in a methodical way. This leads the auditor to hold definite points in his mind, and to understand that when these have been discussed the oration will be over.

Now I think I ought to present briefly the method of using each form of partition. A partition which shows what is agreed upon, and what is not, should turn the subject of agreement to the advantage of the speaker's case, in the following manner: "I agree with my opponents that the mother was killed by her son." In the same way on the other side of the case, "It is agreed that Agamemnon was killed by Clytemnestra." For here each speaker stated what was agreed upon, yet was mindful of the advantage of his own side of the case. Secondly, what is in controversy should be set forth in explaining the point for the judge's decision, how this is discovered has been stated above.

The form of partition which contains a methodical statement of topics to be discussed ought to have the following qualities: brevity, completeness, conciseness. Brevity is secured when no word is used unless necessary. It is useful in this place because the attention of the auditor should be attracted by the facts and topics of the case, and not by extraneous embellishments of style. Completeness is the quality by which we embrace in the partition all forms of argument which apply to the case, and about which we ought to speak, taking care that no useful argument be omitted or be introduced late as an addition to the plan of the speech, for this is faulty and unseemly in the highest degree. Conciseness in the partition is secured if only *genera* of things are given and they are not confused and mixed with their *species*. To explain: a *genus* is a class that embraces several *species*, as *animal*. A *species* is that which is a part of a *genus*, as *horse*. But often the same thing is a genus in relation to one thing and a species in relation to another. For example, man is a species of animal, but a genus of which Thebans or Trojans are species . . . .

I, xxiii, 33 — xxiv, 34

Now that the rules for partition have been stated, it is necessary to remind the orator that throughout the speech he should bear in mind to complete the sections in order one after another as they have been planned in the partition, and that after all have been dispatched he should bring the speech to a close so that nothing be introduced after the conclusion. The old man in the Andria of Terence makes a brief and neat partition of what he wishes his freedman to know: "In this way you will learn my son's manner of life, my plan, and what I wish you to do in the matter." And his narrative follows the plan laid down in the partition: first, his son's manner of life,

"For after he had left the school of youth . . ."

then his plan:

"And now I am anxious . . ."

then what he wishes Sosia to do, which was the last point in the partition, is stated last:

"Now your task is . . ."

Just as he turned his attention first to each point as it arose, and after dispatching them all stopped speaking, so I favour turning our attention to each topic and when all have been dispatched, winding up the speech.

Now it seems desirable to give in turn the rules about *confirmation* as is demanded by the regular order of the speech. Confirmation or proof is the part of the oration which by marshalling arguments lends credit, authority, and support to our case. For this section of the speech there are definite rules which will be divided among the different kinds of cases. But

I think that it will not be inconvenient to set forth in the beginning, without any attempt at order or arrangement, a kind of raw material for general use from which all arguments are drawn, and then later to present the way in which each kind of case should be supported by all the forms of argumentation derived from this general store.

All propositions are supported in argument by attributes of persons or of actions. We hold the following to be the attributes of persons: name, nature, manner of life, fortune, habit, feeling, interests, purposes, achievements, accidents, speeches made . . . .

I, xxix, 44 – xxx, 47

All argumentation drawn from these topics which we have mentioned will have to be either probable or irrefutable. For, to define it briefly, an argument seems to be a device of some sort to demonstrate with probability or prove irrefutably.

Those things are proved irrefutably which cannot happen or be proved otherwise than as stated; for example, "If she has borne a child, she has lain with a man." This style of argument which is used for rigorous proof, generally in speaking takes the form of a dilemma, or of an enumeration or of a simple inference. A dilemma is a form of argument in which you are refuted, whichever alternative you grant, after this fashion: "If he is a scoundrel, why are you intimate with him? If he is an honest man, why accuse him?" Enumeration is a form of argument in which several possibilities are stated, and when all but one have been disproved, this one is irrefutably demonstrated; the following is an example: "He must have been killed by the defendant either because of his enmity to him, or through fear or hope or to gratify a friend; if none of these statements is true, he cannot have been killed by the defendant. For a crime cannot be committed without a motive. If there was no enmity, and no fear, and no hope of any advantages from his death and his death was of no interest to any friend of the defendant, it therefore follows that the defendant did not kill him." A simple inference arises from a necessary consequence, as follows: "If you say that I did this at that time, but at that particular time I was overseas, it follows that I not only did not do what you say, but that I was not even in a position to do it." And it will be necessary to keep a sharp watch that this kind of argument cannot be refuted in any way, so that the proof may not contain in itself only a form of argument and a mere appearance of a necessary conclusion, but rather that the argument may rest on rigorous reasoning.

That is probable which for the most part usually comes to pass, or which is a part of the ordinary beliefs of mankind, or which contains in itself some resemblance to these qualities, whether such resemblance be true or false. In the class of things which for the most part usually come to pass are probabilities of this sort: "If she is his mother, she loves him." "If he is avaricious, he disregards his oath." Under the head of ordinary beliefs or opinions come probabilities of this sort: "Punishment awaits the wicked in the next world." "Philosophers are atheists." Resemblance is seen mostly in contraries, in analogies, and in those things which fall under the same principle. In contraries, as follows: "For if it is right for me to pardon those who have wronged me unintentionally, I ought not to be grateful to those who have assisted me because they could not help it." In analogies, thus: "For as a place without a harbour cannot be safe for ships, so a mind without integrity cannot be relied on by friends." In the case of those things which fall under the same principle, probability is considered after this fashion: "For if it is not disgraceful for the Rhodians to farm out their customs-duties, neither is it disgraceful for Hermocreon to take the contract." Arguments of this kind are sometimes rigorous – for example: "Since there is a scar, there has been a wound" – sometimes they are only plausible, for instance: "If there was much dust on his shoes, he must have been on a journey. . . ."

I, xlviii, 89

On the other hand, the very nature of the argumentation may be shown to be faulty for the following reasons: if there is any defect in the argumentation itself or if it is not adapted to prove what we purpose to prove. To be specific, there will be a defect in the argument itself if it is wholly false, general, common, trifling, far-fetched, a bad definition, controvertible, self-evident, disputable, discreditable, offensive, "contrary," inconsistent, or adverse. . . .

I, li, 97 - lii, 98

Hermagoras puts the digression next, and then finally the peroration. In this digression he thinks a passage should be introduced unconnected with the case and the actual point to be decided; it might contain praise of oneself or abuse of the opponent, or lead to some other case which may supply confirmation or refutation not by argument but by adding emphasis by means of some amplification. If anyone thinks this is a proper division of a speech, he may follow Hermagoras' rule. For some of the rules for amplification and praise and vituperation have already been given, and the rest will be given in the proper place. But we do not think that this should be listed among the regular parts of the speech, because we disapprove of digressing from the main subject except in case of "commonplaces"; and this topic is to be discussed later. Moreover, I am of the opinion that praise and vituperation should not be made a separate part, but should be closely interwoven with the argumentation itself. Now we shall discuss the peroration.

The peroration is the end and conclusion of the whole speech; it has three parts, the summing-up, the *indignatio* or exciting of indignation or ill-will against the opponent, and the *conquestio* or the arousing of pity and sympathy.

The summing-up is a passage in which matters that have been discussed in different places here and there throughout the speech are brought together in one place and arranged so as to be seen at a glance in order to refresh the memory of the audience. If this is always treated in the same manner, it will be perfectly evident to everyone that it is being handled according to some rule or system. But if it is managed in different ways it will be possible to avoid both this suspicion and the boredom which comes from repetition. Therefore it will be proper at times to sum up in the manner which the majority of speakers employ, because it is easy, *i.e.* to touch on each single point and so to run briefly over all the arguments. At times, however, it is well to take the harder course and state the topics which you have set out in the partition and promised to discuss, and to recall to mind the lines of reasoning by which you have proved each point, in this fashion: "We have demonstrated this, we have made this plain." At times one may inquire of the audience what they might rightly wish to have proved to them. Thus the auditor will refresh his memory and think that there is nothing more that he ought to desire . . . .

I, liii, 100

The *indignatio* is a passage which results in arousing great hatred against some person, or violent offence at some action. In discussing this topic we wish it to be understood at the beginning that *indignatio* is used in connexion with all the topics which we laid out when giving rules for confirmation. In other words, all the attributes of persons and things can give occasion for any use of amplification that may be desired, or any method of arousing enmity. . .

I, iv, 106 – 108

Conquestio (lament or complaint) is a passage seeking to arouse the pity of the audience. In this the first necessity is to make the auditor's spirit gentle and merciful that he may be more easily moved by the *conquestio*. This ought to be done by the use of "commonplaces" which set forth the power of fortune over all men and the weakness of the human race. When such a passage is delivered gravely and sententiously, the spirit of man is greatly abased and prepared for pity, for in viewing the misfortune of another he will contemplate his own weakness. After that the first topic with which to evoke pity is that by which it is shown what prosperity they once enjoyed and from what evils they now suffer. The second employs a division according to time, and shows in what troubles they have been, still are, and are destined to be. The third, in which each separate phase of misfortune is deplored; for example, in lamenting the death of a son, one might mention the delight that his father took in his childhood, his love, his hope for the boy's future, the comfort he derived from him, the careful training, and whatever in a similar case can be said in bewailing any misfortune. The fourth, in which one recounts shameful, mean, and ignoble acts and what they have suffered or are likely to suffer that is unworthy of their age, race, former fortune, position or preferment. The fifth, in which all misfortunes are presented to view one by one, so that the auditor may seem to see them, and may be moved to pity by the actual occurrence, as if he were present, and not by words alone. The sixth, in which it is shown that one is in distress contrary to all expectation, and when he looked forward to receiving some benefit, he not only did not gain it, but fell into the greatest distress. The seventh, in which we turn to the audience and ask them when they look at us to think of their children or parents or some one who ought to be dear to them. The eighth, in which something is said to have happened which ought not, or that something did not happen which ought to have happened: for example, "I was not present, I did not see him, I did not hear his last words, I did not catch his last breath."

QUINTILIAN: INSTITUTIO ORATORIA

Translated by H. E. Butler

Presented below is Quintilian's philosophical approach to arrangement with his heavy stress on the role of the prosecutor, a major emphasis for classical writers. This section, from Book VII, is considerably different from and more interesting than the highly technical discussions of arrangement by Cicero in his De Inventione *and in the* Rhetorica Ad Herennium.

VII, Preface 1 — i, 37.

I think that enough has been said on the subject of invention. For I have dealt not merely with the methods by which we may instruct the judge, but also with the means of appealing to his emotions. But just as it is not sufficient for those who are erecting a building merely to collect stone and timber and other building materials, but skilled masons are required to arrange and place them, so in speaking, however abundant the matter may be, it will merely form a confused heap unless arrangement be employed to reduce it to order and to give it connexion and firmness of structure. Nor is it without good reason that arrangement is treated as the second of the five departments of oratory, since without it the first is useless. For the fact that all the limbs of a statue have been cast does not make it a statue: they must be put together; and if you were to interchange some one portion of our bodies or of those of other animals with another, although the body would be in possession of all the same members as before, you would none the less have produced a monster. Again even a slight dislocation will deprive a limb of its previous use and vigour, and disorder in the ranks will impede the movements of an army. Nor can I regard as an error the assertion that order is essential to the existence of nature itself, for without order everything would go to wrack and ruin. Similarly if oratory lack this virtue, it cannot fail to be confused, but will be like a ship drifting without a helmsman, will lack cohesion, will fall into countless repetitions and omissions, and, like a traveller who has lost his way in unfamiliar country, will be guided solely by chance without fixed purpose or the least idea either of starting-point or goal.

The whole of this book, therefore, will be devoted to arrangement, an art the acquisition of which would never have been such a rarity, had it been possible to lay down general rules which would suit all subjects. But since cases in the courts have always presented an infinite variety, and will continue to do so, and since through all the centuries there has never been found one single case which was exactly like any other, the pleader must rely upon his sagacity, keep his eyes open, exercise his powers of invention and judgment and look to himself for advice. On the other hand, I do not deny that there are some points which are capable of demonstration and which accordingly I shall be careful not to pass by.

Division, as I have already stated, means the division of a group of things into its component parts, *partition* is the separation of an individual whole into its elements, *order* the correct disposition of things in such a way that what follows coheres with what precedes, while *arrangement* is the distribution of things and parts to the places which it is expedient that they should occupy. But we must remember that *arrangement* is generally dependent on expediency, and that the same question will not always be discussed first by both parties. An example of what I mean, to quote no others, is provided by Demosthenes and Aeschines, who adopt a different order in the trial of Ctesiphon, since the accuser begins by dealing with the legal question involved, in which he thought he had the advantage, whereas the advocate for the defence treats practically every other topic before coming to the question of law, with a view to preparing the judges for a consideration of the legal aspect of the case. For it will often be expedient for the parties to place different points first; otherwise the pleading would always be determined by the good pleasure of the prosecution. Finally, in a case of mutual accusation, where both parties have to defend themselves before accusing their antagonist, the order of everything must necessarily be different. I shall therefore set forth the method adopted by myself, about which I have never made any mystery: it is the result in part of instruction received from others, in part of my own reasoning.

When engaged in forensic disputes I made it a point to make myself familiar with every circumstance connected with the case. (In the schools, of course, the facts of the case are definite and limited in number and are moreover set out before we begin to declaim: the Greeks call them *themes,* which Cicero translates by *propositions.*) When I had formed a general idea of these circumstances, I proceeded to consider them quite as much from my opponent's point of view as from my own. The first point which I set myself to determine (it is easy enough to state, but is still all-important) was what each party desired to establish and then what means he was likely to adopt to that end. My method was as follows. I considered what the prosecutor would say first: his point must either be admitted or controversial: if admitted, no question could arise in this connexion. I therefore passed to the answer of the defence and considered it from the same standpoint: even there the point was sometimes one that was admitted. It was not until the parties ceased to agree that any question arose. Take for example the following case. "You killed a man." "Yes, I killed him." Agreed, I pass to the defence, which has to produce the motive for the homicide. "It is lawful," he urges, "to kill an adulterer with his paramour." Another admitted point, for there is no doubt about the law. We must look for a third point where the two parties are at variance. "They were not adulterers," say the prosecution; "They were," say the defence. Here then is the question at issue: there is a doubt as to the facts, and it is therefore a question of *conjecture.* Sometimes even the third point may be admitted; it is granted that they were adulterers. "But," says the accuser, "you had no right to kill them, for you were an exile" or "had forfeited your civil rights." The question is now one of law. On the other hand, if when the prosecution says, "You killed them," the defence at once replies, "I did not," the issue is raised without more delay.

If it requires some search to discover where the dispute really begins, we must consider what constitutes the first question. The charge may be simple, as for example "Rabirius killed Saturninus," or complex like the following: "The offence committed by Lucius Varenus falls under the law of assassination: for he procured the murder of Gaius Varenus, the wounding of Gnacus Varenus and also the murder of Salarius." In the latter case there will be a number of propositions, a statement which also applies to civil suits as well. But in a complex case there may be a number of *questions* and *bases*: for instance the accused may deny one fact, justify another and plead technical grounds to show that a third fact is not actionable. In such cases the pleader will have to consider what requires refutation and where that refutation should be placed.

As regards the prosecutor, I do not altogether disagree with Celsus, who, though no doubt in so doing, he is following the practice of Cicero, insists with some vehemence on the view that the first place should be given to some strong argument, but that the strongest should be reserved to the end, while the weaker arguments should be placed in the middle, since the judge has to be moved at the beginning and forcibly impelled to a decision at the end. But with the defence it is different: the strongest arguments as a rule require to be disposed of first, for fear that the judge through having his thoughts fixed on those arguments should regard the defence of other points with disfavour. Sometimes, however, this order is subject to alteration; for example if the minor arguments are obviously false and the refutation of the most serious argument a matter of some difficulty, we should attack it last of all, after discrediting the prosecution by demonstrating the falsity of the former, thereby disposing the judges to believe that all their arguments are equally unreliable. We shall, however, require to preface our remarks by explaining why we postpone dealing with the most serious charge, and by promising that we will deal with it at a later stage: otherwise the fact that we do not dispose of it at once may give the impression that we are afraid of it. Charges brought against the past life of the accused should generally be dealt with first in order that the judge may be well-disposed to listen to our defence on that point on which he has to give his verdict. But Cicero in the *pro Vareno* postpones his treatment of such charges to the conclusion, being guided not by the general rule, but by the special circumstances of the case.

When the accusation is simple, we must consider whether to give a single answer to the charge or several. In the former case, we must decide whether the question is one of fact or of law: if it is one of fact, we must deny the fact or justify it: if, on the other hand, it is a question of law, we must decide on what special point the dispute arises and whether the question turns on the letter or the intention of the law. We shall do this by considering what the law is which gives rise to the dispute, that is to say under what law the court has been constituted. In scholastic themes, for example, the laws are sometimes stated merely with a view to connecting the arguments of the cases. Take the following case: "A father who recognises a son whom he has exposed in infancy, shall only take him back after paying for his keep. A disobedient son may be disinherited. A man who took back a son whom he had exposed orders him to marry a wealthy neighbour. The son desires to marry the daughter of the poor man who brought him up." The law about children who have been exposed affords scope for emotional treatment, while the decision of the court turns on the law of disinheritance. On the other hand, a question may turn on more laws than one, as in cases of αντινομία or contradictory laws. It is by consideration of such points as these that we shall be able to determine the point of law out of which the dispute arises.

As an example of complex defence I may quote the *pro Rabirio*: "If he had killed him, he would have been justified in so doing: but he did not kill him." But when we advance a number of points in answer to a single proposition, we must first of all consider everything that can be said on the subject, and then decide which out of these points it is expedient to select and where to put them forward. My views on this subject are not identical with those which I admitted a little while ago on the subject of *propositions* and on that of *arguments* in the section which I devoted to *proofs*, to the effect that we may sometimes begin with the strongest. For when we are defending, there should always be an increase of force in the treatment of questions and we should proceed from the weaker to the stronger, whether the points we raise are of the same or of a different character. Questions of law will often arise from one ground of dispute after another, whereas questions of fact are always concerned with one point; but the order to be followed is the same in both cases. We must, however, deal first with points that differ in character. In such cases the weakest should always be handled first, for the reason that there are occasions when after discussing a question we make a concession or present of it to our opponents: for we cannot pass on to others without dropping those which come first. This should be done in such a way as to give the impression not that we regard the points as desperate, but that we have deliberately dropped them because we can prove our case without them. Suppose that the agent for a certain person claims the interest on a loan as due under an inheritance. The question may here arise whether such a claim can be made by an agent. Assume that, after discussing the question, we drop it or that the argument is refuted. We then raise the question whether the person in whose name the action is brought has the right to employ an agent. Let us yield this point also. The case will still admit of our raising the question whether the person in whose name the suit is brought is heir to the person to whom the interest was due and again whether he is sole heir. Grant these points also and we can still raise the question whether the sum is due at all? On the other hand, no one will be so insane as to drop what he considers his strongest point and pass to others of minor importance. The following case from a scholastic theme is of a similar character. "You may not disinherit your adopted son. And if you may disinherit him *quā* adopted son, you may not disinherit one who is so brave. And if you may disinherit one who is so brave, you may not disinherit him because he has not obeyed your every command; and if he was bound to obey you in all else, you may not disinherit him on the ground of his choice of a reward; and even if the choice of a reward may give just ground for disinheriting, that is not true of such a choice as he actually made." Such is the nature of dissimilarity where points of law are concerned. Where, however, the question is one of fact, there may be several points all tending to the same result, of which some may be dropped as not essential to the main issue, as for instance if a man accused of theft should say to his accuser, "Prove that you had the property, prove that you lost it, prove that it was stolen, prove that it was stolen by me." The first three can be dropped, but not the last.

I used also to employ the following method. I went back from the ultimate *species* (which generally contains the vital point of the case) to the first general question or descended from the *genus* to the ultimate *species,* applying this method even to deliberative themes. For example, Numa is deliberating whether to accept the crown offered him by the Romans. First he considers the general question, "Ought I to be a king?" Then, "Ought I to be king in a foreign state? Ought I to be king at Rome?

Are the Romans likely to put up with such a king as myself?" So too in controversial themes. Suppose a brave man to choose another man's wife as his reward. The ultimate *species* is found in the question whether he is allowed to choose another man's wife. The *general* question is whether he should be given whatever he chooses. Next come questions such as whether he can choose his reward from the property of private individuals, whether he can choose a bride as his reward, and if so, whether he can choose one who is already married. But in our search for such questions we follow an order quite different from that which we employ in actual speaking. For that which as a rule occurs to us first, is just that which ought to come last in our speech: as for instance the conclusion, "You have no right to choose another man's wife." Consequently undue haste will spoil our division of the subject. We must not therefore be content with the thoughts that first offer themselves, but should press our inquiry further till we reach conclusions such as that he ought not even to choose a widow: a further advance is made when we reach the conclusion that he should choose nothing that is private property, or last of all we may go back to the question next in order to the general question, and conclude that he should choose nothing inequitable. Consequently after surveying our opponent's proposition, an easy task, we should consider, if possible, what it is most natural to answer first. And, if we imagine the case as being actually pleaded and ourselves as under the necessity of making a reply, that answer will probably suggest itself. On the other hand, if this is impossible, we should put aside whatever first occurs to us and reason with ourselves as follows: "What if this were not the case?" We must then repeat the process a second and a third time and so on, until nothing is left for consideration. Thus we shall examine even minor points, by our treatment of which we may perhaps make the judge all the better disposed to us when we come to the main issue. The rule that we should descend from the *common* to the *particular* is much the same, since what is *common* is usually *general.* For example, "He killed a tyrant" is *common,* while "A tyrant was killed by his son, by a woman or by his wife" are all *particular.*

I used also to note down separately whatever was admitted both by my opponent and myself, provided it suited my purpose, and not merely to press any admissions that he might make, but to multiply them by partition, as for example in the following controversial theme: — "A general, who had stood against his father as a candidate and defeated him, was captured: the envoys who went to ransom him met his father returning from the enemy. He said to the envoys, 'You are too late.' They searched the father and found gold in his pockets. They pursued their journey and found the general crucified. He cried to them, 'Beware of the traitor.' The father is accused." What points are admitted by both parties? "We were told that there had been treason and told it by the general." We try to find the traitor. "You admit that you went to the enemy, that you did so by stealth, that you returned unscathed, that you brought back gold and had it concealed about your person." For an act of the accused may sometimes be stated in such a way as to tell heavily against him, and if our statement makes a real impression on the mind of the judge, it may serve to close his ears to all that is urged by the defence. For as a general rule it is of advantage to the accuser to mass his facts together and to the defence to separate them.

I used also, with reference to the whole material of the case, to do what I have already mentioned as being done with arguments, namely, after first setting forth all the facts without exception, I then disposed of all of them with the one exception of the fact which I wished to be believed. For example, in charges of collusion it may be argued as follows. "The means for securing the acquittal of an accused person are strictly limited. His innocence may be established, some superior authority may intervene, force or bribery may be employed, his guilt may be difficult to prove, or there may be collusion between the advocates. You admit that he was guilty; no superior authority intervened, no violence was used and you make no complaint that the jury was bribed, while there was no difficulty about proving his guilt. What conclusion is left to us save that there was collusion?" If I could not dispose of all the points against me, I disposed of the majority. "It is acknowledged that a man was killed: but he was not killed in a solitary place, such as might lead me to suspect that he was the victim of robbers; he was not killed for the sake of plunder, for nothing was taken from him; he was not killed in the hope of inheriting his property, for he was poor: the motive must therefore have been hatred, since you are his enemy." The task not merely of division, but of invention as well, is rendered materially easier by this method of examining all possible arguments and arriving at the best by a process of elimination. Milo is accused of killing Clodius. Either he did or did not do the deed. The best policy would be to deny the fact, but that is impossible. It is admitted then that he killed him. The act must then have been either right or wrong. We urge that it was right. If so, the act must have either been deliberate or under compulsion of necessity, for it is impossible to plead ignorance. The intention is doubtful, but as it is generally supposed to have existed, some attempt must be made to defend it and to show that it was for the good of the state. On the other hand, if we plead necessity, we shall argue that the fight was accidental and unpremeditated. One of the two parties then must have lain in wait for the other. Which was it? Clodius without doubt. Do you see how inevitably we are led to the right method of defence by the logical necessity of the facts? We may carry the process further: either he wished to kill Clodius, who lay in wait for him, or he did not. The safer course is to argue that he did not wish to kill him. It was then the slaves of Milo who did the deed without Milo's orders or knowledge. But this line of defence shows a lack of courage and lessens the weight of our argument that Clodius was rightly killed. We shall therefore add the words, "As every man would have wished his slaves to do under similar circumstances." This method is all the more useful from the fact that often we can find nothing to say that really pleases us and yet have got to say something. Let us therefore consider every possible point; for thus we shall discover what is the best line for us to pursue, or at any rate what is least bad. Sometimes, as I have already said in the appropriate context, we may make good use of the statement of our opponent, since occasionally it is equally to the purpose of both parties.

UNIT FOUR: STYLE

QUINTILIAN: INSTITUTIO ORATORIA

Translated by H. E. Butler

As in his philosophical discussion of arrangement, Quintilian offers a theoretical, but equally practical, consideration of style. Unlike most of the rhetorical treatises which had preceded the Institutes, *Quintilian's Book X suggests that the best way to obtain an eloquent style is to read, write, and practice extensively. While he believes that* elocutio *is the most difficult part of rhetoric and that it ought to be the chief object of study, Quintilian warns against an excessive attention to stylistic perfection, to the exclusion of the content of the message. He argues that when a man has something important to say, based on his own frequency of reading, writing, and speaking, a natural beauty of style is assured. In the first section printed below, Quintilian defines the first essential of good style as clearness, marked by propriety and the correct rhetorical ornamentation. In the second section, he discusses one form of ornamentation, the trope, and in the third section selected, he discusses the figure. Quintilian's extensive treatment of tropes and figures formed the basis for a large number of the treatises written on them during the Renaissance when many writers believed that their use constituted the whole art of rhetoric.*

VIII, i, 1 — ii, 24

What the Greeks call φράσις, we in Latin call *elocutio* or style. Style is revealed both in individual words and in groups of words. As regards the former, we must see that they are Latin, clear, elegant and well-adapted to produce the desired effect. As regards the latter, they must be correct, aptly placed and adorned with suitable figures. I have already, in the

Reprinted by permission of the publisher and THE LOEB CLASSICAL LIBRARY from H. E. Butler, translator, Quintilian, *Institutio Oratoria*, Cambridge, Mass.: Harvard University Press.

portions of the first book dealing with the subject of grammar, said all that is necessary on the way to acquire idiomatic and correct speech. But there my remarks were restricted to the prevention of positive faults, and it is well that I should now point out that our words should have nothing provincial or foreign about them. For you will find that there are a number of writers by no means deficient in style whose language is precious rather than idiomatic. As an illustration of my meaning I would remind you of the story of the old woman at Athens, who, when Theophrastus, a man of no mean eloquence, used one solitary word in an affected way, immediately said that he was a foreigner, and on being asked how she detected it, replied that his language was too Attic for Athens. Again Asinius Pollio held that Livy, for all his astounding eloquence, showed traces of the idiom of Padua. Therefore, if possible, our voice and all our words should be such as to reveal the native of this city, so that our speech may seem to be of genuine Roman origin, and not merely to have been presented with Roman citizenship.

Clearness results above all from *propriety* in the use of words. But *propriety* is capable of more than one interpretation. In its primary sense it means calling things by their right names, and is consequently sometimes to be avoided, for our language must not be obscene, unseemly or mean. Language may be described as mean when it is beneath the dignity of the subject or the rank of the speaker. Some orators fall into serious error in their eagerness to avoid this fault, and are afraid of all words that are in ordinary use, even although they may be absolutely necessary for their purpose. There was, for example, the man who in the course of a speech spoke of "Iberian grass," a meaningless phrase intelligible only to himself. Cassius Severus, however, by way of deriding his affectation, explained that he meant Spanish broom. Nor do I see why a certain distinguished orator thought "fishes conserved in brine" a more elegant phrase than the word which he avoided. But while there is no special merit in the form of *propriety* which consists in calling things by their real names, it is a fault to fly to the opposite extreme. This fault we call *impropriety,* while the Greeks call it ἄκυρον As examples I may cite the Virgilian, "Never could I have hoped for such great woe," or the phrase, which I noted had been corrected by Cicero in a speech of Dolabella's, "To bring death," or again, phrases of a kind that win praise from some of our contemporaries, such as, "His words fell from the cross."[1] On the other hand, everything that lacks appropriateness will not necessarily suffer from the fault of positive *impropriety,* because there are, in the first place, many things which have no proper term either in Greek or Latin. For example, the verb *iaculari* is specially used in the sense of "to throw a javelin," whereas there is no special verb appropriated to the throwing of a ball or a stake. So, too, while *lapidare* has the obvious meaning of "to stone," there is no special

---

[1] Presumably in the sense, "He spoke like one in bodily pain."

word to describe the throwing of clods or potsherds. Hence abuse or *catachresis* of words becomes necessary, while metaphor, also, which is the supreme ornament of oratory, applies words to things with which they have strictly no connexion. Consequently *propriety* turns not on the actual term, but on the meaning of the term, and must be tested by the touchstone of the understanding, not of the ear. The second sense in which the word *propriety* is used occurs when there are a number of things all called by the same name: in this case the original term from which the others are derived is styled the *proper* term. For example, the word *vertex* means a whirl of water, or of anything else that is whirled in a like manner: then, owing to the fashion of coiling the hair, it comes to mean the top of the head, while finally, from this sense it derives the meaning of the highest point of a mountain. All these things may correctly be called *vertices,* but the *proper* use of the term is the first. So, too, *solea* and *turdus* are employed as names of fish, to mention no other cases. The third kind of *propriety* is found in the case where a thing which serves a number of purposes has a special name in some one particular context; for example, the proper term for a funeral *song* is *naenia,* and for the general's *lent augurale.* Again, a term which is common to a number of things may be applied in a *proper* or special sense to some one of them. Thus we use *urbs* in the special sense of Rome, *venales* in the special sense of newly-purchased slaves, and *Corinthia* in the special sense of bronzes, although there are other cities besides Rome, and many other things which may be styled *venales* besides slaves, and gold and silver are found at Corinth as well as bronze. But the use of such terms implies no special excellence in an orator. There is, however, a form of *propriety* of speech which deserves the highest praise, that is to say, the employment of words with the maximum of significance, as, for instance, when Cato said that "Caesar was thoroughly sober when he undertook the task of overthrowing the constitution," or as Virgil spoke of a "thin-drawn strain," and Horace of the "shrill pipe," and "dread Hannibal." Some also include under this head that form of *propriety* which is derived from characteristic epithets, such as in the Virgilian phrases, "sweet unfermented wine," or "with white teeth." But of this sort of propriety I shall have to speak elsewhere. *Propriety* is also made to include the appropriate use of words in metaphor, while at times the salient characteristic of an individual comes to be attached to him as a *proper* name: thus Fabius was called "Cunctator," the Delayer, on account of the most remarkable of his many military virtues. Some, perhaps, may think that words which mean more than they actually say deserve mention in connexion with clearness, since they assist the understanding. I, however, prefer to place *emphasis* among the ornaments of oratory, since it does not make a thing intelligible, but merely more intelligible.

Obscurity, on the other hand, results from the employment of obsolete words, as, for instance, if an author should search the records of the priests, the earliest treaties and the works of long-forgotten writers with the deliberate design of collecting words that no man living understands. For there are persons who seek to gain a reputation for erudition by such means as this, in order that they may be regarded as the sole depositories of certain forms of knowledge. Obscurity may also be produced by the use of words which are more familiar in certain districts than in others, or which are of a technical character, such as the wind called "Atabalus," or a "sack-ship," or *in malo cosanum.* Such expressions should be avoided if we are pleading before a judge who is ignorant of their meaning, or, if used, should be explained, as may have to be done in the case of what are called homonyms. For example, the word *taurus* may be unintelligible unless we make it clear whether we are speaking of a bull, or a mountain, or a constellation, or the name of a man, or the root of a tree.

A greater source of obscurity is, however, to be found in the construction and combination of words, and the ways in which this may occur are still more numerous. Therefore, a sentence should never be so long that it is impossible to follow its drift, nor should its conclusion be unduly postponed by transposition or an excessive use of *hyperbaton.* Still worse is the result when the order of the words is confused as in the line

"In the midmost sea
Rocks are there by Italians altars called."

Again, parenthesis, so often employed by orators and historians, and consisting in the insertion of one sentence in the midst of another, may seriously hinder the understanding of a passage, unless the insertion is short. For example, in the passage where Vergil describes a colt, the words

"Nor fears he empty noises,"

are followed by a number of remarks of a totally different form, and it is only four lines later that the poet returns to the point and says,

"Then, if the sound of arms be heard afar,
How to stand still he knows not."

Above all, ambiguity must be avoided, and by ambiguity I mean not merely the kind of which I have already spoken, where the sense is uncertain, as in the clause *Chremetem audivi percussisse Demean,* but also that form of ambiguity which, although it does not actually result in obscuring the sense, falls into the same verbal error as if a man should say *visum a se hominem librum scribentem* (that he had seen a man writing a book). For although it is clear that the book was being written by the man, the sentence is badly put together, and its author has made it as ambiguous as he could.

Again, some writers introduce a whole host of useless words; for, in their eagerness to avoid ordinary methods of expression, and allured by false ideals of beauty they wrap up everything in a multitude of words simply and solely because they are unwilling to make a direct and simple statement of the facts: and then they link up and involve one of those long-winded clauses with others like it, and extend their periods to a length beyond the compass of mortal breath. Some even expend an infinity of toil to acquire this vice, which, by the way, is nothing new: for I learn from the pages of Livy that there was one, a teacher, who instructed his pupils to make all they said obscure, using the Greek word σκότισον ("darken it"). It was this same habit that gave rise to the famous words of praise, "So much the better: even I could not understand you." Others are consumed with a passion for brevity and omit words which are actually necessary to the sense, regarding it as a matter of complete indifference whether their meaning is intelligible to others, so long as they know what they mean themselves. For my own part, I regard as useless words which make such a demand upon the ingenuity of the hearer. Others, again, succeed in committing the same fault by a perverse misuse of figures. Worst of all are the phrases which the Greeks call ἀδιανόητα, expressions which, though their meaning is obvious enough on the surface, have a secret meaning, as for example in the phrase *cum ductus est caecus secundum viam stare,* or where the man, who is supposed in the scholastic theme to have torn his own limbs with his teeth, is said to have *lain upon himself.* Such expressions are regarded as ingenious, daring and eloquent, simply because of their ambiguity, and quite a number of persons have become infected by the belief that a passage which requires a commentator must for that very reason be a masterpiece of elegance. Nay, there is even a class of hearer who find a special pleasure in such passages; for the fact that they can provide an answer to the riddle fills them with an ecstasy of self-congratulation, as if they had not merely heard the phrase, but invented it.

For my own part, I regard clearness as the first essential of a good style: there must be propriety in our words, their order must be straightforward, the conclusion of the period must not be long postponed, there must be nothing lacking and nothing superfluous. Thus our language will be approved by the learned and clear to the uneducated. I am speaking solely of clearness in style, as I have already dealt with clearness in the presentation of facts in the rules I laid down for the *statement of the case.* But the general method is the same in both. For if what we say is not less nor more than is required, and is clear and systematically arranged, the whole matter will be plain and obvious even to a not too attentive audience. For we must never forget that the attention of the judge is not always so keen that he will dispel obscurities without assistance, and bring the light of his intelligence to bear on the dark places of our speech. On the contrary, he will have many other thoughts to distract him unless what we say is so clear that our words will thrust themselves into his mind even when he is not giving us his attention, just as the sunlight forces itself upon the eyes. Therefore our aim must be not to put him in a position to understand our argument, but to force him to understand it. Consequently we shall frequently repeat anything which we think the judge has failed to take in as he should. We shall say, for example, "I fear that this portion of our case has been somewhat obscurely stated: the fault is mine, and I will therefore re-state it in plainer and simpler language"; for the pretended admission of a fault on our part creates an excellent impression. . . .

VIII, v, 35 − vi, 29

I will now proceed to the next subject for discussion, which is, as I have said, that of *tropes*, or *modes*, as the most distinguished Roman rhetoricians call them. Rules for their use are given by the teachers of literature as well. But I postponed the discussion of the subject when I was dealing with literary education, because it seemed to me that the theme would have greater importance if handled in connexion with the ornaments of oratory, and that it ought to be reserved for treatment on a larger scale.

By a *trope* is meant the artistic alteration of a word or phrase from its proper meaning to another. This is a subject which has given rise to interminable disputes among the teachers of literature, who have quarrelled no less violently with the philosophers than among themselves over the problem of the *genera* and *species* into which *tropes* may be divided, their number and their correct classification. I propose to disregard such quibbles as in no wise concern the training of an orator, and to proceed to discuss those *tropes* which are most necessary and meet with most general acceptance, contenting myself merely with noting the fact that some *tropes* are employed to help out our meaning and others to adorn our style, that some arise from words used *properly* and others from words used *metaphorically*, and that the changes involved concern not merely individual words, but also our thoughts and the structure of our sentences. In view of these facts I regard those writers as mistaken who have held that *tropes* necessarily involved the substitution of word for word. And I do not ignore the fact that as a rule the *tropes* employed to express our meaning involve ornament as well, though the converse is not the case, since there are some which are intended solely for the purpose of embellishment.

Let us begin, then, with the commonest and by far the most beautiful of *tropes*, namely, *metaphor*, the Greek term for our *translatio*. It is not merely so natural a turn of speech that it is often employed unconsciously or by uneducated persons, but it is in itself so attractive and elegant that however distinguished the language in which it is embedded it shines forth with a light that is all its own. For if it be correctly and appropriately applied, it is quite impossible for its effect to be commonplace, mean or unpleasing. It adds to the copiousness of language by the interchange of words and by borrowing, and finally succeeds in accomplishing the supremely difficult task of providing a name for everything. A noun or a verb is transferred from the place to which it properly belongs to another where there is either no *literal* term or the *transferred* is better than the *literal.* We do this either because it is necessary or to make our meaning clearer or, as I have already said, to produce a decorative effect. When it secures none of these results, our metaphor will be out of place. As an example of a necessary metaphor I may quote the following usages in vogue with peasants when they call a vinebud *gemma,* a gem (what other term is there which they could use?), or speak of the *crops being thirsty* or the *fruit suffering.* For the same reason we speak of a *hard* or *rough* man, there being no *literal* term for these temperaments. On the other hand, when we say that a man is *kindled to anger* or *on fire with greed* or that he has *fallen into error,* we do so to enhance our meaning. For none of these things can be more literally described in its own words than in those which we import from elsewhere. But it is a purely ornamental metaphor when we speak of *brilliance of style, splendour of birth, tempestuous public assemblies, thunderbolts of eloquence,* to which I may add the phrase employed by Cicero in his defence of Milo where he speaks of Clodius as the *fountain*, and in another place as *the fertile field and material* of his client's *glory.* It is even possible to express facts of a somewhat unseemly character by a judicious use of metaphor, as in the following passage:

> "This do they lest too much indulgence make
> The field of generation slothful grow
> And choke its idle furrows."

On the whole *metaphor* is a shorter form of *simile,* while there is this further difference, that in the latter we compare some object to the thing which we wish to describe, whereas in the former this object is actually substituted for the thing. It is a comparison when I say that a man did something *like a lion,* it is a metaphor when I say of him, *He is a lion.* Metaphors fall into four classes. In the first we substitute one living thing for another, as in the passage where the poet, speaking of a charioteer, says,

> "The steersman then
> With mighty effort wrenched his charger round."

or when Livy says that Scipio was continually *barked at* by Cato. Secondly, inanimate things may be substituted for inanimate, as in the Virgilian:

>   "And gave his fleet the rein,"

or inanimate may be substituted for animate, as in

>   "Did the Argive bulwark fall by sword or fate?"

or animate for inanimate, as in the following lines:

>   "The shepherd sits unknowing on the height
>   Listening the roar from some far mountain brow."

But, above all, effects of extraordinary sublimity are produced when the theme is exalted by a bold and almost hazardous metaphor and inanimate objects are given life and action, as in the phrase

>   "Araxes' flood that scorns a bridge,"

or in the passage of Cicero, already quoted, where he cries, "What was that sword of yours doing, Tubero, the sword you drew on the field of Pharsalus? Against whose body did you aim its point? What meant those arms you bore?" Sometimes the effect is doubled, as in Virgil's.

>   "And with venom arm the steel."

For both "to arm the steel" and "to arm with venom" are metaphors. These four kinds of metaphor are further subdivided into a number of *species,* such as transference from rational beings to rational and from irrational to irrational and the reverse, in which the method is the same, and finally from the whole to its parts and from the parts to the whole. But I am not now teaching boys: my readers are old enough to discover the *species* for themselves when once they have been given the *genus.*

While a temperate and timely use of metaphor is a real adornment to style, on the other hand, its frequent use serves merely to obscure our language and weary our audience, while if we introduce them in one continuous series, our language will become allegorical and enigmatic. There are also certain metaphors which fail from meanness, such as that of which I spoke above:

>   "There is a rocky wart upon the mountain's brow."

or they may even be coarse. For it does not follow that because Cicero was perfectly justified in talking of "the sink of the state," when he desired to indicate the foulness of certain men, we can approve the following passage from an ancient orator: "you have lanced the boils of the state." Indeed

Cicero himself has demonstrated in the most admirable manner how important it is to avoid grossness in metaphor, such as is revealed by the following examples, which he quotes: — "The state was gelded by the death of Africanus," or "Glaucia, the excrement of the senate-house." He also points out that a metaphor must not be too great for its subject or, as is more frequently the case, too little, and that it must not be inappropriate. Anyone who realises that these are faults, will be able to detect instances of them only too frequently. But excess in the use of metaphor is also a fault, more especially if they are of the same species. Metaphors may also be harsh, that is, far-fetched, as in phrases like "the snows of the head" or "Jove with white snow the wintry Alps bespewed." The worst errors of all, however, originate in the fact that some authors regard it as permissible to use even in prose any metaphors that are allowed to poets, in spite of the fact that the latter aim solely at pleasing their readers and are compelled in many cases to employ metaphor by sheer metrical necessity. For my own part I should not regard a phrase like "the shepherd of the people" as admissible in pleading, although it has the authority of Homer, nor would I venture to say that winged creatures "swim through the air," despite the fact that this metaphor has been most effectively employed by Virgil to describe the flight of bees and of Daedalus. For metaphor should always either occupy a place already vacant, or if it fills the room of something else, should be more impressive than that which it displaces.

What I have said above applies perhaps with even greater force to *synecdochè*. For while *metaphor* is designed to move the feelings, give special distinction to things and place them vividly before the eye, *synecdochè* has the power to give variety to our language by making us realise many things from one, the whole from a part, the *genus* from a *species*, things which follow from things which have preceded; or, on the other hand, the whole procedure may be reversed. It may, however, be more freely employed by poets than by orators. For while in prose it is perfectly correct to use *mucro,* the point, for the whole sword, and *tectum,* roof, for a whole house, we may not employ *puppis,* stern, to describe a ship, nor *abies,* fir, to describe planks; and again, though *ferrum,* the steel, may be used to indicate a sword, *quadrupes* cannot be used in the sense of horse. It is where numbers are concerned that *synecdochè* can be most freely employed in prose. For example, Livy frequently says, "The Roman won the day," when he means that the *Romans* were victorious; on the other hand, Cicero in a letter to Brutus says, "We have imposed on the people and are regarded as orators," when he is speaking of himself alone. This form of *trope* is not only a rhetorical ornament, but is frequently employed in everyday speech. Some also apply the term *synecdochè* when something is assumed which has not actually been expressed, since one word is then discovered from other words, as in the sentence,

"The Arcadians to the gates began to rush;"

when such omission creates a blemish, it is called an *ellipse.* For my own part, I prefer to regard this as a figure, and shall therefore discuss it under that head. Again, one thing may be suggested by another, as in the line,

"Behold, the steers
Bring back the plough suspended from the yoke,"

from which we infer the approach of night. I am not sure whether this is permissible to an orator except in arguments, when it serves as an indication of some fact. However, this has nothing to do with the question of style.

It is but a short step from *synecdochè* to *metonymy,* which consists in the substitution of one name for another, and, as Cicero tells us, is called *hypallage* by the rhetoricians. These devices are employed to indicate an invention by substituting the name of the inventor, or a possession by substituting the name of the possessor. Virgil, for example, writes:

"Ceres by water spoiled,"

and Horace:

"Neptune admitted to the land
Protects the fleets from blasts of Aquilo."

If, however, the process is reversed, the effect is harsh. But it is important to enquire to what extent *tropes* of this kind should be employed by the orator. For though we often hear "Vulcan" used for fire and to say *vario Marte pugnatum est* for "they fought with varying success" is elegant and idiomatic, while *Venus* is a more decent expression than *coitus,* it would be too bold for the severe style demanded in the courts to speak of *Liber* and *Ceres* when we mean bread and wine. Again, while usage permits us to substitute that which contains for that which is contained, as in phrases such as "civilised cities," or "a cup was drunk to the lees," or "a happy age," the converse procedure would rarely be ventured on by any save a poet: take, for example, the phrase:

"Ucalegon burns next."

It is, however, perhaps more permissible to describe what is possessed by reference to its possessor, as, for example, to say of a man whose estate is being squandered, "the man is being eaten up." Of this form there are innumerable species. For example, we say "sixty thousand men were slain by Hannibal at Cannae," and speak of "Virgil" when we mean "Virgil's poems"; again, we say that supplies have "come," when they have been "brought," that a "sacrilege," and not a "sacrilegious man" has been detected, and that a man possesses a knowledge of "arms," not of "the art of arms." The type which indicates cause by effect is common both in poets and orators. As examples from poetry I may quote:

"Pale death with equal foot knocks at the poor man's door"

and

"There pale diseases dwell and sad old age;"

while the orator will speak of "headlong anger," "cheerful youth" or "slothful case."

The following type of *trope* has also some kinship with *synecdochè*. For when I speak of a man's "looks" instead of his "look," I use the plural for the singular, but my aim is not to enable one thing to be inferred from many (for the sense is clear enough), but I merely vary the form of the word. Again, when I call a "gilded roof" a "golden roof," I diverge a little from the truth, because gilding forms only a part of the roof. But to follow out these points is a task involving too much minute detail even for a work whose aim is not the training of an orator.

Antonomasia, which substitutes something else for a proper name, is very common in poets: it may be done in two ways: by the substitution of an epithet as equivalent to the name which it replaces, such as "Tydides," "Pelides," or by indicating the most striking characteristics of an individual, as in the phrase "Father of gods and king of men . . . ."

IX, i, 1 – 25

In my last book I spoke of *tropes*. I now come to *figures,* called σχήματα in Greek, a topic which is naturally and closely connected with the preceding. For many authors have considered *figures* identical with *tropes,* because whether it be that the latter derive their name from having a certain form or from the fact that they effect alterations in language (a view which has also led to their being styled *motions*), it must be admitted that both these features are found in *figures* as well. Their employment is also the same. For they add force and charm to our matter. There are some again who call *tropes, figures,* Artorius Proculus among them. Further the resemblance between the two is so close that it is not easy to distinguish between them. For although certain kinds differ, while retaining a general resemblance (since both involve a departure from the simple and straightforward method of expression coupled with a certain rhetorical excellence), on the other hand some are distinguished by the narrowest possible dividing line: for example, while *irony* belongs to *figures of thought* just as much as to *tropes, periphrasis, hyperbaton* and *onomatopoea* have been ranked by distinguished authors as *figures of speech* rather than *tropes.*

It is therefore all the more necessary to point out the distinction between the two. The name of *trope* is applied to the transference of expressions from their natural and principal signification to another, with a view to the embellishment of style or, as the majority of grammarians define it, the transference of words and phrases from the place which is strictly theirs to another to which they do not properly belong. A *figure,* on the other hand, as is clear from the name itself, is the term employed when we give our language a conformation other than the obvious and ordinary. Therefore the substitution of one word for another is placed among *tropes,* as for example in the case of *metaphor, metonymy, antonomasia, metalepsis, synecdochè, catachresis, allegory* and, as a rule, *hyperbole,* which may, of course, be concerned either with words or things. *Onomatopoea* is the creation of a word and therefore involves substitution for the words which we should use but for such creation. Again although *periphrasis* often includes the actual word whose place it supplies, it still uses a number of words in place of one. The *epithet* as a rule involves an element of *antonomasia* and consequently becomes a *trope* on account of this affinity. *Hyperbaton* is a change of order and for this reason may exclude it from *tropes.* None the less it transfers a word or part of a word from its own place to another. None of these can be called *figures.* For a *figure* does not necessarily involve any alteration either of the order or the strict sense of words. As regards *irony,* I shall show elsewhere how in some of its forms it is a *trope,* in others a *figure.* For I admit that the name is common to both and am aware of the complicated and minute discussions to which it has given rise. They, however, have no bearing on my present task. For it makes no difference by which name either is called, so long as its stylistic value is apparent, since the meaning of things is not altered by a change of name. For just as men remain the same, even though they adopt a new name, so these artifices will produce exactly the same effect, whether they are styled *tropes* or *figures,* since their values lie not in their names, but in their effect. Similarly it makes no difference whether we call a *basis* conjectural or negative, or concerned with fact or substance, provided always that we know that the subject of enquiry is the same. It is best therefore in dealing with these topics to adopt the generally accepted terms and to understand the actual thing, by whatever name it is called. But we must note the fact that *trope* and *figure* are often combined in the expression of the same thought, since figures are introduced just as much by the metaphorical as by the literal use of words.

There is, however, a considerable difference of opinion among authors as to the meaning of the name, the number of *genera* and the nature and number of the *species* into which figures may be divided. The first point for consideration is, therefore, what is meant by a *figure*. For the term is used in two senses. In the first it is applied to any form in which thought is expressed, just as it is to bodies which, whatever their composition, must have some shape. In the second and special sense, in which it is called a *schema,* it means a rational change in meaning or language from the ordinary and simple form, that is to say, a change analogous to that involved by sitting, lying down on something or looking back. Consequently when a student tends to continuous or at any rate excessive use of the same cases, tenses, rhythms or even feet, we are in the habit of instructing him to vary his *figures* with a view to the avoidance of monotony. In so doing we speak as if every kind of language possessed a *figure*: for example *cursitare* and *lectitare* are said to have the same figure, that is to say, they are identical in formation. Therefore in the first and common sense of the word everything is expressed by *figures.* If we are content with this view, there is good reason for the opinion expressed by Apollodorus (if we may trust the statement of Caecilius on this point) to the effect that he found the rules laid down in this connexion quite incomprehensible. If, on the other hand, the name is to be applied to certain attitudes, or I might say gestures of language, we must interpret *schema* in the sense of that which is poetically or rhetorically altered from the simple and obvious method of expression. It will then be true to distinguish between the style which is devoid of figures (or ἀσχημάτιστος) and that which is adorned with figures (or ἐσχηματισμένη). But Zoilus narrowed down the definition, since he restricted the term *schema* to cases when the speaker pretends to say something other than that which he actually does say. I know that this view meets with common acceptance: it is, in fact, for this reason that we speak of *figured* controversial themes, of which I shall shortly speak. We shall then take a *figure* to mean a form of expression to which a new aspect is given by art.

  Some writers have held that there is only one kind of *figure,* altogether they differ as regards the reasons which lead them to adopt this view. For some of them, on the ground that a change of words causes a corresponding change in the sense, assert that all *figures* are concerned with words, while others hold that *figures* are concerned solely with the sense, on the ground that words are adapted to things. Both these views are obviously quibbling. For the same things are often put in different ways and the sense remains unaltered though the words are changed, while a *figure of thought* may include several *figures of speech.* For the former lies in the conception, the latter in the expression of our thought. The two are frequently combined, however, as in the following passage: "Now, Dolabella, [I have no pity] either for you or for your children": for the device by which he turns from the judges to Dolabella is a *figure of thought,* while *iam iam* ("now") and *liberum* ("your children") are *figures of speech.*

It is, however, to the best of my knowledge, generally agreed by the majority of authors that there are two classes of *figure,* namely *figures of thought,* that is of the mind, feeling or conceptions, since all these terms are used, and *figures of speech,* that is of words, diction, expression, language or style: the name by which they are known varies, but mere terminology is a matter of indifference. Cornelius Celsus, however, to *figures of thought* and *speech* would add those produced by "glosses"; but he has merely been led astray by an excessive passion for novelty. For who can suppose that so learned a man was ignorant of the fact that "glosses" and "reflexions" both come under the heading of thought? We may therefore conclude that, like language itself, figures are necessarily concerned with thought and with words.

As, however, in the natural course of things we conceive ideas before we express them, I must take *figures of thought* first. Their utility is at once great and manifold, and is revealed with the utmost clearness in every product of oratory. For although it may seem that proof is infinitesimally affected by the *figures* employed, none the less those same *figures* lend credibility to our arguments and steal their way secretly into the minds of the judges. For just as in sword-play it is easy to see, parry, and ward off direct blows and simple and straightforward thrusts, while side-strokes and feints are less easy to observe and the task of the skilful swordsman is to give the impression that his design is quite other than it actually is, even so the oratory in which there is no guile fights by sheer weight and impetus alone; on the other hand, the fighter who feints and varies his assualt is able to attack flank or back as he will, to lure his opponent's weapons from their guard and to outwit him by a slight inclination of the body. Further, there is no more effective method of exciting the emotions than an apt use of figures. For if the expression of brow, eyes and hands has a powerful effect in stirring the passions, how much more effective must be the aspect of our style itself when composed to produce the result at which we aim? But, above all, *figures* serve to commend what we say to those that hear us, whether we seek to win approval for our character as pleaders, or to win favour for the cause which we plead, to relieve monotony by variation of our language, or to indicate our meaning in the safest or most seemly way.

But before I proceed to demonstrate what *figures* best suit the different circumstances, I must point out that their number is far from being as great as some authorities make out. For I am not in the least disturbed by the various names which the Greeks more especially are so fond of inventing. First of all, then, I must repudiate the views of those who hold that there are as many types of *figure* as there are kinds of emotion, on the ground, not that emotions are not qualities of the mind, but that a figure, in its strict, not its general sense, is not simply the expression of anything you choose to select. Consequently the expression in words of anger, grief, pity, fear, confidence or contempt is not a *figure,* any more than persuasion, threats, entreaty or excuse. But superficial observers are deceived by the fact that they find *figures* in all passages dealing with such themes, and select examples of them from speeches; whereas in reality there is no department of oratory which does not admit such *figures*. But it is one thing to admit a *figure* and another to be a *figure*; I am not going to be frightened out of repeating the term with some frequency in my attempt to make the facts clear. My opponents will, I know, direct my attention to special figures employed in expressing anger, in entreating for mercy, or appealing to pity, but it does not follow that expressions of anger, appeals to pity or entreaties for mercy are in themselves *figures*. Cicero, it is true, includes all ornaments of oratory under this head, and in so doing adopts, as it seems to me, a middle course. For he does not hold that all forms of expression are to be regarded as *figures*, nor, on the other hand, would he restrict the term merely to those expressions whose form varies from ordinary use. But he regards as figurative all those expressions which are especially striking and most effective in stirring the emotions of the audience.

CICERO: ORATOR

Translated by H. M. Hubbell

Cicero's Orator, *written in 46 B.C. in the form of a letter to Marcus Junius Brutus, delineates Cicero's conception of the ideal orator. As the last of his rhetorical works, it discusses questions raised about his earlier work and defends his own use of the middle and grand styles of oratory in his career. Almost the entire treatise is devoted to* elocutio *or style, and thus, he approaches the ideal orator primarily through the concept of the three styles available to the orator. Beginning the prooemium to his treatise, Cicero comments on the difficult task Brutus has assigned him, describing the ideal orator. He suggests that true eloquence requires both excellence in thinking and in expression, and the great orator must master the three styles, the plain, the middle, and the grand. Cicero divides style into language and delivery, saying that style for the orator is different from that used by the philosopher, the sophist, the historian, and the poet. In the section printed below he expands his thesis that the orator is the man who can speak in the courts or deliberative assemblies "so as to prove, please, or persuade." John Edwin Sandys, remarking that the* Orator *belongs to the "aesthetics of oratory," states that it is evident that "the living image of his own oratorical greatness forms the foundation on which he builds his ideal fabric. His own speeches supply him with examples of every variety of oratorical excellence. . . ."*[1]

Reprinted by permission of the publishers and THE LOEB CLASSICAL LIBRARY from H. M. Hubbell, translator, Cicero, *Orator,* Cambridge, Mass.: Harvard University Press.

[1]John Edwin Sandys, *M. Tulli Ciceronis ad M. Brutum Orator* (Cambridge, England, 1885), pp. lviii, lxiv.

XX, 69 – XXIX, 101

The man of eloquence whom we seek, following the suggestion of Antonius, will be one who is able to speak in court or in deliberative bodies so as to prove, to please and to sway or persuade. To prove is the first necessity, to please is charm, to sway is victory; for it is the one thing of all that avails most in winning verdicts. For these three functions of the orator there are three styles, the plain style for proof, the middle style for pleasure, the vigorous style for persuasion; and in this last is summed up the entire virtue of the orator. Now the man who controls and combines these three varied styles needs rare judgement and great endowment; for he will decide what is needed at any point, and will be able to speak in any way which the case requires. For after all the foundation of eloquence, as of everything else, is wisdom. In an oration, as in life, nothing is harder than to determine what is appropriate. The Greeks call it πρέπον; let us call it *decorum* or "propriety." Much brilliant work has been done in laying down rules about this; the subject is in fact worth mastering. From ignorance of this mistakes are made not only in life but very frequently in writing, both in poetry and in prose. Moreover the orator must have an eye to propriety not only in thought but in language. For the same style and the same thoughts must not be used in portraying every condition in life, or every rank, position or age, and in fact a similar distinction must be made in respect of place, time and audience. The universal rule, in oratory as in life, is to consider propriety. This depends on the subject under discussion, and on the character of both the speaker and the audience. The philosophers are accustomed to consider this extensive subject under the head of duties – not when they discuss absolute perfection, for that is one and unchanging; the literary critics consider it in connexion with poetry; orators in dealing with every kind of speech, and in every part thereof. How inappropriate it would be to employ general topics and the grand style when discussing cases of stillicide[1] before a single referee, or to use mean and meagre language when referring to the majesty of the Roman people. This would be wrong in every respect; but others err in regard to character – either their own or that of the jury, or of their opponents; and not merely in the statement of facts, but often in the use of words. Although a word has no force apart from the thing, yet the same thing is often either approved or rejected according as it is expressed in one way or another. Moreover, in all cases the question must be, "How far?" For although the limits of propriety differ for each subject, yet in general too much is more offensive than too little. Apelles said that those painters also make this error, who do not know when they have done enough. This is an important topic, Brutus, as you well know, and requires another large volume; but for our present discussion the following will be enough: Since

[1] The legal technicalities about water dripping from a roof on adjoining property.

we say "This is appropriate" — a word we use in connexion with everything we do or say, great or small, — since, I repeat, we say "This is appropriate" and "That is not appropriate," and it appears how important propriety is everywhere (and that it depends upon something else and is wholly another question whether you should say "appropriate" or "right"; — for by "right" we indicate the perfect line of duty which every one must follow everywhere, but "propriety" is what is fitting and agreeable to an occasion or person; it is important often in actions as well as in words, in the expression of the face, in gesture and in gait, and impropriety has the opposite effect); the poet avoids impropriety as the greatest fault which he can commit; he errs also if he puts the speech of a good man in the mouth of a villain, or that of a wise man in the mouth of a fool; so also the painter in portraying the sacrifice of Iphigenia, after representing Calchas as sad, Ulysses as still more so, Menelaus as in grief, felt that Agamemnon's head must be veiled, because the supreme sorrow could not be portrayed by his brush; even the actor seeks for propriety; what, then, think you, should the orator do? Since this is so important, let the orator consider what to do in the speech and its different divisions: it is certainly obvious that totally different styles must be used, not only in the different parts of the speech, but also that whole speeches must be now in one style, now in another.

It follows that we must seek the type and pattern of each kind — a great and arduous task, as we have often said; but we should have considered what to do when we were embarking; now we must certainly spread our sails to the wind, no matter where it may carry us. First, then, we must delineate the one whom some deem to be the only true "Attic" orator. He is restrained and plain, he follows the ordinary usage, really differing more than is supposed from those who are not eloquent at all. Consequently the audience, even if they are no speakers themselves, are sure they can speak in that fashion. For that plainness of style seems easy to imitate at first thought, but when attempted nothing is more difficult. For although it is not full-blooded, it should nevertheless have some of the sap of life, so that, though it lack great strength, it may still be, so to speak, in sound health. First, then, let us release him from, let us say, the bonds of rhythm. Yes, the orator uses certain rhythms, as you know, and these we shall discuss shortly; they have to be employed with a definite plan, but in a different style of speech; in this style they are to be wholly eschewed. It should be loose but not rambling; so that it may seem to move freely but not to wander without restraint. He should also avoid, so to speak, cementing his words together too smoothly, for the hiatus and clash of vowels has something agreeable about it and shows a not unpleasant carelessness on the part of a man who is paying more attention to thought than to words. But his very freedom from periodic structure and cementing his words together will make it necessary for him to look to the other requisites. For the short and concise clauses must not be handled carelessly, but there is such a thing even as a careful negligence. Just as some women are said to be handsomer when unadorned — this very lack of ornament becomes them — so this plain style gives pleasure even when unembellished: there is something in both cases which lends greater charm, but without showing itself. Also all noticeable ornament, pearls as it were, will be excluded; not even curling-irons will be used; all cosmetics, artificial white and red, will be rejected; only elegance and neatness will remain. The language will be pure Latin, plain and clear; propriety will always be the chief aim. Only one quality will be lacking, which Theophrastus mentions fourth among the qualities of style — the charm and richness of figurative ornament. He will employ an abundance of apposite maxims dug out from every conceivable hiding place; this will be the dominant feature in this orator. He will be modest in his use of what may be called the orator's stock-in-trade. For we do have after a fashion a stock-in-trade, in the stylistic embellishments, partly in thought and partly in words. The embellishment given by words is twofold, from single words and from words as they are connected together. In the case of "proper" and ordinary words, that individual word wins approval which has the best sound, or best expresses the idea; in the case of variations from the common idiom we approve the metaphor, or a borrowing from some source, or a new formation or the archaic and obsolete (yet even obsolete and archaic words are to be classed as "proper" except that we rarely use them). Words when connected together embellish a style if they produce a certain symmetry which disappears when the words are changed, though the thought remains the same; for the figures of thought which remain even if the words are changed are, to be sure, numerous, but relatively few are noticeable. Consequently the orator of the plain style, provided he is elegant and finished, will not be bold in coining words, and in metaphor will be modest, sparing in the use of archaisms, and somewhat subdued in using the other embellishments of language and of thought. Metaphor he may possibly employ more frequently because it is of the commonest occurrence in the language of townsman and rustic alike. The rustics, for example, say that the vines are "bejewelled," the fields "thirsty," the crops "happy," the grain "luxuriant." Any of these metaphors is bold enough, but there is a similarity to the source from which the word is borrowed, or if a thing has no proper term the borrowing seems to be done in order to make the meaning clear, and not for entertainment. The restrained speaker may use this figure a little more freely than others, but not so boldly as if he were speaking in the grandest style. Consequently impropriety — the nature of which should be plain from what has been said about propriety — appears here too, when a metaphor is far-fetched, and one is used in the plain style which would be appropriate in another. This unaffected orator whom certain people call "Attic," and rightly so, except that he is not the only "Attic" — this orator will also use the symmetry that enlivens a group of words with the embellishments that the

Greeks call σχήματα, figures as it were, of speech. (They apply the same word also to figures of thought.) He will, however, be somewhat sparing in using these. For as in the appointments of a banquet he will avoid extravagant display, and desire to appear thrifty, but also in good taste, and will choose what he is going to use. There are, as a matter of fact, a good many ornaments suited to the frugality of this very orator I am describing. For this shrewd orator must avoid all the figures that I described above, such as clauses of equal length, with similar endings, or identical cadences, and the studied charm produced by the change of a letter, lest the elaborate symmetry and a certain grasping after a pleasant effect be too obvious. Likewise if repetition of words requires some emphasis and a raising of the voice, it will be foreign to this plain style of oratory. Other figures of speech he will be able to use freely, provided only he breaks up and divides the periodic structure and uses the commonest words and the mildest of metaphors. He may also brighten his style with such figures of thought as will not be exceedingly glaring. He will not represent the State as speaking or call the dead from the lower world, nor will he crowd a long series of iterations into a single period. This requires stronger lungs, and is not to be expected of him whom we are describing or demanded from him. For he will be rather subdued in voice as in style. But many of these figures of thought will be appropriate to this plain style, although he will use them somewhat harshly: such is the man we are portraying. His delivery is not that of tragedy nor of the stage; he will employ only slight movements of the body, but will trust a great deal to his expression. This must not be what people call pulling a wry face, but must reveal in a well-bred manner the feeling with which each thought is uttered.

A speech of this kind should also be sprinkled with the salt of pleasantry, which plays a rare great part in speaking. There are two kinds, humour and wit. He will use both; the former in a graceful and charming narrative, the latter in hurling the shafts of ridicule. Of this latter there are several kinds, but now we are discussing another subject. We here merely suggest that the orator should use ridicule with a care not to let it be too frequent lest it become buffoonery; nor ridicule of a smutty nature, lest it be that of low farce; nor pert, lest it be impudent; nor aimed at misfortune, lest it be brutal, nor at crime, lest laughter take the place of loathing: nor should the wit be inappropriate to his own character, to that of the jury, or to the occasion; for all these points come under the head of impropriety. He will also avoid far-fetched jests, and those not made up at the moment but brought from home; for these are generally frigid. He will spare his friends and dignitaries, will avoid rankling insult; he will merely prod his opponents, nor will he do it constantly, nor to all of them nor in every manner. With these exceptions he will use wit and humour in a way in which none of these modern "Attics" do, so far as I know, though this is certainly an outstanding mark of Attic style. For my part, I judge this to be the pattern of the plain orator — plain but great and truly Attic; since whatever is witty and wholesome in speech is peculiar to the Athenian orators. Not all of them, however, are humorous. Lysias is adequate and so is Hyperides; Demades is said to have excelled them all, Demosthenes is considered inferior. Yet it seems to me that none is cleverer than he; still he is not witty so much as humorous; the former requires a bolder talent, the latter a greater art.

The second style is fuller and somewhat more robust than the simple style just described, but plainer than the grandest style which we shall presently discuss. In this style there is perhaps a minimum of vigour, and a maximum of charm. For it is richer than the unadorned style, but plainer than the ornate and opulent style. All the ornaments are appropriate to this type of oration, and it possesses charm to a high degree. There have been many conspicuous examples of this style in Greece, but in my judgement Demetrius of Phalerum led them all. His oratory not only proceeds in calm and peaceful flow, but is lighted up by what might be called the stars of "transferred" words (or metaphor) and borrowed words. By "transferred" I now mean, as often before, words transferred by resemblance from another thing in order to produce a pleasing effect, or because of lack of a "proper" word; by "borrowed" I mean the cases in which there is substituted for a "proper" word another with the same meaning drawn from some other suitable sphere. It is, to be sure, a "transfer" when Ennius says

I am bereft of citadel and town,

but a "transfer" of quite a different kind than when he says

Dread Africa trembled with terrible tumult.

The latter is called ὑπαλλαγή or "hypallage" by the rhetoricians, because as it were words are exchanged for words; the grammarians call it μετωνυμία or "metonymy" because nouns are transferred. Aristotle, however, classifies them all under metaphor and includes also the misuse of terms, which they call κατάχρησις or "catachresis," for example, when we say a "minute" mind instead of "small"; and we misuse related words on occasion either because this gives pleasure or because it is appropriate. When there is a continuous stream of metaphors, a wholly different style of speech is produced; consequently the Greeks call it ἀλληγορία or "allegory." They are right as to the name, but from the point of view of classification Aristotle does better in calling them all metaphors. The Phalerian uses these very frequently, and they are attractive to a degree; and although he has many metaphors, yet the cases of metonymy are more numerous than in any other orator. To the same oratorical style — I am discussing the mean and tempered style — belong all figures of language, and many of thought. This speaker will likewise develop his arguments with breadth and erudition, and use commonplaces without undue emphasis. But why speak at length? It is commonly the philosophic schools which produce such orators: and unless he be brought face to face with the more robust speaker, the orator whom I am describing will find approval on his own merits. It is, as a matter of fact, a brilliant and florid, highly coloured and polished style in which all the charms of language and thought are intertwined. The sophists are the source from which all this has flowed into the forum, but scorned by the simple and rejected by the grand, it found a resting-place in this middle class of which I am speaking.

The orator of the third style is magnificent, opulent, stately and ornate; he undoubtedly has the greatest power. This is the man whose brilliance and fluency have caused admiring nations to let eloquence attain the highest power in the state; I mean the kind of eloquence which rushes along with the roar of a mighty stream, which all look up to and admire, and which they despair of attaining. This eloquence has power to sway men's minds and move them in every possible way. Now it storms the feelings, now it creeps in; it implants new ideas and uproots the old. But there is a great difference between this and the other styles. One who has studied the plain and pointed style so as to be able to speak adroitly and neatly, and has not conceived of anything higher, if he has attained perfection in this style, is a great orator, if not the greatest. He is far from standing on slippery ground, and, when once he gets a foothold, he will never fall. The orator of the middle style, whom I call moderate and tempered, once he has drawn up his forces, will not dread the doubtful and uncertain pitfalls of speaking. Even if not completely successful, as often happens, he will not run a great risk; he has not far to fall. But this orator of ours whom we consider the chief, – grand, impetuous and fiery, if he has natural ability for this alone, or trains himself solely in this, or devotes his energies to this only, and does not temper his abundance with the other two styles, he is much to be despised. For the plain orator is esteemed wise because he speaks clearly and adroitly; the one who employs the middle style is charming; but the copious speaker, if he has nothing else, seems to be scarcely sane. For a man who can say nothing calmly and mildly, who pays no attention to arrangement, precision, clarity or pleasantry – especially when some cases have to be handled entirely in this latter style, and others largely so, – if without first preparing the ears of his audience he begins trying to work them up to a fiery passion, he seems to be a raving madman among the sane, like a drunken reveller in the midst of sober men.

We have him now, Brutus, the man whom we are seeking, but in imagination, not in actual possession. If I had once laid my hands on him, not even he with his mighty eloquence would have persuaded me to let him go. But we have certainly discovered that eloquent orator whom Antonius never saw. Who is he, then? I will describe him briefly, and then expand the description at greater length. He in fact is eloquent who can discuss commonplace matters simply, lofty subjects impressively, and topics ranging between in a tempered style. You will say, "There never was such a man." I grant it; for I am arguing for my ideal, not what I have actually seen, and I return to that Platonic Idea of which I had spoken; though we do not see it, still it is possible to grasp it with the mind. For it is not an eloquent *person* whom I seek, nor anything subject to death and decay, but that absolute quality, the possession of which makes a man eloquent. And this is nothing but abstract eloquence, which we can behold only with the mind's eye. He, then, will be an eloquent speaker — to repeat my former definition — who can discuss trivial matters in a plain style, matters of moderate significance in the tempered style, and weighty affairs in the grand manner.

ARISTOTLE: THE RHETORIC

Translated by Richard Claverhouse Jebb

In introducing the metaphor, Aristotle remarks: "To learn easily is by nature, pleasant to all. Words contain meaning. As a result, whatever words impart new knowledge to us are pleasantest. But glosses are not understood and we already know proper words. It is a metaphor which most produces knowledge (1410 b 10)." The metaphor, then, bridges the gap between what is unknown and what we do know. Since, as Lane Cooper suggests, the central thought of the Poetics, *that the plot itself is the soul of tragedy, is itself a metaphor,*[1] *it is no wonder that both in the* Poetics *and in the* Rhetoric, *Aristotle places such a heavy value on the metaphor. In these two brief excerpts from Book III of the* Rhetoric, *Aristotle amplifies the description of the metaphor he gave in the* Poetics *and considers the inappropriate metaphor and the simile.*

III, ii, 3 – iv, 4

Deviation from the ordinary idiom makes diction more impressive; for, as men are differently impressed by foreigners and by their fellow-citizens, so are they affected by styles. Hence we ought to give a foreign air to our language; for men admire what is far from them, and what is admired is pleasant. In the case of *metrical* composition there are many things which produce this effect, and which are in place *there*; for the things and persons concerned are more out of the common. In prose the opportunities are much fewer, the subject-matter being humbler. Even in

Reprinted from Richard Claverhouse Jebb, translator, Aristotle, *The Rhetoric of Aristotle*, Cambridge, England: At the University Press.

[1] Lane Cooper, Introduction, Aristotle, *On the Art of Poetry*, translated by Lane Cooper (Boston, 1913), p. xx.

poetry, if fine language were used by a slave, or by a very young man, or about mere trifles, it would be somewhat unbecoming; even in poetry, there is a sliding scale of propriety. We must disguise our art, then, and seem to speak naturally, not artificially; the natural is persuasive, the artificial is the reverse; for men are prejudiced against it, as against an insidious design, just as they are suspicious of doctored wines. The difference is the same as between the voice of Theodôros and that of other actors; *his* voice seems to belong to the speaker, — *theirs*, to other men. A successful illusion is wrought, when the composer picks his words from the language of daily life; this is what Euripides does, and first hinted the way to do.

Language is composed of nouns and verbs, — nouns being of the various classes which have been examined in the *Poetics*. Strange words, compound words, words coined for the occasion, should be used sparingly and rarely: — *where*, we will say by and by. The reason of this has been given already: — the effect is too odd to be fitting. Accepted terms, proper terms, and metaphors, are alone available for the diction of prose. This appears from the fact that all men confine themselves to these: all men in talking use metaphors, and the accepted or proper terms for things; so it is plain that, if the composer is skilful, the foreign air will be given, the art may be concealed, and he will be clear. And this, we saw, is the excellence of rhetorical language. Equivocal terms are the class of words most useful to the sophist, for it is with the help of these that he juggles; synonyms are most useful to the poet. By synonyms in ordinary use I mean, for instance, 'to go' and 'to walk': — these are at once accepted and synonymous terms.

The nature of each of these kinds of words, — the number of sorts of metaphor, — and the supreme importance of metaphor both in poetry and in prose, have been explained, as we said, in the *Poetics*. In prose the greater pains ought to be taken about metaphor, inasmuch as prose depends on fewer resources than verse. Clearness, pleasure, and distinction, are given in the highest degree by metaphor; and the art of metaphor cannot be taught. Our metaphors, like our epithets, should be suitable. This will result from a certain proportion; if this is lost, the effect will be unbecoming, since the contrast between opposites is strongest when they are put side by side. As a crimson cloak suits a young man, what (we must inquire) suits an old man? The same dress will not suit him. If we wish to adorn, we must take our metaphor from something *better* in the same class of things; if to depreciate, from something *worse*. Thus (opposites being in the same class) it would be an example of this to say that the beggar 'prays' or that the man who prays 'begs'; as both are forms of asking. So Iphikrates said that Kallias was a 'begging priest,' not a 'torch-bearer'; and Kallias replied that he must be uninitiated, or he would not call him a 'begging priest,' but a 'torch-bearer': both are concerned with a god, but one is a title of honour, the other of dishonour. Some people call actors 'creatures of Dionysos,' but they call themselves 'artists.' Both terms are metaphors, the one calumnious, the other complimentary. Again, pirates nowadays call themselves 'purveyors.' So we may speak of the wrong-doer as 'making a mistake,' or the erring man as 'guilty of a wrong.' We may say that the thief has merely 'taken,' or that he has 'plundered.' The expression in the Têlephos of Euripides –

> '*Ruling* the oar,
> And, having landed on the Mysian coast,'. . .

is unsuitable, because the word 'to rule' is above the dignity of the subject; so no illusion is produced. There is another fault, which may arise from the form of a word, when the sound which this symbolises is not pleasant. Thus Dionysios 'the brazen' in his elegiacs calls poetry the 'scream of Kalliopê,' both being sounds; the metaphor from inarticulate sounds, however, is unworthy. Again, the metaphors, by which we give names to nameless things, must not be far-fetched, but drawn from things so kindred, and so similar, that the affinity appears at first sight: as in the well-known riddle –

> 'I saw a man who had glued bronze to a man with fire.'

The operation has no name; but, both processes being applications, he has called the application of the cupping-instrument a 'glueing.' As a general rule, good riddles supply good metaphors; for metaphors are in the nature of riddles, and so of course the metaphors are happy. Also, metaphors should be taken from beautiful things: – the beauty or ugliness of a word consisting, as Likymnios says, either in the sound or in the sense. There is yet a third consideration, which answers the sophistic argument. Bryson said that there could be no such thing as foul language, if the *meaning* is the same, whether we use this or that term. This is false. One term may be more appropriate than another, more in the image of our thought, better suited to set it before the eyes. Again, this term and that term do not describe the thing in the same aspect and so, on this ground also, one of them must be regarded as fairer or fouler than another. Both words denote the fair or foul things, but not *qua* fair or foul; or, if so, yet in different degrees. Our metaphors must be taken from this quarter, – from things beautiful in sound or in significance, – beautiful to the eye, or to some other sense. It makes a difference whether we say, for instance, 'rosy-fingered morn,' or 'crimson-fingered,' or worse still, 'red-fingered.' In using epithets, too, we may characterise an object either from its mean or base side, as, 'Orestes, the matricide' or from its better side, as, 'avenger of his father.' Thus Simônides, when the winner of the mule-race offered him a small fee, declined to write, on the ground that he did not like to write about half-asses. But, when the pay was made enough, he wrote –

'Hail, daughters of wind-swift steeds!'

(yet they were the daughters of the asses too). Then, without changing one's word, one may extenuate it. This extenuation consists in making less either of the evil or of the good: as Aristophanes in the *Babylonians* jokingly uses 'coinlet' for 'coin,' 'cloaklet' for 'cloak,' 'gibelet' for 'gibe,' – 'plaguelet' &c. – Both in metaphors and in epithets, however, we must be cautious and observe the mean.

Frigidities of style have four sources. First, compound words. Thus Lykophron[1] speaks of the *'many-faced* heaven (above) the *high-peaked* earth'; – and the *'narrow-channelled* shore.' Gorgias spoke of 'the *beggar-poet* flatterer'; 'forsworn or *ultra-veracious.'* Alkidamas[2] has – 'the soul filling with passion, and the face becoming *flame-hued'*; 'he thought that their zeal would prove *doom-fraught'*; he describes 'the persuasiveness of his speech' as 'end-fulfilling'; and 'the floor of the sea' as 'dark-hued.' All these phrases seem poetical, because they are composite.

This is one source of frigidity. Another is the use of strange words. Thus, with Lykophron, Xerxes is a 'mammoth man,' Skiron a 'fell wight'; Alkidamas offers a 'playful theme' to poetry, and speaks of the 'distraughtness of a man's nature' – 'whetted with the untempered anger of his thought.'

A third cause is the use of lengthy, unsuitable or frequent epithets. In poetry it is fitting to say *'white* milk'; but in prose such epithets are either somewhat unsuitable, or, when too abundant, they betray the trick, and make it clear that this is poetry. It is right enough to use some epithets: they relieve the monotony, and give an air of distinction to our style; but we should aim at a mean, for too much art does more harm than utter carelessness: the latter is not good, but the other is positively bad. This is why Alkidamas seems frigid; his epithets are not the mere seasoning but the actual meat, so thickly packed and over-grown and obtrusive are they. It is not 'sweat' but 'the *damp* sweat'; not 'to the Isthmian games' but 'to the *solemn festival* of the Isthmian games.' It is not 'the laws,' but 'those laws which are *the kings of the state'*; not 'with a rush,' but 'with the *impulse rushing from his soul.'* He does not say 'having taken to himself a school of the Muses,' but 'to *Nature's* school of the Muses'; (he speaks of)

[1] The rhetorician and sophist. Several of the following phrases may have come from a panegyric on Theseus and other Athenian heroes.

[2] Alkidamas, a rhetorician and sophist of the fourth century, who was a pupil of Gorgias. He is the reputed author of two extant declamations. The first of these, *On the Sophists,* argues in favour of an aptitude for extemporaneous discourse, as contrasted with the elaborately written compositions of Isokrates. The second purports to be a speech of Odysseus attacking Palamedes, and is less likely to be his genuine work. Aristotle's quotations apparently came from a lost work in praise of philosophy and culture, and from a discourse on the *Odyssey....*

the solicitude of his soul as *'sullen-visaged'*; (he says) not, 'the winner of favour,' but 'the winner of *multitudinous* favour.' Again — *'dispenser* of pleasure to the hearers'; 'he hid it (not among branches, but) among the branches *of the wood.'* 'He veiled' — not his body, but — 'the *shame* of his body.' He calls the soul's desire *'mirror-like'* — (this being a compound word, as well as an epithet, so that we get poetry); and, in the same way, the excess of his depravity as *'abnormal.'* Hence, by using poetic language, they make their style absurd and frigid owing to the impropriety, — and obscure, owing to the wordiness; for, when the speaker reiterates what is already understood, he overclouds and darkens the sense. People generally use compound words, when there is no name for a thing, and when the compound is easy, — as *'pastime'*; but, if this is carried too far, it becomes distinctly poetical. Thus, compound words are most useful to writers of dithyrambs, — the dithyramb being sonorous; — rare words to epic poetry, since the rarity has grandeur and boldness; metaphor, to iambic verse, — iambic verse being, as we have said, the present metre of tragedy.

The fourth and last source of frigidity is metaphor. Metaphors, too, may be unsuitable, either from their absurdity (comic poets have their metaphors), or from an excess of tragic grandeur: — they are obscure, when they are far-fetched. Thus Gorgias spoke of events being 'fresh, with the blood in them still'; 'you sowed this shameful seed, and have reaped this evil harvest.' This is too poetical. Again, Alkidamas calls philosophy 'a fort planted on the domain of the laws,' and the *Odyssey* 'a fair mirror of human life.' He speaks of 'offering no such playful theme to poetry.' All these phrases fail to be winning, for the reasons just given. The address of Gorgias to the swallow, which had polluted his head in its flight, is a masterpiece of the tragic style. 'Nay,' he said, 'this is unseemly, Philomela.' The act would not have been unbecoming in a bird, but was unbecoming in a girl. It was judicious reproach, then, to call her what she *was,* and not what she *is.*

The Simile, too, is a metaphor; the difference is but small. When the poet says of Achilles, 'he sprang on them like a lion,' this is a simile. When he says 'The lion sprang on them,' this is a metaphor; for, as both the animals are brave, he has transferred the name of 'lion' to Achilles. The simile, too, is available in prose; rarely, however, as it is poetical. Similes must be used like metaphors; for they *are* metaphors, differing in the point stated.

The following are examples of similes. Androtion said of Idrieus[1] that he was 'like curs which have been unchained — they rush on one, and bite; — and so Idrieus, freed from his bonds, is savage.' Theodamas said that

---

[1] The Athenian orator and Atthidographer, Androtion, was sent as envoy to Mausôlus, prince of Caria (377–351), who was succeeded by his brother Idrieus. Nothing is known of the imprisonment of the latter, which must have preceded his accession.

'Archidâmos was like Euxenos, − without his knowledge of geometry,' − and, *vice versa,* Euxenos will be 'an Archidâmos, who knows geometry.' In Plato's *Republic,* those who strip the dead are compared to 'curs who bite the stones, while they do not touch the thrower'; the people are likened to 'the captain of a ship, who is strong but a little deaf'; the verses of poets to 'persons, who have bloom, without beauty'; these seem different, when their prime is passed, and similarly with verses, when resolved into prose. Perikles said of the Samians that they were 'like children who took the sop, but cried'; and of the Boeotians, that they were 'like oaks; for an oak is shattered by an oak, so are the Boeotians by their wars with each other.' Demosthenes compared the people to 'sea-sick voyagers'; Demokrates[1] compared public speakers to 'nurses who swallow the morsel, and, in doing so, just touch the children with the saliva.' Antisthenes said that the lean Kêphisodotos was 'like incense − his consumption gives pleasure.' All these may be used either as similes, or as metaphors. Metaphors, which have gained applause, will, of course, serve as similes too; and similes, with the explanation omitted, will be metaphors. A 'Proportional' metaphor[2] must always apply reciprocally to both of two things in the same class; thus, if a bowl is the shield of Dionysos, it is fitting to call a shield the bowl of Ares. . . .

III, x, 1 − xi, 13

All men take a natural pleasure in learning quickly; words denote something; and so those words are pleasantest which give us *new* knowledge. Strange words have no meaning for us; common terms we know already; it is *metaphor* which gives us most of this pleasure. Thus, when the poet calls old age 'a dried stalk,' he gives us a new perception by

[1] Notorious for his bitter and offensive sayings. Two of the name are mentioned in Isaeus and Demosthenes respectively, but nothing worth mentioning is known of either.

[2] In the *Poetics,* xxi 4, Aristotle defines metaphor as 'the imposition of a foreign name' by means of a *transference* 'either from genus to species, or from species to genus, or from species to species, or proportionally.' Of these four kinds of 'metaphor' the first two are simply cases of *synechdoche,* as (1) the generic *vessel* for the specific *ship,* or (2) the specific *sail* for the generic *ship.* The third is *metonymy,* as 'rob' for 'cut off,' both being species of 'taking away.' It is only the fourth kind, the *proportional metaphor* that corresponds to our use of the word. Here there are always four terms, and as *a* is to *b,* so is *c* to *d*; for example, as the *shield* is to *Ares,* so is the *bowl* to *Dionysos.* The 'shield' and the 'bowl' both fall under the same *genus,* viz. 'the characteristic badge of a deity'; and both can be reciprocally transferred. Thus, a bowl can be called the 'shield of Dionysos,' and a shield 'the bowl of Ares.' The latter phrase was actually used by the dithyrambic poet, Timotheos: − ἤπει δ᾽ ἥρως θ᾽ ὅπλον · φιάλην Αρεως κατὰ Τιμοθεον᾽ Athen. 433 D. Similarly, as the 'evening' is to the 'day,' so is 'old age' to 'life'; hence we may call evening the 'old age of the day,' and old age the 'evening of life' (*Poet.* xxi 6).

means of the common *genus*; for both the things have lost their bloom. Now poets' similes have the same effect; hence, when they are good, they have this sprightliness. A simile, as has been said before, is a metaphor with a preface; for this reason it is less pleasing because it is more lengthy; nor does it affirm that *this* is *that*; and so the mind does not even inquire into the matter. It follows that a smart style, and a smart enthymeme, are those, which give us a new and rapid perception. Hence superficial enthymemes are not popular — meaning by 'superficial' those which are obvious to all, and which demand no inquiry — nor, again, those which, when stated, are not understood; but either those which convey knowledge, as soon as they are uttered, though this knowledge was not possessed before; or those, behind which the intelligence lags only a little; for here there is a sort of acquisition: whereas, in the other cases, there is neither sort. In respect to *sense,* then, these are the popular enthymemes. In respect to *style,* the popular *form* is the antithetic, for example, — 'regarding the peace, which the rest of the world enjoys in common, as a war upon their private interests,' where war is contrasted with peace. The popular *words* are the metaphorical, — the metaphor being neither remote, since this is hard to see at a glance, nor trite, for this excites no emotion. The third condition is, that the thing should be set before the eyes; for the hearer should see the action as present, not as future. We must aim, then, at these three things, — Metaphor, Antithesis, Actuality.

Metaphors are of four kinds, — the most popular being those 'from analogy.' Such was the saying of Perikles that the youth, who had perished in the war, had vanished from the city in such sort as if the spring were taken out of the year. And so Leptines said in reference to the Lacedaemonians that we 'must not suffer Greece to lose one of her two eyes.' When Chares was anxious to give account of his conduct in the Olynthiac war, Kêphisodotos expressed indignation, saying that Chares proposed to give his account 'while his grasp was upon the people's throat.' On another occasion, when he was urging the Athenians to make an expedition to Euboea, he said that 'they must go out with the decree of Miltiades for their commissariat. The Athenians having made truce with Epidauros and the seaboard, Iphikrates expressed his irritation by saying that 'they had been stripped of their stores for the campaign.' Peitholaos described the Paralos as 'the people's cudgel,' and Sestos as 'the meal-shop of the Peiraeus.' Perikles urged the removal of that 'eyesore' of the Peiraeus, AEgina. Moerokles said he was no worse than such an one — naming a respectable citizen; that person was scoundrel for 33 1/3 per cent, he for ten per cent. Or, take the iambic line of Anaxandrides about the delay of his daughters to get married —

'The bridals of my girls are *overdue.*'

Or the saying of Polyeuktos about a certain apoplectic Speusippos, — that he 'could not keep quiet, although fortune and his disease had put him in the pillory.' Kêphisodotos called triremes, 'painted mills': and Diogenes described taverns as 'the public messes of Attica.' AEsion spoke of their 'having poured the city into Sicily'; – this is a metaphor, and puts the thing before the eyes. 'So that Hellas *cried aloud*' – this is, in a way, metaphorical and vivid. Again, Kêphisodotos warned the city not to have too many *concourses*. Isokrates used the same term in reference to the 'concourse' at the festivals. In the *Funeral Oration*, it is said that 'Greece might well cut off her hair at the grave of those who fell at Salamis, deeming her freedom buried with their valour,' The saying that 'Greece might well mourn, since her valour *was buried in that grave*' is a vivid metaphor; while the juxtaposition of *valour* and *freedom* gives a certain antithesis. Again, Iphikrates said – 'the path of my speech lies through the midst of the deeds of Chares'; this is a metaphor of proportion, and the phrase 'through the midst' is graphic. Again, to speak of 'summoning dangers to the rescue of dangers' is a vivid metaphor. Lykoleôn said in defence of Chabrias – 'They did not revere even his symbol of supplication, the brazen statue'; this is a metaphor for the time, but not for all times; it serves, however, to give vividness; it is when he is in danger, that his statue is a suppliant, – that (of course) lifeless image of life, the record of public services. 'In every way studying to be spiritless'; – a metaphor, since 'studying' implies *increasing* something. And 'God has *kindled* intellect to be a light in the soul'; both intellect and light *show* something. – 'We are not composing but *postponing* our wars': – both things are of the future, – postponement, and the kind of peace in question. It is a metaphor to say 'this treaty is a *trophy* much nobler than those won on battlefields; these commemorate small things and a single issue; the treaty is a momument of the whole war': – for both 'trophy' and 'treaty' are tokens of victory. Or – 'Cities render heavy accounts to the censure of mankind': – the account being a sort of just penalty.

We have seen, then, that smartness depends on 'proportional' metaphor, and on 'setting things before the eyes.' We must now explain what we mean by 'setting things before the eyes,' and by what methods this is effected. This is my definition – those words 'set a thing before the eyes,' which describe it in an active state. For instance, to say that a good man is 'four-square' is a metaphor, since both the man and the square are complete; but it does not describe an active state. This phrase, on the other hand, '*in the flower of* his vigour'; or this, 'at large, like a sacred animal,' – are images of an active state. And, in the verse –

'From thence the Greeks, then, *darting* with their feet,'

the word 'darting' gives both actuality and metaphor – for it means swiftness. Or, we may use the device, often employed by Homer, of giving life to lifeless things by means of metaphor. In all such cases he wins applause by describing *an active state*: as in these words –

'Back again plainward rolled the *shameless* stone.'
'The arrow *flew.*'
'The arrow *eager* to fly on.'
'The spears stuck in the ground *quivering* with hunger for the flesh.'
'The spear-point shot *quivering* through his breast.'

In all these cases the thing is shown in an active state by being made alive; — 'to be shameless,' 'to quiver,' &c., are active states. These terms are applied with the help of a proportional metaphor; — as the stone is to Sisyphos, so is the shameless man to the victim of shamelessness. This, again, is among his admired images for lifeless things —

'Curved, white-crested — some in front, and more behind —.'

All such expressions make the thing moving and living — and an active state is movement.

Metaphors, as has been said before, must be taken from appropriate but not obvious things; just as in philosophy acuteness is shown by discerning resemblance between things apart; as Archytas said that 'an arbitrator and an altar were the same thing' — for each is a refuge for injured innocence. Or, one might say that 'an anchor and a swing were identical'; for each is the same sort of thing, with the difference between 'above' and 'below.' To speak of States having been 'put on the same level' is to use the same phrase of things which are far apart, equalisation being here the point in common between a superficies and political resources.

Now smartness, too, is given, as a rule, by means of metaphor, with the addition of a deception. The fact that the hearer has learned something is made plainer by its contrast with his expectation; the mind seems to say — 'Indeed! So I was wrong.' The smartness of apophthegms, too, depends on a meaning beyond the mere words — as when Stêsichoros says, 'the grasshoppers will sing to themselves on the ground.' Good riddles are pleasing for the same reason; there is a new perception and there is a metaphor. The like is true of what Theodôros calls 'novelty' in style. This happens when the thing is a surprise, and, as he says, does not answer to our presentiment; like those words, formed by a change, which comic writers use. Jokes which depend on the change of a letter have this effect: they deceive. And so in verse; the hearer is disappointed by the line, —

'Statelily stept he along, and under his feet were his — chilblains':

one expected 'sandals.' (This kind of point, however, must be obvious on the instant.) The verbal joke depends on a meaning which is not proper to the word, but twists it; for instance, the saying of Theodoros about Nikon the citharaplayer — 'θ ράττειϲε': he affects to mean, — θ ράττειϲε, — and deceives us; for he has another meaning. So, when this is perceived, it gives pleasure (of course, if the hearer does not understand that Nikon is a Thracian, he will see no point in it). Or this — 'you want him to find his Mede.' (Both kinds of smartness must be used seasonably.) Of the same sort are such pleasantries as saying that, 'for the Athenians the ἀρχὴ θάλαττης was not the ἀρχὴ κακῶν — they benefited by it: or that, as Isokrates said, the ἀρχή was an ἀρχὴ κακῶν for the city. In each case the thing said is unexpected, and, at the same time, its truth is recognised. In the latter case, there would be no point in saying that ἀρχή is ἀρχη' were there not a double meaning; in the former case, the ἀρχή which is the subject of the negation has a different sense from that first named. In all such instances, however, the merit of the pun, or of the metaphor, depends on its fitness. Thus, in saying that Ἀνάσχετος is οὐκ ἀνασχετός' there is a pun with the negative; but it is fitting only if Anaschetos is disagreeable. Again: —

'Thou canst be too much our stranger-friend';

[or] 'Thou canst be too much,' &c., is equivalent to saying, 'The stranger must not always be a stranger'; for this same word ξένος means 'alien.' Of the same kind is the admired saying of Anaxandrides,

'Well is it to die ere one has done a deed worthy of death,'

for this is equivalent to saying — 'It is a worthy thing to die, without being worthy to die,' or 'without doing deeds worthy of death.' The species of diction is the same in all these cases; but, the more compact and the more antithetical the expression, the greater the applause. The reason is, that our new perception is made clearer by the antithesis, and quicker by the brevity. Further, the saying must always have, either a personal application, or a merit of expression, if it is to be striking as well as true. It may be true and yet trite: thus, 'one ought to die innocent' is true, but not smart. 'Wife and husband should be well matched' — this is not smart. Smartness depends on having both qualities: thus 'it is worthy of a man to die, while he is unworthy of death.' The greater the number of conditions which the saying fulfils, the greater seems the smartness: as, for instance, when the words are metaphorical, and the metaphor of a certain kind, — with antithesis, parallelism of structure, and actuality.

Similes, also, of an effective kind, as has been said above, are in a sense metaphors; for, like the 'proportional' metaphor, they always involve two terms. For instance, a shield (we say) is 'the goblet of Ares,' — a bow is a 'chordless lyre.' Thus stated, it is not a *simple* metaphor; it would be a *simple* metaphor to say that the bow is a lyre, or the shield a goblet. There are similes, also, of this simple kind, — as the comparison of a flute-player to an ape, or of a shortsighted man to a sputtering lamp (since both wink). But the happy simile is where there is a 'proportional' metaphor: — as one may compare a shield to a 'goblet of Ares,' a ruin to the 'rag of a house,' or say that Nikêratos is a 'Philoktêtês stung by Pratys,' — to use the comparison of Thrasymachos, when he saw Nikêratos defeated in recitation by Pratys, and with long hair and still squalid. It is in these things that poets are most hissed for failure, or most applauded for success — as when they make it come just right thus —

'Curly as stalks of parsley are his legs.'
'Just like Philammon struggling with the sand-bag.'

All things of this kind, too, are similes; and that similes are metaphors has been often said.

Proverbs, again, are 'metaphors from species to species.' Suppose for instance that one introduces something in the expectation of profiting by it himself, and then is injured, he says 'This is like the Carpathian and the hare'; — since both he and the Carpathian have had the fate in question.

The sources and the theory of smartness in style may now be considered as explained. It may be added that hyperboles of the most popular kind are also metaphors; — as the hyperbole about the man with the black eye — 'You would have taken him for a basket of mulberries': — the bruise being something purple; but the *quantity* of the purple makes the exaggeration. The formula, '*like* so or so,' may be a hyperbole differently stated. '*Like* Philammon struggling with the sand-bag' — otherwise— 'You would have thought that he was Philammon boxing with the sand-bag.' 'With legs curling *like* parsley'; otherwise — 'You would have thought he was not on legs, but on stalks of parsley, so curly are they.' Hyperbole is boyish, for it expresses vehemence. Hence it is most used by angry people: —

'Not if his gifts to me were as the sand or the dust: I will not marry the daughter of Agamemon son of Atreus, never, though she should vie in beauty with golden Aphroditê, and in skill with Athênê.'

(Hyperbole is most used by the Attic orators.) For the reason given above, it does not suit an elderly speaker.

CICERO: DE ORATORE

Translated by E. W. Sutton and H. Rackham

"It is with formal rhetoric that the theory of the laughable is subsequently to be bound...."[1] *While Aristotle formulated the theory, and there is evidence to suggest that other Greek rhetoricians such as Gorgias and Plato considered the laughable, it was left to Cicero to set down the theory in precise terms, something which he says cannot be done. Cicero suggests that there are two sorts of wit, irony and raillery, neither of which can be taught. Having said this, he continues the dialogue in Book II, section 57 and following printed below, and discusses the functions of the laughable as a form of style and its limitations. Later in the book he discusses the varied kinds of wit and how they may be used.*

II, lvii, 233 — lxi, 252.

"And so, Caesar, I too beg you, if you think proper, to discuss fully this type of jesting, and to state your views, lest haply one branch of oratory should be thought to have been passed over, with your approval, in such company as this, and in a conversation so carefully elaborated."
"Assuredly, Crassus," replied Caesar, "seeing that you are collecting a boon companion's 'shot', I will not run away and so give you any occasion for complaint...."
"As regards laughter there are five matters for consideration: first its nature; second, its source; third, whether willingness to produce it becomes an orator; fourth, the limits of his licence; fifth, the classification of things laughable.

Reprinted by permission of the publishers and THE LOEB CLASSICAL LIBRARY from E. W. Sutton and H. Rackham, translators, Cicero, *De Oratore*, Cambridge, Mass.: Harvard University Press.

[1] Mary A. Grant, *The Ancient Rhetorical Theories of the Laughable*, University of Wisconsin Studies in Language and Literature, No. 21 (1924), p. 24.

"Now the first of these topics, the essential nature of laughter, the way it is occasioned, where it is seated, and how it comes into being, and bursts out so unexpectedly that, strive as we may, we cannot restrain it, and how at the same instant it takes possession of the lungs, voice, pulse, countenance and eyes, – all this I leave to Democritus[1] : for it does not concern the present conversation, and, even if it did, I should still not be ashamed to show ignorance of something which even its professed expositors do not understand.

"Then the field or province, so to speak, of the laughable (this being our next problem), is restricted to that which may be described as unseemly or ugly; for the chief, if not the only, objects of laughter are those sayings which remark upon and point out something unseemly in no unseemly manner.

"And again, to come to our third topic, it clearly becomes an orator to raise laughter, and this on various grounds; for instance, merriment naturally wins goodwill for its author; and everyone admires acuteness, which is often concentrated in a single word, uttered generally in repelling, though sometimes in delivering an attack; and it shatters or obstructs or makes light of an opponent, or alarms or repulses him; and it shows the orator himself to be a man of finish, accomplishment and taste; and, best of all, it relieves dullness and tones down austerity, and, by a jest or a laugh, often dispels distasteful suggestions not easily weakened by reasonings.

"But the limits within which things laughable are to be handled by the orator, that fourth question we put to ourselves, is one calling for most careful consideration. For neither outstanding wickedness, such as involves crime, nor, on the other hand, outstanding wretchedness is assailed by ridicule, for the public would have the villainous hurt by a weapon rather more formidable than ridicule; while they dislike mockery of the wretched, except perhaps if these bear themselves arrogantly. And you must be especially tender of popular esteem, so that you do not inconsiderately speak ill of the well-beloved.

"Such then is the restraint that, above all else, must be practised in jesting. Thus the things most easily ridiculed are those which call for neither strong disgust nor the deepest sympathy. This is why all laughing-matters are found among those blemishes noticeable in the conduct of people who are neither objects of general esteem nor yet full of misery, and not apparently merely fit to be hurried off to execution for their crimes; and these blemishes, if deftly handled, raise laughter. In ugliness too and in physical blemishes there is good enough matter for jesting, but here as elsewhere the limits of licence are the main question.

---

[1]An eminent Greek physicist of the 5th century B.C.; known as "the laughing philosopher."

As to this, not only is there a rule excluding remarks made in bad taste, but also, even though you could say something with highly comical effect, an orator must avoid each of two dangers: he must not let his jesting become buffoonery or mere mimicking. We shall more readily understand examples of each kind when we come to the actual classification of things laughable.

"For there are two types of wit, one employed upon facts, the other upon words. Upon facts, whenever any tale is told, some anecdote for instance, just as you, Crassus, alleged one day, in a speech against Memmius, that Memmius 'had made a mouthful of Largus's arm,' when brawling with him at Tarracina over a lady-love; it was a spicy story, but every word of your own fabrication. You wound up by relating that the letters M.M.L.L.L. were inscribed on every wall in Tarracina, and that some ancient inhabitant answered, when you asked what they meant, 'Mordacious Memmius lacerates Largus's limb.' You see plainly how graceful, choice and well befitting an orator is a jest of this sort, whether you have some truth you can relate, – which for all that may be sprinkled with fibs, – or whether you are only fabricating. Now the beauty of such jesting is, that you state your incidents in such a way, that the character, the manner of speaking and all the facial expressions of the hero of your tale, are so presented that those incidents seem to your audience to take place and to be transacted concurrently with your description of them. Another sort of jest depending on facts, is that which is generally derived from what may be called vulgarized mimicry, as when on another occasion, Crassus was adjuring an adversary in the words, 'By your rank, by your lineage!' What else had the assembly to laugh at in this than that mimicry of facial expression and intonation? But when he went on to say, 'By your statuary,' and lent a touch of action to the word by stretching out his arm, we laughed quite consumedly. To this class belongs Roscius's famous representation of an old man, when he quavers out, 'For you, son Antipho, I'm planting these.' I think I am listening to testy Eld personified. However this particular kind of laughing-matter is all such as to need extreme circumspection in the handling of it. For if the caricature is too extravagant, it becomes the work of buffoons in pantomine, as also does grossness. It behoves the orator to borrow merely a suspicion of mimicry, so that his hearer may imagine more than meets his eye; he must also testify to his own well-bred modesty, by avoiding all unseemly language and offensive gestures.

"These then are the two kinds of the jesting that is founded on facts; and they are appropriate to continuous irony, wherein the characters of individuals are sketched and so portrayed, that either through the relation of some anecdote their real natures are understood, or, by the infusion of a trifle of mimicry, they are found out in some fault sufficiently marked to be laughed at.

' As regards words, however, the laughter is awakened by something pointed in a phrase or reflection. But just as, with the former kind, both in narrative and in mimicry, all likeness to buffoons in pantomime is to be avoided, so in this latter case the orator must scrupulously shun all buffoonish raillery. How then shall we distinguish from Crassus, from Catulus, and from the others, your familiar acquaintance Granius, or my own friend Vargula? Upon my word, I have never considered this matter, for all of them are witty, none indeed more so than Granius. The first point to make, I think, is that we should not feel bound to utter a witticism every time an occasion offers. A very small witness once came forward. 'May I examine him?' said Philippus. The president of the Court, who was in a hurry, answered, 'Only if you are short.' 'You will not complain,' returned Philippus, 'for I shall be just as short as that man is.' Quite comical; but there on the tribunal sat Lucius Aurifex, and he was even tinier than the witness: all the laughter was directed against Lucius, and the joke seemed merely buffoonish. And so those shafts which may light upon unintended victims, however featly they may be winged, are none the less essentially those of a buffoon. . . .

"Regard then to occasions, control and restraint of our actual raillery, and economy in bon-mots, will distinguish an orator from a buffoon, as also will the fact that we people speak with good reason, not just to be thought funny, but to gain some benefit, while those others are jesting from morning to night, and without any reason at all. Thus, when Aulus Sempronius was on canvassing bent, along with Marcus his brother, and embraced Vargula, what good did it do Vargula to shout 'Boy, drive away these buzzers?' His object was to get a laugh — to my mind the very poorest return for cleverness. The right occasion therefore for speaking out we shall fix by our own wisdom and discretion: would that we had some theory of the use of these qualities! though intuition is the sovereign directress.

"Now let us summarize the essential natures of the chief sources of laughter. Let our first distinction, then, be this, that a witty saying has its point sometimes in facts, sometimes in words, though people are most particularly amused whenever laughter is excited by the union of the two. But remember this, that whatever subjects I may touch upon, as being sources of laughing-matters, may equally well, as a rule, be sources of serious thoughts. The only difference is that seriousness is bestowed austerely and upon things of good repute, jesting upon what is a trifle unseemly, or, so to speak, uncouth; for example, we can, in identical terms, praise a careful servant, and make fun of one who is good-for-nothing. There is humour in that old remark of Nero's about a thievish servant, 'that he was the only member of the household against whom nothing was sealed up or locked away,' a description frequently applied to a trusty servant also, and that too word for word. In fact all kinds of remarks are derived from identical sources. For his mother's words to Spurius Carvilius, who was sadly lame from a wound received on national service, and for that reason shy of walking abroad, 'No no, my Spurius, go out! and let every step you take remind you of your gallantry,' are noble and dignified. But what Glaucia said to Calvinus, who was limping, 'Where is that old saying — Can he be hobbling? Nay, but he is wobbling,' is merely absurd. Yet both observations were derived from what the contemplation of lameness might suggest. Scipio's pun, 'Is there an idler knave than this Naevius?', was intended for austerity. But there was a spark of humour in the remark of Philippus to a malodorous individual, 'I perceive that you are stinking me out.' Yet both kinds of pun lie in the verbal echo that survives the change in a letter.

"Bons-mots prompted by an equivocation are deemed the very wittiest, though not always concerned with jesting, but often even with what is important. What Publius Licinius Varus said to the great Africanus the elder, when he was adjusting a garland to his head at a banquet, and it tore again and again, was praiseworthy and creditable: 'Don't be astonished,' said he, 'if it does not fit, for it is on a Head of vast capacity.' Yet from the same category comes, 'He is bald enough, seeing that he is bald in diction.' So, to bore you no further, there is no source of laughing-matters from which austere and serious thoughts are not also to be derived.

"There is also this to be noted, that all is not witty that is laughable. For can there be anything so droll as a pantaloon? Yet it is for his face, his grimaces, his mimicry of mannerisms, his intonation, and in fact his general bearing, that he is laughed at. Humorous I am able to call him, but humorous for a low comedian, and not in the sense in which I would have an orator humorous.

"Accordingly this kind of wit, though raising as much laughter as any, is not at all our kind: it caricatures peevishness, fanaticism, mistrust, pomposity and folly, characters which are laughed at for their own sakes, masks which we do not put on, but attack. Another kind, quite comical, consists in mimicry, but this we may employ only by stealth, if at all, and but momentarily, as fuller use of it does not befit the well-bred. A third kind is grimacing, which is beneath our dignity. A fourth is indecency, not only degrading to a public speaker, but hardly sufferable at a gentlemen's dinner-party. When all these modes, then, are withheld from this branch of oratory, the residue of wit depends apparently either on the facts or on the language, in accordance with the distinction I have already drawn. For the joke which still remains witty, in whatever words it is couched, has its germ in the facts; that which loses its pungency, as soon as it is differently worded, owes all its humour to the language.

DEMETRIUS: "ON STYLE"

Translated by G. M. A. Grube

J. W. H. Atkins writes: "There ... emerged a body of criticism which represented a solid contribution to the subject [of style], and which, while rivalling in interest anything that had gone before, was destined to have considerable influence on the work of later ages. The outstanding contributors were Tacitus, Demetrius, 'Longinus' and Quintilian, all great names in the history of criticism. "[1] *Although Grube argues that the date of composition for "On style" may be as early as 270 B.C. and questions whether it was authored by Demetrius of Phalerum, a contemporary of Theophrastus, he agrees with Atkins and Kennedy that it is the only extant critical text on style between Aristotle and the Roman writers of the first century B.C. Grube reminds the modern reader that "On Style" and* On The Sublime *are "rhetorical only in the Greek sense, for they concern themselves with all literature and rhetoric as only one of the literary genres. ... And since the Greeks discovered literature and developed it almost to perfection in nearly all its genres, it is not surprising that all these works are, or should be, of considerable interest to literary students, as to all would-be writers, and that they can still illuminate our own literary taste in an age that is much less concerned with language as an art – a τέχνη. "*[2]

Demetrius identifies four types of style. His initial discussion of these types and his detailed account of the forceful style are presented below.

Reprinted by permission of the publishers from G. M. A. Grube, translator, Demetrius, *A Greek Critic: Demetrius On Style,* Toronto, University of Toronto Press.

[1] J. W. H. Atkins, *Literary Criticism in Antiquity, II* (Cambridge, England, 1934), p. 175.

[2] G. M. A. Grube, p. v.

There are four simple types of style: the plain, the grand, the elegant, and the forceful. The rest are combinations of these, but not all combinations are possible: the elegant can be combined with both the plain and the grand, and so can the forceful; the grand alone does not mix with the plain; these two face one another as opposite extremes. That is why some critics recognize only these last two as styles, and the other two as intermediate. They class the elegant rather with the plain, because the elegant is somewhat slight and subtle; while the forceful, which has weight and dignity, is classed with the grand.

Such a theory is absurd. With the exception of the two opposite extremes mentioned (the plain and the grand), we find combinations of all these types in the Homeric epic, in the works of Plato, Xenophon, Herodotus, and many other writers who display a frequent mixture of grandeur, forcefulness, and charm, so that the number of types is such as we have indicated, and the manner of expression appropriate to each will be seen in what follows. . . .

The Forceful or Intense Style

As for forcefulness, it follows from what has been said that it, too, shows itself in the same three ways as the previous styles. Certain things are forceful in themselves so that those who speak about them are thought to be forceful even when they do not speak forcefully. When Theopompus, for example, describes the Piraeus with its flute-girls and brothels, and the male flute-players as singing and dancing, he uses words which have an intensity of their own; although his style is feeble, it is considered forceful.

As regards word-arrangement, forcefulness follows if, firstly, short phrases take the place of clauses. Length dissolves vehemence, and a more forceful effect is attained where much is said in a few words. An example of this is the warning of the Spartans to Philip: "Dionysius [is] in Corinth." If they had amplified this and said: "Dionysius has lost his throne and is now a beggarly schoolteacher in Corinth," this would have been a statement of fact rather than a taunt.

The Spartans were always naturally inclined to brevity of speech. Brevity is more forceful and commanding, while it is more appropriate to speak at length in requests and supplications.

Symbola (tokens) also have force, because they resemble brevity of speech. From a little that is said one must understand a great deal, just as in the case of tokens. In this way "The grasshoppers will sing to you from the ground" is more forceful for being spoken by *allegoria* than if he had simply said: "Your trees shall be cut down."

The periods should be securely knotted at the end, for the periodic structure which brings us round to an end is forceful, while a looser structure is simpler and a sign of simpler character. All early writers used this simpler style, for the ancients were simple men.

And so, in the forceful style, we should avoid the old-fashioned in character and rhythm, but rather resort to the forcefulness now in fashion. The rhythm should make the sentence come to a definite stop, as in the first sentence of Demosthenes' speech against Leptines which clings to the rhythm I mentioned.

Violence contributes to forcefulness in word-arrangement, for harsh sounds are often forceful, like rough roads. We have an example in the same passage of Demosthenes.

We should avoid antitheses and balanced clauses in the periods. They make for weight but not for forcefulness, and frequently result in frigidity instead of force, as in Theopompus' attack on the friends of Philip where the antithesis destroys the intensity. The excessive elaboration, or rather the poor technique, attracts the attention of the reader who is quite untouched by anger.

The subject itself will often compel us to adopt a compact and forceful word-arrangement, as in this passage of Demosthenes: "If any one of them had been convicted, you would not have proposed this bill; and, if you are now convicted, no one else will make such a proposal." The subject itself and the steps in the argument clearly demanded a word-arrangement that grows out of them; no one could easily have constructed the sentence differently, not even if he did violence to the subject-matter. For in adopting a certain sentence-structure we are often carried along by the subject like people running downhill.

It also contributes to forcefulness to put the most forceful expression at the end as Antisthenes did. Its force will be blunted in the middle of other words. For if anyone changes the order of the words, though he says the same thing, he will not be thought to do so.

The kind of antithesis which I condemned in Theopompus is inappropriate even in Demosthenes, where he says: "You were the temple-servant, I was the initiate; you were the teacher, I the pupil; you were a minor actor, I was a spectator; you were hissed, I hissed." The exact correspondence of parallel clauses is poor art; it is more like a jest than an expression of anger.

When being forceful, it is appropriate to use periods continuously, although this is not suitable in other styles. For if one period follows another the effect will be as of metre following metre, and a forceful metre at that, like choliambs.

These continuous periods should at the same time be short, that is, periods of two clauses, for the effect of periods consisting of many clauses is beautiful rather than forceful.

Brevity is so useful in this style that it is often even more forceful *not* to say something, as when Demosthenes says: "Now I might remark — but I myself certainly do not wish to say anything offensive, and my accuser has the advantage in slandering me."

And, by the gods, even obscurity is frequently forceful. For what is implied is more forceful, whereas what is explained is thought common-place.

Sometimes discordant sounds (kakophônia) are forceful, especially if the subject matter demands it, as in Homer's line: "The Trojans shivered when they saw the writhing snake." This could have been said more euphoniously while preserving the metre, but then neither the poet nor the snake would have seemed as forceful.

From this example we can deduce similar examples: instead of πάντα ἂν ἔγραψεν we might write ἔγραψεν ἂν and παρεγένετο οὐχί for οὐ παρεγένετο·

Sometimes forcefulness may be attained by ending with a connective like δέ or τε· We are taught to avoid such endings but they are often useful, as in "he gave him no praise although he deserved it, he insulted him though"; or like "Schoinos and Skolon too . . . ," but in the Homeric lines the connectives at the end give an impression of grandeur.

A sentence like the following (with repetition of the connective τε) will sometimes be forceful too. For pleasant smoothness is characteristic of the elegant, not of the forceful manner, and these (two) styles seem most opposed to one another.

Forcefulness of a kind often results from an admixture of playfulness, as in comedy and all works written in the Cynic manner. So Crates says:

"There is a land of Pêra (= wallet) in the midst of the wine-dark ocean."

Another example is Diogenes' announcement at Olympia. After the race in armour he ran forward and proclaimed himself Olympian victor over all men in personal worth and beauty. The words excite both laughter and wonder, and have a gentle hidden sting in them.

Still another example is what Diogenes said to the beautiful youth. In wrestling with him Diogenes had an erection, and when the boy got scared and leapt away "Don't worry," said the philosopher, "I'm not your equal there." The surface meaning is funny, but the hidden significance has a certain forcefulness. And this is true of all Cynic discourse as a whole. To put it briefly: it is like a dog that fawns and bites at the same time.

Orators too will sometimes use this sort of pointed jest as they have done in the past. As Lysias said to the old woman's lover that "her teeth were easier to count than her fingers." These words put the old woman in a most forceful and ridiculous light. And so with Homer's "I shall eat Nobody last."

Forceful Figures

We shall now discuss how forcefulness can arise from use of figures. First, from figures of thought; for example that which is called *paraleipsis*:

"I make no mention of Olynthus, Methone, Apollonia, and the thirty-two cities in Thrace." With these words the orator has said all he wanted to say, and he says he will not mention them in order to give the impression that he has even more dreadful things to say.

Aposiôpêsis, which was mentioned before, has the same character; it also makes for forcefulness.

The figure of thought called *prosôpopoiia* can also be used with forceful effect: "Consider that it is your forefathers who are reproaching you and saying such things to you, or Greece, or your own city in the form of a woman. . . ."

Or as in Plato's Funeral Speech: "Children, that your fathers were brave men. . . ." He does not speak in his own person but in that of their fathers. To bring them in as *dramatis personae* makes the passage much more real and forceful; indeed it becomes a dramatic presentation.

The different figures and forms of thought may be used as stated. We have said this much by way of examples. As for figures of speech, a varied choice of them will make the style more forceful.

There is anadiplôsis: "Thebes, Thebes, our neighbouring city, has been snatched from the middle of Greece." The repeated word gives forcefulness.

Then there is that called anaphora, as in: "You call him against yourself as a witness, you call him against the laws as a witness, you call him against the people as a witness." This is a triple figure. It is, as already stated, an epanaphora, because the same words are repeated at the beginning of each clause; it is an asyndeton because there are no connectives; it is an homoioteleuton because every clause ends with the same words. The forcefulness is due to the combination of all three figures. If one said: "You call him as a witness against yourself, the laws, and the people," the figures would disappear, and so would the force of the passage.

We should realize, however, that lack of connectives, more than anything else, produces forcefulness: "He walks through the market, puffing out his cheeks, raising his eyebrows, keeping in step with Pythocles." If you join these clauses by connectives, the effect is much gentler.

The figure called *klimax* should also be used, as Demosthenes uses it in: "I did not say these things and then refuse to move a proposal; I did not move a proposal and fail to go as an envoy; I did not go as an envoy and fail to persuade the Thebans." This passage is like a man climbing higher and higher. If you were to put it like this: "After my speech, and after moving a proposal I went as an envoy, and persuaded the Thebans," he would be narrating facts, but saying nothing forceful.

In general, figures of speech give the speaker an opportunity for histrionic delivery in debate, that is for forcefulness, and this is especially true when connectives are omitted. So much for figures of both kinds.

Forceful Diction

The diction should in every respect be the same as in the grand style, except that it is not used with the same end in view, and metaphors too contribute to forcefulness; for example: "Python, that bold torrent of oratory rushing upon you...."

Similes too can be used, as by Demosthenes where he says: "This decree made the danger which then threatened the city pass away like a cloud."

Long comparisons, however, are unsuited to forcible passages because of their length: "As a noble inexperienced hound leaps at a boar recklessly...." There is beauty and precision in this image, but forcefulness requires a vehement brevity, like men aiming blows in a close fight.

The use of a compound word can also be forceful; and common usage forms many forceful compounds. Many such can be found in the speeches of the orators.

One should try to use words appropriate to the subject. If an action is violent and wicked, we say a man perpetrated it, or, according to the nature of the deed, that he committed, performed, or executed it.

A sudden rise in emotional tension is not only impressive but forceful, as where Demosthenes says: "It is not necessary to keep your hands in the folds of your cloak when you are speaking, Aeschines, but you should keep them there when on an embassy."

And again in the passage: "When he was appropriating Euboea..." the *epanastasis* does not aim at grandeur but at forcefulness. And this happens when, in the middle of what we are saying, we are emotionally aroused and denounce somebody. The first example was a denunciation of Aeschines, here of Philip.

It is also forceful to ask your audience questions without giving the answer. "When Philip was appropriating Euboea, and made it a base against Attica, was he doing wrong, was he breaking the peace, or was he not?" He embarrasses his audience, and seems to prove them wrong, and they have no answer. But if one changes this to read: "Philip did wrong and broke the peace," it is like a piece of obvious information and does not put them in the wrong.

The figure called *epimonê*, dwelling on a point longer than is required to state the facts, may also contribute to forcefulness. Here is an example from Demosthenes: "A dread disease, men of Athens, has fallen upon Greece...." Put differently, it would not have been forceful.

Euphemism, as it is called, can also be forceful, when bad things are given fair names, and impiety is made to sound pious. The Athenian who proposed that the golden Victories should be melted down, and the gold used for war purposes, did not say bluntly: "Let us melt down the Victories to prosecute the war." That would have sounded like a bad omen and an insult to the goddesses. He put it more euphemistically: "We shall have the Victories to help us with the war." Put in this way it did not sound like destroying the Victories, but seeking their help.

There are, too, the forceful expressions of Demades. These are of a peculiar and strange kind; their force results from three things: expressive words, a kind of allêgoria, and hyperbole.

When he said, for example, "Alexander is not dead or the whole world would smell his corpse," the use of "smell" instead of "be aware of" is a hyperbole and at the same time has an element of allêgoria, while to say that the whole earth would be aware of it pointedly expresses Alexander's power. The phrase is startling as a combination of these three figures at the same time. What is startling is always forceful, for it inspires fear.

Here is another example of the same kind: "This decree was not drafted by me; the war itself drafted it, with Alexander's sword as its pen." And again: "The power of Macedon, with Alexander gone, is like a blinded Cyclops."

On another occasion he said: "Our city, no longer the warrior of Salamis, but a slippered old dame greedily gulping her gruel." The old woman implies weakness and exhaustion, and he expresses this feeble state hyperbolically; "gulping her gruel" also means that the city was spending its war resources on public feasts and banquets.

This must suffice about Demades' forcefulness; its use involves a certain risk, and it is hard to imitate; it has a poetic flavour, if indeed veiled meanings, hyperboles, and expressive words are poetical, but the poetic is here mixed with the comic.

Innuendo

What we call innuendo is employed by the speakers of our own day in a ridiculous manner, with a vulgar expressiveness which may be said to make the meaning obvious, but it is a true figure if used for two purposes: good taste and discretion.

To preserve appearances, as when Plato wants to censure Aristippus and Cleombrotus for living daintily in Aegina while Socrates was for many days imprisoned in Athens, and for not crossing the straits to their friend and teacher, although the distance was less than twenty-five miles. He does not blame them explicitly, for that would have been mere abuse, but he expresses his feelings tactfully as follows: Phaedo is asked who was with Socrates and enumerates those present. Then he is asked whether Aristippus and Cleombrotus were there too and he says: "No, for they were in Aegina." The point of all that precedes is made clear by the words 'they were in Aegina." And the result is much more forceful in that the facts themselves, rather than the speaker, seem to point to the enormity of their conduct. Although it was presumably quite safe for Plato to attack Aristippus and his friends, yet he prefers to do so by innuendo.

Frequently, however, when we are speaking to a dictator or some other violent individual and we want to censure him, we are of necessity driven to do so by innuendo. So when Craterus of Macedon was insolently receiving Greek envoys while lying on a high golden couch and clad in royal purple, Demetrius of Phalerum censured him by using this figure: "We too received these envoys at one time, and Craterus there was among them." For by pointing to him with the word "there" (τοῦτον) all the insolence of Craterus is pointed to and censured by using the figure.

The same kind of device is seen in what Plato said to Dionysius when the latter was telling lies and going back on a promise he had made. "It was not I, Plato, who made any agreement with you, but, by the gods, you did so yourself." These words prove Dionysius a liar, and the form of speech has both dignity and discretion.

Men often speak equivocally. If one wishes to speak like that, and also one's censure not to sound like censure, then what Aeschines said about Telauges is a model to follow. Almost his whole account of the man leaves one puzzled as to whether he is expressing admiration for him or satirizing him. This kind of writing is ambiguous; although it is not irony, yet there are indications of irony.

Innuendo may also be used in another way, like this: men and women in positions of power dislike any reference to their faults. When we are advising them on a course of action, therefore, we shall not speak frankly. We should either blame others who have acted in a similar way, we may, for example, condemn the despotic severity of Phalaris when talking to Dionysius; or again we shall praise others, be it Gelon or Hiero, who have acted in the opposite way and say they were like fathers or teachers to their Sicilian subjects. As he hears these things, Dionysius is being admonished, but he is not being censured; moreover he will envy the praise bestowed on Gelon, and he will want to deserve such praise himself.

There are many such occasions in the company of despotic rulers. Philip, for example, had only one good eye, and any reference to a Cyclops angered him, indeed any reference to eyes. Hermias, ruler of Atarneus, though in other ways gentle, found it difficult to endure any reference to knives or surgical operations, because he was a eunuch. I mention these things to draw attention to the proper way to speak to princes, and that it very much requires the circumspect manner of speech which is called innuendo.

Moreover, great and powerful popular assemblies frequently need to be addressed in the same manner as despots, as did the people of Athens when they were masters of Greece and nurtured such flatterers as Cleon and Cleophon. Flattery is ugly, but censure is dangerous; that manner is best which lies between the two, namely innuendo.

And sometimes we shall praise even the wrongdoer, not for what he did wrong, but for what he did right. You will tell a bad-tempered man that you heard him praised for the gentleness he displayed yesterday when so and so was in the wrong and that he is an example to his fellow-citizens. For everybody likes to be a model to himself, and wants to be praised more and more, indeed to be praised continually.

Different Modes of Speech

Just as from the same wax one man will make a dog, another an ox, a third a horse, so the same subject-matter can be expressed in the pointed and accusatory manner of Aristippus: "Men leave property to their children, but they do not leave along with it the knowledge of how to use the legacy," and this is the Aristippean manner; or it can be put as a suggestion, as Xenophon mostly does: "One should not leave only property to one's children, but also the knowledge of how to use it."

Then there is the peculiar manner called Socratic, which seems to have been emulated especially by Aeschines and Plato. Here the above advice becomes a question, something like this: "Well, my boy, how much money did your father leave you? Quite a lot, more than you can easily account for? — Quite a lot, Socrates — Then surely he also left you the knowledge of how to use it?" The boy is in difficulties before he realizes it; he is made aware of his ignorance, and set on the path of education. All these different manners are suitably in character, and certainly not the proverbial Scythian manner of speech.

This type of writing was very successful at the time it was first discovered; people were struck by its vivid imitation of actual conversation and its high-minded exhortations.

So much for the various forms of expression into which a subject can be moulded, and for innuendos.

Forcible Arrangement

Smoothness in the arrangement of words, as especially affected by the school of Isocrates, who avoid all hiatus, is not very suitable in the forceful style. A hiatus often increases forcefulness, its avoidance deprives the passage of force, for the echoing sound of the clashing vowels contributes to its forcefulness.

Indeed what is unpremeditated and spontaneous itself makes a more forceful impression, especially when we show our anger at a wrong we have suffered. The care which a smooth and melodious arrangement betrays belongs not to the expression of anger but to jest or display.

Just as we mentioned that the figure of omitted connectives contributes to forcefulness, so does an altogether loose word-arrangement. A proof of this is found in Hipponax. When he wants to attack his enemies he breaks his rhythm, makes it halting instead of straightforward, less rhythmical, and this suits the forcefulness of his attack. Rhythm which is smooth to the ear is more appropriate to eulogy than to censure. So much for hiatus.

The Vice of Coarseness

There is, as we would expect, a faulty style neighbouring on the forceful, and this we call the coarse. There is coarseness of subject-matter where an author openly speaks of things ugly and unmentionable, as when the man who was accusing Timandra of prostitution filled the courtroom with descriptions of her basin, her instruments, her rush-mat, and many other such unseemly details.

The arrangement of words appears coarse when it is jerky; also when the clauses are quite unconnected, like fragments of speech. Continuous long periods, too, which make a reader pant for breath not only surfeit but repel him.

The choice of words can make disagreeable even subjects which are pleasing in themselves, as when Clitarchus says of a kind of bee: "it feeds on the countryside, and rushes into hollow oaks." You would think he was talking about a wild bull or the Erymanthian boar instead of a bee. The passage is both coarse and frigid, and indeed these two faults are close neighbours.

LONGINUS: ON THE SUBLIME

Translated by A. O. Prickard

For a treatise whose authorship is doubtful, whose date of composition can only be postulated at somewhere between the end of the first century A.D. and the beginning of the third century A.D., and whose significance was literally unrecorded until the discovery of the manuscript in 1554, its influence on the development of modern style is unparalleled except for Aristotle's Poetics.[1] *As Grube suggests, Longinus is not commenting on the three major styles prevalent at that time, nor is he trying to define style: "Longinus is not thinking so much of great books (as we are apt to do) or of particularly successful sayings or sentences (as his fellow critics mostly did) but of supremely great passages in great authors."[2]*

In the excerpts included, Longinus is writing to his friend Terentianus concerning the marks and sources of sublimity, and concludes that sublimity raises man almost to the intellectual greatness of God.

I – II

I am almost relieved at the outset from the necessity of showing at any length that Sublimity is always an eminence and excellence in language; and that from this, and this alone, the greatest poets and writers of prose have attained the first place and have clothed their fame with immortality.

Reprinted by permission of the publishers from A. O. Prickard, translator, Longinus, *On The Sublime,* Oxford: The Clarendon Press, 1906.

[1] See Churton Collins, *Studies in Poetry and Criticism* (London, 1905); W. Hamilton Fyfe, Introduction, Aristotle, *The Poetics* and "Longinus" *On The Sublime,* translated by W. Hamilton Fyfe (Cambridge, Mass., 1965), p. xviii; G. M. A. Grube, Introduction, Longinus, *On Great Writing (On The Sublime),* translated and introduced by G. M. A. Grube (Indianapolis, 1957), p. viii.

[2] G. M. A. Grube, *op. cit.,* p. xii.

For it is not to persuasion but to ecstasy that passages of extraordinary genius carry the hearer: now the marvellous, with its power to amaze, is always and necessarily stronger than that which seeks to persuade and to please: to be persuaded rests usually with ourselves, genius brings force sovereign and irresistible to bear upon every hearer, and takes its stand high above him. Again, skill in invention and power of orderly arrangement are not seen from one passage nor from two, but emerge with effort out of the whole context; Sublimity, we know, brought out at the happy moment, parts all the matter this way and that, and like a lightning flash, reveals, at a stroke and in its entirety, the power of the orator. These and suchlike considerations I think, my dear Terentianus, that your own experience might supply.

We, however, must at once raise this further question; is there any art of sublimity or of its opposite? For some go so far as to think all who would bring such terms under technical rules to be entirely mistaken. 'Genius,' says one, 'is inbred, not taught; there is one art for the things of genius, to be born with them.' All natural effects are spoilt, they think, by technical rules, and become miserable skeletons. I assert that the reverse will prove true on examination, if we consider that Nature, a law to herself as she mostly is in all that is passionate and lofty, yet is no creature of random impulse delighting in mere absence of method; that she is indeed herself the first and originating principle which underlies all things, yet rules of degree, of fitting occasion, of unerring practice, and of application can be determined by method and are its contribution; in a sense all greatness is exposed to a danger of its own, if left to itself without science to control, 'unsteadied, unballasted,' abandoned to mere velocity and uninstructed venture; greatness needs the spur often, it also needs the bit. What Demosthenes shows to be true of the common life of men – that of all good things the greatest is good fortune, but a second, not inferior to the first, is good counsel, and that where the latter is wanting the former is at once cancelled – we may properly apply to literature; here Nature fills the place of good fortune, Art of good counsel. Also, and this is most important, it is only from Art that we can learn the very fact that certain effects in literature rest on Nature and on her alone. If, as I said, the critic who finds fault with earnest students, would take all these things into his account, he would in my opinion no longer deem inquiry upon the subjects before us to be unnecessary or unfruitful. . . .

VI – IX

It is possible, my friend, to do this [escape the vices mingled with the sublime – *Eds.*], if we could first of all arrive at a clear and discriminating knowledge of what true sublimity is. Yet this is hard to grasp: judgement of style is the last and ripest fruit of much experience. Still, if I am to speak in the language of precept, it is perhaps not impossible, from some such remarks as follow, to attain to a right decision upon the matter.

We must, dear friend, know this truth. As in our ordinary life nothing is great which it is a mark of greatness to despise; as fortunes, offices, honours, kingdoms, and such like, things which are praised so pompously from without, could never appear, at least to a sensible man, to be surpassingly good, since actual contempt for them is a good of no mean kind (certainly men admire, more than those who have them, those who might have them, but in greatness of soul let them pass); even so it is with all that is elevated in poetry and prose writings; we have to ask whether it may be that they have that image of greatness to which so much careless praise is attached, but on a close scrutiny would be found vain and hollow, things which it is nobler to despise than to admire. For it is a fact of Nature that the soul is raised by true sublimity, it gains a proud step upwards, it is filled with joy and exultation, as though itself had produced what it hears. Whenever therefore anything is heard frequently by a man of sense and literary experience, which does not dispose his mind to high thoughts, nor leave in it material for fresh reflection, beyond what is actually said; while it sinks, if you look carefully at the whole context, and dwindles away, this can never be true sublimity, being preserved so long only as it is heard. That is really great which gives much food for fresh reflection; which it is hard, nay impossible, to resist; of which the memory is strong and indelible. You may take it that those are beautiful and genuine effects of sublimity which please always, and please all. For when men of different habits, lives, ambitions, ages, all take one and the same view about the same writings, the verdict and pronouncement of such dissimilar individuals give a powerful assurance, beyond all gainsaying, in favour of that which they admire.

Now there are five different sources, so to call them, of lofty style, which are the most productive; power of expression being presupposed as a foundation common to all five types, and inseparable from any. First and most potent is the faculty of grasping great conceptions, as I have defined it in my work on Xenophon. Second comes passion, strong and impetuous. These two constituents of sublimity are in most cases native-born, those which now follow come through art: the proper handling of figures, which again seem to fall under two heads, figures of thought, and figures of diction; then noble phraseology, with its subdivisions, choice of words, and use of tropes and of elaboration; and fifthly, that cause of greatness which includes in itself all that preceded it, dignified and spirited composition. Let us now look together at what is included under each of these heads, premising that Caecilius has passed over some of the five, for instance, passion. If he did so under the idea that sublimity and feeling are one and the same thing, coexistent and of common origin, he is entirely wrong. For some passions may be found which are distinct from sublimity and are humble, as those of pity, grief, fear; and again, in many cases, there is sublimity without passion; take, besides countless other instances, the poet's own venturesome lines on the Aloadae:

> Upon Olympus Ossa, leafy Pelion
> On Ossa would they pile, a stair to heaven;

and the yet grander words which follow:

> Now had they worked their will.

In the Orators, again, speeches of panegyric, pomp, display, exhibit on every hand majesty and the sublime, but commonly lack passion: hence Orators of much passion succeed least in panegyric, and again the panegyrists are not strong in passion. Or if, on the other hand, Caecilius did not think that passion ever contributes to sublimity, and, therefore, held it undeserving of mention, he is quite in error. I should feel confidence in maintaining that nothing reaches great eloquence so surely as geniune passion in the right place; it breathes the vehemence of frenzy and divine possession, and makes the very words inspired.

After all, however, the first element, great natural genius, covers far more ground than the others: therefore, as to this also, even if it be a gift rather than a thing acquired, yet so far as is possible we must nurture our souls to all that is great, and make them, as it were, teem with noble endowment. How? you will ask. I have myself written in another place to this effect: − 'Sublimity is the note which rings from a great mind.' Thus it is that, without any utterance, a notion, unclothed and unsupported, often moves our wonder, because the very thought is great: the silence of Ajax in the book of the Lower World is great, and more sublime than any words. First, then, it is quite necessary to presuppose the principle from which this springs: the true Orator must have no low ungenerous spirit, for it is not possible that they who think small thoughts, fit for slaves, and practise them in all their daily life, should put out anything to deserve wonder and immortality. Great words issue, and it cannot be otherwise, from those whose thoughts are weighty. So it is on the lips of men of the highest spirit that words of rare greatness are found. . . .

XI − XII

Closely connected with the excellencies which I have named is that called Amplification; in which, when the facts and issues admit of several fresh beginnings and fresh halting-places, in periodic arrangement, great phrases come rolling upon others which have gone before, in a continuously ascending order. Whether this be done by way of enlarging upon commonplace topics, or of exaggeration, or of intensifying facts or reasoning, or of handling deeds done or suffering endured (for there are numberless varieties of amplification), the orator must in any case know that none of these can possibly stand by itself without sublimity as a perfect structure. The only exceptions are where pity or depreciation are required; in all other processes of amplification, take away the sublime, and you will take soul out of body; they are effective no longer, and become nerveless and hollow unless braced by passages of sublimity. But, for clearness' sake, I must shortly lay down wherein the difference lies between my present precepts, and what I said above (there I spoke of a sketch embracing the principal ideas and arranging them into one); and the broad difference between Amplification and Sublimity.

I am not satisfied with the definition given by the technical writers. Amplification is, they say, language which invests the subject with greatness. Of course this definition may serve in common for sublimity, and passion, and tropes, since they, too, invest the language with greatness of a particular kind. To me it seems that they differ from one another in this, that Sublimity lies in intensity, Amplification also in multitude; consequently sublimity often exists in a single idea, amplification necessarily implies quantity and abundance. Amplification is — to define it in outline — an accumulation of all the parts and topics inherent in a subject, strengthening the fabric of the argument by insistence; and differs in this from rhetorical proof that the latter seeks to demonstrate the point required. . . .

[*Here about six pages have been lost.*]

In richest abundance, like a very sea, Plato often pours into an open expanse of grandeur. Hence it is, I think, that, if we look to style, the Orator, appealing more strongly to passions, has a large element of fire and of spirit aglow; Plato, calm in his stately and dignified magnificence, I will not say, is cold, but is not so intense. It is on these and no other points, as it seems to me, dear Terentianus (that is, if we as Greeks are allowed to form an opinion), that Cicero and Demosthenes differ in their grand passages. Demosthenes' strength is in sheer height of sublimity, that of Cicero in its diffusion. Our countryman, because he burns and ravages all in his violence, swift, strong, terrible, may be compared to a lightning flash or a thunderbolt. Cicero, like a spreading conflagration, ranges and rolls over the whole field; the fire which burns is within him, plentiful and constant, distributed at his will now in one part, now in another, and fed with fuel in relays. These are points on which you can best judge: certainly

the moment for the sublimity and tension of Demosthenes is where
accumulated invective and strong passion are in play, and generally where
the hearer is to be hard struck: the moment for diffusion is where he is to
be flooded with detail, as it is always appropriate in enlargement upon
commonplaces, in perorations and digressions, and in all passages written
for the style and for display, in scientific and physical exposition, and in
several other branches of literature. . . .

XIV

Therefore even we, when we are working out a theme which requires lofty
speech and greatness of thought, do well to imagine within ourselves how,
if need were, Homer would have said this same thing, how Plato or
Demosthenes, or, in history, Thucydides would have made it sublime. The
figures of those great men will meet us on the way while we vie with them,
they will stand out before our eyes, and lead our souls upwards towards
the measure of the ideal which we have conjured up. Still more so if we
add to our mental picture this; how would Homer, were he here, have
listened to this phrase of mine? or Demosthenes? how would they have
felt at this? Truly great is this competition, where we assume for our own
words such a jury, such an audience, and pretend that before judges and
witnesses of that heroic build we undergo a scrutiny of what we write. Yet
more stimulating than all will it be if you add: 'If I write this, in what
spirit will all future ages hear me?' If any man fear this consequence, that
he may say something which shall pass beyond his own day and his own
life, then all which such a soul can grasp must needs be barren, blunted,
dull; for it posthumous fame can bring no fulfilment. . . .

XXXVI

Hence, when we speak of men of great genius in literature, where the
greatness does not necessarily fall outside the needs and service of man, we
must at once arrive at the conclusion, that men of this stature, though far
removed from flawless perfection, yet all rise above the mortal: other
qualities prove those who possess them to be men, sublimity raises them
almost to the intellectual greatness of God. No failure, no blame; but
greatness has our very wonder. What need still to add, that each of these
great men is often seen to redeem all his failures by a single sublimity, a
single success; and further, which is most convincing, that if we were to
pick out all the failures of Homer, Demosthenes, Plato, and the other
greatest writers, and to mass them together, the result would be a small, an
insignificant fraction of the successes which men of that heroic build
exhibit everywhere. Therefore every age and all time, which envy itself can

never prove to be in its dotage, has bestowed upon them the assured prizes of victory; it guards and keeps them to this day safe and inalienable, and will as it seems, keep them

> As long as waters flow and poplars bloom.

To the writer, however, who objects that the faulty Colossus is not better work than the Spearman of Polycleitus I might say much, but I say this. In Art the most accurate work is admired, in the works of Nature greatness. Now it is by Nature that man is a being endowed with speech; therefore in statues we seek what is like man, in speech what surpasses, as I said, human standards. Yet it is right (for our precept returns to the early words of this treatise), because the success of never failing is in most cases due to Art, the success of high although not uniform excellence, to Genius, that, therefore, Art should ever be brought in to aid Nature; where they are reciprocal the result should be perfection. It was necessary to go thus far towards a decision upon the points raised: let every one take the view which pleases him, and enjoy it.

ST. AUGUSTINE:
ON CHRISTIAN DOCTRINE

Translated by D. W. Robertson, Jr.

Charles Sears Baldwin, in his article, "St. Augustine and the Rhetoric of Cicero," calls Augustine's fourth book one of the most fruitful of all discussions of style in preaching.[1] *Augustine adapts Cicero's three-fold purpose of oratory, to teach (*docere*), to delight (*delectare*), and to move (*movere*) to the three styles found in the* Orator, *plain (*tenue*), moderate (*medium*), and grand (*grande*). Augustine applies to the preacher Cicero's definition of the orator: "He, then, shall be called eloquent who can speak small things quietly, larger things proportionally, great things greatly (*Orator, xxix, 21*)." Augustine exemplifies in the excerpts below the first style which he calls* genus submissum *by St. Paul's epistle to the Galatians; the second style which he calls* genus temperatum *from the epistles to Timothy and to the Romans as having the charm of aptness; and the third style which he calls* genus grande *as having the force of emotional appeal.*

IV, xvii, 34 — xx, 39

He who seeks to teach in speech what is good, spurning none of these three things, that is, to teach, to delight, and to persuade, should pray and strive that he be heard intelligently, willingly, and obediently. When he does this well and properly, he can justly be called eloquent, even though he fails to win the assent of his audience. To these three things — that he should teach, delight, and persuade — the author of Roman eloquence himself seems to have wished to relate three other things when he said,

[1]Charles Sears Baldwin, "St. Augustine and the Rhetoric of Cicero," *Proceedings of the Classical Association,* 22 (1925), p. 31.

"He therefore will be eloquent who can speak of small things in a subdued manner, of moderate things in a temperate manner, and of grand things in a grand manner."[1] It is as though he had added these to the three mentioned previously and said, "He is therefore eloquent who in order to teach, can speak of small things in a subdued manner, and in order to please, can speak of moderate things in a temperate manner, and in order to persuade, can speak of great things in a grand manner."

He could have demonstrated these three things as he explains them in legal cases, but he could not have done so in ecclesiastical questions of the kind with which the speech which we wish to cultivate will be called upon to concern itself. In legal questions those things are called "small" which are concerned in cases involving money; they are called "great" when they have to do with human welfare or life. Those cases in which neither of these is to be judged and nothing is advanced to make the listener judge or act, but what is said is set forth only to please him, the matter is said to be as if in between and on this account called middling or "moderate." "Moderate" comes from *modus,* "measure," so that we do not speak properly when we use "moderate" pejoratively to mean "small." Among our orators, however, everything we say, especially when we speak to the people from the pulpit, must be referred, not to the temporal welfare of man, but to his eternal welfare and to the avoidance of eternal punishment, so that everything we say is of great importance, even to the extent that pecuniary matters, whether they concern loss or gain, or large or small amounts of money, should not be considered "small" when they are discussed by the Christian teacher. For neither is justice small, since we ought to maintain it even with reference to small amounts of money, for, as the Lord says, "He that is faithful in that which is least, is faithful also in that which is greater." Therefore, what is least is least, but to be faithful in what is least is great. Just as in the nature of a circle all lines drawn from the center to the circumference are equal, and the same holds true whether we are examining a large disc or a very small coin, in the same way when justice is applied to small things justice itself is not diminished.

When the Apostle spoke of worldly cases (and which of them is not concerned with money?) he said: "Dare any of you, having a matter against another, go to be judged before the unjust, and not before the saints? Know you not that the saints shall judge this world? And if the world shall be judged by you, are you unworthy to judge the smallest matters? Know you not that we shall judge angels? How much more things of this world! If therefore you have judgments of things pertaining to this world, set them to judge, who are the most despised in the church. I speak to your shame. Is it so that there is not among you any one wise man, that is able to judge between his brethren? But brother goeth to law with

---

[1] Cic. *Orat.* 29. 101. *Submissus* is here translated "subdued" rather than "plain" or "simple," both of which would be misleading in this context.

brother, and that before unbelievers. Already indeed there is plainly a fault among you, that you have lawsuits one with another. Why do you not rather take wrong? Why do you not rather suffer yourselves to be defrauded? But you do wrong and defraud, and that to your brethren. Know you not that the unjust shall not possess the kingdom of God?" What so angers the Apostle that he upbraids, reproves, reproaches, and threatens in this way? Why is it that he shows his emotion with such repeated bitter expressions? Finally, why does he speak of such small things in such a grand manner? Did that worldly business merit it? Not at all. He did this on account of justice, charity, piety, which, as no sober mind will doubt, are great even in the smallest things.

Certainly, if we were advising men how they should act in worldly cases, either for themselves or for their friends, before ecclesiastical judges, we should rightly urge them to speak in a subdued manner as if of small things. But when we are speaking of the eloquence of those men whom we wish to be teachers of things which will liberate us from eternal evil or lead us to eternal good, wherever these things are discussed, either before the people or in private, either with one or with several, either with friends or with enemies, either in extended speech or in conversation, either in treatises or in books, either in long letters or in short, they are great things. Unless, perhaps, because a cup of cold water is a small and most insignificant thing, we should also regard as small and most insignificant the promise of the Lord that he who gives such a cup to one of His disciples "shall not lose his reward." Or when our teacher in the Church makes a sermon on this text, he should feel that he is speaking about a small thing so that he should speak, not in a moderate manner and not in a grand manner, but in a subdued manner. When we happen to speak about this matter before the people, and God assists so that we do not speak ineptly, does not a certain flame rise up as if from that cold water which even inflames the cold breasts of men to perform acts of mercy in the hope of heavenly reward?

Nevertheless, although our teacher should speak of great things, he should not always speak about them in the grand manner, but in a subdued manner when he teaches something, in a moderate manner when he condemns or praises something. But when something is to be done and he is speaking to those who ought to do it but do not wish to do it, then those great things should be spoken in the grand manner in a way appropriate to the persuasion of their minds. And sometimes concerning one and the same important thing, he speaks in a subdued manner if he teaches, in a moderate manner if he is praising it, and in a grand manner if he is moving an adverse mind to conversion. For what is greater than God? Should nothing then be learned about Him? Or should he who teaches the unity of the Trinity use nothing except the subdued style so that he may make a thing very difficult to understand comprehensible in so far as is possible? Or should ornaments and not proofs be sought here? Or is the listener to be persuaded to do something and not rather instructed that he may learn? Again, when God is praised either on His own account or because of His works, what an appearance of beautiful and splendid diction arises in him who praises Him as he is able, whom no one praises adequately and whom no one in one way or another fails to praise! And if He is not worshiped, or if idols are worshiped with Him or before Him, or demons, or creatures of any kind, the orator should speak in a grand style of how great that evil is so that men may be averted from it.

That what I say may be more plain, here is an example from the Apostle Paul of the subdued style: "Tell me, you that desire to be under the law, have you not read the law? For it is written that Abraham had two sons: the one by a bondwoman, and the other by a freewoman. But he who was of the bondwoman, was born according to the flesh: but he of the freewoman was by promise. Which things are said by an allegory. For these are the two testaments: the one from mount Sina, engendering unto bondage, which is Agar: For Sina is a mountain in Arabia, which hath affinity to that Jerusalem which now is, and is in bondage with her children. But that Jerusalem which is above, is free: which is our mother." Again, where he reasons, and says; "Brethren (I speak after the manner of man) yet a man's testament, if it be confirmed, no man despiseth, nor addeth to it. To Abraham were the promises made and to his seed. He saith not, 'And to his seeds,' as of many: but as of one, 'And to thy seed,' which is Christ. Now this I say, that the testament which was confirmed by God, the law which was made after four hundred and thirty years, doth not disannul, to make the promise of no effect. For if the inheritance be of the law, it is no more of promise. But God gave it to Abraham by promise." And since it might occur to the mind of the listener to ask, "Why, then, was the Law given, if there is no inheritance from it?", he introduces this himself and says as if asking, "Why then was the law?" Then he answers, "It was set because of transgressions, until the seed should come, to whom he made the promise, being ordained by angels in the hand of a mediator. Now a mediator is not of one: but God is one." And here occurs an objection which he himself proposed, "Was the law then against the promises of God?" And he answers, "God forbid." And he gives a reason, saying, "For if there had been a law given which could give life, verily justice should have been by the law. But the scripture hath included all under sin, that the promise, by the faith of Jesus Christ, might be given to them that believe," etc. Or similar examples could be cited. It is relevant to teaching not only to explain those things that are hidden and to solve the difficulties of questions, but also, while these things are being done, to introduce other questions which might by chance occur, lest what is said be rendered improbable or be refuted by them. But they should be introduced in such a way that they are answered at the same time, lest we introduce something we cannot remove. However, it sometimes happens that when questions contingent upon the main question, and still other questions contingent upon these, are introduced and solved, the process of reasoning is extended to such a length that the disputant, unless he has a very strong and vigorous memory, cannot return to the original topic. Nevertheless, it is good practice to refute such objections as may occur, lest one appear where there is no one to refute it, or lest it occur to someone who is present but is silent about it so that he goes away with less benefit. . . .

IV,xx,42 — xxvi, 56

The grand style differs from the moderate style not so much in that it is adorned with verbal ornaments but in that it is forceful with emotions of the spirit. Although it uses almost all of the ornaments, it does not seek them if it does not need them. It is carried along by its own impetus, and if the beauties of eloquence occur they are caught up by the force of the things discussed and not deliberately assumed for decoration. It is enough for the matter being discussed that the appropriateness of the words be determined by the ardor of the heart rather than by careful choice. For if a strong man is armed with a gilded and bejeweled sword, and he is fully intent on the battle, he does what he must with the arms he has, not because they are precious but because they are arms. Yet he is himself the same, and very powerful, even when "wrath provides a weapon as he seeks one." The Apostle urges that the evils of this world are to be suffered for the sake of the evangelical ministry, since all things may be tolerated with the solace of God's gifts. It is a great subject, and it is grandly presented, nor are the ornaments of speech lacking: "Behold," he says, "now is the acceptable time; behold, now is the day of salvation. Giving no offense to any man, that our ministry be not blamed: But in all things let us exhibit ourselves as the ministers of God, in much patience, in tribulation, in necessities, in distresses, In stripes, in prisons, in seditions, in labours, in watchings, in fastings, In chastity, in knowledge, in long-suffering, in sweetness, in the Holy Ghost, in charity unfeigned, In the word of truth, in the power of God; by the armour of justice on the right hand and on the left; Through honour and dishonour, through evil report and good report; as deceivers, and yet true; as unknown, and yet known; As dying, and behold we live; as chastised, and not killed; As sorrowful, yet always rejoicing; as needy, yet enriching many; as having nothing, and possessing all things." Behold him still fervent: "Our mouth is open to you, O ye Corinthians, our heart is enlarged," and so on, but it would take too long to follow it all.

Again, he urges the Romans to conquer the persecutions of this world by charity, with a sure hope in the help of God. He speaks both grandly and ornately: "And we know that to them that love God, all things work together unto good, to such as, according to his purpose, are called to be saints. For whom he foreknew, he also predestinated to be made conformable to the image of his Son; that he might be the firstborn amongst many brethren. And whom he predestinated, them he also called. And whom he called, them he also justified. And whom he justified, them he also glorified. What shall we say then to these things? If God be for us, who is against us? He that spared not even his own Son, but delivered him up for us all, how hath he not also, with him, given us all things! Who shall accuse against the elect of God? God that justifieth? Who is he that shall condemn? Christ Jesus that died, yea that is risen also again; who is at the right hand of God, who also maketh intercession for us? Who then shall separate us from the love of Christ? Shall tribulation? or distress? or famine? or nakedness? or danger? or persecution? or the sword? As it is written. For thy sake we are put to death all the day long. We are accounted as sheep for the slaughter. But in all these things we overcome, because of him that hath loved us. For I am sure that neither death, nor life, nor angels, nor principalities, nor powers, nor things present, nor things to come, nor might, nor height, nor depth, nor any other creature shall be able to separate us from the love of God, which is in Christ Jesus our Lord."

Although almost all of the Epistle to the Galatians is written in the subdued style, except the beginning and the end, which are in the moderate style, nevertheless he inserts one passage with such emotion that, without any ornaments like those in the passages quoted as examples heretofore, it cannot be spoken except in the grand style. "You observe," he says, "days, and months, and times, and years. I am afraid of you, lest perhaps I have laboured in vain among you. Be ye as I, because I also am as you: brethren, I beseech you. You have not injured me at all. And you know how through infirmity of the flesh, I preached the gospel to you heretofore: and your temptation in my flesh, You despised not, nor rejected, but received me as an angel of God, even as Christ Jesus. Where is then your blessedness? For I bear you witness, that if it could be done, you would have plucked out your own eyes, and would have given them to me. Am I then become your enemy, because I tell you the truth? They are zealous in your regard not well: but they would exclude you, that you might be zealous for them. But be zealous for that which is good in a good thing always: and not only when I am present with you. My little children, of whom I am in labour again, until Christ be formed in you. And I would willingly be present with you now, and change my voice: because I am ashamed for you." Are contrary words set against their contraries here, or are things arranged climactically, or are *caesa* and *membra* and *circuitus* used? Yet not on that account is the grand emotion which we feel in the fervor of this eloquence diminished.

Although these apostolic words are clear, they are also profound, and they are so written and commended to posterity that not only the reader or hearer but even the expositor has a task to perform if he is not content with their surfaces and seeks their depths. On this account, let us examine these styles of speaking in those who by reading the Scriptures became proficient in the knowledge of divine and salutary truths and are at the same time ministers of the Church. The blessed Cyprian uses the subdued style in that book where he discusses the sacrament of the chalice. There he resolves the question as to whether or not the Lord's chalice should contain water alone or water mixed with wine. By way of example, something from this discussion may be used. After the beginning of his epistle, he sets out to resolve the question: "You know that we have been admonished to follow the Lord's example in offering the chalice, and that nothing should be done by us other than that which the Lord first did for us, so that the chalice which is offered in His commemoration should contain water mixed with wine. For since Christ says, 'I am the true vine,' the blood of Christ is not water at all but wine. Nor can it be held that His blood, by which we are redeemed and vivified, is in the chalice when it contains no wine, through which the blood of Christ is shown, as is foretold by all the mysteries and testimonies of the Scriptures. Thus we find in Genesis concerning the sacrament that Noah prefigured it, and presented a figure of the Lord's Passion in that he drank wine, that he became inebriated, that he was naked in his house, that he lay naked with his limbs and thighs exposed, that the nakedness of the father was pointed out by his second son but covered by the oldest and youngest, and that other things happened which it is not necessary to refer to here, since it is enough to understand that when Noah showed the type of truth to come, he drank not water but wine, and so expressed the image of the Lord's Passion. Again, we see the Lord's sacrament prefigured in the priest Melchisedech, according to what the holy Scripture testifies, saying, 'But Melchisedech the king of Salem, bringing forth bread and wine, for he was the priest of the most high God, blessed [Abraham].' The Holy Spirit declares in the Psalms that Melchisedech bore the type of Christ, saying in the person of the Father to the Son, 'Thou art a priest forever according to the order of Melchisedech.'" These and the other things which follow in this epistle are in the manner of the subdued style, as the reader may easily discover.

St. Ambrose also, when he is urging a very important matter concerning the Holy Spirit, so that he may show it to be equal with the Father and the Son, nevertheless uses the subdued manner of speaking. For the thing discussed does not need verbal ornaments, nor motions of the affections to persuade, but evidence as proof. Thus among other things at the beginning of this work he says, "Gedeon was disturbed by the divine message when he heard that, although thousands of people were failing, the Lord would free his people from their enemies through one man. He offered the kid of goats and placed its flesh together with unleavened loaves on the rock in accordance with the precept of the Angel, and poured the broth on them. When the Angel touched these things together with the tip of the rod he was carrying, fire arose from the rock so that the sacrifice which was offered was consumed. This evidence seems to show that the rock bore the type of the Body of Christ, for it is written, 'and they drank of the spiritual rock that followed them, and the rock was Christ.' This clearly refers not to His divinity but to His flesh, which has flooded the thirsty hearts of the people with the unfailing stream of His blood. Then it was also announced in this mystery that Lord Jesus in the crucifixion of His flesh should abolish not only crimes committed but also the lusts of the heart. For the flesh of the kid refers to the guilt of actions, the broth to the evils of concupiscence, as in the passage, 'For...a multitude of people...burned with desire...and said, Who will give us flesh to eat?' That the angel extended the rod and touched the rock from which fire came forth shows that the flesh of the Lord, filled with the Holy Spirit, would burn away all the sins of the human condition. Whence the Lord Himself says, 'I am come to cast fire on the earth.' " The passage continues, in which he is concerned with teaching and offering proof.

This praise of virginity from Cyprian is in the moderate style: "Now we address ourselves to virgins, who because of their greater glory deserve our greater care. They are the flower of the seed of the Church, the beauty and ornament of spiritual grace, the joyful inward nature of praise and honor, a whole and uncorrupted work, an image of God reflecting the sanctity of the Lord, the more illustrious part of the flock of Christ. The glorious fruitfulness of Mother Church rejoices in them and in them profusely flowers. The more glorious virginity adds to her number, the more the joy of the Mother increases." And in another place at the end of the epistle, he says, " 'As we have borne the image of the earthly, let us bear also the image of the heavenly.' This image virginity bears; integrity bears it; sanctity and truth bear it. Those mindful of the discipline of God bear it, maintaining justice with religion, stable in faith, humble in fear, strong to bear all, meek to sustain injuries, eager to perform works of mercy, united and harmonious in fraternal peace. Each of these, O good virgins, you should observe, love, and fulfill your duties, you who, devoting yourselves to God and to Christ, should lead the way, being in a greater and better status, to the Lord to whom you have dedicated yourselves. You who are advanced in years should teach the younger; you who are younger, assist the ministry of the older and be an incitement to your peers; inspire one another with mutual encouragement; urge one another to glory by examples of virtue; persevere strongly, go forward spiritually, and attain your end happily; remember us when virginity begins to be honored in you."

Ambrose also in a moderate but ornamented style sets forth to religious virgins, as it were in an example, what they should imitate in their manners. He says, "She was a virgin not only in body but also in mind. Her sincere disposition was not stained by any traces of deceit. She was humble in heart, grave in discourse, prudent in mind, sparing in speech, studious in learning. She placed her hope, not in the uncertainty of wealth, but in the prayer of the poor man. She was attentive to her work, shamefast in speech. She customarily sought not man but God as the guide to her mind. She injured no one, but had good will toward all; she assented to her elders, and did not envy her equals; she fled boasting, followed reason, loved virtue. When did this one injure her parents, even with a glance? When did she quarrel with her relatives? When did she disdain the humble? When did she deride the weak? When did she avoid the needy? She was accustomed to visit only those gatherings of men at which mercy would not be ashamed nor shame terrified. There was no arrogance in her eyes, no boldness in her voice, no shamelessness in her actions. Her bearing was not too faint, her gait not too loose, her voice not too sensual, so that the very appearance of her body was an image of her mind and a figure of probity. Certainly a good house should be recognizable at its threshold, and should show at the very entrance that no darkness lies within, as if the light of the lamp inside illuminates the exterior. Why should I describe her sparingness with food, her insistent kindness, the one excessive beyond nature, the other almost less than nature itself? In the one there was no intermission of time, in the other days of fasting were doubled; and when the desire to eat appeared, the food offered was often only of such a character as to prevent death, not to minister to delights," etc. I have offered this as an example of the moderate style, since he is not here urging that anyone take vows of virginity who has not already done so, but simply explaining how those who have already taken such vows should act. For in order that the mind may be moved toward a proposal of such importance, it must be excited and inflamed by the grand style. But the martyr Cyprian wrote concerning the habit of virgins and not of taking vows of virginity. However, this bishop arouses them with great eloquence even to this.

But I shall now offer examples of the grand manner of speaking concerning a subject which both men have discussed. Both men have condemned those women who color, or discolor, their features with paint. When the first discusses this matter, he says, among other things, "If an artist had depicted the face and form of a man and indicated the quality of his body with colors rivaling those of the original, and when the likeness was complete and finished another set his hand to it, as if being more skillful he would reshape the picture already made, this would be seen as a grave injury to the first artist and a reason for just indignation. Do you think that you can with impunity commit such a rash and wrongful act offensive to God the artist? Even though you may not be shameless concerning men nor defiled in mind by alluring rouges, you make yourself worse than an adulteress by corrupting and defiling those things which are

God's. What you think ornaments you, what you think makes you more beautiful, is an attack on the divine work, a corruption of the truth. The voice of the Apostle warns: 'Purge out the old leaven, that you may be a new paste, as you are unleavened. For Christ our pasch is sacrificed. Therefore let us feast, not with the old leaven, nor with the leaven of malice and wickedness; but with the unleavened bread of sincerity and truth.' Are sincerity and truth preserved when those things which are sincere are polluted and truth is changed into falsehood by adulterating colors and the tricks of cosmetics? Your Lord says, 'Thou canst not make one hair white or black'; and you, in order to refute the word of your Lord, wish to be stronger. With brazen audacity and sacrilegious contempt you dye your hair; as an evil omen of the future, your hair already presages flames." It would take too long to insert all that follows.

Ambrose discusses such things. "From these things," he says, "proceed incentives to vices in that they paint their faces with artificial colors when they are afraid to displease men, and the adulterated face implies an adulteration of chastity. What a piece of foolishness is this, to change the image of nature and to seek a picture, and in dreading the adverse judgment of their husbands on their faces to reveal their own! For she passes a judgment on herself who desires to change that which is natural to her; thus when she seeks to please others she reveals her own prior displeasure. What more veracious judge do we need, woman, than yourself, when you are afraid to be seen? If you are beautiful, why do you hide? If you are ugly, why do you lie in implying that you are beautiful, since you will have neither the reward of your own conscience nor that of another's deception? If he loves another, you wish to please another; and you are angry if he loves another and was taught by you to be adulterous. You are the bad teacher of your own injury. For even she who has suffered from it flees from the art of the pander, and although she is a wicked woman, she sins not against another but against herself. Crimes of adultery are almost more endurable, for there shame is corrupted while here nature is adulterated." It is sufficiently apparent, I think, that women are vehemently urged by this eloquence not to adulterate their appearance with rouge and to be shameful and fearful. Thus we recognize that the style is neither subdued nor moderate, but altogether grand. And in these two whom from among all writers I chose to quote, and in many writings of other ecclesiastical authors who say good things and say them well, that is, as the matter demands, acutely, ornately, or ardently, these three styles may be found. And students may learn them by assiduous reading, or hearing, accompanied by practice.

But no one should think that it is contrary to theory to mix these three manners; rather, speech should be varied with all types of style in so far as this may be done appropriately. For when one style is maintained too long, it loses the listener. When transitions are made from one to another, even though the speech is long, it proceeds more effectively, although each style has its own varieties in the discourse of eloquent men by means of which the senses of the audience are not permitted to cool or languish. However, the subdued style alone can be tolerated more readily for a period of time than the grand style alone. Indeed, the more the mind of the listener is aroused so that he may agree with us, the less time it can be maintained in that state, once it has been sufficiently aroused. Thus we must be cautious lest when we wish to arouse what is already aroused, it may fall from that height to which it was brought by our stimulating it. When those things which must be said in the subdued style have been interposed, we return effectively to those things which must be said in the grand style, so that the impetus of our speech ebbs and flows like the sea. Whence it is true that if the grand style must be used for a protracted time, it should not be used alone, but should be varied by the intermingling of other styles. But the whole speech is said to be in that style which is used most in it so that it predominates.

It is important to consider what style should be used to vary what other style, and what style should be employed in specific places. Thus even in the grand style the beginning of the discourse should always, or almost always, be moderate. And it is within the power of the speaker that he say some things in the subdued style which might be spoken in the grand style so that those things which are spoken in the grand style may seem more grand by comparison and be rendered more luminous as if by shadows. But in whatever style the difficulties of questions are to be solved, there is need for acumen, which the subdued style appropriates to itself. Thus this style is to be used with either of the other two when such matters appear in them. In the same way when praise or blame is a part of the matter, and neither the condemnation nor the liberation of anyone, nor assent to any other action is being urged, the moderate style should be employed, no matter which of the other two is being used. Therefore in the grand style the two others have a place, and the same is true of the subdued style. The temperate style sometimes but not always needs the subdued style if, as I have said, a question arises to be solved, or, when some things which could be expressed with ornament are left plain and spoken in the subdued manner so that certain extravagances, so to speak, of ornament may seem more eminent. But the temperate style does not need the grand style, for it is used for purposes of delight rather than for persuasion.

If a speaker is applauded frequently and vigorously, he should not think that for that reason he is speaking in the grand style; for the acumen revealed in the subdued style and the ornaments of the moderate style may produce the same result. For the grand style frequently prevents applauding voices with its own weight, but it may bring forth tears. Thus when I was dissuading the populace of Caesarea in Mauretania from civil war, or rather from a war worse than civil which they called "Caterva" — for not only the citizens themselves, but relatives, brothers, even parents and children, divided themselves into two parts for several successive days at a certain time of the year and solemnly fought each other with stones, and each killed whomever he could — I pleaded in the grand style in so far as I was able that they should cast forth from their hearts and customs such a ferocious and inveterate evil. But I did not think that I had done anything when I heard them applauding, but when I saw them weeping. They indicated by applause that they were being taught or pleased, but tears indicated that they were persuaded. When I saw these, I believed that the terrible custom handed down by their fathers and grandfathers and from still more remote times, which had besieged their hearts like an enemy, or rather taken them, had been overcome, even before the victory had been demonstrated. As soon as the speech was finished, I directed their hearts and lips to giving thanks to God. And behold! by the grace of Christ, nothing similar has been attempted there for eight years or more. There are many other experiences through which we have learned what effect the grand style of a wise speaker may have on men. They do not show it through applause but rather through their groans, sometimes even through tears, and finally through a change of their way of life.

And many are changed through the subdued style, but in such a way that they know what they did not know before, or believe what they did not formerly believe, not in such a way that they do what they know they should do, although they have not desired to do so. To bend hardness of this kind the grand style is necessary. But when praises and vituperations are eloquently spoken, although they belong to the moderate style, they so affect some that they are not only delighted by the eloquence of praising or blaming, but also desire to live in a praiseworthy way and to avoid living in a way that should be blamed. But is it true that all who are delighted are changed as in the grand style all who are persuaded act, or in the subdued style all who are taught know, or believe to be true, what they did not know before?

Hence it is to be concluded that the purpose that these two styles seek to effect is especially important to those who would speak with wisdom and eloquence. That which the moderate style urges, that is, that the eloquence itself be pleasing, is not to be taken up for its own sake, but in order that things which may be usefully and virtuously spoken, if they require neither a teaching nor a moving eloquence, may have a knowing and sympathetic audience which sometimes may assent more readily or adhere more tenaciously to that which is being said because of the delight aroused by that eloquence. For it is the universal office of eloquence, in any of these three styles, to speak in a manner leading to persuasion; and the end of eloquence is to persuade of that which you are speaking. In any of these three styles an eloquent man speaks in a manner suitable to persuasion, but if he does not persuade, he has not attained the end of eloquence. Thus in the subdued style he persuades his listener that what he says is true; he persuades in the grand style that those things which we know should be done are done, although they have not been done. He persuades in the moderate style that he himself speaks beautifully and with ornament. Of what use is this to us? Let those seek this end who glory in their language, and who display themselves in panegyrics and other speeches of this kind, neither moving the listener to do anything nor teaching him anything, but simply pleasing him. We, however, refer this end to another end, that is, so that in addition to what we desire to bring about when we speak in the grand style we also desire this: that good habits be loved and evil avoided. Or, if men are seen not to be so hostile to the action which we are urging that the grand style is necessary, or if they are already practicing it, that they do so more assiduously we use the moderate style. Thus we use the ornaments of the moderate style not ostentatiously but prudently, not content with its end that the audience be pleased, but rather using them in such a way that they assist that good which we wish to convey by persuasion.

Thus those three ends which we described above for a man who speaks wisely if he would also speak eloquently, that is, that he should so speak that he is heard intelligently, willingly, and obediently, are not to be taken so that one of the three styles is attributed to each one so that the subdued style pertains to understanding, the moderate style to willingness, and the grand style to obedience; rather, in such a way that the orator always attends to all three and fulfills them all as much as he can, even when he is using a single style. We do not wish to tire the listener, even when we speak in the subdued style, but we desire rather that he hear not only intelligently but also willingly. And why do we employ divine testimonies in what we say in order to teach, except that we may be heard obediently, that is, that we may be believed with the aid of Him to whom it is said, "Thy testimonies are become exceedingly credible"? What does he desire who explains something to learners even in the subdued style but to be believed? And who would wish to hear him unless he could retain his listener with some sweetness of discourse? Who does not know that, if he is not heard with understanding, neither is he heard willingly or obediently? Frequently the subdued style, when it solves difficult questions and demonstrates in unexpected ways, when it brings to light and sets forth most acute principles from I know not what caverns, as it were, in an unexpected way, when it shows an adversary's error and reveals that what he seemed to say uncontrovertibly is false, and especially if a certain beauty is added to it, not deliberately sought but in some way natural, and a few rhythmic closings are used, not ostentatiously but, as I say, as if necessary, arising from the things discussed themselves, then it excites such acclamations that it is hardly recognized as being subdued. It does not come forth armed or adorned but, as it were, nude, and in this way crushes the sinews and muscles of its adversary and overcomes and destroys resisting falsehood with its most powerful members. Why is it that those using this style are frequently and greatly applauded unless for the reason that truth thus demonstrated, defended, and placed in triumph is a source of delight? And in this subdued style our teacher and speaker should so conduct himself that he is heard not only intelligently but also willingly and obediently.

RHETORICA AD HERENNIUM

Translated by Harry Caplan

Among modern students of rhetoric, the canons of delivery and memory have seldom been accorded the respect or emphasis given them by some of the ancients. Except for brief comments on rehearsal in public speaking texts, the subject of memory as a formal part of rhetoric has all but disappeared, so that now memoria *is commonly referred to as the "lost canon." But as one critic points out, "at least a third of the justification for outlining which appears in modern textbooks is undeclared talk about* Memoria. *The ancients did not have our concepts of 'outline' or 'logical structure' and were conditioned by their culture in other ways to concentrate on* words. *Their problem, then, was to command masses of word detail, where we think of commanding relations of ideas. Hence, theories of* Memoria *and advice about learning to command one's discourse were very different from ours. The canon did not die out, the considerations changed." Because of an embarrassing overemphasis on delivery by nineteenth-century elocutionists, and because they wish to direct students to ideas rather than techniques, most modern writers on public speaking have been wary of too explicit instruction on management of voice and body during the speech. Aristotle, too, had his doubts about the dignity of studying delivery and passed over the subject with the hope that some actor would one day produce a work on delivery. Recent writers on oral interpretation have demonstrated the extent to which the concept of vocal delivery can aid in the analysis of both prose and poetry, and communication theorists are newly interested in the "silent language" of gesture. It appears that delivery, though not so important as the canons of invention, arrangement, and style, needs to be given due consideration in both written and oral composition.*

Reprinted by permission of the publishers of THE LOEB CLASSICAL LIBRARY from Harry Caplan, translator, [Cicero], *Ad. C. Herennium Libri IV de Ratione Dicendi (Rhetorica ad Herennium),* Cambridge, Mass.: Harvard University Press.

The unknown author of the Rhetorica Ad Herennium *presented in his treatise a concise treatment of delivery and the oldest extant statement on memory. A textbook rather than a theoretical discussion, the* Ad Herennium *is a clear, practical, prescriptive exposition of what the young student needed to know about public speaking. As such, it is useful to modern scholars who wish to assess the state of the art at this period, and who find in the* Ad Herennium *a compact treatment of the whole range of rhetorical method.*

III, xi, 19 — xxiv, 40

Many have said that the faculty of greatest use to the speaker and the most valuable for persuasion is Delivery. For my part, I should not readily say that any one of the five faculties is the most important; that an exceptionally great usefulness resides in the delivery I should boldly affirm.[1] For skilful invention, elegant style, the artistic arrangement of the parts comprising the case, and the careful memory of all these will be of no more value without delivery, than delivery alone and independent of these. Therefore, because no one has written carefully on this subject — all have thought it scarcely possible for voice, mien, and gesture to be lucidly described, as appertaining to our sense-experience — and because the mastery of delivery is a very important requisite for speaking, the whole subject, as I believe, deserves serious consideration.

Delivery, then, includes Voice Quality and Physical Movement. Voice Quality has a certain character of its own, acquired by method and application. It has three aspects: Volume, Stability, and Flexibility. Vocal volume is primarily the gift of nature; cultivation augments it somewhat, but chiefly conserves it. Stability is primarily gained by cultivation; declamatory exercise augments it somewhat, but chiefly conserves it. Vocal flexibility — the ability in speaking to vary the intonations of the voice at pleasure — is primarily achieved by declamatory exercise. Thus with regard to vocal volume, and in a degree also to stability, since one is the gift of nature and the other is acquired by cultivation, it is pointless to give any other advice than that the method of cultivating the voice should be sought from those skilled in this art. It seems, however, that I must

---

[1] *Cf* Quintilian, 11. 3. 2: "But delivery itself has a marvellously powerful effect in oratory; for the nature of the material we have composed in our minds is not so important as how we deliver it;" 11. 3. 7: "Cicero also thinks action to be the dominant element in oratory;" 11. 3. 5-6: "For my part I would affirm that a mediocre speech supported by all the power of delivery will have more force than the best speech devoid of that power. That is why Demosthenes, asked what was primary in the whole task of oratory, gave the palm to delivery, and gave it second and third place as well. . . . So that we may assume that he thought it to be not merely the first, but the only virtue of oratory" (*cf.* also Philodemus, *Rhet.*, ed. Sudhaus, 1. 196; Cicero, *Brutus* 37.

discuss stability in the degree that it is conserved by a system of declamation, and also vocal flexibility (this is especially necessary to the speaker), because it too is acquired by the discipline of declamation.

We can, then, in speaking conserve stability mainly by using for the Introduction a voice as calm and composed as possible. For the windpipe is injured if filled with a violent outburst of sound before it has been soothed by soft intonations. And it is appropriate to use rather long pauses — the voice is refreshed by respiration and the windpipe is rested by silence. We should also relax from continual use of the full voice and pass to the tone of conversation; for, as the result of changes, no one kind of tone is spent, and we are complete in the entire range. Again, we ought to avoid piercing exclamations, for a shock that wounds the windpipe is produced by shouting which is excessively sharp and shrill, and the brilliance of the voice is altogether used up by one outburst. Again, at the end of the speech it is proper to deliver long periods in one unbroken breath, for then the throat becomes warm, the windpipe is filled, and the voice, which has been used in a variety of tones, is restored to a kind of uniform and constant tone. How often must we be duly thankful to nature, as here! Indeed what we declare to be beneficial for conserving the voice applies also to agreeableness of delivery, and, as a result, what benefits our voice likewise finds favour in the hearer's taste. A useful thing for stability is a calm tone in the Introduction. What is more disagreeable than the full voice in the Introduction to a discourse? Pauses strengthen the voice. They also render the thoughts more clear-cut by separating them, and leave the hearer time to think. Relaxation from a continuous full tone conserves the voice, and the variety gives extreme pleasure to the hearer too, since now the conversational tone holds the attention and now the full voice rouses it. Sharp exclamation injures the voice and likewise jars the hearer, for it has about it something ignoble, suited rather to feminine outcry than to manly dignity in speaking. At the end of the speech a sustained flow is beneficial to the voice. And does not this, too, most vigorously stir the hearer at the Conclusion of the entire discourse? Since, then, the same means serve the stability of the voice and agreeableness of delivery, my present discussion will have dealt with both at once, offering as it does the observations that have seemed appropriate on stability, and the related observations on agreeableness. The rest I shall set forth somewhat later, in its proper place.

Now the flexibility of the voice, since it depends entirely on rhetorical rules, deserves our more careful consideration. The aspects of Flexibility are Conversational Tone, Tone of Debate, and Tone of Amplification. The Tone of Conversation is relaxed, and is closest to daily speech. The Tone of Debate is energetic, and is suited to both proof and refutation. The Tone of Amplification either rouses the hearer to wrath or moves him to pity.

Conversational tone comprises four kinds: the Dignified, the Explicative, the Narrative, and the Facetious. The Dignified, or Serious, Tone of Conversation is marked by some degree of impressiveness and by vocal restraint. The Explicative in a calm voice explains how something could or could not have been brought to pass. The Narrative sets forth events that have occurred or might have occurred. The Facetious can on the basis of some circumstance elicit a laugh which is modest and refined.

In the Tone of Debate are distinguishable the Sustained and the Broken. The Sustained is full-voiced and accelerated delivery. The Broken Tone of Debate is punctuated repeatedly with short, intermittent pauses, and is vociferated sharply.

The Tone of Amplification includes the Hortatory and the Pathetic. The Hortatory, by amplifying some fault, incites the hearer to indignation. The Pathetic, by amplifying misfortunes, wins the hearer over to pity.

Since, then, vocal flexibility is divided into three tones, and these in turn subdivide into eight others, it appears that we must explain what delivery is appropriate to each of these eight subdivisions.

(1)For the Dignified Conversational Tone it will be proper to use the full throat but the calmest and most subdued voice possible, yet not in such a fashion that we pass from the practice of the orator to that of the tragedian. (2) For the Explicative Conversational Tone one ought to use a rather thin-toned voice, and frequent pauses and intermissions, so that we seem by means of the delivery itself to implant and engrave in the hearer's mind the points we are making in our explanation. (3) For the Narrative Conversational Tone varied intonations are necessary, so that we seem to recount everything just as it took place. Our delivery will be somewhat rapid when we narrate what we wish to show was done vigorously, and it will be slower when we narrate something else done in leisurely fashion. Then, corresponding to the content of the words, we shall modify the delivery in all the kinds of tone, now to sharpness, now to kindness, or now to sadness, and now to gaiety. If in the Statement of Facts there occur any declarations, demands, replies, or exclamations of astonishment concerning the facts we are narrating, we shall give careful attention to expressing with the voice the feelings and thoughts of each personage. (4) For the Facetious Conversational Tone, with a gentle quiver in the voice, and a slight suggestion of a smile, but without any trace of immoderate laughter, one ought to shift one's utterance smoothly from the Serious Conversational tone to the tone of gentlemanly jest.

Since the Tone of Debate is to be expressed either through the Sustained or the Broken, when the (5) Sustained Tone of Debate is required, one ought moderately to increase the vocal volume, and, in maintaining an uninterrupted flow of words, also to bring the voice into harmony with them, to inflect the tone accordingly, and to deliver the words rapidly in a full voice, so that the voice production can follow the fluent energy of the speech. (6) For the Broken Tone of Debate we must with deepest chest tones produce the clearest possible exclamations, and I advise giving as much time to each pause as to each exclamation.

For (7) the Hortatory Tone of Amplification we shall use a very thin-toned voice, moderate loudness, an even flow of sound, frequent modulations, and the utmost speed. (8) For the Pathetic Tone of Amplification we shall use a restrained voice, deep tone, frequent intermissions, long pauses, and marked changes.

On Voice Quality enough has been said. Now it seems best to discuss Physical Movement.

Physical movement consists in a certain control of gesture and mien which renders what is delivered more plausible. Accordingly the facial expression should show modesty and animation, and the gestures should not be conspicuous for either elegance or grossness, lest we give the impression that we are either actors or day labourers. It seems, then, that the rules regulating bodily movement ought to correspond to the several divisions of tone comprising voice. To illustrate: (1) For the Dignified Conversational Tone, the speaker must stay in position when he speaks, lightly moving his right hand, his countenance expressing an emotion corresponding to the sentiments of the subject — gaiety or sadness or an emotion · intermediate. (2) For the Explicative Conversational Tone, we shall incline the body forward a little from the shoulders, since it is natural to bring the face as close as possible to our hearers when we wish to prove a point and arouse them vigorously. (3) For the Narrative Conversational Tone, the same physical movement as I have just set forth for the Dignified will be appropriate. (4) For the Facetious Conversational Tone, we should by our countenance express a certain gaiety, without changing gestures.

(5) For the Sustained Tone of Debate, we shall use a quick gesture of the arm, a mobile countenance, and a keen glance. (6) For the Broken Tone of Debate, one must extend the arm very quickly, walk up and down, occasionally stamp the right foot, and adopt a keen and fixed look.

(7) For the Hortatory Tone of Amplification, it will be appropriate to use a somewhat slower and more deliberate gesticulation, but otherwise to follow the procedure for the Sustained Tone of Debate. (8) For the Pathetic Tone of Amplification, one ought to slap one's thigh and beat one's head, and sometimes to use a calm and uniform gesticulation and a sad and disturbed expression.

I am not unaware how great a task I have undertaken in trying to express physical movements in words and portray vocal intonations in writing. True, I was not confident that it was possible to treat these matters adequately in writing. Yet neither did I suppose that, if such a treatment were impossible, it would follow that what I have done here would be useless, for it has been my purpose merely to suggest what ought to be done. The rest I shall leave to practice. This, nevertheless, one must remember: good delivery ensures that what the orator is saying seems to come from his heart.

Now let me turn to the treasure-house of the ideas supplied by Invention, to the guardian of all the parts of rhetoric, the Memory.

The question whether memory has some artificial quality, or comes entirely from nature, we shall have another, more favourable, opportunity to discuss. At present I shall accept as proved that in this matter art and method are of great importance, and shall treat the subject accordingly. For my part, I am satisfied that there is an art of memory – the grounds of my belief I shall explain elsewhere. For the present I shall disclose what sort of thing memory is.

There are, then two kinds of memory: one natural, and the other the product of art. The natural memory is that memory which is imbedded in our minds, born simultaneously with thought. The artificial memory is that memory which is strengthened by a kind of training and system of discipline. But just as in everything else the merit of natural excellence often rivals acquired learning, and art, in its turn, reinforces and develops the natural advantages, so does it happen in this instance. The natural memory, if a person is endowed with an exceptional one, is often like this artificial memory, and this artificial memory, in its turn, retains and develops the natural advantages by a method of discipline. Thus the natural memory must be strengthened by discipline so as to become exceptional, and, on the other hand, this memory provided by discipline requires natural ability. It is neither more nor less true in this instance than in the other arts that science thrives by the aid of innate ability, and nature by the aid of the rules of art. The training here offered will therefore also be useful to those who by nature have a good memory, as you will yourself soon come to understand. But even if these, relying on their natural talent, did not need our help, we should still be justified in wishing to aid the less well-endowed. Now I shall discuss the artificial memory.

The artificial memory includes backgrounds and images. By backgrounds, I mean such scenes as are naturally or artifically set off on a small scale, complete and conspicuous, so that we can grasp and embrace them easily by the natural memory – for example, a house, an intercolumnar space, a recess, an arch, or the like. An image is, as it were, a figure, mark, or portrait of the object we wish to remember; for example, if we wish to recall a horse, a lion, or an eagle, we must place its image in a definite background. Now I shall show what kind of backgrounds we should invent and how we should discover the images and set them therein.

Those who know the letters of the alphabet can thereby write out what is dictated to them and read aloud what they have written. Likewise, those who have learned mnemonics can set in backgrounds what they have heard, and from these backgrounds deliver it by memory. For the backgrounds are very much like wax tablets or papyrus, the images like the letters, the arrangement and disposition of the images like the script, and the delivery is like the reading. We should therefore, if we desire to memorize a large number of items, equip ourselves with a large number of backgrounds, so that in these we may set a large number of images. I likewise think it obligatory to have these backgrounds in a series, so that we may never by confusion in their order be prevented from following the images — proceeding from any background we wish, whatsoever its place in the series, and whether we go forwards or backwards — nor from delivering orally what has been committed to the backgrounds.

For example, if we should see a great number of our acquaintances standing in a certain order, it would not make any difference to us whether we should tell their names beginning with the person standing at the head of the line or at the foot or in the middle. So with respect to the backgrounds. If these have been arranged in order, the result will be that, reminded by the images, we can repeat orally what we have committed to the backgrounds, proceeding in either direction from any background we please. That is why it also seems best to arrange the backgrounds in a series.

We shall need to study with special care the backgrounds we have adopted so that they may cling lastingly in our memory, for the images, like letters, are effaced when we make no use of them, but the backgrounds, like wax tablets, should abide. And that we may by no chance err in the number of backgrounds, each fifth background should be marked. For example, if in the fifth we should set a golden hand, and in the tenth some acquaintance whose first name is Decimus, it will then be easy to station like marks in each successive fifth background.

Again, it will be more advantageous to obtain backgrounds in a deserted than in a populous region, because the crowding and passing to and fro of people confuse and weaken the impress of the images, while solitude keeps their outlines sharp. Further, backgrounds differing in form and nature must be secured, so that, thus distinguished, they may be clearly visible; for if a person has adopted many intercolumnar spaces, their resemblance to one another will so confuse him that he will no longer know what he has set in each background. And these backgrounds ought to be of moderate size and medium extent, for when excessively large they render the images vague, and when too small often seem incapable of receiving an arrangement of images. Then the backgrounds ought to be neither too bright nor too dim, so that the shadows may not obscure the images nor the lustre make them glitter. I believe that the intervals between backgrounds should be of moderate extent, approximately thirty feet; for, like the external eye, so the inner eye of thought is less powerful when you have moved the object of sight too near or too far away.

Although it is easy for a person with a relatively large experience to equip himself with as many and as suitable backgrounds as he may desire, even a person who believes that he finds no store of backgrounds that are good enough, may succeed in fashioning as many such as he wishes. For the imagination can embrace any region whatsoever and in it at will fashion and construct the setting of some background. Hence, if we are not content with our ready made supply of backgrounds, we may in our imagination create a region for ourselves and obtain a most serviceable distribution of appropriate backgrounds.

On the subject of backgrounds enough has been said; let me now turn to the theory of images.

Since, then, images must resemble objects, we ought ourselves to choose from all objects likenesses for our use. Hence likenesses are bound to be of two kinds, one of subject-matter, the other of words. Likenesses of matter are formed when we enlist images that present a general view of the matter with which we are dealing; likenesses of words are established when the record of each single noun or appellative is kept by an image.

Often we encompass the record of an entire matter by one notation, a single image. For example, the prosecutor has said that the defendant killed a man by poison, has charged that the motive for the crime was an inheritance, and declared that there are many witnesses and accessories to this act. If in order to facilitate our defence we wish to remember this first point, we shall in our first background form an image of the whole matter. We shall picture the man in question as lying ill in bed, if we know his person. If we do not know him, we shall yet take some one to be our invalid, but not a man of the lowest class, so that he may come to mind at once. And we shall place the defendant at the bedside, holding in his right hand a cup, and in his left tablets, and on the fourth finger a ram's testicles.[1] In this way we can record the man who was poisoned, the inheritance, and the witnesses. In like fashion we shall set the other counts of the charge in backgrounds successively, following their order, and whenever we wish to remember a point, by properly arranging the patterns of the backgrounds and carefully imprinting the images, we shall easily succeed in calling back to mind what we wish.

When we wish to represent by images the likenesses of words, we shall be undertaking a greater task and exercising our ingenuity the more. This we ought to effect in the following way:

Iam domum itionem reges Atridae parant.
"And now their home-coming the kings, the sons of Atreus, are making ready."

---

[1] According to Macrobius, *Sat.* 7. 13. 7-8, the anatomist spoke of a nerve which extends from the heart to the fourth finger of the left hand (the *digitus medicinalis*), where it interlaces into the other nerves of that finger; the finger was therefore ringed, as with a crown. *Testiculi* suggests *testes* (witnesses). Of the Scrotum of the ram purses were made; thus the money used for bribing the witnesses may perhaps. . .be suggested.

If we wish to remember this verse, in our first background we should put Domitius, raising hands to heaven while he is lashed by the Marcii Reges[1] — that will represent "Iam domun itionem reges" ("And now their home-coming the kings,"); in the second background, Aesopus and Cimber, being dressed as for the roles of Agamemnon and Menelaüs in *Iphigenia* — that will represent "Atridae parant" ("the sons of Atreus, are making ready"). By this method all the words will be represented. But such an arrangement of images succeeds only if we use our notation to stimulate the natural memory, so that we first go over a given verse twice or three times to ourselves and then represent the words by means of images. In this way art will supplement nature. For neither by itself will be strong enough, though we must note that theory and technique are much the more reliable. I should not hesitate to demonstrate this in detail, did I not fear that, once having departed from my plan, I should not so well preserve the clear conciseness of my instruction.

Now, since in normal cases some images are strong and sharp and suitable for awakening recollection, and others so weak and feeble as hardly to succeed in stimulating memory, we must therefore consider the cause of these differences, so that, by knowing the cause, we may know which images to avoid and which to seek.

Now nature herself teaches us what we should do. When we see in everyday life things that are petty, ordinary, and banal, we generally fail to remember them, because the mind is not being stirred by anything novel or marvellous. But if we see or hear something exceptionally base, dishonourable, extraordinary, great, unbelievable, or laughable, that we are likely to remember a long time. Accordingly, things immediate to our eye or ear we commonly forget; incidents of our childhood we often remember best. Nor could this be so for any other reason than that ordinary things easily slip from the memory while the striking and novel stay longer in mind. A sunrise, the sun's course, a sunset, are marvellous to no one because they occur daily. But solar eclipses are a source of wonder because they occur seldom, and indeed are more marvellous than lunar eclipses, because these are more frequent. Thus nature shows that she is not aroused by the common, ordinary event, but is moved by a new or striking occurrence. Let art, then, imitate nature, find what she desires, and follow as she directs. For in invention nature is never last, education never first; rather the beginnings of things arise from natural talent, and the ends are reached by discipline.

We ought, then, to set up images of a kind that can adhere longest in the memory. And we shall do so if we establish likenesses as striking as possible; if we set up images that are not many or vague, but doing

---

[1]The scene is doubtless our author's own creation. Rex was the name of one of the most distinguished families of the Marcian *gens*; the Domitian (of plebeian origin) was likewise a celebrated *gens*.

something; if we assign to them exceptional beauty or singular ugliness; if we dress some of them with crowns or purple cloaks, for example, so that the likeness may be more distinct to us; or if we somehow disfigure them, as by introducing one stained with blood or soiled with mud or smeared with red paint, so that its form is more striking, or by assigning certain comic effects to our images, for that, too, will ensure our remembering them more readily. The things we easily remember when they are real we likewise remember without difficulty when they are figments, if they have been carefully delineated. But this will be essential — again and again to run over rapidly in the mind all the original backgrounds in order to refresh the images.

I know that most of the Greeks who have written on the memory have taken the course of listing images that correspond to a great many words, so that persons who wished to learn these images by heart would have them ready without expending effort on a search for them. I disapprove of their method on several grounds. First, among the innumerable multitude of words it is ridiculous to collect images for a thousand. How meagre is the value these can have, when out of the infinite store of words we shall need to remember now one, and now another? Secondly, why do we wish to rob anybody of his initiative, so that, to save him from making any search himself, we deliver to him everything searched out and ready? Then again, one person is more struck by one likeness, and another more by another. Often in fact when we declare that some one form resembles another, we fail to receive universal assent, because things seem different to different persons. The same is true with respect to images: one that is well-defined to us appears relatively inconspicuous to others. Everybody, therefore, should in equipping himself with images suit his own convenience. Finally, it is the instructor's duty to teach the proper method of search in each case, and, for the sake of greater clarity, to add in illustration some one or two examples of its kind, but not all. For instance, when I discuss the search for Introductions, I give a method of search and do not draught a thousand kinds of Introductions. The same procedure I believe should be followed with respect to images.

Now, lest you should perchance regard the memorizing of words either as too difficult or as of too little use, and so rest content with the memorizing of matter, as being easier and more useful, I must advise you why I do not disapprove of memorizing words. I believe that they who wish to do easy things without trouble and toil must previously have been trained in more difficult things. Nor have I included memorization of words to enable us to get verse by rote, but rather as an exercise whereby to strengthen that other kind of memory, the memory of matter, which is of practical use. Thus we may without effort pass from this difficult training to ease in that other memory. In every discipline artistic theory is of little avail without unremitting exercise, but especially in mnemonics theory is almost valueless unless made good by industry, devotion, toil, and care. You can make sure that you have as many backgrounds as possible and that these conform as much as possible to the rules; in placing the images you should exercise every day. While an engrossing preoccupation may often distract us from our other pursuits, from this activity nothing whatever can divert us. Indeed there is never a moment when we do not wish to commit something to memory, and we wish it most of all when our attention is held by business of special importance. So, since a ready memory is a useful thing, you see clearly with what great pains we must strive to acquire so useful a faculty. Once you know its uses you will be able to appreciate this advice. To exhort you further in the matter of memory is not my intention, for I should appear either to have lacked confidence in your zeal or to have discussed the subject less fully than it demands.

APPENDIX:
CHRONOLOGY OF CLASSICAL RHETORIC*

B.C.

c. 1200   Achaean capture of Troy.

c. 900   HOMER and the Greek epics.

814   Traditional date of founding of Carthage.

800–700   Greek lyric poets.

753   Traditional date of founding of Rome.

500–450   Major Greek dramatists.

500   EMPEDOCLES OF AGRIGENTUM (b. c. 500 or 480-, d. c. 430): Sicilian philosopher, scientist; "inventor of rhetoric."

500   PERICLES (b. 500-, d. 429): Athenian statesman and orator; "Funeral Oration" ascribed to him by Thucydides.

500   ANAXAGORAS (b. 500-, d. 428): Greek philosopher saved from death by the eloquence of Pericles.

499–449   Persian Wars.

496   GORGIAS OF LEONTINI (b. 496-, d. 388; or b. 483-, d. 375): Sicilian rhetorician and sophist; noted for his figures of speech called the Gorgianic figures; Platonic dialogue bears his name; two of his declamations and fragments of three speeches extant.

*In compiling this chronology, the editors gratefully acknowledge particularly the usefulness of Sir Paul Harvey, *The Oxford Companion to Classical Literature* (Oxford, 1966); Sir William Smith, *Smaller Classical Dictionary* (New York, 1958); George Kennedy, *The Art of Persuasion in Greece* (Princeton, 1963); M. L. Clarke, *Rhetoric at Rome* (London, 1966); and G. L. Hendrickson, translator of Cicero, *Brutus* (Cambridge, 1962).

Abbreviations used: c. (circa); b. (born); d. (died); fl. (flourished).

485   PROTAGORAS (b. 485-, d. 415; or b. 481-, d. 411): first to call himself a sophist.

?485   PRODICUS OF CEOS (fl. 431–404): sophist; contemporary of Socrates.

480   ANTIPHON (b. 480-, d. 411): first of ten Attic orators; 15 orations extant.

c. 470   CORAX (b. c. 470-, d. ?): Sicilian rhetorician; author of first work on the art of forensic rhetoric called "The Art of Rhetoric."

c. 470   TISIAS (b. c. 470-, d. ?): Sicilian rhetorician; student of Corax.

469   SOCRATES (b. 469-, d. 399): Athenian philosopher and teacher; major oratorical work paraphrased as Plato's *Apology*; founder of formal logic, induction and universal definition; sought truth through dialectic; major interpreters Plato and Xenophon; chief speaker in Plato's dialogues.

462–429   Supremacy of PERICLES.

460   DEMOCRETES OF ABDERA (also Democritus, b. 460-, d. c. 370): Greek philosopher; his rhetoric praised by Cicero.

458   LYSIAS (b. 458-, d. 380): Attic orator and logographer (ghostwriter); author of more than 200 orations of which 34 have survived.

457   THUCYDIDES (b. 457-, d. 401): Athenian statesman and historian; his history of the Peloponnesian War relates arguments for and against proposed actions in the form of orations representing the substance of what was said by participants.

457   THRASYMACHUS OF CALCHEDON (b. 457-, d. c. 400): teacher of rhetoric; developed Attic prose; created the "middle style"; a character in Plato's *Phaedrus*.

450   Establishment of the Twelve Tables.

450   HIPPIAS OF ELIS (b. 450-, d. ?): sophist and contemporary of Socrates; two minor Platonic dialogues named after him.

c. 440   ANTISTHENES (b. c. 440-, d. ?): founder of the Cynic School of Philosophy.

c. 440   ANDOCIDES (b. c. 440-, d. ?): Attic orator; three speeches extant; renowned for his natural and persuasive eloquence.

436   ISOCRATES (b. 436-, d. 338): Attic orator; student of Gorgias, Prodicus, and probably Socrates; teacher of rhetoric at Chios; founder of rhetorical school at Athens; logographer; extant treatises on rhetoric include "Antidosis" and "Against the Sophists"; 21 orations extant of which the most famous is the "Panegyric"; believed rhetoric a primary training for citizenship; had considerable influence on Cicero.

431–404   Peloponnesian War.

429   PLATO (b. 429 or 428-, d. 347; or b. 420-, d. 348): philosopher, poet, founder of the Academy; disciple of Socrates, teacher of Aristotle; author of three broad groups of dialogues: nine which represent Socrates as the chief speaker examining the views offered him by questioners, 13 which also present Socrates as the major speaker and are thought to give Plato's own views or his interpretation of Socrates' views (including his two major treatises on rhetoric, the *Gorgias* and the *Phaedrus*), and six dialogues written toward the end of his life; as a critic of sophistic rhetoric he compared it to "cookery" or "flattery" in the *Gorgias*, while dialectic is "the king of men," but in the *Phaedrus*, he acknowledged that rhetoric can be good if based on truth as found from dialectic.

c. 427?   THEODORUS OF BYZANTIUM (fl. c. 427): rhetorician and contemporary of Plato.

c. 427?   POLUS (b. c. 427?-, d. ?): sophist; student of Gorgias; character in Plato's *Gorgias.*

c. 427?   ALCIDAMUS (b. c. 427?-, d.?): rhetorician.

c. 425   LYCOPHRON (b. c. 425-, d. ?): Greek poet; writer of tragedies; author of treatise on comedy; rhetorician.

420   ISAEUS (b. 420-, d. 348): Attic orator and logographer; founder of rhetorical school at Athens at which Demosthenes may have been a student; 11 orations extant.

404   Surrender of Athens; Thirty Tyrants in power.

404–371   Spartan supremacy.

c. 400?   ZOILUS (b. c. 400?-, d. ?): rhetorician and critic; author of nine books of criticism on Homer.

c. 396   LYCURGUS (b. c. 396-, d. 324): Attic orator; disciple of
            Plato and Isocrates; one oration extant.

390   Sack of Rome by the Gauls.

389   AESCHINES (b. 389-, d. 314): Athenian orator; attacked by
            Demosthenes in "On the Crown"; established school of
            eloquence at Rhodes; several orations extant.

389   HYPERIDES (b. 389-, d. 322): Attic orator; portions of his
            orations discovered in Egypt in 1847 and 1892.

384   ARISTOTLE (b. 384-, d. 322): student of Plato, philosopher,
            scientist, rhetorician; teacher of Alexander the Great; director
            of the Lyceum in Athens; some 400 works attributed to him,
            including 14 surviving fragments of dialogues on philosophy,
            collections of data obtained by systematic research which are
            now mostly lost, and his major treatises which were lost until
            the first century B.C. (including six treatises on logic, treatises
            on metaphysics, natural philosophy, ethics and politics, and
            the *Rhetorica*, which has remained perhaps the most
            influential work on that subject, and his *Poetica* which has
            served as a major force in the study of literary criticism).

384   DEMOSTHENES (b. 384 or 383-, d. 322): Athenian statesman
            and orator; student of Isaeus; logographer; 61 orations extant
            although authenticity of authorship for some is in question;
            major orations included "The Philippics" used as a model for
            Cicero, "On the Crown," and "On the Peace"; considered by
            Quintilian as the greatest of Greek orators, whose orations
            should be memorized.

c. 380   ANAXIMENES (b. c. 380-, d. 320): thought to be the author
            of *Rhetorica ad Alexandrum*, a sophistic handbook written
            about 330.

372   THEOPHRASTUS OF ERESUS (b. 372 or 371-, d. 287):
            student of Aristotle and his successor as head of the
            Peripatetic school of philosophy; teacher of Dinarchus and of
            Demetrius of Phalerum; rhetorician; author of writings
            developing the philosophy of Aristotle; author of treatise "On
            Style" which was praised by Cicero.

370?   DEMADES (b. 370?-, d. 319): Athenian orator; bitter enemy
            of Demosthenes.

366   CALLISTRATUS (fl. 366): eloquent Athenian orator and
            statesman.

363–292   Major comic dramatists.

362   ZENO (b. 362-, d. 264; or b. 335-, d. 263): founder of the
          Stoic philosophy which encouraged an austere style of
          oratory.

c. 360   DINARCHUS (b. c. 360-, d. ?): last of the ten Attic orators;
          three orations extant.

c. 354   DEMETRIUS OF PHALERUM (b. c. 354- or 345-, d. c. 283):
          student of Theophrastus; Athenian statesman, orator,
          philosopher and poet; author of works on literature, politics
          and oratory, and treatise entitled "On Style"; this authorship
          may belong to another Demetrius.

340   Latin War.

336–323   ALEXANDER THE GREAT, King of Macedon.

331   CLEANTHES (b. 331- d. 230): Stoic philosopher and
          successor of Zeno.

312   APPIUS CLAUDIUS CAECUS (fl. 312-280): Roman censor;
          first notable Roman orator; his funeral orations praised by
          Cicero.

310   CALLIMACHUS (b. 310-, d. 240): Alexandrine poet,
          grammarian, and bibliographer; a vigorous literary feud
          developed between him and his former student Appollonius
          Rhodius.

c. 300?   HEGESIAS OF MAGNESIA (b. c. 300?-, d. 250?): biographer
          of Alexander the Great; orator of the Asiatic school of
          oratory.

c. 295   APPOLLONIUS RHODIUS (b. c. 295-, d. 215): poet,
          grammarian, and rhetorician; his teaching of rhetoric met such
          success that Rhodians honored him with the title "The
          Rhodian."

285   LYCOPHRON (b. 285-, d. 247): poet.

282   CHRYSIPPUS (b. 282-, d. 206; or b. 280- d. 207): Stoic
          philosopher; successor of Cleanthes.

270   HERMARCHUS (fl. 270): rhetorician of Mytilene; disciple
          and successor of Epicurus the philosopher.

264–241   First Punic War.

234   CATO THE CENSOR (b. 234-, d. 149): Roman statesman and
           orator; 150 of his orations known to Cicero; distrusted Greek
           culture and forbade Greek philosophers and rhetoricians to
           reside at Rome.

c. 234   ERATOSTHENES (fl. c. 234): historian, philosopher, literary
           critic.

215, 200–196, 171–167, 149–148   Four Macedonian Wars.

c. 195   ARISTOPHANES OF BYZANTIUM (fl. c. 195): head of the
           Alexandrian Library; said to have invented or regularized
           Greek accents.

c. 186   GAIUS LAELIUS (b. c. 186-, d. ?): Roman statesman and
           orator; surnamed "Sapiens" (the Wise) for his wide learning
           and philosophical attainments; principal character in Cicero's
           dialogue "Concerning Friendship."

185   SCIPIO AEMILIANUS (b. 185-, d. 129): Roman statesman
           and orator; patron of Greek and Latin letters; regarded by
           Cicero as the greatest of Romans.

c. 166   DIONYSIUS THE THRACIAN (b. c. 166-, d. ?): author of the
           first systematic Greek grammar, still extant.

c160?   HERMAGORAS OF TEMNOS (b. c. 160?-, d. c. 110?): first
           distinguished teacher of rhetoric after Isocrates; author of
           treatise on rhetoric, now lost, in which he modified the
           Aristotelian parts of rhetoric by dividing political questions
           into two classes — *theses* (controversies not involving specific
           individuals) and *hypotheses* (specific controversies involving
           definite persons and events) — and by calling the crucial point
           at issue the *stasis* (later called *status* by Cicero).

146   Achaean War; destruction of Corinth by the Romans.

143   MARCUS ANTONIUS (b. 143-, d. 87): Roman statesman;
           considered by Cicero one of the greatest orators of his period;
           a principal character in Cicero's dialogue *De Oratore*.

140   LUCIUS LICINIUS CRASSUS (b. 140-, d. 91): also
           considered by Cicero one of the great Roman orators; a chief
           character in Cicero's *De Oratore*.

c. 135   POSIDONIUS (b. c. 135-, d. c. 51): Stoic philosopher; to the
           extent that Aristotle is thought to have influenced the early
           Greek culture, Posidonius is thought to have affected the
           Hellenistic period.

133   TIBERIUS SEMPRONIUS GRACCHUS (fl. 133): Roman tribune, reformer, and orator; highly praised by Cicero.

133–122   Tribunate of the Gracchi.

c. 130   ARCHEDEMUS OF TARSUS (b. c. 130-, d. ?): simplified Hermagoras' system of stasis.

c130   ATHENAEUS (b. c. 130-, d. ?): opponent of Archedemus; called Hermagoras' *thesis* a part of *hypothesis*; treated delivery extensively.

128   QUINTUS MUCIUS CAEVOLA (fl. 128-117, d. 88): Roman statesman, jurist, and orator; speaker in Cicero's *De Oratore.*

121   GAIUS SEMPRONIUS GRACCHUS (b. ?-, d. 121): Roman tribune, reformer, and orator; highly praised by Cicero.

c. 120   APPOLLONIUS OF ALABANDA (b. c. 120-, d.   ?): rhetorician; taught rhetoric at about 100 B.C.

116   MARCUS TERRENTIUS VARRO (b. 116-, d. 27): Roman poet, satirist, jurist, and grammarian; author of systematic treatise on Latin grammar; called "the most learned of Romans" by Quintilian.

114   HORTENSIUS HORTALUS (b. 114-, d. 50): Cicero's chief rival in the law courts and leading Roman orator of the period until Cicero's success in the trial of Verres; Cicero called him a genius in the *Brutus* and praised him in *De Oratore* for his grand Asian style of oratory; Ciceronian dialogue, now lost, named for him.

c. 112   ORBILIUS PUPILLIUS (b. c. 112-, d. c. 17): Roman grammarian; teacher of Horace.

109   TITUS POMPONIUS ATTICUS (b. 109-, d. 32): Roman scholar; intimate friend of Cicero to whom he wrote his famous letters; publisher of Cicero's works.

106   MARCUS TULLIUS CICERO (b. 106-, d. 43): Roman statesman, jurist, orator, and rhetorician; studied rhetoric and philosophy under Philo the Academic and Diodotus the Stoic at Rome, and later under Molo and Posidonius at Rhodes; made his first extant speech in the law courts in 81, entitled "Pro Quinctio" facing Hortensius as his opponent; became one of the three leading Roman advocates and eventually surpassed the other two; delivered his first political oration "De Lege Manila" in 66 B.C.; elected consul in 64 B.C.; gave his four

Catilinarian orations in 63 B.C.; was forced into exile in 58 after Caesar became consul in 59, but returned in 57; turned to his philosophical and rhetorical treatises, writing (1) in 55 *De Oratore*, which he authored to replace his youthful *De Inventione*, (2) in about 53, a small manual on the parts of the oration, "Partitiones Oratoriae," (3) between 46 and 44, his history of Roman oratory, *Brutus*, as well as his description of the ideal speaker, *Orator*, an abstract of the "Topics" of Aristotle, and a small treatise concerning the best kind of orator, *De Optimo Genere Oratorum*, which he intended as an introduction to his translations, now lost, of the speeches of Aeschines and Demosthenes' "On the Crown," (4) in 45 B.C., "Hortensius," now lost, and other philosophical works; after Caesar's assassination in 44, Cicero became politically active again, delivering his 14 "Philippic" orations against Mark Anthony, for which Anthony had him murdered in 43; Cicero's rhetorical and oratorical influence extended to Quintilian, Ambrose, Jerome, Augustine, and Petrarch (who rediscovered several of his lost rhetorical works), and to much of the literature of the Renaissance.

105   APPOLODARUS OF PERGAMUM (b. 105-, d. 23): promulgated Isocrates' scholastic rhetoric.

102   GAIUS JULIUS CAESAR (b. 102 or 100-, d. 44): Roman ruler, historian, and orator of the Attic school; Cicero disliked him and worked for Pompey, but was forced to give an oration thanking him for clemency and praised him in the *Brutus*.

c. 100   DEMETRIUS OF PERGAMUM (b. c. 100-, d. ?): rhetorician.

95   QUINTUS MUCIUS SCAEVOLA (fl. 95): Pontifex Maximus; consul, orator, teacher of Cicero; noted by Cicero for his concise use of language.

92–88   Civil War between Marius and Sulla.

88–84, 74–63   Three Mithridatic Wars.

86–82   *Rhetorica ad Herennium*, treatise on oratory in four books; long thought a work of Cicero, but probably authorship belongs to Cornificius.

82   GAIUS LICINIUS CALVUS (b. 82-, d. 47): celebrated Roman poet and forensic orator.

c. 80   APPOLLONIUS OF ALABANDA, surnamed Molon (b. c. 80-, d. ?): taught rhetoric at Rhodes; gave instruction to Cicero.

78? MARCUS JUNIUS BRUTUS (b. 78-, d. 42): conspirator in the assassination of Caesar; an eminent orator whose name Cicero gave to his history of Roman oratory.

c. 75 GAIUS AURELIUS COTTA (fl. 75): Roman consul in 75 B.C.; distinguished orator; speaker in Cicero's "De Natura Deorum" and *De Oratore.*

c. 73 THEODORUS OF GADARA (b. c. 73 B.C.-, d.6 A.D.): author of a ' techne" reemphasizing Aristotle's rhetoric.

70 VIRGIL (b. 70-, d. 19): Rome's foremost poet.

65 HORACE (b. 65-, d. 8): Roman poet, author of "The Art of Poetry."

63 Conspiracy of Catiline.

60 First Triumvirate.

60? DIONYSIUS OF HALICARNASSUS (b. 60?-, d. 8, fl. 25): celebrated Greek historian and rhetorician who lived at Rome; 11 of his 22 volumes on the history of Rome extant; among his chief rhetorical works were "On the Arrangement of Words," "On the Ancient Orators," and "On the Eloquence of Demosthenes"; his most famous statement remains "The style is the man."

c. 55 SENECA THE ELDER (b. 55-, d. 37 A.D.): Spanish Roman; called "the Rhetorician"; assembled for his sons a collection of "Controversiae" (debates on imaginary problems in criminal and civil law cases) and a collection of "Suasioriae" (monologues on deliberative themes of ancient history).

58–51 Caesar's conquest of Gaul.

49–48 Civil War between Caesar and Pompey.

44 Assassination of Caesar.

43 Second Triumvirate, followed by Second Civil War; assassination of Cicero.

42 Battle of Philippi.

31 Battle of Actium.

27–14 A.D. The reign of the empire of Augustus.

c. 10   VERRIUS FLACCUS (fl. c. 10): a Roman freedman at time of
           Augustus; grammarian and teacher; author of treatise "On the
           Meaning of Words."

c. 4   LUCIUS ANNAEUS SENECA (b. c. 4 B.C.-, d. 65 A.D.): son
           of Seneca the Elder; called "the Philosopher"; statesman,
           philosopher, rhetorician, and forensic orator; tutor to Nero; 12
           of his dialogues are extant, including some dealing with
           rhetorical and philosophical exercises; author of moral essays,
           124 Epistles used widely by Christian writers, seven books on
           natural phenomena, and nine tragedies.

A.D.

1?   CAECILIUS OF CALACTE (fl. 1 A.D.?): Greek rhetorician at
           Rome in the period of Augustus; author of treatise "On the
           Character of the ten Orators" now lost.

1–100?   "Longinus on the Sublime": a Greek work of unknown date
           and authorship, analyzing the quality of writing that
           constitutes sublimity and finding it in the eloquence of ideas.

14   VALERIUS MAXIMUS (fl. 14- 27): compiler of nine books of
           anecdotes "Facta et Dicta Memorabilia" to be used by orators.

23   PLINY THE ELDER (b. 23 or 24-, d. 79): statesman,
           historian, and orator; author of books on military science,
           oratory, grammar, biography, and history which are lost; and
           author of *Naturalis Historia* in 37 volumes which is extant.

c. 30   DION CHRYSOSTOM (fl. 30): Greek philosopher and orator
           living at Rome; called "the golden-mouthed"; his collection of
           discourses in Greek on political, literary, and philosophical
           subjects is extant.

c. 35   QUINTILIAN (b. c. 35-, d. c. 95; or b. 40-, d. 118): Spanish
           Roman; first teacher of rhetoric at Rome to receive state
           salary; forensic orator; author of a lost treatise "On the Cause
           of the Corruption of Eloquence"; two collections of
           "Declamations" on rhetorical themes are attributed, perhaps
           incorrectly, to him; author of *Institutio Oratoria* in 12 books
           which synthesizes earlier rhetoric, gives childhood training
           rules for the future orator, and contains the famous
           description of the orator as "the good man speaking well"; its
           influence was considerable at first but the volumes were lost
           until 1470 when it acquired a major influence among
           educators in the Renaissance.

37   QUINTUS REMMIUS PALAEMON (fl. 37): Roman grammarian and teacher.

c. 46   PLUTARCH (b. c. 46- d. c. 120): Greek biographer and moral philosopher; author of treatises on 23 parallel Greek and Roman lives and four single lives, in which rhetorical criticism is offered of the oratory of Pericles, Demosthenes, Brutus, Julius Caesar, Cicero, and others; author of 83 treatises on moral conduct and related subjects entitled "Moralia."

c. 50?   RUTILIUS LUPUS (fl. c. 50?): translator of four books on figures of speech by Gorgias.

50?   JULIUS RUFINIANUS (fl. 50?): author of treatise on figures of speech.

c. 55   PUBLIUS (?) CORNELIUS TACITUS (b. c. 55-, d. 117): Roman historian, student of rhetoric, orator, and author of "Dialogue Concerning Orators."

61   PLINY THE YOUNGER (b. 61-, d. 113): student of Quintilian; Roman statesman, orator, essayist, and poet; he took particular pride in his oratory, but received his greatest fame for his ten volumes of *Letters* which are extant.

65   GAIUS PETRONIUS ARBITER (b. ?-, d. 65): "Arbiter of Taste" to Nero; probable author of "Satyricon" which satirizes poetry, rhetoric, grammar, and customs of that period.

c. 69   SUETONIUS TRANQUILLUS (b. c. 69-, d. 160): Roman historian; author of *De Viris Illustribus,* which included brief treatises ''Concerning Illustrious Grammarians'' and "Concerning Illustrious Rhetoricians."

70   Destruction of Jerusalem.

100–200?   APOLLONIUS DYSCOLUS (fl. second century): author of Greek treatises which first placed Greek grammar on a scientific basis; author of various works, mostly lost, on the parts of speech and syntax.

100–200?   HERODIAN (fl. second century): author of treatise in 21 books on Greek accents.

100?   MARCUS CORNELIUS FRONTO (b. 100?-, d. 166?): forensic Roman orator; advocate of return to style and language of older Romans; author of letters on literature, oratory, and the study of words.

101   HERODES ATTICUS (b. 101-, d. 177): Greek orator and
           rhetorician; instructor of Emperor Marcus Aurelius.

114–117, 161–166   Parthian Wars.

c. 115   LUCIAN (b. c. 115-, d. c. 200): former rhetorician and
           philosopher who became an author of satirical dialogues
           against rhetoric, philosophy, and the morality of his day.

150   TERTULLIAN (b. c. 150-160-, d. 230): an influential
           Christian writer who was later declared a heretic; author of
           "The Apology," a treatise defending Christian beliefs and
           written in the form of an oration.

161   HERMOGENES OF TARSUS (fl. 161-180): Greek
           rhetorician; author of "Concerning the Parts of Stasis,"
           "Concerning Invention of Oratory," "Concerning the Type of
           Orators," and "Concerning Eloquence."

180   JULLIUS POLLUX (fl. 180): lexicographer and author of an
           extant list of Attic words and technical terms.

c. 200   ALEXANDER OF APHRODISIAS (fl. c. 300): the most
           important early commentator on Aristotle.

c. 200   ATHENAEUS OF NAUCRATIS (fl. c. 200): Greek writer on
           the sophists.

c. 200   DIOGENES LAERTIUS (b. c. 200-, d. 250): author of a ten
           volume *Lives and Opinions of Eminent Philosophers* which
           included the lives of several celebrated rhetoricians.

c. 200   FLAVIUS PHILOSTRATUS (fl. 200): one of the four
           Philostratus (all authors) living in this period; teacher of
           rhetoric at Athens and later at Rome.

c. 210   PHILOSTRATUS III (fl. c. 210): thought to be author in
           Greek of a treatise called *Lives of the Sophists* which was a
           history of the orators and rhetoricians from Protagoras to
           about 200 A.D.

220   CASSIUS LONGINUS (b. 200-, d. 273): eminent Greek writer
           on rhetoric and philosophy; his extant treatise on "The Art of
           Rhetoric" survives; scholars believe he is not author of "On
           the Sublime."

c. 235   APSINES OF GADARA IN PHOENICIA (fl. c. 235):
           rhetorician.

c. 250   CAECILLIUS FIRMIANUS LACTANTIUS (b. c. 250-, d. c. 317): an African pagan who became professor of rhetoric at Nicomedia and then became Christian; wrote in an oratorical Ciceronian prose and was called the Christian Cicero.

c. 270   AQUILA ROMANUS (fl. c. 270): author of treatise on figures of speech.

285–305   Reign of Diocletian.

300   MARIUS (QUINTUS FABIUS LAURENTIUS) VICTORINUS (b. 300-, d. 363): Latin rhetorician and teacher of Jerome; author of treatise "Explanation of the Rhetoric of Marcus Tullius Cicero"; translator of Aristotle's "Categories" and "On Interpretation."

c. 300   NONIUS MARCELLUS (b. c. 300-, d. c. 350): Roman grammarian and encyclopaedist for Constantine; part of encyclopaedia deals with the diction of the older Latin writers.

c. 310   DECIMUS MAGNUS AUSONIUS (b. c. 310-, d. c. 395); teacher of rhetoric for 30 years; writer of verse which demonstrated better his skill of rhetoric than poetic creation.

c. 314   LIBANIUS (b. c. 314-, d. 393): a rhetorician of Antioch who founded a rhetorical school at Constantinople; author of an extant life of Demosthenes and synopses of his orations.

c. 315   APTHONIUS OF ANTIOCH (b. 315-, d. ?): Greek rhetorician; author of an introduction to a study of rhetoric called "Progymnasmata," a series of rhetorical exercises which were used in the schools for several centuries.

c. 325   C. CHIRIUS FORTUNATIANUS (fl. c. 325): author of "Ars Rhetorica."

c. 325   SULPICIUS VICTOR (fl. c. 325): author of "Institutiones Oratoriae," largly copied from Quintilian.

330   Establishment of Constantinople.

c. 330   C. JULIUS VICTOR (fl. c. 330): author of "Ars Rhetorica."

c. 340   AMBROSE (b. c. 340-, d. 397): Christian bishop and writer; used Cicero's oratorical style as a model; author of numerous important sermons.

c. 340   JEROME (b. c. 340-, d. 420): Christian writer; translator of the *Vulgate*; his admiration for pagan literature, including the works of Cicero, was in conflict with his belief that he should subscribe only to Christian literature and the "Verbum" Word of God.

345   QUINTUS AURELIUS SYMMACHUS (b. 345-, d. 405): Roman nobleman and orator whose eloquence was acknowledged by Ambrose.

347   CHRYSOSTOM (JOANNES CHRYSOSTOMUS) (b. 347-, d. 407): archbishop of Constantinople; author of many extant sermons, often filled with sophistic excesses, which he condemned.

c. 350?   AELIUS DONATUS (fl. c. 350?): Latin grammarian and rhetorician; author of "Ars Grammatica," a Latin grammar used throughout the middle ages.

c. 350?   SERVIUS MARIUS HONORATUS (fl. c. 350-400?): Latin grammarian.

354   AUGUSTINE (b. 354-, d. 430): teacher of pagan rhetoric at Thagaste, Carthage, Rome, and Milan; converted by Ambrose to Christianity; author of numerous treatises and sermons defending Christianity, including the treatise "On Christian Doctrine," in which he developed the first Christian rhetoric.

c. 360   THEMISTIUS (fl. c. 360): rhetorician of Paphalognia who taught at Constantinople; surnamed "The Eloquent"; 33 of his orations are extant, many of them panegyrics on the emperors.

c. 370   AELIUS THEON OF ALEXANDRIA (b. c. 370-, d. ?): author of rhetorical exercises entitled "Progymnasmata."

395   Defeat of Attila the Hun.

c. 400   MARTIANUS CAPELLA (fl. c. 400): an African writer of allegories; encyclopaedist of the seven liberal arts: the trivium — grammar, logic, and rhetoric, and the quadrivium — geometry, arithmetic, astronomy, and music.

c. 430   JULIUS SEVERIANUS (fl. c. 430): author of "The Precepts of the Art of Rhetoric."

430?   GRILLIUS (fl. 430?): author of "Commentary on the Rhetoric of Cicero."

c. 431   SIDONIUS APPOLLINARIS (b. c. 431- d. ?): politician, bishop, and panegyric orator of Gaul.

476   End of the Western Empire.

SELECTED BIBLIOGRAPHY

RHETORIC AND GENERAL BACKGROUND

Adams, John Q., *Lectures On Rhetoric And Oratory*. New Intro. by J. Auer and J. Banninga (New York, 1962).

Aristotle, *Ars Rhetorica*. Ed. by W. D. Ross (Oxford, 1959).

_____ ,*Art of Poetry: A Greek View of Poetry and Drama* (Oxford, 1940).

_____ ,*On Poetry and Style*. Tr. by G. M. A. Grube (Indianapolis, 1958).

_____ ,*Poetics*. Tr. by S. H. Butcher, intro. by Francis Fergusson (New York, 1961).

_____ ,*Posterior Analytics*. Tr. by E. S. Foster (Cambridge, England, 1961).

_____ ,*Rhetoric of Aristotle*. Tr. by Lane Cooper (New York, 1967).

_____ ,*The Rhetoric of Aristotle*. With a Commentary, by ... Edward Meredith Cope; revised and edited ... by John Edwin Sandys. 3 vols. (Cambridge, England, 1877).

_____ ,*The Rhetoric of Aristotle*. Tr. by R. C. Jebb, intro. by J. E. Sandys (Cambridge, England, 1909).

_____ ,*The Works of Aristotle*. Tr. by J. A. Smith and W. D. Ross. 11 vols. (Oxford, (1908-1931).

Atkins, J. W. H., *Literary Criticism in Antiquity: A Sketch of its Development*, 2 vols. (Cambridge, England, 1934).

Augustine, *On Christian Doctrine*. Tr. by D. W. Robertson (Indianapolis, 1958).

_____ ,*Writings of Saint Augustine*, 18 vols. (New York, 1947-1959).

Avery, Catherine B., ed., and Jotham Johnson, editorial consultant, *The New Century Classical Handbook* (New York, 1962).

Bailey, Dudley, ed., *Essays on Rhetoric* (New York, 1965).

Baird, A. Craig, *Rhetoric: A Philosophical Inquiry* (New York, 1965).

Baldry, H. C., *The Unity of Mankind in Greek Thought* (London, 1965)

Baldwin, C. S., *Ancient Rhetoric and Poetic* (New York, 1924).

———, *Medieval Rhetoric and Poetic* (New York, 1928).

———, *Renaissance Literary Theory and Practice* (New York, 1959).

———, *"St. Augustine and the Rhetoric of Cicero,"* Proceedings of the Classical Association, 22 (1925), pp. 24-46.

Beaumont, Charles Allen, *Swift's Classical Rhetoric* (Athens, Georgia, 1961).

Bell, J. H., and A. Cohn, *Rhetoric in a Modern Mode with Selected Readings* (Glencoe, Ill., 1968).

Berquist, Goodwin F., Jr., "An Ancient Who is Not Antiquated [Isocrates]," *Today's Speech*, 2 (April, 1954), pp. 11-13.

Black, E., "Plato's View of Rhetoric," *Quarterly Journal of Speech*, 44 (1958), pp. 361-74.

———, *Rhetorical Criticism* (London, 1967).

Blair, Hugh, *An Abridgement of Lectures on Rhetoric*. Ed. by J. L. Blake (Concord, Mass., 1830).

———, *Lectures on Rhetoric and Belles Lettres* (Philadelphia, 1829).

Bluck, R. S., "Plato, *Gorgias* 493c 1-3," *Classical Review*, 13 (1963), pp. 263-264.

Bonner, S. F., *The Education of a Roman: A Lecture for Schools* (Liverpool, 1950).

———, *Roman Declamation in the Late Republic and Early Empire* (Liverpool, 1949).

Booth, W. C., "Revival of Rhetoric," *PMLA*, 80 (May, 1965), pp. 8-12.

Bosmajian, Haig A., ed., *Readings in Speech* (New York, 1965).

Bower E. W., "Some Technical Terms in Roman Education," *Hermes*, 89 (1961), pp. 462-477.

Bowsky, William, ed., *Studies in Medieval and Renaissance History*, 3 vols. (Lincoln, 1964, 1965, 1966).

British and Continental Rhetoric and Elocution. Microfilm, 16 reels (Ann Arbor, 1953).

Brockriede, W. E., "Dimensions of the Concept of Rhetoric," *Quarterly Journal of Speech*, 54 (Feb., 1968), pp. 1-12.

———, "Toward a Contemporary Aristotelian Theory of Rhetoric," *Quarterly Journal of Speech*, 52 (1966), pp. 33-40.

Brownstein, Oscar L., "Plato's *Phaedrus*: Dialectic as the Genuine Art of Speaking," *Quarterly Journal of Speech*, 51 (1965), pp. 392-398.

Bryant, Donald C., *Papers in Rhetoric* (St. Louis, 1940).

——— , "Rhetoric: Its Functions and Its Scope," *Quarterly Journal of Speech*, 39 (1953), pp. 401-424.

——— ,ed., *The Rhetorical Idiom* (Ithaca, 1958).

Burke, Kenneth, *A Rhetoric of Motives* (New York, 1950).

——— , "Rhetoric — Old and New," *Journal of General Education*, 5 (1951), pp. 202-209.

Campbell, George, *Philosophy of Rhetoric*. Ed. by L. Bitzer (Carbondale, 1963).

Caplan, Harry, and others, eds., *Of Eloquence: Studies in Ancient and Medieval Rhetoric* (Ithaca, 1966).

Carmack, William R., "A History of Greek Rhetoric and Oratory," *Quarterly Journal of Speech*, 49 (1963), pp. 325-328.

Cary, Max, and others, *Oxford Classical Dictionary* (Oxford, 1967).

Chroust, Anton-Hermann, "Aristotle's Earliest 'Course of Lectures on Rhetoric.' " *L'Antiquité Classique*, 33 (1964), pp. 58-72.

——— , "Aristotle's First Literary Effort: The *Gryllus*, A Lost Dialogue on the Nature of Rhetoric," *Revue Des Etudes Grecques*, 78 (1965), pp. 576-591.

——— , "The First Thirty Years of Modern Aristotelian Scholarship (1912-1942)," *Classica et Mediaevalia*, 24 (1963), pp. 27-57.

Cicero, *Brutus*, Tr. by G. L. Hendrickson (Cambridge, Mass., 1952).

——— ,*De Inventione, De Optimo Genere Oratorum*, and *Topica*. Tr. by H. M. Hubbell (Cambridge, Mass., 1949).

——— ,*De Oratore*. Books I and II tr. by E. W. Sutton, completed, with an intro. by H. Rackham (Cambridge, Mass., 1939).

——— ,*De Oratore*. Book III, Together with *De Fato, Paradoxa Stoicorum*, and *De Partitione Oratoria*. Tr. by H. Rackham (Cambridge, Mass., 1940).

——— ,*Orator*. Tr. by H. M. Hubbell (Cambridge, Mass., 1952).

——— , *Rhetorica*. Ed. by A. S. Wilkins (Oxford, 1903).

[———],*Rhetorica Ad Herennium*. Tr. by Harry Caplan (Cambridge, Mass., 1954).

Clark, D. L., *Rhetoric and Poetry in the Renaissance* (Magnolia, Mass., 1967).

——— ,*Rhetoric in Greco-Roman Education* (New York, 1957).

——— , "Some Values of Roman Declamatio, the Controversia as a School Exercise in Rhetoric," *Quarterly Journal of Speech*, 35 (1949), pp. 280-283.

Clarke, M. L., *Classical Education in Britain (1500-1900)* (Cambridge, England, 1959).

———, *Rhetoric at Rome: A Historical Survey* (London, 1953).

Classical, Medieval and Renaissance Studies in Honor of B. L. Ullman, 2 vols. (Rome, 1964).

Colton, Robert E., "Juvenal on Recitations," *Classical Bulletin,* 42 (1966), pp. 81-85.

Cooper, Lane, *The Poetics of Aristotle, its Meaning and Influence* (Ithaca, 1927).

Corbett, Edward P. J., *Classical Rhetoric for the Modern Student* (New York, 1965).

———,"Rhetoric and Teachers of English," *Quarterly Journal of Speech,* 51 (1965), pp. 375-381.

———,"The Usefulness of Classical Rhetoric," *College Composition and Communication,* 14 (1963), pp. 162-164.

Coulter, James A., "The Relation of the Apology of Socrates to Gorgias' Defense of Palamedes and Plato's Critique of Gorgianic Rhetoric," *Harvard Studies in Classical Philology,* 68 (1964), pp. 269-303.

Crocker, Lionel, and Paul A. Carmack, eds., *Readings in Rhetoric* (Springfield, Ill., 1965).

Cushman, Helen V., "Corax — Secretary or Rhetorician?" *Pennsylvania Speech Annual,* 20 (1963), pp. 8-10.

D'Alton, J. F., *Roman Literary Theory and Criticism* (New York, 1931).

Dalzell, Alexander, "C. Asinius Pollio and the Early History of Public Recitation at Rome," *Hermathena,* 86 (1955), pp. 20-28.

Dearin, Ray D., "Aristotle on Psychology and Rhetoric," *Central States Speech Journal,* 17 (1966), pp. 277-282.

DeQuincey, Thomas, *Selected Essays on Rhetoric.* Ed. by F. Burwick (Carbondale, 1967).

Dieter, Otto A., "*Arbor Picta*: The Medieval Tree of Preaching," *Quarterly Journal of Speech,* 51 (1965), pp. 123-144.

———,"Classics and Speech," *Quarterly Journal of Speech,* 37 (1951), pp. 479-482.

———,"The Rhetor Stone," *Quarterly Journal of Speech,* 51 (1965), pp. 426-432.

Dorsch, T. S., tr., *Classical Literary Criticism* (New York, 1967),

Downey, Glanville, "Education and Public Programs as Seen by Themistius," *Transactions of the American Philological Association,* 86 (1955), pp. 291-307.

———,"Education in the Christian Roman Empire, Christian and Pagan Theories Under Constantine and His Successors," *Speculum,* 32 (1957), pp. 48-61.

Duff, J. Wight, *A Literary History of Rome from the Origins to the Close of the Golden Age.* 3rd ed. (London, 1953).

Duhamel, Pierre Albert, "The Function of Rhetoric as Effective Expression," *Journal of the History of Ideas,* 10 (1949), pp. 344-356.

Ferguson, J. L. A. Thompson, A. R. Hands, and W. A. Laidlaw, *Studies in Cicero* (Rome, 1962).

Fisher, J., "Plato on Writing and Doing Philosophy," *Journal of the History of Ideas,* 27 (April, 1966), pp. 163-172.

Fisher, Walter Ray, "Rhetoric, a Pedagogic Definition," *Western Speech,* 25 (1961), pp. 168-170.

Fleshler, Helen, "Plato and Aristotle on Rhetoric and Dialectic," *Pennsylvania Speech Annual,* 20 (1963), pp. 11-17.

Flynn, Lawrence J., "Aristotle: Art and Faculty of Rhetoric," *Southern Speech Journal* (Summer, 1956), pp. 244-254.

Gilbert, Neal Ward, "Concepts of Method in the Renaissance and Their Ancient and Medieval Antecedents." Unpublished Ph.D. dissertation, Columbia University, 1956.

Gomperz, T., *Greek Thinkers,* 4 vols. (London, 1901-1902).

Grant, Michael, *Roman Literature* (Cambridge, England, 1954).

Greene, William Chace, "The Spoken and the Written Word," *Harvard Studies in Classical Philology,* 60 (1951), pp. 23-59.

Grote, George, *A History of Greece* (London, 1851).

Grube, G. M. A., "Educational, Rhetorical, and Literary Theory in Cicero," *The Phoenix,* 16 (1962), pp. 234-257.

Grute, Harold, "Cicero's Attitude to the Greeks," *Greece and Rome,* 9 (1962), pp. 142-159.

Harrison, E. L., "Was Gorgias a Sophist?" *The Phoenix,* 18 (1964), pp. 183-192.

Havelock, Eric A., *Preface to Plato* (Oxford, 1963).

Hill, Forbes Iverson, "The Genetic Method in Recent Criticism on the *Rhetoric* of Aristotle." Unpublished Ph.D. dissertation, Cornell University, 1963.

Hoerber, Robert G., "Love or Rhetoric in Plato's *Phaedrus?*" *Classical Bulletin,* 34 (1958), p. 33.

Howell, Wilbur Samuel, "Classical and European Traditions of Rhetoric and Speech Training," *Southern Speech Journal,* 23 (1957), pp. 73-78.

—— , *Logic and Rhetoric in England: 1500-1700* (Princeton, 1956).

Howes, Raymond F., ed., *Historical Studies of Rhetoric and Rhetoricians* (Ithaca, 1961).

Hubbell, Harry M., *The Influence of Isocrates on Cicero, Dionysius, and Aristides* (New Haven, 1914).

Isocrates, *Works* Books I and II tr. by George Norlin, and Book III tr. by Larue Van Hook. 3 vols. (London, 1928 and 1929, and Cambridge, Mass., 1954).

Jebb, R. C., *Attic Orators, From Antiphon to Isaeos* (London, 1876).

Jenkinson, Edna M., "Further Studies in the Curriculum of the Roman Schools of Rhetoric in the Republican Period," *Symbolae Osloenses*, 31 (1955), pp. 124-130.

Jennrick, Walter A., "Classical Rhetoric in the New Testament," *Classical Journal*, 44 (1948), pp. 30-32.

Johannsen, Richard L., "The Greek Rhetoricians on Deistic Reference," *Central States Speech Journal* (Winter, 1962), pp. 100-105.

Johnson, R., "Isocrates' Methods of Teaching," *American Journal of Philology*, 80 (1959), pp. 25-36.

———,"The Poet and the Orator," *Classical Philology*, 54 (1959), pp. 173-176.

Jordan, John E., *Using Rhetoric* (New York, 1965).

Kennedy, George, *The Art of Persuasion in Greece* (Princeton, 1963).

———,"An Estimate of Quintilian," *American Journal of Philology*, 83 (1962), pp. 130-146.

Kenney, E. J., "Juvenal: Satirist or Rhetorician?" *Latomus*, 22 (1963), pp. 704-720.

Kerferd, G. B., "The First Greek Sophists," *Classical Review*, 64 (1950), pp. 8-10.

Kiernan, Thomas P., ed., *Aristotle Dictionary* (New York, 1962).

King, Donald B., "The Appeal to Religion in Greek Rhetoric," *Classical Journal*, 50 (1955), pp. 363–371, 376.

Kinsey, T. E., "A Mistake by Cicero?" *Latomus*, 24 (1965), pp. 120-121.

Kirk, J. W., "Lucian and the Rhetoric of the Second Century," *Southern Speech Journal*, 26 (Fall, 1960), pp. 70-80.

Knowles, David, *The Evolution of Medieval Thought* (Baltimore, 1963).

Kovacs, Ruth S., "The Aesopic Fable in Ancient Rhetorical Theory and Practice." Unpublished Ph.D. dissertation, University of Illinois, 1950.

Kristeller, Paul Oskar, "Renaissance Aristotelianism," *Greek, Roman and Byzantine Studies*, 6 (1965), pp. 157-174.

Larson, Richard, *Rhetoric* (Indianapolis, 1967).

LaRusso, Dominic A., "A Neoplatonic Dialogue: Is Rhetoric an Art? An Introduction and a Translation," *Speech Monographs*, 32 (1965), pp. 393-440.

Laughton, Eric, *Rhetoric and the Roman Heritage, Inaugural Lecture* (Sheffield, 1953).

Lee, Irving J., "Some Conceptions of Emotional Appeal in Rhetorical Theory," *Speech Monographs,* 6 (1939), pp. 66-86.

Levinson, Ronald B., "Plato's *Phaedrus* and the New Criticism," *Archiv Fur Geschichte Der Philosophie,* 46 (1964), pp. 293-309.

Lewis, C. S., *Medieval and Renaissance Literature* (Cambridge, England 1966).

Lodge, R. C., *Plato's Theory of Education* (New York, 1947).

McCord, Clarence W., "On Sophists and Philosophers," *Southern Speech Journal,* 29 (1963), pp. 146-149.

Momigliano, Arnaldo, ed., *The Conflict Between Paganism and Christianity in the Fourth Century* (Oxford, 1963).

Moody, Ernest A., "The Medieval Contribution to Logic," *Studium Generale,* 19 (1966), pp. 443-452.

Morrison, J. S., "An Introductory Chapter in the History of Greek Education," *Durham University Review,* 41 (1949), pp. 55-63.

Mourant, John A., ed., *Introduction to the Philosophy of St. Augustine* (University Park, Penna., 1964).

Murphy, James J., "Aristotle's *Rhetoric* in the Middle Ages," *Quarterly Journal of Speech,* 52 (1966), pp. 109-115.

———,"Cicero's Rhetoric in the Middle Ages," *Quarterly Journal of Speech,* 53 (1967), pp. 334-341.

———,"Modern Elements in Medieval Rhetoric," *Western Speech,* 28 (1964), pp. 206-211.

———,"St. Augustine and the Christianization of Rhetoric," *Western Speech,* 22 (Winter, 1958), pp. 24-29.

———,"Saint Augustine and the Debate about a Christian Rhetoric," *Quarterly Journal of Speech,* 46 (1960), pp. 400-410.

Nadeau, Ray, "*Rhetorica Ad Herennium,* Commentary and Translation of Book I," *Speech Monographs,* 16 (1949), pp. 57-68.

Nichols, Marie H., *Rhetoric and Criticism* (Baton Rouge, 1963).

Nobles, W. Scott, "The Paradox of Plato's Attitude toward Rhetoric," *Western Speech,* 21 (Fall, 1957), pp. 206-210.

North, Helen F., "The Use of Poetry in the Training of the Ancient Orator," *Traditio,* 8 (1952), pp. 1-33.

Olbricht, Thomas H., "The Education of a Fourth-Century Rhetorician [St. Basil]," *Western Speech,* 29 (1965), pp. 29-36.

Olian, Jay R , "Ancient Rhetoric and Moral Theory." Unpublished Ph.D. dissertation, Northwestern University, 1965.

Otto, Walter F., *Dionysius: Myth and Cult*. Tr. with intro. by Robert B. Palmer (Bloomington, Ind., 1965).

Petronius, *The Satyricon*. Tr. by William Arrowsmith (New York, 1960).

Plato, *The Dialogues of Plato*. Ed. by B. Jowett, revisions by D. J. Allan and H. E. Dale. 4 vols, 4th ed. (New York, 1953).

———, *Gorgias*. Tr. with intro. by W. C. Helmbold (New York, (1952).

———, *Gorgias*. Revised text with intro. and commentary by E. R. Dodds (New York, 1959).

Quintilian, *Institutio Oratoria*. Tr. by H. E. Butler. 4 vols. (London, 1922).

Ragsdale J. Donald, "Brevity in Classical Rhetoric," *Southern Speech Journal*, 31 (1965), pp. 20-27.

Ramage, Edwin S., "Cicero on Extra-Roman Speech," *Transactions of the American Philological Association*, 92 (1961), pp. 481-494.

———, *"Urbanitas*: Cicero and Quintilian: A Contrast in Attitudes," *American Journal of Philology*, 84 (1963), pp. 390-414.

Rayment, C. S., "Ancient Rhetoric (1957-1963)" [A Bibliography], *Classical World*, 57 (1964), pp. 241-251.

———, "A Current Survey of Ancient Rhetoric," *Classical World*, 52 (1958), pp. 75-76; 78-80; 82-84; 86-91.

Reid, L., "Discipline of Speech," *Speech Teacher*, 16 (Jan., 1967), pp. 1-10.

Rhetorica Ad Alexandrum. Tr. by H. Rackham (Cambridge, Mass., 1957).

Rice, George P., Jr., "Aristotle's *Rhetoric* and Introductory Public Address," *Western Speech* (May, 1943), pp. 2-5.

Richards, Ivor, *A Philosophy of Rhetoric* (Oxford, 1967).

Roberts, W. R., *Greek Rhetoric and Literary Criticism* (New York, 1928).

Rockas, Leo, *Modes of Rhetoric* (New York, 1964).

Rosenfield, Lawrence W., "Aristotle and Information Theory: A Comparison of the Influence of Causal Assumptions on Two Theories of Communication." Unpublished Ph.D. dissertation, Cornell University, 1963.

Sandys, John E., *History of Classical Scholarship*, 3 vols. (Cambridge, England, 1958).

Sattler, William M., "Some Platonic Influences on the Rhetorical Works of Cicero," *Quarterly Journal of Speech*, 35 (1949), pp. 164-169.

Schnakel, Peter J., "Plato's *Phaedrus* and Rhetoric, " *Southern Speech Journal*, 32 (1966), pp. 124-132.

Schwartz, Joseph, and John A. Rycenga, eds., *The Province of Rhetoric* (New York, 1965).

Sinaiko, Herman, *Love, Knowledge, and Discourse in Plato: Dialogue and Dialectic in the Phaedrus, Republic, Parmenides* (Chicago, 1965).

Solmsen, Frederich, "Aristotle and Cicero on the Orator's Playing upon Feelings," *Classical Philology*, 33 (1938), pp. 390-404.

──── ,"The Aristotelian Tradition in Ancient Rhetoric," *American Journal of Philology*, 62 (1941), pp. 35-50 and 169-190.

Steinman, Martin, Jr., ed., *New Rhetorics* (New York, 1966).

Studies in Rhetoric and Public Speaking in Honor of James A. Winans (New York, 1962). [Reprint of 1925 edition.]

Suetonius, *On Grammarians and Rhetoricians.* Tr. by J. C. Rolfe (London, 1939).

"Symposium: The Rhetoric of the English Renaissance," *Western Speech*, 28 (1964), pp. 69-105.

Tacitus, *Agricola, Germania, Dialogus.* Ed. and tr. by W. H. Fyfe (Oxford, 1908).

Taylor, John Hammond, "St. Augustine and the Hortensius of Cicero," *Studies in Philology*, 60 (1963), pp. 487-498.

Thompson, L. S., *A Bibliography of American Doctoral Dissertations in Classical Studies and Related Fields* (Hamden, Conn., 1968).

Thonssen, Lester, *Selected Readings in Rhetoric and Public Speaking* (Bronx, N. Y., 1942).

Thonssen, Lester, and A. C. Baird, *Speech Criticism* (New York, 1948).

Tisdale, R., and R. Miles, *Introduction to Rhetoric* (New York, 1967).

Van Straaten, M., and G. J. De Vries, "Some Notes on the *Rhetoric* of Aristotle," *Mnemosyne*, 17 (1964), pp. 140-147.

Veatch, Henry B., *Rational Man: The Modern Interpretation of Aristotelian Ethics* (Bloomington, Ind., 1962).

Walsh, James J., *Aristotle's Conception of Moral Weakness* (New York, 1963).

Warry, J. G., *Greek Aesthetic Theory: A Study of Callistic and Aesthetic Concepts in the Works of Plato and Aristotle* (London, 1962).

Weaver, Richard M., *The Ethics of Rhetoric* (Chicago, 1953).

Webster, T. B. L., "Communication of Thought in Ancient Greece," *Studies in Communication Contributed to the Communication Research Center, University College, London* (London, 1955), pp. 125-146.

Whately, Richard, *Elements of Rhetoric.* Ed. by D. Ehninger (Carbondale, 1963).

Wilson, Thomas, *The Arte of Rhetorique* (1553). A facsimile reproduction with an introduction by Robert Hood Bowers (Gainesville, Fla., 1962).

Winterbottom, Michael, "Some Problems in Quintilian, Book Two," *Philologus,* 108 (1964), pp. 119-127.

Winterowd, W. R., *Rhetoric: A Synthesis* (New York, 1968).

INVENTION AND ARRANGEMENT

Abel, D. Herbert. "Emphasis by Proportion: A Classical Rhetorical Practice," *Classical Bulletin,* 41 (1964), pp. 81-84.

Backes, James G., "Aristotle's Theory of Stases in Forensic and Deliberative Speech in the *Rhetoric,*" *Central States Speech Journal,* 12 (1960), pp. 6-8.

Bird, Otto, "The Tradition of the Logical Topics: Aristotle to Ockham," *Journal of the History of Ideas,* 23 (1962), pp. 307-323.

Brake, Robert J., "Classical Conceptions of 'Places': A Study in Invention." Unpublished Ph.D. dissertation, Michigan State University, 1965.

_____ ,"A Reconsideration of Aristotle's Concept of Topics," *Central States Speech Journal* (May, 1965), pp. 106-112.

Church, David A., and Robert S. Cathcart, "Some Concepts of the Epicheireme in Greek and Roman Rhetoric," *Western Speech,* 29 (1965), pp. 140-147.

Clarke, Martin L., "The Thesis in the Roman Rhetorical Schools of the Republic," *Classical Quarterly,* 45 (1951), pp. 159-166.

Carrino, Elnora, "Conceptions of Dispositio in Ancient Rhetoric." Unpublished Ph.D. dissertation, University of Michigan, 1959.

Dick, Robert C., "Topoi: An Approach to Inventing Arguments," *Speech Teacher,* 13 (1964), pp. 313-319.

Dieter, Otto Alvin Loeb, "Stasis," *Speech Monographs,* 17 (1950), pp. 345-369.

Ehninger, Douglas Wagner, "The Classical Doctrine of Invention," *Gavel,* 39 (1957), pp. 59-62, 70.

Flynn, Lawrence J., "The Aristotelian Bases for the Ethics of Speaking," *Speech Teacher,* 6 (1957), pp. 179-187.

Greene, Murray, "Aristotle's Circular Movement as a Logos Doctrine," *Review of Metaphysics,* 19 (1965), pp. 115-132.

Grimaldi, William, "Rhetoric and the Philosophy of Aristotle," *Classical Journal,* 53 (1958), pp. 371-375.

Harrington, Elbert W., *Rhetoric and the Scientific Method of Inquiry, A Study of Invention.* University of Colorado Studies Series in Language and Literature, no. 1 (Boulder, 1948).

Hauser, Gerard A., "The Example in Aristotle's Rhetoric: Bifurcation or Contradiction?" *Philosophy and Rhetoric,* 1 (Spring, 1968), pp. 78-90.

Huby, Pamela M., "The Date of Aristotle's Topics and Its Treatments of the Theory of Ideas," *Classical Quarterly,* 12 (1962), pp. 72-80.

Hughes, Richard E., "The Contemporaneity of Classical Rhetoric [In Argumentation]," *College Composition and Communication,* 16 (1965), pp. 157-159.

Knapp, Mark, and James McCroskey, "The Siamese Twins: Inventio and Dispositio," *Today's Speech,* 14 (April, 1966), pp. 17-18.

Lloyd, G. E. R., *Polarity and Analogy: Two Types of Argumentation in Early Greek Thought* (Cambridge, England, 1966).

Macksoud, S. J. "Greco-Roman Nonartistic Proofs and Modern Concepts of Evidence," *Classical Journal,* 62 (Feb., 1968), pp. 220-222.

McBurney, James H., "The Place of the Enthymeme in Rhetorical Theory," *Speech Monographs,* 3 (1936), pp. 49-74.

Meador Prentice A., Jr., "The Classical *Epicheireme:* A Re-examination," *Western Speech,* 30 (1966), pp. 151-155.

———,"Minucian, *On Epicheiremes:* An Introduction and a Translation," *Speech Monographs,* 31 (1964), pp. 54-63.

Nadeau, Ray, "An Analysis of the Commonplaces," *Quarterly Journal of Speech,* 49 (1963), pp. 328-331.

———,"Classical Systems of Stases in Greek: Hermagoras to Hermogenes," *Greek, Roman and Byzantine Studies,* 2 (1959), pp. 51-71.

———,"Hermogenes' *On Stasis:* A Translation With an Introduction and Notes," *Speech Monographs,* 31 (1964), pp. 361-424.

———,"Some Aristotelian and Stoic Influences on the Theory of Stases," *Speech Monographs,* 26 (1959), pp. 248-254.

Oates, Whitney J., *Aristotle and the Problem of Value* (Princeton, 1963).

Ochs, Donovan Joseph, "The Tradition of the Classical Doctrines of Rhetorical Topoi." Unpublished Ph.D. dissertation, State University of Iowa, 1966.

Renehan, Robert, "Aristotle's Definition of Anger," *Philologus,* 107 (1963), pp. 61-74.

Rose, Lynn E., "Premise Order in Aristotle's Syllogistic," *Phronesis,* 11 (1966), pp. 154-158.

Rosenfield, Lawrence W., "Rhetorical Criticism and An Aristotelian Notion of Process," *Speech Monographs,* 33 (1966), pp. 1-16.

Sattler, William M., "Conceptions of *Ethos* in Ancient Rhetoric," *Speech Monographs,* 14 (1947), pp. 55-65.

Schick, Thomas, "Cicero and Pathetical Appeal in Oratory," *Classical Bulletin,* 42 (1965), pp. 17-18.

Segal, Charles P., "Gorgias and the Psychology of the Logos," *Harvard Studies in Classical Philology,* 66 (1962), pp. 99-155.

Steele, Edward D., "The Role of the Concept of Choice in Aristotle's Rhetoric," *Western Speech,* 27 (1963), pp. 77-83.

Wiley, Earl W., "Aristotle's *Topoi:* Patterns of Persuasion," *Ohio Speech Journal,* 2 (1963), pp. 5-14.

Abbott, Kenneth M., "Rhetoric and Latin Literary Forms," *Quarterly Journal of Speech,* 36 (1950), pp. 457-461.

STYLE

Abel, D. Herbert, "Paradox or Oxymoron," *Classical Bulletin* 34 (1957), p. 23.

Allen, Don Cameron, "Style and Certitude," *Journal of English Literary History,* 15 (1948), pp. 167-175.

Aristotle's Poetics and English Literature: A Collection of Critical Essays. Ed. with intro. by Elder Olsen (Chicago, 1965).

Blanshard, Brand, "Philosophical Style," *Yale Review,* 42 (1953), pp. 547-578.

Clark, Donald Lemen, "Imitation — Theory and Practice in Roman Rhetoric," *Quarterly Journal of Speech,* 37 (1951), pp. 11-22.

Coleric, E., *Introduction to Latin Style and Rhetoric* (Malta, 1959).

Coleman, Robert, "Two Linguistic Topics in Quintilian," *Classical Quarterly,* 13 (1963), pp. 1-18.

Cooper, Lane, ed., *Theories of Style* (London, 1907).

Croll, Morris W., *Style, Rhetoric, and Rhythm: Essays by Morris W. Croll.* Ed. by J. Max Patrick and Robert O. Evans with John M. Wallace and R. J. Schoeck (Princeton, 1966).

Cunningham, Maurice P., "Some Principles of Latin Phrasing, Quintilian II, 3, 35-38 on *Aeneid* L, 1-3," *Classical Weekly,* 47 (1953), pp. 17-22.
—— ,"A Theory of the Latin Sentence," *Classical Philology,* 60 (1965), pp. 24-28.

Denniston, John B., *Greek Prose Style* (New York, 1953).

Douglas, A. E., "M. Calidus and the Atticists," *Classical Quarterly,* 49 (1955), pp. 241-247.

Dover, Kenneth J., *Greek Word Order,* (Cambridge, England, 1960).

Grube, G. M. A., "The Date of Demetrius *On Style,*" *The Phoenix,* 18 (1964), pp. 294-302.

——— ,ed., *A Greek Critic: Demetrius on Style* (Toronto, 1961).

——— , *The Greek and Roman Critics* (London, 1965).

——— ,"Thrasymachus, Theophrastus and Dionysius of Halicarnassus," *American Journal of Philology,* 73 (1952), pp. 251-267.

Hartung, Charles V., "The Persistence of Tradition in Grammar," *Quarterly Journal of Speech,* 48 (1962), pp. 174-186.

Herrick, Marvin T., "Some Neglected Sources of Admiratio," *Modern Language Notes,* 62 (1947), pp. 222-226.

Hill, James J., "The Aesthetic Principles of the *Peri Hupsous* [of Longinus]," *Journal of the History of Ideas,* 27 (1966), pp. 265-274.

Hubbell, Harry M., "Cicero on Styles of Oratory," *Yale Classical Studies,* 19 (1966), pp. 171-186.

Huseman, Richard C., "The Concept of Appropriateness as an Element of Style in Classical Rhetoric." Unpublished Ph.D. dissertation, University of Illinois, 1965.

Kennedy, George A., "Aristotle on the Period," *Harvard Studies in Classical Philology,* 63 (1968), pp. 283-288.

——— ,"Prolegomena and Commentary on Quintilian VIII." Unpublished Ph.D. dissertation, Harvard University, 1954.

——— ,"Theophrastus and Stylistic Distinctions," *Harvard Studies in Classical Philology,* 62 (1957), pp. 93-104.

Kleve, Knut, "The Unum Verabilissimum and Plato's Mystical Style," *Symbolae Osloenses,* 37 (1961), pp. 88-95.

Kriel, D. M., "The Forms of the *Sententia* in Quintilian VIII, 5, 3, 24," *Acta Classica, Proceedings of the Classical Association of South Africa,* 4 (1961), pp. 80-90.

Laughton, Eric, "Cicero and the Greek Orator," *American Journal of Philology,* 82 (1961), pp. 27-49.

Lelievre, F. J., "The Basis of Ancient Parody," *Greece and Rome,* 1 (1954), pp. 66-81.

Longinus, *On Great Writing (On the Sublime).* Tr. by G.M.A. Grube (Indianapolis, 1957).

——— ,*On Sublimity.* Tr. by D. A. Russell (Oxford, 1965).

Martin, Howard H., "Style in the Golden Age," *Quarterly Journal of Speech,* 43 (1957), pp. 374-382.

Muilenburg, James, *A Study in Hebrew Rhetoric: Repetition and Style* (Leiden, Netherlands, 1953).

Murphy, Paul R., "Archaism and Colloquialism in the Use of a Latin Negative Pattern," *American Journal of Philology,* 79 (1958), pp. 44-51.

Pomeroy, Ralph Stanley, "Aristotle and Cicero: Rhetorical Style," *Western Speech,* 25 (1961), pp. 25-32.

Rayment, Charles Sanford, "Functional Parallelism in Ancient Rhetoric," *Classical Bulletin,* 25 (1949), pp. 21-22.

————,"How Realistic Are Quintilian's Themes?" *Classical Bulletin,* 27 (1952), pp. 43-45.

Reid, Ronald F., "Books: Some Suggested Readings on the History of Ancient Rhetorical Style," *Central States Speech Journal,* 11 (1960), pp. 116-122.

Rist, J. M., "Demetrius the Stylist and Artemon the Compiler," *The Phoenix,* 18 (1964), pp. 2-8.

Robbins, Charles, "Rhetoric in Latin Word Order," *Classical Journal,* 47 (1951), pp. 78-83.

Schenkeveld, D. M., *Studies in Demetrius on Style* (Amsterdam, 1965).

Shurr, William, "Cicero and English Prose Style," *Classical Bulletin,* 37 (1961), pp. 49-50.

Sprott, S. E., "Cicero's Theory of Prose Style," *Philological Quarterly,* 34 (1955), pp. 1-17.

"Symposium: Elocutio," *Western Speech,* 26 (1962), pp. 5-28.

Temmer, M. J., "Style and Rhetoric," *Yale French Studies,* No. 35, pp. 20-28.

Thompson, J. A. K., *Classical Influences On English Prose* (London, 1956).

Turbayne, Colin Murray, *The Myth of Metaphor* (New Haven, Conn., 1962).

van Rooy, C. A., *Studies in Classical Satire and Related Literary Theory* (Leiden, Netherlands, 1965).

Wilder, Amos N., *The Language of the Gospel: Early Christian Rhetoric* (New York, 1964).

MEMORY AND DELIVERY

Balcer, Charles L., "The Vocal Aspect of Delivery Traced Through Representative Works in Rhetoric and Public Speaking — Aristotle to Rush," *Central States Speech Journal,* 11 (Autumn, 1959), pp. 27-34.

Bolton, Janet, "The Garnishing of the Manner of Utterance," *Western Speech* (Spring, 1964), pp. 83-91.

Hudson, Williams H., "Impromptu Speaking," *Greece and Rome,* 18 (1949), pp. 28-31.

Mathews, Gareth B., "Augustine on Speaking from Memory," *American Philosophical Quarterly,* 2 (1965), pp. 157-160.

Meissner, W. W., "A Historical Note on Retention," *Journal of Germanic Philology,* 59 (1958), pp. 229-236.

Nadeau, Ray, "Delivery in Ancient Times: Homer to Quintilian," *Quarterly Journal of Speech,* 50 (1964), pp. 53-60.

Sonkowsky, Robert P., "An Aspect of Delivery in Ancient Rhetorical Theory," *Transactions of the American Philological Association,* 90 (1959), pp. 256-274.

Yates, Frances A., *The Art of Memory* (Chicago, 1966).

INDEX

Abraham, 187, 276, 279
aberration, 192
abridgment, 192
Academe, 128
Academicians, 123
Academy, the, 95, 102, 105, 129
accusation and defense, 30, 36, 60,
    64, 73-74, 145, 149, 155, 162,
    167, 169, 192
Achelous, 28
Achilles, 61, 162-163, 165, 244
actuality, 246, 249
Acumenus, 31
Adonis, 39
Adrastus, 32
advocacy, 171-179
Aesop, 157-158
Aesopus, [Claudius], 297
AEsion, 247
Aemilius, Marcus, 175
Aeschines, 95, 207, 261, 263-264
affections, 150 (*see also* emotion)
Africanus, the Elder, 225, 255
Agamemnon, 108-109, 200, 234,
    250, 297
Agar, 276
Agathon, 156
Agesipolis, 167
Ajax, 168-169, 269
Alexander, 262
Alexandros, 166
Alkidamas, 166, 243-244
allegoria, 257, 262
allegory, 224-228, 237, 276
Aloadae, the, 269
Alphesiboea, 164
ambiguity, 145, 185, 220, 263
Ambrose, 279, 282
Ammon, 37-38
amplification, 71, 155, 157, 192,
    198, 204, 269-271

anadiplosis, 259
analogy, argument from, 65, 203
anaphora, 260
Anaschetos, 249
Anaxagoras, 21, 33, 128
Anaxandrides, 246, 249
Anaximenes, 63
Androcles the Pittheaen, 169
Androtion, 244
anger, 150, 152, 258
Antipho, 253
Antiphon, 168
Antisthenes, 245, 258
antithesis, 246-247, 249, 258
Antonius, 171-179, 233, 238
Antonius, Marcus, 92, 99, 101-107,
    121, 171-179, 251-255
antonomasia, 227-228
Apelles, 233
Aphrodite, 29, 170, 250
Apolonius, 101
apophthegms, 248
aposiopesis, 260
Appius, 199
Apollodorus, 229
appropriateness, 44, 277
aptness, 273
Aquilius, Manius, 173-174
Aquilo, 226
Archelaos, 166
Archidamos, 245
Archilochos, 166
Archytas, 248
Areiopagos, 54, 167
Ares, 245, 249-250
argument, 30, 54-62, 64-65, 82,
    131, 137, 144, 149-153,
    154-170, 191-192, 194-195,
    201-203, 209, 246, 270 (*see al-
    so* commonplaces, invention,
    stasis, and topics)

argumentum, 198-199
Aristeides, 165
Aristippos, 167
Aristippus, 128, 262, 264
Aristogeiton, 166
Aristophanes, 243
  The Babylonians, 243
Aristophon, 165
Aristotle, 53-62, 91, 95-97,
  149-170, 171, 191-192, 194,
  237, 240-250, 256, 266, 289
  Analytics, 58-59
  Methodica, 58
  Poetics, 240-241, 245n, 266
  Rhetoric, 58-62, 95-97, 149-170,
  191-192, 194, 196, 240-250
Aristotelian dialogue, 92
arrangement, 28, 191-213, 264,
  267, 289
art, 34, 44, 54, 78, 144, 156, 195,
  267, 272, 293-294, 297
artificial parallel, 157-158
artificial proof, 55-57
Artorius Proculus, 227
Ascelepiod, 33
Asclepiades, 99
Asinii, 121
Asinius, Pollio, 218
asyndeton, 260
Athene, 250
Athenian orators, 237
Atreus, 250, 296-297
attention, 221-222, 282
Attic, 234-237, 250
attributes of persons, 202
audience analysis, 35, 149, 172
Augustine, 117, 133-139, 180-188,
  273-286
  De Doctrina Christiana, 133-139,
  180-188, 273-286
Aulus Sempronius, 254
Aurifex, Lucius, 254
Autocles, 167

backgrounds, 294-298
balanced clauses, 258
basis, 143-148, 208, 228 (*see also
  stasis*)
belief, 150
blame (*see* praise and blame)
brevity, 200, 221, 249, 257-258,
  261
Bromius, 84
Brutus, 121, 146, 225, 232-239,
  290

Bryson the sophist, 242
buffoonery, 236, 253-254

Caccilius, 229, 268-269
Caepio, 175-176
caesa, 278
Caesar, 113, 219, 251-255
Calchas, 234
Callicles, 3-5
Calliope, 23
Calvinus, 255
Calvus, 113, 121
Carbo, Gaius, 94, 113
Carneades, 95-96, 123
Cassius Severus, 218
catachresis, 219, 228, 237
Cato, 146, 219-223
Cato the Censor, 123
Cato, Gaius, 113
Cato, Marcus, 118, 131
Catulus, 254
cause, 145-148
causidici, 121
Celsus, Cornelius, 144, 208, 230
censor perpetuus, 116
Cephalus, 28
Ceres, 226
Chabrias, 247
Chaeremon, 170
Chalcedonian, 31
character, 46, 49, 57, 149, 155,
  161, 171, 178, 233, 258, 264
  (*see also ethos*)
Chares, 246-247
Charidemus, 168
charity, 186
Charmadas, 95, 102-104
chaste language, 109
Cheilon, 166
Choliambs, 258
Christ, Jesus, 276, 278-280, 284
Christian rhetoric, 133-139, 180-
  188, 273-286
Chrysippus, 96, 120
Cicero, 76, 91-107, 109, 112, 114,
  120-121, 125, 128, 131, 138,
  146, 171-179, 193, 196-206,
  208-209, 218, 223-226,
  232-239, 251-255, 270,
  [273-274], 290n
  De Inventione, 193, 196-205,
  206, 251-255
  De Oratore, 91-107, 125, 171-179
  Orator, 232-239, 273-274
  Partitiones Oratoriae, 196

Cicero *(Cont.)*
 "Pro Rabirio," 209
 "Pro Vareno," 209
Ciceronian style, 112
Cicilia, 102
Cimber, 297
circuitus, 278
clarity, 217-218, 221
classes of speech, 35, 40
Cleanthes, 120
Cleombrotus, 262
Cleon, 263
Cleophon, 263
climax, 260, 270, 278
 vs. anti-climax, 208-210
Clitarchus, 265
Clitomachus, 95
Clodius, 146, 212, 223
Clytemnestra, 200
coarseness, 265
Colossus, 272
comic, 262
common to the particular, 211
commonplaces, 60, 63, 97, 154-155, 166, 177, 179, 203-207, 271 *(see also* topics)
communication theorists, 289
comparison, 145, 157, 177-178, 223
competence, 145
completeness, 200-201
composition, 268
compound word, 243-244, 261
conciliation, 136
conciseness, 200-201
conclusion, 194, 291
confirmation, 30, 197, 201-203
conjecture, 79-80, 144-148, 208-209 *(see also stasis)*
connectives, 260, 264, 298
conquestio, 204-205
constitutions of states, 69
content *vs.* manner, 138
contention, 26
contraries, 203
contrast, 191-192
controversial theme, 211, 229
conversational tone, 291-293
Corax, 3, 104
Cotta, [Gaius Aurelius], 92
Cotta, Lucius, 175
Crassus, Lucius Licenius, 92, 101, 107, 113-114, 125, 173-175, 251-255
Craterus of Macedon, 263

Crates, 259
credibility *(see ethos)*
criticism, 256
Critolaus the Peripatetic, 95
Ctesiphon, 207
cupidity, 186
Curius, 129
Cyclops, 262-263
Cycnus (Kyknos), 163
Cynic, 259
Cyprian, 279-281

Daedalus, 225
Darius, 22, 157
debate, 99, 123, 128
Decius, 129
declamation, 290-291
decorum, 233
deductive reasoning, 154-160
defense *(see* accusation and defense)
definition, 127, 144-147
delectare (to delight), 273-289
deliberative oratory, 9-10, 25, 55, 60, 64, 66, 81, 84, 86, 101, 114, 127, 144, 157, 161, 191-192, 210-211, 232
delight, to *(delectare)*, 273-289
delivery, 179, 194, 232, 236, 253, 260, 289-295
Demades, 237, 262
Demetrius, 256-265
 "On Style," 256-265
Demetrius of Phalerum, 256, 263
democracy, 69
Democrates, 245
Democritus, 96, 174, 252
demonstration, 57, 82, 191
demonstrative oratory, 144, 158 *(see also* epideictic)
Demosthenes, 79, 98, 103, 108-109, 120-121, 128, 164, 207, [234], 237, 245, 258, 260-261, 267, 270-271, 290n
deprecation, 155
dialectic, 30, 32, 39, 55-56, 78-79, 84, 86-87, 100, 126-127, 191
diction, 179, 240, 257-265, 268
Didius, Titus, 175
differentiation, 127
digression, 203, 271
dilemma, 202
Diodorus, 95
Diogenes, 247, 259
Diomede, 163

Diomedes, 168
Diomedon, 164
Dionysios the Brazen, 242
Dionysius, 29, 257, 263
Dionysos, 60, 242, 245
discipline, 294, 297
discordant sounds, 259
discovery, 134, 143, 163, 174 (*see also* invention)
dispositio (*see* arrangement)
disputatious exercises, 114
dissuasion, 64, 71, 149, 169
dithyramb, 244
distinction and classification, 127
division, 146, 192, 194, 207, 212 (*see also* arrangement)
docere (to teach), 273-289
Dolabella, 113, 218, 229
Domitian, 116-117
Domitius, 114, 296
Dorieus, 59
Draco, 170
Drusus, 105

ecstasy, 267
Eld, 253
Elis, 31
ellipse, 226
elocutio (*see* style)
elocution, 289
eloquence, 93, 102, 104-105, 109, 114-115, 121, 125, 135-139, 273-286
embellishment, 194
emotion, 25, 54, 57, 97, 103, 144, 149, 163, 172-179, 206, 230, 261, 273, 277-279, 293
emphasis, 219
Encolpius, 108
enigmatic language, 224
Ennius, 237
enthymeme, 54-62, 149-153, 154-170, 246 (*see also* syllogism)
enumeration, 202 (*see also* 212)
epanaphora, 260
epanastasis, 261
epic poetry, 244
Epicureans, 76, 78, 82
Epicurus, 78, 81-84, 128
epideictic oratory, 61, 64-76, 83-85, 155, 191
epideixis 82, 84 (*see also* style)
epilogue, 191-192
epimonê, 261

epithets, 227-228, 241-244
Erato, 23
Eristics, 43
Eros, 29
Eryximachus, 31
Esau, 187
ethos, 15, 49, 57, 103, 119, 122, 149-151, 161, 171, 250 (*see also* argument, invention)
ethics, 126-128
eulogy, 64, 71, 73, 176, 264 (*see also* epideictic oratory)
euphemism, 261-262
euphony, 259
Euripides, 32, 108-109, 170
  Iphigenia, 297
  Medea, 170
  Telephos, 242
Euthynos, 156
Euxenos, 245
Evenus, 30
evidence, 136-137, 279
example, 57-59, 157, 160
exercise, 299
exhortation, 61-62, 64, 149, 167
exordium, 197-198 (*see also* arrangement)
expediency and inexpediency, 65-71, 157
exposition, 136

Fabius, 219
fable, 157
Fabricius, 124, 129
fabula, 198
facial expression, 293
facts, 156-162
faith, hope, and charity, 184-185
fallible sign, 59
fashion, 258
fear, 177-178
figures, 32, 217-218, 221, 226-231, 259-260, 268
  of diction, 268
  of speech, 32, 227-230, 235-236, 260
  of thought, 227-230, 236, 259-260, 268
flattery, 263
flexibility of voice, 290-292
forensic oratory, 9-10, 25, 36, 45, 54-55, 59, 64, 73, 81, 84, 86-87, 123-125, 130, 144, 191-192, 206-213, 232
formulae, 131

foul language, 242
fragments of speech, 265
friendship, 149-153
frigidity, 258

Galba, Servius, 94, 98
Gedeon, 279
Gelon, 263
generalization, 160
Genesis, 279
genius, 267, 272
genus, 156, 201, 210, 271
genus grande, 273
genus submissum, 273
genus temperatum, 273
gesture, 289-290, 293
Glaucia, 225, 255
glosses, 123, 230, 240
Good, the, 162-163
goodness, 27, 118
good-will, 150, 171, 179, 252 (*see also ethos*)
Gorgias, 2-21, 22, 25, 31, 106, 243-244, 251
grammar, 79, 83
grammatice, 77
grandeur, 259
Granius, 254
greatness or smallness, 154-155, 157
grimacing, 255

Hannibal, 219, 227
Harmodios, 165, 166
hate, 149, 177-178
Hector, 163, 165
Hecuba, 170
Helen, 167
Hellas, 247
Hellenistic rhetoric, 193
Hermagoras, 144, 203
Hermarchus, 78
Hermes, 28
Hermias, ruler of Atarneus, 263
Hermocreon, 203
Herodicos, 170
Herodicus, 4
Herodotus, 257
hiatus, 264
Hiero, 263
Hippias of Elis, 31, 58
Hippocrates, 33-34
Hipponax, 264
historia, 198-199
historical parallel, 157-158

Homer, 41, 166, 225, 247, 259, 271
Odyssey, 243-244
Homeric epic, 257
homiletics (*see* Augustine)
homoioteleuton, 260
honorable, the, 157, 163
hope, 177-178
Horace, 219, 226
humor, 236-237
hypallage, 226
hyperbaton, 220, 228
hyperbole, 228, 250, 262
Hyperides, 98, 109, 237

iambic verse, 244
Idrieus, 244
images, 247-248, 294-295, 298-299
imitation, 137, 144, 282
impropriety, 218, 236
inartificial proofs, 56-57
indecency, 255
indignatio, 204
indispensable conditions, 72
induction, 57-59, 154, 157-158
inference, 127
inflection, 292
innuendo, 262-264
insinuation, 197
instruction and persuasion, 138
intelligence, 150 (*see also ethos*)
intensity, 257-265, 270
interpretation, 183-184
introduction, 30, 194-195, 197, 233, 291, 298
invention (*inventio*), 92, 134, 143, 174, 196, 206, 212-213, 267, 289, 290, 298
investigation, 64, 74
Iphicrates, 166, 168, 241, 246-247
Iphigenia, 234
irony, 228, 251, 253, 263
Isaeus, 245n
Ismênias, 166
Isocrates, 41, 43-46, 47-52, 91, 167-168, 243, 247, 249, 264
"Against the Sophists," 43-46
"Antidosis," 47-52
issue (*see stasis*)

Jason, 170
jealousy, 179
Jerome, 117, 193
jest, 258-259, 264, 292
jokes, 248

Jove, 225
joy, 177-178
justice, 10-11, 16, 27, 87, 123, 157-163, 274-275

kakophônia, 259
Kallias, 58, 152, 241
Kalliope, 242
Kallippos, 167
   art of, 169
Karkinos, 170
Kêphisodotos, 245-247
Konon, 167, 170

Lailius, Gaius, 93, 98
language, 172, 218, 224, 232, 241-242, 256 (*see also* style)
Largus, 253
laughable, the, 251-255
laughter, 251-255, 292
law, the, 145, 209
letter *vs.* spirit of, 145-147
Lentulus, 91
Leôdamas, 169
Leptines, 258
Leukothea, 170
Liber, 226
Libyan fables, 157
Licymnius, 31
Likymnios, art of, 192, 242
literature, 256, 267
Livy, 218, 221, 223, 225
locution, 186
logical structure, 289
logos, 134-144, 149, 154-170 (*see also* argument, invention)
[Longinus], *On the Sublime*, 256, 266-272
loose structure, 257-258, 264
"lost canon," 289
love, 177
Lucilius, 110
Lyceum, 105
Lycurgus, 22, 98, 166
Lycymnius, 31
Lykoleon, 247
Lykophron, 243
Lypitheides, 66
lyric poets, 109
Lysias, 22-42, 237, 259

Macrobius, 296
Mantias, 166
Marcellus, Marcus, 98
Marcii Reges, 297

Marcus, 254
Marius, Gaius, 174
Maternus, 112
Mausolus, 244n
maxims, 157-161, 177, 235
meaning of words, 240, 242
Medea, 170
Medieval rhetoric, 193, 196
medium (style), 273
Megara, 60
Melchisedech, 279
Meleager, 168
membra, 278
Memmius, 253
memory (*memoria*), 30, 192, 195, 204, 268, 277, 289-290, 293-299
Menedemus, 102-103
Menelaus, 234, 297
Messalla, 112
Messeniakos, 163
metalepsis, 228
metaphor, 219, 222-225, 228, 235, 237, 240-250, 261
metonymy, 226, 228, 237, 245n
metrical composition, 240, 258
Metrodorus, 78, 83, 95
Micio, 199
Midas, 29
mien, 290, 293
Milo, 146, 212, 223
Miltiades, 246
mimicry, 255
Mixidêmidês, 167
mnemonics (*see* memory)
Mnesarchus, 95, 102
modes of speech, 222, 264
modulation, 292
Moerokles, 246
motions, 227
motives, 149, 187
movere (to move, persuade), 10, 34-35, 267, 273-286
Mucius, 106, 129

Nacvius, 255
narration, 30, 54, 83, 191-192, 194, 197-200
nature, 103, 105, 122, 144, 267-268, 272, 290-291, 293-294, 297
   vs. instruction, 103
natural talent, 105
Naucratis of Egypt, 37
Neptune, 226

Nero, 254
Nestor, 25
Nikânor, 164
Nikeratos, 250
Nikon, 248-249
Noah, 279
Norbanus, Gaius, 173, 175, 177
Numa, 210

obscurity, 219, 220, 259
occasion, 44
Odysseus, 24, 168-169, 234, 243, [259]
Oeneus, 165
oligarchy, 69
onomatopoea, 228
opinion *vs.* truth, 104
oral interpretation, 289
orator:
  functions of, 118, 126, 144, 273
  ideal, 33, 92, 107, 118-131, 232, 238-239
  knowledge of, 25, 104, 125, 128-130
  moral qualities of, 91, 97, 118, 121-123, 129
  qualifications of, 25, 91, 162
orator-philosopher, 91, 125
orator-statesman, 91, 128
orators of Greece, 128
order, 207
Orestes, 242
originality, 44
ornamentation, 135, 217, 222, 235, 277, 279, 280, 283
Osee, 187

Pacuvius, 174
Palamedes, 26, 243
Pamphilos, art of, 169
Pan, 28, 41
Panactus, 95, 101
panegyric, 62, 82, 269 (*see also* epideictic)
pantaloon, 255
paraleipsis, 259-260
parallelism, 249
parenthesis, 220
Parian, 30
Paris, 165, 167
partition, 197, 200-201, 207, 211
parts of discourse, 28, 30, 83 (*see also* arrangement)
parts *vs.* whole, 72
passion, 268-271 (*see also* emotion)

pathos (*see* emotion)
Patroklos, 62, 165
Paul, the Apostle, 273, 277, 282
  "Epistle to the Galatians," 278
pause, 291-292
Peisistratos, 60
Peitholaos, 246
Pelides, 227
Pentheus, 170
Pericles, 12, 32-33, 128, 245-246
  "The Funeral Oration," 247
periodic structure, 236, 257, 265, 270
Peripatetics, 95, 129, 194
periphrasis 228
peroration, 197, 203, 205, 271
Petronius, *Satyricon*, 108
Phaedo, 262
Phaedrus, 22-42, 91
Phalaris, 157-158, 263
Pharsalus, 224
Philammon, 250
Philip, 165, 257-258, 263
Philippus, 254-255
Philodemus, *Rhetorica*, 76-90, 290n
Philoktetis, 250
Philomela, 244
philosophy, 41, 44, 50, 76-77, 97, 102, 125-126
Phocis, 165
physical movement, 290, 293
Pindar, 109
Piso, Marcus, 106
pity, 204-205
Plato, 3-21, 22-42, 43, 91, 96, 103, 108, 128, 174, 191, 239, 251, 257, 262-264, 270-271
  "Funeral Speech," 259-260
  Gorgias, 3-21, 43, 91, 96
  Phaedrus, 22-42, 91, 191
  Republic, 245
pleasure and pain, 150
plural for the singular, 227
poetic, 133
poetry, 109, 240-241, 243-244
Pollio, Asinius, 11
Pôlos, 170
Polus, 3-21, 31
Polycleitus, *The Spearman*, 272
Polyeuktos, 246
Porcina, Marcus Aemilius, 94
possible and impossible, 61, 154-156
power of expression, 268

practice, 103, 282, 290, 294
  vs. art, 105, 144
pragmaticas, 130
praise and blame, 61-62, 149, 155,
  162, 167, 203, 262-264, 275,
  283-284
Pratys, 250
preaching, 133-139, 180-188,
  273-286
predispositions, 197
premises, 154, 162
probability, 30, 31, 36, 49, 55, 86,
  156-157, 162, 180, 202-203
problem, 191
Prodicus, 31
proem, 54, 83, 191-192
proof, 30, 54-55, 82, 137, 144,
  157-158, 163, 191-192,
  194-195, 201-203, 209, 270,
  279 (*see also* argument, commonplaces, invention, enthymeme, syllogism, and topics)
proportional metaphor, 245,
  247-249
proposition, 163, 194, 208-209
propriety, 37, 44, 208, 217, 219,
  221-222, 233, 243, 261
prose, 240-241
prosopopoiia, 260
Protagoras, 31
proverbs, 250
Psalms, 279
pun, 249, 255
Pyrrho, 128
Pythagoras, 120
Pythocles, 260
Python, 261

quality, 144-148 (*see also stasis*)
question, 15, 55, 143-148,
  206-213, 261, 264, 274,
  276-277 (*see also stasis*)
Quintilian, 116-132, 143-148,
  206-213, 217-231, 256, 290
  Institutes of Oratory, 116-132,
  143-148, 206-213, 217-231

Rabirius, 208
raillery, 251, 254
ramifications, 192
rate, 292
refutation, 30, 73, 169-170, 179,
  191-192, 194-195, 197, 203,
  208, 276

Regulus, 129
Renaissance rhetoric, 217
repetition, 222, 236, 260
rhetor, 79-80, 85, 87, 149, 180
rhetoric:
  and art, 6-7, 34, 44, 54, 78, 106,
    144, 156, 195, 267, 272,
    293-294, 297
  and cookery, 18-21
  deliberative (*see* deliberative ora-
    tory)
  and dialectic, 5, 6, 30, 32, 39, 53,
    55-58, 78-79, 84, 86-87, 100,
    126-127, 191
  epideictic (*see* epideictic oratory)
  and flattery, 19-20
  forensic (*see* forensic oratory)
  and medicine, 80, 134, 172, 188
  and philosophy, 50, 76-77, 97,
    125-126
  and politics, 19, 57, 81
  and special knowledge, 12, 15-16,
    121
  and truth, 12, 15, 23, 35, 40, 43,
    54-55, 57, 83, 122, 134, 286
  as a knack, 18-19, 54, 102, 173
  as prophecy, 81
  as science, 44, 102
  Christian, 133-139, 180-188,
    273-286
  defined, 3-139, 144, 150,
    232-233, 254
  functions of, 118, 126, 144, 273
  Hellenistic, 193
  ideal, 33, 92, 107, 118-132, 232,
    238-239
  in evil men, 122, 173
  Medieval, 193, 196
  moral qualities of, 91, 97, 118,
    121-123, 129
  orator's knowledge, 25, 104, 127,
    128-131
  qualifications of, 25, 91, 162
  Renaissance, 217
Rhetorica ad Alexandrum, 63-75,
  191
Rhetorica ad Herennium, 193-195,
  196, 206, 289-299
rhetorical questions, 261
rhythm, 234-235, 258, 264
riddles, 242, 246
ridicule, 236
Roman education, 193
Rome, rhetoric at, 102, 114, 116,
  123, 129, 133, 193

Roscius, 253
Rufinus, Cornelius, 124
rules, 110, 267, 291, 294

Salamis, 174
Salarius, 208
Sappho, 166
Saturninus, 208
Scaurus, 177
Scaevola, 91, 107
schema, 229
schemata, 227-231, 236
Schoinos, 259
scholastic themes, 209-210, 221
Scipio, 223, 255
Scriptures, 133-139, 180-188,
    273-286
  figurative interpretation of,
    185-189
  literal interpretation of, 185-189
Scythian speech, 264
Sempronius, Gaius, 94
shame, 163
signs, 59-60, 185
silent language, 289
similarity and dissimilarity, 26
simile, 223, 240, 244, 249-251, 261
similitudes, 185
Simonides, 242
simple inference, 202
simple *vs.* complex cases, 208
sincerity, 173 (*see also ethos*)
Sisyphos, 248
Skiron, 243
Skolon, 259
smoothness, 264
Socrates, 3-21, 22-42, 58, 90, 99,
    152, 157, 165, 167, 262, 264
Solon, 22, 41, 98, 166
sophist, 43-46, 50, 76, 79-85, 165,
    191, 238, 241, 243
Sophocles, 32, 108-109, 170
Sosia, 201
soul, the, 38-40
species, 156, 210
speech *vs.* writing, 39
"Speeding On," 192
Speusippos, 246
Spurius Carvilius, 255
stability of voice, 290-291
stasis (*status, basis*), 15, 55, 106,
    127, 143-148, 197, 206-213,
    228, 261, 264, 274, 276-277
statement, 191-192 (*see also*

statement *(Cont.)*
  arrangement)
    of case, 221
    of facts, 194-195, 292
Statute of Appuleius, 176
Stesichoros, 158-160, 248
Stilbôn, 166
Stoics, 77, 95, 102n, 120, 123, 129
Strabax, 168
style, 81, 96, 109, 178-179, 198,
    217, 286, 289-290
  bombastic, 115
  elegant, 257-259
  emotion in, 174
  forceful, 256-265
  frigid, 243-244
  grand (*grande*), 232-233, 257,
    261, 269-286
  in arrangement, 198-199
  levels of, 232-233
  lofty, 268
  medium, 273
  middle, 232-233, 237-238
  moderate, 273-286
  novelty in, 240-241
  ornamentation in, 279-280
  plain, 232-233, 234-237, 257,
    273
  smartness in, 248-250
  subdued, 273-286
  sublimity in, 224, 266
  submissus, 274
  temperate, 283
  tenue, 273
  vs. content, 217
  words in, 217-218
suasion, 169
sublimity, 224, 266
Sulpicius, 92, 105, 171-179
summary, 31
summing-up, 204
syllogism, 57-60, 145, 159, 162,
    163, 170 (*see also* enthymeme)
symbola (tokens), 257
symmetry, 235-236
synecdoche, 225, 227-228, 245n
synonym, 241

Tacitus, 112, 256
  Dialogue on Orators, 112-115
taste, 262
teach, to (*docere*), 273-286
techne, 256
technique, 267, 289, 294, 297
Telamon, 174

Terence, 199
  Andria, 197
Terrentianus, 266-272
terms, 219, 222, 241
Terpsichore, 23
testimony, 137, 158
Teucer, 165
Thamus, 37
Theagenes, 60
themes, 114, 144, 146, 207-208
Themistocles, 12
Theodectes, 166-169
  Alkmaeon, 164
  Law, 166, 168
Theodomas, 244
Theodoros, 25, 30, 170, 192, 241, 248
Theophrastus, 95-97, 218, 235, 256
Theopompus, 257-258
Theseus, 165, 167, 243n
Thettaliskos, 166
Theuth, 37
Thrasybulos, 169-170
Thrasymachus, 25, 30, 33-34, 170, 250
Thucydides, 108, 271
Tiberius, 94
Tilauges, 263
Timandra, 265
Timothy, 273
Tisias, 31, 36-37, 104
tokens, 257
tone, 289, 291-293
topics, 44, 55, 58, 60-61, 154-170, 172, 202
  cause and effect, 169
  character, 172
  common place, 154
  consequence, 167, 170
  definition, 165
  degree, 164
  devising a better course, 170-171
  division, 166
  expediency and inexpediency, 65, 71, 157
  founded on mistakes, 170
  general, 154, 159
  greatness or smallness, 154-155, 157
  identity of cause, 168
  inconsistency, 168
  incredible, 169
  inducements and drawbacks, 169
  induction, 166
  inflections, 164

topics *(Cont.)*
  lines of argument, 154
  opposites, 163-164, 167
  play on names, 170
  parts of subject, 167
  past and future fact, 156-142
  possibility and impossibility, 154-156
  precedence, 166
  probability, 156-157
  public *vs.* private, 168
  relative terms, 164
  resolving paradox, 169
  sense of a word, 166
  size, 155
  special, 60-61
  statements by adversary, 165
  symmetry of results, 168
  time, 165
  universal, 154
tragedy, 32, 244
translatio (metaphor), 222
tropes, 217, 222-228, 268, 270
truth, 12, 15, 24, 35, 40, 43, 54-55, 57, 82, 122-123, 134, 286
Tubero, 224
Tumotheos, 245n
Twelve Tables, 98, 145
Tydides, 227
Tyndaridae, 165

Ucalegon, 226
Urania, 23

Varenus, Gaius, 208
Varenus, Lucius, 208
Vargula, 254
variety, 291
Varus, Publius Licinius, 255
Vatinius, 113
Venus, 226
Verbum (Word of God), 133, 182, 186
verbum (word of man), 133
vexation, 177-178
vice, 186
Victor, Jules, 117
  Ars Rhetorica, 117
Victories, the, 261-262
Virgil, 122, 218-220, 224-225
virtue, 118, 125, 150, 186
vituperation, 64, 71, 73
vivacity, 198-199
voice, 289-293
volume, 290, 292

Vulcan, 226

wisdom *vs.* eloquence, 136-139
wit, 236-237, 251-254
witness, 60, 158
words:
  archaic, 235
  arrangement, 257-265
  borrowed, 237
  choice of, 235, 268
  coined, 235
  embellishment by, 235
  expressive, 262
  ordinary, 235
  proper and metaphorical, 222,
    235
  rare, 244

words *(Cont.)*
  strange, 243
  transferred, 237
  useless, 221
wrath, 177-179

Xenophanes, 168, 170
Xenophon, 257, 264, 268
Xerxes, 243

Zeno, 26, 120
  Elatie Palamedes, 26
Zeno of Sidon, 76
Zerxes, 157
Zeus, 25, 38
Zeuxis, 10
Zoilus, 229